D0490235

GORDON BROWN
SPEECHES 1997–2006

GORDON BROWN
SPEECHES 1997–2006

with introductory comments by

Kofi Annan, Helen Clark, Linda Colley, Lord Ralf Dahrendorf,
Al Gore, Alan Greenspan, Wangaari Maathai, Nelson Mandela,
Trevor Phillips, J.K. Rowling, Sir Jonathan Sacks,
Sir Derek Wanless and Sir Magdi Yacoub

edited by

WILF STEVENSON

BLOOMSBURY

First published in Great Britain 2006

Speeches of Gordon Brown Crown copyright © 2006

Selection, introduction and commentary copyright © Wilf Stevenson, 2006

Copyright in the introductory comments to each chapter and listed
in the contents page remains with the individual contributors.

All royalties are being donated to the Jennifer Brown Research Laboratory within
the University of Edinburgh's Research Institute for Medical Cell Biology.

The right of the author, editor and contributors to this
work has been asserted by them in accordance with
the Copyright, Designs and Patents Act, 1998.

A CIP catalogue record for this book is available from the British Library.

ISBN 0747588376
ISBN-13 9780747588375

10 9 8 7 6 5 4 3 2 1

Typeset by Hewer Text UK Ltd, Edinburgh
Printed in Great Britain by Clays Ltd, St Ives plc

The paper this book is printed on is certified by the © Forest Stewardship Council
1996 A.C. (FSC). It is ancient-forest friendly. The printer holds FSC chain
of custody SGS-COC-2061

FSC

Mixed Sources
Product group from well-managed
forests and other controlled sources

Cert no. SGS-COC-2061
www.fsc.org
© 1996 Forest Stewardship Council

There is a golden thread which runs through British history, of the individual standing firm against tyranny and then of the individual participating in their society. It is a thread that runs from that long-ago day in Runnymede in 1215, on to the Bill of Rights in 1689 to not just one, but four great Reform Acts within less than a hundred years. And the tensile strength of that golden thread comes from countless strands of common continuing endeavour in our villages, towns and cities, the efforts and achievements of ordinary men and women, united by a strong sense of responsibility, who, long before de Tocqueville found civic associations to be at the heart of America, defined Britain by its proliferation of local clubs, associations, societies and endeavours – a Britain where liberty did not descend into licence and where freedom was exercised with responsibility.

Gordon Brown, Hugo Young Memorial Lecture
December 2005

CONTENTS

ACKNOWLEDGEMENTS

Gordon Brown has been unstinting in his support for this anthology, and without his agreement to quote from his speeches, there would be no book.

I am very grateful to Kofi Annan, Helen Clark, Linda Colley, Lord Ralf Dahrendorf, Wangaari Maathai, Nelson Mandela, Trevor Phillips, J.K. Rowling, Sir Jonathan Sacks, Sir Derek Wanless and Sir Magdi Yacoub for agreeing to contribute introductions to the various chapters of the book. Al Gore and Alan Greenspan kindly allowed me to quote comments made by them when speaking publicly about Gordon Brown.

Margaret Vaughan helped considerably with the introductory chapter. Shriti Vadera, Spencer Livermore, Michael Jacobs, Beth Russell and Damian McBride all helped to research the speeches, check dates and provide ancillary materials. I am particularly indebted to Cathy Koester for tracking down copies of the originals, and cross-referencing the dates on which the speeches were given, and I am also grateful to Sue Nye, Gil McNeil and Sarah Brown for their support of the project at various stages.

Liz Calder and Bill Swainson and the team at Bloomsbury have managed the publication process with great skill, and have been a pleasure to work with.

EDITOR'S NOTE

The speeches given by Gordon Brown in the period 1997–2006, which is the span of this collection, fall into several distinct types. There are speeches which advance the work of the Treasury, often fitted in around the Budget and Comprehensive Spending Review, which serve to contextualise or to advance what it is possible to say in those sometimes rather formulaic parliamentary occasions. But there are also speeches which deal with ideas and political philosophy, sometimes in areas which might appear at first glance to be remote from direct Treasury interest. The speeches on British-ness, for example, raise fascinating questions about our history and our place in the modern world; and some of the material around the question of how best to advance the public interest offers radical insights into the role and purpose of government. These have often not had the audience they deserve.

Gordon Brown's speeches have not been collected and published before, although some have been published individually. This collection of speeches is drawn, with permission, from those given by Gordon Brown since he became Chancellor of the Exchequer in May 1997 until January 2006. There were many fine speeches delivered before 1997 which could have been included here (and indeed part of one has been). However the self-discipline adopted by the party in the run-up to the 1997 election, combined with the fact that speeches in opposition are naturally constrained, made it difficult to match those speeches with those given once Labour assumed power. Spring 2006 has been used as a cut-off date simply because there was an opportunity to publish this collection in the autumn of 2006.

The speeches selected for inclusion in this book have been divided into an introductory chapter, and nine main chapters, although there are several occasions where material in one chapter spans more than one of these rather arbitrary divisions. In each chapter, an attempt has been made to track how the ideas have developed, by including extracts from successive iterations of speeches on related themes. And because the speeches are arranged chronologically, some sections are repeated, sometimes with little or no variation. Where the context needed it, or where the flow required it, these passages have been retained. In each chapter, at least one speech has been given more or less complete. Similarly, the introduction to each chapter contains an overview of all the speeches in that chapter, but as an aid to the reader a number of passages are repeated to provide the specific context for the particular speech.

Inevitably, in transforming what were live events into print, some of the colour and the texture of the original have been lost. I hope, however, that those who were present when these speeches were delivered will recognise what is included here, and that those who read them afresh will respond to the flow of ideas which spring from the text. The book traces the development of Gordon Brown's thinking over nine years in government. It makes fascinating reading for anyone interested in the political process who wishes to understand how ideas developed in opposition have been modified and energised by the experience of government, and the unpredictable circumstances of a changing world.

Wilf Stevenson
London, April 2006

1

MOVING BRITAIN FORWARD

I am pleased that Gordon Brown's speeches have been collected for publication. Reading them gives an insight into the man behind the politician, and the values behind the policies. These are values we share: values of fairness and liberty and, above all, justice. Gordon Brown brings determination to the fight against international poverty, and it is rooted in a sense of justice that extends beyond Britain's shores. His speeches show a vision of a better world for all, a vision to which he is deeply committed.

Nelson Mandela

Politicians make speeches. In the past, great speeches were treated as big events, the content analysed and widely discussed. Think of the Midlothian speeches of Gladstone; the wartime speeches of Winston Churchill; domestic politicians like David Lloyd George and Nye Bevan; statesmen like Nelson Mandela, Fidel Castro, Mahatma Gandhi and Vaclav Havel; American orators such as Abraham Lincoln, Roosevelt, Martin Luther King and, of course, the Kennedys. And there are speeches which characterise whole movements, such as Emmeline Pankhurst's paean to suffragism; speeches which speak directly to the heart: who will forget the drama of Earl Spencer's funeral tribute to Princess Diana? Speeches have sustained dictators and fanned the flames of revolution and anarchy; but they have also inspired the oppressed, empowered the many against the few, and brought down dictators. Speeches have shaped our world, and though in a changing world they are prepared, delivered and reported in ways that might astonish Gladstone, Gandhi and even Churchill, they still have the power to move us to thought and action.

Despite growing use of the web to publish such material, speeches these days are rarely collected and studied. They are still made, but all too often the media treatment gets in the way of the content. No major speech in the UK happens these days without the impact on the tabloids being calculated; a broadsheet editor being briefed; a BBC *Newsnight* slot sought; and the *Today Programme* interview rehearsed. And why not? It is how messages are delivered these days, and there is some benefit in terms of the intensity of the coverage. The unfortunate by-product, however, is that all we may hear of a major speech is a series of sound bites; or at best a short article based on one or two of the ideas. It is rare for a set-piece speech to be widely circulated and discussed.

And yet, politicians continue to prepare and to deliver set-piece speeches, usually lasting forty minutes to an hour, usually at a conference or a seminar. The hundred or so attendees who hear these speeches will be stimulated by the best of them, but little will be passed on to the wider world. Even when they are shown on television, the live event does not translate well to the small screen. This is most obvious at political party conferences for which the big speeches have to serve two audiences – the party faithful in the hall and, albeit heavily mediated, the general public.

A lot of attention is paid to the major parliamentary occasions, such as the Budget or the Pre-Budget Report. But the rules and conventions of that intense debating chamber are significant barriers in themselves. Some media coverage can be expected for other non-parliamentary slots in the calendar such as the Lord Mayor's Banquets and the CBI and TUC conferences. But the same reservations apply. These events have their own agendas, which can distance the ordinary citizen, and television and press coverage devoted to these occasions is declining.

Huge amounts of time and effort go into major speeches, which may go through dozens of drafts before delivery. While the main thrust of any speech is usually fixed early on, it is not unusual for key speeches to have several people contributing ideas and passages and to be worked on until the very last minute. And on the day, some politicians, perhaps inspired by the occasion, will take oratorical flight from their notes, adding to and re-phrasing passages, despite the fact that the text may have been issued to journalists. The advice to the press, 'check against delivery', is no idle threat!

Public oratory is a strange art, since it depends on the theatricality of the staging, the presentational skills of the speaker, the expectation of the audience and what actors call the 'truth' of the performance. But it also depends heavily on the power of the ideas contained in the speech, which have to be deployed on a large scale, and be more robust, if they are to hold an audience for up to an hour, often in cramped surroundings and conditions. A live event rarely translates well into print, let alone television, but a good test of the most powerful oratory is to see how well the live event stands up to subsequent reading.

Gordon Brown is one of the few senior politicians on the contemporary British scene who has consistently given major speeches on topics which range across the political economy. His interests are broad, his scholarship used to great effect, and his passion and commitment come through on every occasion. But these speeches rarely get reported – it is almost as if the reporters sent to cover the speech are trained only to record the economic content of his speeches, whatever their actual focus.

Reading them again for this collection, it is hard not to be inspired by the passion of his convictions, the coherence of his vision and the rigour of his arguments. As a trained historian the Chancellor is clearly concerned to understand where ideas and policies come from and by whom they have been deployed in the past. He is always concerned to make explicit the connections between the guiding principles used by those of the democratic left and the policies which are derived from these writings. And he is anxious to show how policies will impact on present and future generations.

Some have questioned whether Gordon Brown makes one set of speeches for his Labour audiences and another for the City, but a close reading of them belies this rather trite criticism. Though varying in tone and style, the Chancellor's speeches stand as a coherent whole – as those of very few politicians do – because they reflect long thought and a coherent view of Britain, of our responsibilities to one another as citizens, and of Britain's role in the world. His vision is that of a Britain founded on liberty, responsibility and fairness: hence his interest in Britishness and British values, and the ideals and policies that flow from them. He starts from a dauntingly wide view of the individual in the changing global economy: men and women whose potential needs both encouragement and opportunity; men and women who are not alone, selfish or isolated, but living together in villages, towns and cities; living in communities within which we have responsibilities towards each other. It is a view that owes as much to the thinking of David Hume and Adam Smith – the two major figures of the Scottish Enlightenment – as it does to the growth of the concept of Britishness: a Britishness of liberty and civic duty that first flourished at around the same time, and in the twentieth century expanded to include a new fairness and opportunity for all.

And his vision of an opportunity-driven, dynamic market at one with a fair, open and responsible society is, he argues, more relevant in the age of the global economy than ever before. Globalisation, he says, brings both unrivalled opportunities and rising risks. To maximise opportunity and to minimise risk, people need both an open and enterprising economy where the creative, the dynamic and the hard working can prosper; and a fair society which offers proper insurance against what are even bigger risks. But he does not seek a 'handout society'. His emphasis on the potential of the individual makes poverty of aspiration one of his greatest concerns; young people must be both prepared and challenged to discover and achieve their full potential.

The power to shape opportunities for the citizens of a country is given to very few people in a generation. It is right that we who are affected by the decisions these fellow citizens will take on our behalf should know the formation and thinking of our senior politicians. Their speeches are one way of gaining such an insight. The speeches gathered here reflect the work of a formidable and widely-read intellect trained in the analytic skills of the historian but also – and far more importantly – inspired by a vision of what the political process can achieve for our society and our nation: a vision not simply of Rab Butler's 'art of the possible' but of Isaiah Berlin's 'practical wisdom' too.

2

TOWARDS A MODERN ECONOMY

Kirkcaldy – the birthplace, in 1723, of Adam Smith and, by extension, of modern economics – is also, of course, where your Chancellor of the Exchequer was reared. I am led to ponder to what extent the Chancellor's renowned economic and financial skills are the result of exposure to the subliminal intellect-enhancing emanations of this area.

Alan Greenspan
Adam Smith Memorial Lecture, Kirkcaldy, Scotland
6 February 2005

I am [. . .] especially honored to be sharing the platform this afternoon with my good friend Gordon Brown. The Chancellor, as you heard a short while ago, has achieved an exemplary record as steward of the economy of the United Kingdom and, indeed, is without peer among the world's economic-policy makers. Gordon, I would like to thank you in particular for your leadership of the Group of Seven this past year. It has been a challenging year, and your voice and vision have been indispensable to the G7's efforts to maintain global stability and growth in the face of terrorism, further rises in global oil prices, and protectionist pressures.

Alan Greenspan
Acceptance of honorary degree, along with Gordon Brown MP
New York University
14 December 2005

In this chapter are speeches which set out the policies which have transformed the British economy since 1997. It has become a common-place to assert that the defining characteristic of the new Labour government was the decision to make the Bank of England independent, within a few days of taking office in May 1997. Indeed, looking back, it sometimes seems that that decision was the only one taken in the economic field. Most commentators now agree that the decision to make monetary decisions independent of political influence (within a long-term framework where the objective, set by government, is to promote high and stable levels of growth and employment) has been a major plank in the creation of a stable macro-economic climate in the UK, leading to huge economic, social and political benefits. But what is not always picked up is that the decision to make the Bank of England independent was only one of a raft of carefully planned and executed macro-economic policy decisions which also led into a range of micro-economic decisions aimed at equipping all nations and regions of the UK for the challenges of the future, including higher levels of investment, improved competitiveness and improving employment opportunity through the modernisation of the Welfare State.

This chapter begins with extracts from the speeches about the decision to make the Bank of England responsible for interest-rate setting, and the creation of the independent regulator for the financial-services industry. These speeches, taken together, set out the new government's macro-economic policy, and given how close they were to the general election are remarkable in that they set out such a coherent and comprehensive vision of what was to come. In both style and content, the announcement of Bank of England independence, only five days after the general election, was a tangible sign of the new energy and commitment of the Chancellor and of his determination to make stability the corner-stone of the government's economic policy. The speech on the establish-ment of the FSA is also a re-statement of the government's economic policy, with its reference to the task of government, at all times, to ensure a long-term and stable framework; economic fundamentals that are sound; that objectives for policy are clearly understood; and that public decisions are made in an orderly and transparent way.

The reference in the latter speech to the government's approach to the Euro masks the pressure the government was under at that time to define the likely approach to economic and monetary union, and a good example of the speeches about the 'five economic tests' is given in the

December 1997 speech made to an American audience, which is included here not just because it gives a succinct rationale and context for
the tests themselves, but also because it explains very clearly that there is
no overriding constitutional barrier to UK membership, and confirms
that the government's position was that if there was 'sustainable convergence', that would provide the basis for Britain to move forward to a
single currency, should parliament and the people so decide.

In June 2001, shortly after the general election, the Chancellor set out
his thinking for the second term in a statement entitled 'Enterprise for
All'. This marks a development in thinking from the aims of the first
term, which were focused on high and stable levels of growth and
employment, to raising productivity. There are two aspects of this
approach: radical reform and modernisation of product, capital and
labour markets to create a truly entrepreneurial culture open to all; and a
step change in competitive pressures within the British economy, which
he suggested was essential if we were to deliver faster productivity rises
than our industrial competitors. Although not as headline-grabbing as
the decision to make the Bank of England independent, there is a
symmetry in the plans outlined in this statement to make British competition decisions – and the competition authorities – fully independent
of political influence. The aim of the statement was 'to send a message to
the entrepreneurial, the innovative and dynamic: that if you were starting
up, growing a business, investing, taking people on, seeking new capital
or working your way up in business – the government was on your side'. It
was, in short, a message about how a party with a successful economic
record was committed to building on and improving the position it had
created so successfully in the first term.

In a speech at the Growing Business Awards on 5 December 2002, the
Chancellor returned to his concerns about supply-side, or micro-economic, issues which he felt should be addressed in the drive to create a
modern economy. In particular, he focused on the role of government in
raising the UK's productivity with the aim of creating an entrepreneurial
culture, where all have the opportunity to realise their potential – to
acquire skills, to work their way up, become self-employed or start a
business – and 'to rise as far as their talents and potential can take them'.
And he suggested that the context for this included a need to change the
history in the UK of 'inadequate investment, low skills, boardroom
complacency, workplace resistance to change, cartels and restrictive
practices'. The speech rehearsed many of the arguments discussed

before in this area, but the overall aim was clear: creating an enterprise culture, so that more and more people are encouraged to start their own businesses, and more is done to improve the rate of business creation, particularly in high-unemployment communities.

Rightly proud of the success of the UK economy, the Chancellor has been anxious to draw this experience to the attention of European neighbours, and to reform the approach and processes in the EU. The fullest exposition of this approach is given in the speech made by the Chancellor to the Centre for European Reform at Church House, London, on 10 March 2003. Entitled 'The Road to Full Employment: Economic Reforms for a More Flexible and Dynamic Britain and Europe', the speech took place just before the Iraq conflict, and in the wake of 9/11, and is influenced by this. None the less the speech focuses on changes required to the economies of countries in the European Union so as to bring about modern ways of achieving high and stable levels of growth and employment. In particular the Chancellor focuses on the role of governments in the modern world, setting out three areas of concern: the need for stability, because investment will flow most to those countries that are the most stable, and ever more rapidly away from those that risk stability; the need to create the best environment for high-quality investment – through policies for education, research and development, and infrastructure; and how enhancing productivity and competitiveness in a more open economy demands a new flexibility in labour, capital and product markets, and a commitment to root out inflexibilities, at both a national and increasingly at a regional level. This is an important speech, not just because of the message it sends to Europe, but because it encapsulates much of the thinking about the macro-economic and micro-economic policies which have been employed by the Treasury under this Chancellor. However, it goes further than this, giving a social-inclusion context for much of the economic thinking. The Chancellor is fond of quoting a maxim used by John Smith QC MP, the leader of the Labour Party 1992–4, that 'economic efficiency and social justice are two sides of the same coin'. This speech is a good exposition of how this maxim (and the related 'prudence for a purpose' maxim of Gordon Brown) have been implemented under the Labour government since 1997. As he concludes: Britain has a unique opportunity to be, once again, a beacon to the world, advancing enterprise and fairness together – a dynamic vibrant economy that is the first economy in the new era of globalisation to match flexibility with fairness and, in doing so, attain the high levels of growth and employment that are the best route to prosperity for all.

On 2 December 2005, the Chancellor opened the Advancing Enterprise Conference in London, and gave a *tour d'horizon* of the current range of polices in place, as he says, to ensure that 'Britain is made for globalisation and globalisation is made for Britain'. He stresses the framework for stability put in place in 1997, and which has turned Britain from a stop–go economy into one of the world's most stable economic environments. And he rehearses many of the achievements in the supply side of the economy, arguing that Britain is a leader in the world's fastest-growing, most wealth-creating sectors at the cutting edge of global advance – in capital markets and financial services; in science and innovation; in creativity and enterprise; in skills and education. A Britain that is the preferred international marketplace not just for European companies but also for growing Chinese, Indian and other companies; and the location of choice for the headquarters of multi-national companies.

The first speech is an extract from the announcement about the independence of the Bank of England, delivered on 6 May 1997, a few days after the general election.

The central economic objectives of the new government are high and stable levels of growth and employment. Our aim therefore is to rebuild British economic strength with a modern industrial base, high levels of investment and a culture of entrepreneurship that, through economic opportunity for all, unlocks British economic potential.

This can only happen if we build from solid foundations of prudent economic management and sound finance. The enemy of growth, and the investment necessary for it, is the instability of short periodic bursts of high growth followed by recession. So we must break from the short-termism of the past – the economic instability that has characterised the British economy not just in recent years but for most of the century. That is why I want British economic success to be built on the solid rock of prudent and consistent economic management, not the shifting sands of boom and bust.

Now is the time for long-termism. This is the time to set the British economy on a new long-term course that will deliver high levels of growth and employment through lasting stability.

. . .

Price stability is, as I have said, an essential precondition for the government's objectives of high and sustainable levels of growth and employment. The question is how to achieve the long-term stability that we seek?

As the Prime Minister and I have always made clear, this is a new government that is going to move beyond the old dogmas of the past, and provide a modern and lasting framework for economic prosperity. I have said on repeated occasions that we must tackle the underlying weakness of the British economy – low investment, skill shortages and inadequate infrastructure – all of which have beset the British economy in recent years. These problems are themselves some of the underlying causes of inflation. I have also made clear that reform is required to put monetary policy on a stable, long-term footing. In a speech in May 1995 and subsequently in our 1995 policy document, 'A New Economic Future for Britain', I set out my view of the proper roles of the government and the Bank of England in economic policy.

Government has a responsibility to the public in setting the objectives of economic policy and that means that the government rather than the Bank of England must set the targets for monetary policy. However, as I have repeatedly made clear since 1995, we will only build a fully credible framework for monetary policy if the long-term needs of the economy, not short-term political considerations, guide monetary decision-making. We must remove the suspicion that short-term party-political considerations are influencing the setting of interest rates.

As our election manifesto said: 'We will reform the Bank of England to ensure that decision-making on monetary policy is more effective, open, accountable and free from short-term political manipulation.'

It has become increasingly clear that the present arrangements for policy-making are not generating the confidence that is necessary. That is one reason why Britain has higher long-term interest rates than most of our major competitors. And the perception that monetary policy decisions have been dominated by short-term political considerations has grown.

I am now satisfied that we can put in place, with immediate effect, reforms of the Bank of England to ensure that it can discharge responsibilities for setting interest rates in an effective, open and accountable way. This is the time to take the tough decisions we need for the long-term interests and prosperity of the country. I will not shrink from the tough decisions needed to deliver stability for long-term growth.

I have therefore decided to give the Bank of England operational responsibility for setting interest rates, with immediate effect. The government will continue to set the inflation target and the Bank will have responsibility for setting interest rates to meet the target. The government's policy is set out in a letter I sent to the Governor yesterday, the text of which I am releasing now. It is the government's intention to legislate for these proposals as soon as possible. In the interim, the Governor has agreed to put in place the arrangements that will apply once the legislation has been enacted.

The main elements of the reforms are as follows. In place of the current personalised system of decision-making, decisions will be made by a new nine-member Monetary Policy Committee, on the basis of a majority vote. This is similar to arrangements in other countries, including the USA and other G7 members. In addition to the Governor and two Deputy Governors, nominated by the government, who will sit on the committee, the government will also appoint four members of the Monetary Policy Committee from outside the Bank of England. Openness of decision-making will be ensured by the publication of minutes of proceedings and votes of the Monetary Policy Committee. There will be enhanced requirements for the Bank of England to report to the Treasury Select Committee of the House of Commons to explain and be questioned on their decisions.

The Court of the Bank of England will review the performance of the Bank of England, including that of the Monetary Policy Committee. The Court will be substantially reformed to make it representative of the whole of the United Kingdom and to take account of the full range of Britain's industrial and business sectors.

These changes in accountability and the new breadth of representation on the Court amount to the most radical internal reform to the Bank of England since it was established in 1694 – over 300 years ago.

Britain is, in fact, one of the few major industrial nations in which the central bank does not have operational responsibility for decisions on interest rates. And our record on inflation and interest rates over recent years is poor, while other countries with independent central banks have performed better.

Taken as a whole, these proposals will ensure that decisions are taken for the long-term interests of the economy and not on the basis of short-term political pressures. This is the way to create the stability we need for higher investment and high levels of growth and employment. The changes I have proposed are the right decisions: the right decisions for business which wants to plan ahead with confidence, the right decisions for families who have suffered enough from the uncertainties of short-term economic instability, and the right decisions for Britain.

The specific reforms I am proposing are British solutions, designed to meet British domestic needs for long-term stability. Our monetary reforms provide the platform for stability and are the building block for a new economic policy that will equip us for the challenges of the future: one that takes steps to ensure higher levels of investment, for which I will announce new measures in due course, and improving employment opportunity by the modernisation of the Welfare State. These measures will be addressed in the coming Budget and future Budgets.

But there is, as I have suggested today, a more long-term context. In the last century, Britain was industrially pre-eminent. The history of this century has been one of economic decline, not least because of short-termism and the pursuit of stop–go economics. I am determined that we make the right preparations for long-term national economic success, as we look to the century that lies ahead, so that we can move forward again economically. I am therefore setting in place a long-term policy for long-term prosperity. The ultimate judgement of the success of this measure will not come next week, or indeed in the next year, but in the long term. I am convinced that this radical reform, together with measures we will announce to equip our economy for the challenges ahead, creates the platform of stability upon which Britain can build.

Alongside the Bank of England independence went the creation of an independent regulator for the financial-services industry. In a speech given at the launch of the new Financial Services Authority on 28 October 1997, the Chancellor set out the thinking behind this move, and his aspirations for the future in this important sector of the economy.

I am delighted to be here to mark the launch of Britain's new authority for financial services: the launch of what will be a unique, twenty-first-century, one-stop service for financial-services supervision:

- a single supervisor for all providers of financial services – wholesale and retail;
- from small, local independent financial advisers to big city institutions;
- one that protects everybody – providers and customers; firms and individuals;
- for Britain a single centre of information, advice and supervision;
- one powerful voice internationally, representing the very best standards of supervision in the world.

This is a radical set of reforms. London will be the only major financial centre in the world with a single supervisor. It will put the UK at the cutting edge of financial supervision. It will offer huge competitive advantages for Britain. And I firmly believe that over time it is a model that other world financial centres will follow.

Much has already been achieved since Sir Andrew Large sent his report to me at the end of July. And I want to thank him for his work. And now this launch is the culmination of a great deal of hard work by Howard Davies and his team. And I would like to take this opportunity to thank him and his staff for the commitment and drive that they have brought to the task of building the new supervisor. The three new managing directors – Michael Foot from the Bank of England, Richard Farrant from SFA, and Phillip Thorpe from IMRO – deserve our thanks. I am delighted that they have agreed to join the new supervisor, and I want to wish them well in the task ahead.

There will be published today, along with the launch document, consultation papers on practitioner and consumer input, and on the charging regime during transition.

I am sure that the financial-services industry, and those representing interests of the consumer, will respond to this opportunity to participate in this debate, and to help create a supervisor which meets the needs of both groups. It shows that Britain is building modern institutions and modern procedures to regulate a modern financial market and to provide the stability and regulation it needs.

There is one very pleasant duty that falls to me as Chancellor; it is to announce the name of the new authority that will take regulation into the twenty-first century. The authority takes on the work of seven separate regulatory bodies, all of whom have their distinctive histories, and it will be responsible for the supervision of banks, building societies, investment firms, insurance companies and friendly societies. It will be Britain's financial-services authority for the years ahead. And it will be called exactly that, the Financial Services Authority. And I wish this new regulatory body and the staff who work in it the success it deserves in the years ahead.

Today in my remarks I want to do three things:

- I want to put the changes we are making in regulation and financial policy in their context: our commitment to long-term stability in this country;
- second, I want to set out the new statutory objectives of FSA and thus the reasons for our reforms; and
- third, I want to set out some of the changes that our reforms will bring, to the benefit of financial markets.

First, the reforms to financial-services supervision in their proper context – laying the long-term and lasting foundations for Britain's economic success. When I made my Mansion House speech in June, I set out five long-term objectives to equip our country for all the challenges ahead.

First, a long-term framework for monetary and financial policy that allows businesses, as well as families, a platform of stability from which to plan for the future with confidence. Second, long-term fiscal stability, securing sustainable public finances that allows our national priorities to be met. And just as the first Budget set out the tough fiscal disciplines we will follow and a five-year deficit-reduction plan, our Comprehensive Spending Review will demand rigour in the selection of priorities and efficiency in the use of public money.

Third, equipping ourselves for the future demands the higher levels of investment in business and people that provides the capacity for strong and stable growth, hence our cut in corporation tax and incentives for new investment. Fourth, as important for industries' future skills and staffing, a far-reaching modernisation of the Welfare State to help move people into work and give them the education and training modern work needs. And finally a long-term commitment to Europe, and to constructive engagement in the developed world's largest open market.

Yesterday we showed our commitment to Europe by supporting the principle of economic and monetary union, making it clear that there is no overriding constitutional barrier to our membership, and that the economic tests will be decisive. And by giving the government's position that sustainable convergence would provide the basis for Britain to move forward to a single currency, should parliament and the people so decide, early in the next parliament.

Our first objective, as I said, and the cornerstone of this government's economic policy, is long-term stability. Stability in policy-making is even more necessary in a world of fast-moving global financial markets. It is important that governments and central banks around the world remain vigilant at times of sudden moves in markets. But it is the task of government, at all times, to ensure a long-term and stable framework. It requires economic fundamentals that are sound, that objectives for policy are clearly understood and public decisions that are made in an orderly and transparent way; what Britain has ensured through the institutional reforms and long-term policies that the government has pursued since it came to office.

Today is a key date in the government's programme to lay the foundations for Britain's long-term success by putting in place a new framework for financial and monetary stability. Today the Bank of England Bill is introduced, formally giving operational responsibility for interest rates to the new Monetary Policy Committee, and has its first reading in the House of Commons. Today we are also publishing a joint memorandum of understanding, which sets out how the Treasury, the Bank of England and the new supervisor will work together to deliver our shared objective – financial stability. And today, at this morning's conference, we are marking another milestone – the launch of the new supervisory organisation.

These events, coming together, make this not only a key date in the development of the modern financial-services industry, but a key date for the British economy. I am confident that the new arrangements, taken together, will significantly enhance the credibility of UK monetary policy and improve the workings of the financial markets.

Financial services lie at the heart of a modern, dynamic economy. The effectiveness and competitiveness of all our industries depends upon the quality and availability of the ever increasing array of financial products and services – from current and savings accounts; to pensions and insurance; to securities and derivatives. And in some way, large or small, almost every adult in Britain is a customer of this industry. And our standard of living depends upon it, particularly in retirement.

The UK financial-services industry makes a huge contribution to the nation's prosperity. It represents 7 per cent of national income and employs almost 5 per cent of the workforce – 1 million people. It contributes over £22 billion a year in net overseas earning. The City of London is the most international financial centre in the world. We can take pride that London is home to more US banks than New York, and more Japanese banks than any city except Tokyo. And that there is more international-equity trading on the London stock exchange than any other exchange. The UK financial-services industry is a world leader – it needs a world-class supervisory framework: a framework that is robust, transparent, accountable, one with clear divisions of responsibility, and one that recognises the global reach of the modern financial-services industry.

I believe that the FSA should have statutory objectives. This is a new and important development, but one that is essential to provide clarity in responsibility and proper accountability.

The Bill will set out clear objectives. The areas covered will include:

- to sustain confidence in the UK financial sector and markets;
- to protect consumers by ensuring that firms are competent and financially sound and give their customers confidence in their integrity;
- while recognising customers' own responsibility for their financial decisions, I want it enshrined in law that consumers must be protected;

- to promote the improvement of public understanding of the benefits and risks associated with financial products;
- to monitor, detect and prevent financial crime.

In delivering these specific objectives, the FSA will have a statutory duty:

- to be efficient and economic – to ensure that costs and restrictions on firms are proportionate to the benefits of regulation;
- to facilitate innovation in financial services;
- to take account of the international nature of financial regulation and financial-services business.

These objectives will give the new regulator a clear sense of purpose. And they will provide a benchmark against which performance of the regulator can be measured. And for the first time, the FSA will be required to report to me every year as to how well they have met these statutory objectives.

In a global economy where markets are changing every day, where innovation and diversity are an essential part, the need for a regulator that has power and flexibility has never been greater. Today in Britain we have a profusion of regulatory bodies. It is not uncommon to find a major financial institution that has to deal with half a dozen different regulators, each with different requirements, which creates confusion and adds to cost. At the moment one bank can be supervised by the Bank of England, regulated by the SIB, the SFA, IMRP, the PIA and the DTI, not to mention their international counterparts.

For many years now both the industry and the public have known that the present system, underpinned as it is by the flawed concept of self-regulation, cannot continue. Regulation should be complementary to the business process and not a hindrance. Indeed, the best regulatory system is one that is so good, so efficient that no one ever talks about it. It should be in with the bricks – an essential part of the running of a business. And more than that, it is not just structural reform that is needed, but an awareness that it is the nature and quality of regulation that counts. It is necessary to tread the fine line between sufficient regulation to protect the public interest and over-regulation, where we lose sight of what it is that we are trying to achieve. That is why reform is necessary.

First, structural reform: bringing together the existing self-regulators under one new enhanced body, the FSA. Bringing the regulators together under one roof will reduce the cost to both the regulators and the regulated. It will improve the effectiveness of regulation and ensure that rules are applied consistently. It will create one supervisor that looks at the risks in a firm as a whole, not a number of different regulators looking at their own narrow areas of responsibility. It will improve the flow of information within the regulatory community, end turf wars between the regulators and, I hope, make it easier to attract high-quality people into regulation. The old system was fragmented, inefficient and confusing for investors, and lacked accountability and a clear allocation of responsibilities. Small investors especially did not know where to turn for information or for redress if they had complaints.

And secondly, a recognition that the regulators must have the appropriate response for each section of the market. And one regulator means one approach, a consistent and appropriate set of rules together with a determination to bear down on costs. When the compliance department grows faster than the marketing department something has gone very wrong. The new FSA will reverse that process. I want the FSA to retain the best features of the existing framework, but also to improve upon them:

- keeping a light regulatory touch for wholesale markets while strengthening the regulation of retail markets;
- keeping flexibility in its rule-making. Financial services are fast-moving and rules need to keep abreast of change and not inhibit innovation;
- retaining the vital input of practitioners, and strengthening the input of consumers;
- and we must remember that a regulator is to a large extent only as good as the staff it employs. We want to build on the tremendous expertise in the existing bodies and as Howard Davies will underline we are determined to attract the best staff. And by setting up a regulator with international clout I believe that there are many in the city and in industry who will want the opportunity to work in the FSA.

The draft Bill including fully worked-up objectives will be published for consultation next year. Now begins the time for you to tell us what you need and expect from it.

In creating the Financial Services Authority, but also in every area of monetary and financial policy, the principles underlying our reforms are the same – transparency, accountability and clear divisions of responsibility. The memorandum of understanding establishes both the division of responsibilities for financial stability and supervision and a framework for cooperation between the Treasury, the Bank of England and the Financial Services Authority. This is the only way to establish proper accountability for decision-making. The Treasury, the Bank of England and the FSA will need to work closely together to achieve our common objectives. The arrangements I am announcing today provide for the closest possible cooperation and set out new formal arrangements for the Treasury, the FSA and the Bank of England to follow if problems arise.

The division of responsibilities is based on our four guiding principles:

- clear accountability. Each institution must be accountable for its actions, so each must have unambiguous and well-defined responsibilities;
- transparency. Parliament, the markets and the public must know who is responsible for what;
- no duplication. Each institution must have a clearly defined role, to avoid second-guessing, inefficiency and the duplication of effort. This will help ensure proper accountability;
- regular information exchange. This will help each institution to discharge its responsibilities as efficiently and effectively as possible.

While the prudential supervision of banks and other financial institutions is now the primary responsibility of the Financial Services Authority, the Bank of England Bill lays out the new and additional responsibilities the Bank of England will discharge. The Bill the government is publishing today – a historic reform for the Bank of England – will bring into law the new framework for monetary policy. With its clear rules, procedures and commitment to transparency, and accountability, the Bank will set interest rates to meet the government's inflation target and will do so through the most open and accountable set of procedures of any central bank round the world. The Monetary Policy Committee will be required to publish its decisions, the minutes of its meetings, and a quarterly report.

So these reforms, founded on sound economics, provide the platform for long-term monetary and financial stability, which we need in order to ensure high and stable levels of growth and employment.

Britain now has modern institutions and modern procedures to regulate a modern financial market and to provide the stability and regulation we need in a new global economy.

I am confident they will provide long-term stability and strengthen the position of the United Kingdom financial-services industry as one of the most competitive, sophisticated and dynamic in the world.

The reference in the speech to the government's approach to the Euro masks the pressure the government was under at that time to define the likely approach to economic and monetary union. In the end the position was quite clear: there is no overriding constitutional barrier to our membership, and five economic tests would be decisive. And by confirming that the government's position was that if there was sustainable convergence, that would provide the basis for Britain to move forward to a single currency, should parliament and the people so decide, early in the next parliament, the issue was effectively isolated for the immediate future. A rounded appreciation of this issue is given in the following speech delivered by the Chancellor when speaking at the British-American Chamber of Commerce in New York on 5 December 1997:

. . .

I want to talk to you today about the development of Europe, about Britain's role in it and about how it affects us all. And I will start from the four historic decisions announced by the British government on 27 October 1997:

- first, the commitment of the British government, for the first time, to the principle of currency union in Europe;
- second, our statement that there is no constitutional bar to Sterling's entry;

- third, our statement that we will make our judgement about entry and the timing of entry on the basis of a detailed assessment of the national economic interest;
- fourth, that we would now institute a period of preparations for entry, before a final decision early in the next parliament.

I want to explain what these decisions mean in practical terms for business; and I want to show how our commitment to Europe reflects our wider commitment to a more open, freer and thus stronger international economy.

Now I am delighted to be here because Britain and the USA not only can celebrate together the experience of a shared history, we are also able to celebrate our common values, which continue to bind us ever more closely together. And I like to think that even the most global of economic powers, America, benefits from its strong relationship with Britain and from our shared commitments to liberty; to our countries as lands of opportunity for all; to the virtues of hard work and enterprise; to the value of looking outwards to the world and to free trade and openness.

I like to think of our economies, both of us, as ambassadors for openness and internationalism. Indeed our history and culture make us uniquely outward-looking and open countries, not isolationist and protectionist. And this openness and internationalism is of vital importance in shaping the development of the new global economy. Most of all when the global economy is tested – as it is today – by uncertainties and turbulence.

Global markets have brought us new opportunities, but the recent turmoil in Asia and Latin America illustrates the speed and the volatility with which global markets can react to events when things go wrong in individual countries. In the days before global capital markets, governments could disguise their problems for longer and shelter behind national barriers. Today they can no longer do so. So while the rewards – in investment flows – for doing things well are even greater today, the punishment for those who perform badly is now more instantaneous and more severe than in the past.

Recent events in Thailand, Indonesia and now Korea raise a number of important issues. The scale of the financing packages has dominated the headlines. But we should not forget that the most important response, when a country finds itself in difficulty, is a strong commitment to implement the necessary policy reforms, in conjunction with the IMF and the World Bank.

So the first key lesson I draw from recent events is that, in order that we can step in with financial support without encouraging markets to believe that such financial support is automatic, it is essential that the international financial institutions attach tough conditions to such lending, covering both policy and the conduct of policy.

The second lesson I draw is that crises on this scale, wherever they take place, are of global concern – requiring a global response. Regional cooperation can play its part, but it is in no one's interest if this undermines the importance of the international financial institutions, the IMF and the World Bank.

The third lesson is that when these crises occur we need new ways to respond in tune with today's global and liquid capital markets. That is why I am attracted to the proposal for a new IMF short-term financing facility. Such a facility could combine larger amounts with shorter repayment schedules and a higher interest-rate charge than usual. We need rapid progress to reach agreement on this, and on possible new lending instruments at the World Bank too.

More than any other two countries in the world we, America and Britain, were the moving forces in the creation over fifty years ago of our international financial institutions. These international institutions built for the days of sheltered national economies, must now meet the challenges of the new world of global markets where no economy can shelter for long behind national controls and purely national barriers.

It was Churchill who warned that those who show so little imagination that they attempt to build the present in the image of the past will miss out entirely on the new opportunities of the future. And so, for the era of global markets, we need to think imaginatively and create a new system to prevent crises over the long-term rather than simply cure them when the emergencies arise.

And I believe that the way forward is to match the openness we now have in financial markets with a new openness and transparency in economic policy-making – an openness in the flow of economic information from governments to markets and an openness in the procedures for scrutinising economic information that can build confidence and credibility.

I suggest that the lessons from experience in Mexico, Thailand, Indonesia and now Korea strengthen the case for the code of good practice for promoting openness in fiscal and monetary policy, which I proposed at the IMF interim committee meeting in September, and which is now being drawn up by the IMF. I also believe that in its Article IV consultations the IMF should comment on practices in this area in all member countries as a matter of course.

We need regular public and candid international surveillance by the IMF and of course improved international cooperation in the regulation of banking and securities business. So one answer to the uncertainty and unpredictability of capital flows is the certainty and predictability of information and procedures that can give confidence to the international financial system. So, fundamental to the stability of the international financial system is this long-term commitment to greater openness in the management of all our economies, no matter how difficult this may be for individual countries in the short term.

It is our commitment to stability through clear, open and accountable procedures that has informed our decisions, early in government, to make the Bank of England independent and to legislate for a long-term framework for monetary policy; and to publish a five-year deficit-reduction plan and legislate for a new code for long-term fiscal stability. Our commitment to openness and internationalism also guides our approach to the future of Europe. The European Union, which has been so important to the maintenance of peace in Europe, and is now so important to integrating east and central Europe into Europe, is grounded in a commitment to enterprise, competition, open trade and opportunity for all.

There is now a single market in place between the fifteen countries and 370 million people who now belong to it. Within this fully developed single market, a successful European single currency would have benefits in trade and transaction costs, and for enhanced investment. Unnecessary currency speculation within Europe would be ended for good. Interest rates could be lower. We could have an environment in which new firms and new jobs could grow as freely as they do in the United States.

So there are good economic arguments that support the principle of a single currency. The American economy has grown up with a single currency – even if your central banking system did not take its current shape until well into this century. You take for granted the transparency of pricing, the greater competitive opportunities, the certainty for investment and all the ways in which one currency makes one market work better. These potential benefits will be good for business in Europe too.

So in less than fourteen months from now Europe will start a process whereby businesses in one country selling to another will be able to do so without exchange-rate risk, with lower transaction costs and with more transparent prices. The arguments for European economic and monetary union are economic. And if the economic benefits are clear, it is right – in my view – for the UK to consider being a part of it. There are those, of course, who say monetary union is nothing more than a political project, being pursued for purely political reasons and being implemented on a politically driven timetable. I disagree. Economic and monetary union is about practical economics – growth, jobs, what works for business. And this is, in my view, where the argument should lie. We want a Europe which delivers not constitutional blueprints which are unrealisable but a better future of job opportunities and prosperity.

Of course, there are constitutional implications in transferring decisions about interest rates to a European central bank. The sharing of sovereignty is an important step and should be recognised to be important. But we pool sovereignty in NATO. We pool sovereignty in the single European market. And if this pooling of sovereignty can be shown to be in the the national interest of countries, then it is right in my view for them to consider it.

So I neither subscribe to the dogma that says we must be in a single European currency regardless of the economic consequences or the one that says we must be outside even if the economic arguments for it are compelling. Instead, for me, a decision, and the timing of a decision, comes down to a practical hard-headed assessment of the economic benefits. We will want to examine:

- first, would joining EMU create better conditions for firms making long-term decisions to invest in Britain?
- second, how would adopting the new currency affect our financial services?
- third, whether business cycles and economic structures are sufficiently compatible for us to live comfortably with Euro interest rates on a permanent basis?

- fourth, if problems do emerge, is there sufficient flexibility to deal with them?
- fifth, will joining EMU help to promote higher growth, stability and a lasting increase in jobs?

In short, the tests add up to an assessment of Britain's national economic interest. And they involve an assessment of whether convergence with our European neighbours can be sustained and durable.

Applying these tests I have made clear that membership of a single currency in 1999 would not be in Britain's national economic interest. There is not enough convergence between the economies of Britain and most of Europe. To join in 1999 would risk setting off a short-lived inflationary boom followed by the inevitable bust. It would fly in the face of the government's commitment to economic stability.

Instead, we have said that we need a period of settled convergence before we make a decision on membership and that we are likely to make a judgement early in the next parliament.

So our strategy is to prepare and then, through a referendum of the British people, decide. We have now therefore begun an intensive period of preparation. We are working closely with all sectors of business to ensure that when the Euro arrives elsewhere in Europe – as it will in 1999 – British businesses are in a position to benefit from it. I have asked David Simon, until May the Chairman of BP, and now a Treasury Minister, to take personal charge of our preparations work to ensure that all businesses trading out of the UK are well prepared for the Euro.

We are committed to allowing business to use the Euro in the United Kingdom from 1999. Foreign currencies can already be used in the UK for a wide range of business activities, from filing company accounts to paying certain taxes and issuing shares. Businesses will be able to use the Euro for all these activities in the UK from 1999 and for many others as well. And many British firms are already rising to the challenge of the Euro. Marks and Spencer has decided to put in place the capability to accept the Euro in its shops across the UK. One of our major banks, NatWest Corporate Banking Services, has announced that they will train their staff to handle the Euro and that a range of Euro products and services will be available from early next year. Other firms in Europe are planning to use the Euro for all their transactions with suppliers.

So we are working closely with business to coordinate an effective response to the challenges of the Euro in Britain, based on partnership and a joint commitment to get down together to the serious business of preparing for 1999. And the UK banking system – already by far the most sophisticated and competitive in Europe – will have the capability to process payments in Euros from 1999 for local and national businesses as well as for the international financial market. The Bank of England is leading Euro preparations in the City.

If we have to take any extra steps to ensure that the UK remains the most business-friendly environment in Europe, then we are committed to taking them. So whatever your views on the Euro may be, my message is simple. This British government is determined to maximise your business opportunities after 1999. British economic policies will go on being right for business. Britain will continue to lead Europe towards ever freer trade and more open markets. And Britain will continue to be the best place in Europe from which to exploit the new business opportunities after 1999.

So Britain is now set on a course based on our commitment to the principle of a single currency, and our strategy for preparations now so that, if the government recommends it early in the next parliament, the people of Britain can decide. But I am determined, as I said at the outset, that the Europe that develops out of economic and monetary union is a Europe that is open not protectionist, flexible not sclerotic, and outward-looking not isolationist.

Just as new Labour propose a new and modernised Britain that is more open, more dynamic, and more competitive, so too we also propose a new Europe – more dynamic, competitive, and open, and learning a great deal from the entrepreneurial and flexible labour markets of the American economy. As we start our UK presidency of the European Union we recognise that Europe needs more competitive energy, utilities and telecommunications markets; and we need to open even more the financial services, and the communications and media industries, achieving a more positive balance between competition and regulation.

So the agenda for greater European competitiveness includes completion of the single market and the removal of hidden barriers to trade and competition; reform of the CAP; and the institutional changes necessary for enlargement. We should, of course, retain the British veto, especially in areas like taxation and defence.

Just as Europe is developing a new competition policy, Europe is also now developing a new approach to jobs and to employment – what I call the new European way. We are setting aside the old European model – rightly criticised for being too bureaucratic, over-concerned with regulation, insufficiently attuned to a far more adaptable and flexible economy where technological change is constant. There can be no quick fixes. But there is a new European way for higher growth and employment. This new way recognises we must equip ourselves for a more competitive world where business must be flexible and people must constantly adapt. The new way rejects the failed, old-style over-regulation and inflexibility, which stifled job creation in Europe, just as it rejects governments doing nothing when millions are denied jobs. It states that achieving high and stable levels of growth and employment will require new ap-proaches from national governments in welfare and tax reform, in policies for investment and competition, and in tackling social exclusion.

The new European agenda does not seek to buy temporary jobs by wasteful public-expenditure subsidies to prevent change or to defend irresponsible and unsustainable monetary and fiscal policies. Instead we ensure, within Budget disciplines, that public resources are used more productively and we modernise social-security and tax systems. In this way structural, micro-economic reform goes hand in hand with macro-economic policies for growth.

First, a new approach to welfare – one that recognises unemploy-ment can be structural and technological. So we need to offer men and women new opportunities for work and training. We need a new approach to tax to ensure that tax systems encourage, not penalise, work. A new approach to business – we must recognise small businesses as job creators. Britain has learnt much from successful US experience of venture capital for small firms. I intend to use our European Union presidency to spread the message that small firms plus venture-capital opportunities lead to more jobs throughout Europe. And finally we must all pursue job-enhancing flexibility through an enhanced commitment to education and training.

So this new European way rejects centrally imposed employment solutions that can mean wasteful subsidies and is in tune with the successful policies which have created 9 million jobs over the last five years in the United States. In truth, there is a movement by governments, especially of the centre left, towards more flexible labour markets – witness legislation currently under way in Holland, Sweden and Italy. Skills and productivity are now the key test rather than regulation or deregulation. There is plenty of evidence across Europe that there are new alliances for change in the EU that can be built. And in this way we can show the world that Europe has a new model, combining economic dynamism with social justice, to promote growth and employment through supply-side reform of our economies. And of course maintaining open markets and liberal trade and investment policies are more important than ever to Europe's future.

So this is my view of Europe: a Europe that will become more open, more outward-looking, more competitive, more adaptable to change, more able to provide opportunity to all its citizens. The agenda we want to follow in Europe will allow Europe to make a more effective contribution to promoting free trade and internationalism. So to those who fear the process of change in Europe will make Europe more insular, I reply: greater European integration will not make Europe look inwards, but make it more able to look outwards with more confidence.

Let me say in conclusion: our ambitions for Britain and Europe match the United States' ambitions for itself and we share the same ambition for the world economy. More open, more outward-looking, more internationalist. So Britain and the USA can celebrate today not what we have achieved from our shared histories but what we can achieve by applying our shared values which continue to bind us even more closely together. Shared commitments to liberty, openness and opportunity for all, that have stood the test of time in war and in peace. Shared commitments that have served us well over the course of this century and will, in my view, continue to serve us well in the new century ahead. Our two great countries and our two great continents with our linked destinies moving forward together.

In June 2001, shortly after the general election, the Chancellor set out his thinking for the second term in a statement entitled 'Enterprise for All'. This marks a development in thinking from the aims of the first term, which were focused on high and stable levels of growth and employment, to raising productivity. There are two aspects of this approach: radical reform and modernisation of product, capital and labour markets to create a truly entrepreneurial culture open to all; and a step change in competitive pressures within the British economy, which he suggested was essential if we were to deliver faster productivity rises than our industrial competitors. Although not as headline-grabbing as the decision to make the Bank of England independent, there is a symmetry in the plans outlined in this statement to make British competition decisions – and the competition authorities – fully independent of political influence. The aim of the statement was 'to send a message to the entrepreneurial, the innovative and dynamic: that if you were starting up, growing a business, investing, taking people on, seeking new capital or working your way up in business – the UK government was on your side'. But it was also a mini-Budget, as it ranged from tax adjustments to reforms of the City; education and training issues; and planning and other supply-side measures. It was, in short, a message about how a party with a successful economic record was committed to building on and improving the position it had created so successfully in the first term.

. . .

When four years ago we made the Bank of England independent, we said that the aim of economic policy in Britain should be high and stable levels of growth and employment.

In our first term we put stability and employment creation first. From today our energies – building on the platform of stability and employment creation – must now be directed to raising our country's productivity.

Britain needs radical reform and modernisation of our product, capital and labour markets to create, for the first time, a truly entrepreneurial culture that is not confined to the few but open to all: one where, in every community, people with ideas and initiative have the chance to start and succeed in business.

The new Britain of enterprise for all cannot be built on inadequate investment, low skills, boardroom complacency, workplace resistance to change, or on cartels or restrictive practices from whatever quarter they arise.

So first, competition open to all. Because greater competition at home is the key to greater competitiveness abroad, the Secretary for Industry and I believe that a step change in competitive pressures within the British economy is essential if we are to reach for US levels of productivity growth and to deliver over this decade faster productivity rises than our industrial competitors. In the last parliament we made monetary decisions independent of political influence within a long-term framework where the policy objective is clear, the division of responsibilities is clear, and there is maximum transparency and accountability. In this parliament we must do the same for competition policy.

The approach to competition inherited in 1997 had unclear objectives, Byzantine procedures with inadequate penalties and was not properly transparent. Having laid the foundations with the 1998 Competition Act, and building upon detailed work by Stephen Byers, the Secretary for Industry now intends to make a decisive break with the past. She is setting out today her plans to make British competition decisions – and the competition authorities – fully independent of political influence within a long-term framework where the objective, set by government, is to promote competition and the consumer interest, with transparent procedures and enhanced parliamentary accountability – not just in mergers but also now in complex monopoly decisions.

In the United States, it has long been recognised that cartels are simply a sophisticated form of theft – and that the threat of prison sentences for such clear-cut abuses is the most powerful and effective deterrent. So it is our intention to introduce a new criminal offence for individuals who engage in cartels. We will consult on the details. The new duty to examine all barriers to competition will not exempt the public sector. In future all anti-competitive public-sector regulations will be subjected to competition scrutiny. We will encourage the Office of Fair Trading to recommend changes in government regulations. By next year we will have put in place the framework to deliver a pro-competition regime to match the best in the world.

The small businesses of today are the big businesses of the future. And so, in addition to opening up competition, we are today sending a message to the entrepreneurial, the innovative and dynamic: if you are starting up, growing a business, investing, taking people on, seeking new capital or working your way up in business – we are on your side. So today the government makes proposals to create a

Capital Gains Tax regime for entrepreneurs and business assets that will, overall, be more favourable to enterprise than that of the US.

The Capital Gains Tax rate we inherited was 40p for investments held for one year. We cut it in Budget 2000 to 35p. I now propose a cut to just 20p. For investments held for two years, I propose to cut the rate from 30p to 10p. With this new regime, the Inland Revenue estimates that three-quarters of taxpayers with business assets will pay only a 10p rate. And for non-business assets we will now consider the case for further changes to improve incentives to invest.

The Enterprise Management Incentive scheme helps innovative and growing companies attract the best talent. I now propose to double the reach of the scheme to include all businesses with assets of up to £30m.

For large companies we have already cut Corporation Tax from 33p to 30p, the lowest rate of Corporation Tax in our history. Our approach is one based on a broad base and low tax rates that is stable and transparent, reflecting our belief in fair tax competition – and our opposition to harmful tax competition and niche regimes – so that companies make decisions to exploit real business opportunities. All reflecting our goal to make and keep the UK as the best place for international business. And as we discuss with business the next steps we will take in pursuit of these principles we are, next month, publishing a further consultation document.

It is not enough to offer new incentives for existing businesses. Britain should also be the best place to start a business. Compared with Britain, three times as many Americans say they want to start a business. The chance to start a business should not depend on your background or contacts or just luck. In every area of Britain I want the enterprising to go as far as their talents and potential can take them. Instead of the old Britain under-performing when enterprise was seen to be restricted to a closed circle of the few, the British economy will do best when enterprise is – and is seen to be – open to all.

First, to simplify VAT for half a million small firms, we are publishing details today of a new flat-rate VAT scheme – reducing business costs by up to £1,000 a year. Second, at present companies must compile separate accounts for Companies House and for the purposes of calculating their tax. We are now consulting with business on abolishing the requirement for separate accounts for tax, cutting both red tape and business costs. Third, I can announce that in the Budget of 2002 there will be a cut in small-company Corporation Tax bills. More of small companies' profits will be taxed not at 20p but at half that rate, 10p. Fourth, as we introduce an on-line electronic gateway for small firms to access services, Mr Pat Carter will report on how we put new technology to use to help small firms cut the cost and time of running payroll systems. Fifth, for half a million businesses with turnovers of less than £100,000, we will remove the presumption that fines be levied automatically. In future, automatic VAT fines will be levied only after a written communication is first sent offering advice and help to sort out the problem. Sixth, because small-business growth rests not just on increasing the rewards for success but minimising the costs of failure, the Secretary for Industry will announce major changes to the rules on insolvency. We will abolish administrative receivership – which allows banks to take unilateral control when companies become insolvent – and instead insist they use procedures in which all creditors have a say.

And at a cost of around £10m a year the Treasury will abolish what is called Crown Preference, the right of the Revenue and Customs to have first call for tax payments ahead of other creditors already in the queue.

Finally, to make the enterprise culture work for people and places too long forgotten, I can announce that a £40m community-development venture-capital fund, comprising government, private sector and charities, is to be opened and we will set out, in the next few weeks, the detail of the stamp-duty exemptions, VAT reductions and enhanced capital allowances that will be on offer to encourage new economic activity in high-unemployment areas.

Fresh incentives to start a business will be accompanied by new measures to encourage venture capital – vital to bridging the investment and productivity gaps with our competitors – in all our regions and nations. I can announce today that, following our agreement with the European Commission and backed by £80m of Treasury funding and up to £60m from the EIB, our Regional Development Agencies – leaders in a new industrial policy for Britain's regions – will issue prospectuses for a £1 billion fund. Regional targets are being set out today.

The modern way to personal prosperity is higher earnings through higher skills. To tackle the most serious skills problem in the modern industrialised economies – 7m adults with less than five GCSEs and 3m with no qualifications at all – the new Education Secretary is preparing plans for a step change in the skills of the adult workforce.

Our new British tax-credit system that applies to work and families allows the tax system to pay out money as well as receive money. Because of its strategic national importance to the future of our economy, and because the voluntary approach has not achieved enough so far, we are prepared to apply to workplace training the same radical approach, with the government not only recognising companies' investment in skills when they pay tax, but looking at contributing more through a new workplace-skills tax credit or grant. But we will only move ahead with this reform if the opportunities we offer are matched by new responsibilities accepted by both employers and employees.

A tax credit is already boosting research and development and encouraging innovation among smaller firms. In the next Budget I intend to introduce a new research-and-development tax credit for larger firms.

Britain benefits from entrepreneurial talent joining us from all over the world. In the last parliament we extended the work-permit system and skilled people coming to the UK have risen from 50,000 a year to 150,000 a year. The next step is to attract those with a business track record that demonstrates their value to the economy and, building upon this new scheme, it is our intention to do more.

Closing the productivity gap requires us to raise the quantity and quality of investment in private and public sectors.

Institutional investors control £1.5 trillion in assets, including half the quoted equity markets. We will see through the reforms Paul Myners has prescribed to encourage long-term investment and there will be a further review – as he recommended – on the extent to which our pension funds have risen to the challenge he has laid down.

I can also announce today that Ron Sandler, former Chief Executive of Lloyds and Chief Operating Officer of NatWest Group, will undertake an independent review of the long-term retail-savings industry, including life insurance, a sector which manages more than £1,000 billion in assets. Working closely with the FSA, he will examine the forces and incentives which drive the industry and its approach to investment.

The efficiency we seek in the private sector we demand in the public sector. Having doubled net public investment by 2003–4 to £18 billion per year, and agreed £180 billion of new public and private investment over ten years for transport, government at every level – national, regional and local – must raise its game.

The planning system is a key issue for business and the economy. Much of our planning system is based on the needs of the post-war world. The Secretary for Transport, Local Government and the Regions will now bring forward detailed proposals for modernisation in a Green Paper on reform to the planning system which we will publish later this year and which will strike the right balance in a radically different economy which puts an ever higher premium on speed, efficiency and flexibility – especially to reflect the widely differing needs of all our regions.

Today, Martin Cave, who is conducting the independent review of radio-spectrum management launched in the Budget, is publishing a consultation paper on his approach. His preliminary conclusion is that we need better incentives so that users, in the public or private sectors, do not waste or hoard what has previously been a free good – especially if we are to encourage innovation and productivity in this area.

The same radical programme of reform of capital, product and labour markets we have announced for Britain, we will also pursue in Europe.

Our universities have a major role to play in generating ideas and providing high-level skills crucial for productivity and growth. In the last parliament, we provided substantial new funding, especially for science. The universities too have begun to respond, and a process of culture change is under way. In this parliament we will take this further, ensuring that the right freedoms and incentives are in place for universities, and that talented people from all backgrounds are able and encouraged to get the best education.

If we are to have the deeper and wider entrepreneurial culture we need, we must start in our schools and colleges, and the Secretary for Education and I have asked Sir Howard Davies to examine how we can make progress. We want every young person to hear about business and enterprise in school; every college student to be made aware of the opportunities in business – and to start a business; every teacher to be able to communicate the virtues and potential of business and enterprise.

So as we spread the spirit of enterprise from the classroom to the boardroom, our aim for this parliament is to contribute to the creation of a deeper and wider entrepreneurial culture where enterprise is truly open to all.

In a speech at the Growing Business Awards on 5 December 2002, the Chancellor returned to his concerns about supply-side issues which he felt should be addressed in the drive to create a modern economy. In particular, he focused on the role of government in raising the UK's productivity with the aim of creating an entrepreneurial culture, where all have the opportunity to realise their potential – to acquire skills, to work their way up, become self-employed or start a business – and 'to rise as far as their talents and potential can take them'. And he suggested that the context for this included a need to change the history in the UK of 'inadequate investment, low skills, boardroom complacency, workplace resistance to change, cartels and restrictive practices'.

. . .

At the CBI Conference last month in Manchester, the CBI published their latest survey showing that 95 per cent of businesses say that macro-economic stability is the most influential factor when making investment decisions. And I can assure you tonight that as a government we will take no risks with our hard-won and newly won stability.

. . .

Under the new monetary and fiscal regime that we put in place in 1997 based on independence for the Bank of England: we imposed an inflation target that is symmetrical, designed to combat both deflation and inflation; froze public spending for two years; introduced new fiscal rules to put the public finances in a sustainable position; and systematically reduced the burden of debt – a framework designed not just for times of high growth but to cope with times of global difficulty too.

. . .

If stability is the precondition for growth, enterprise is its driving force, and our energies must also now be directed to raising our country's productivity, creating, for the first time, a truly entrepreneurial culture where all have the opportunity to realise their potential – to acquire skills, to work their way up, become self-employed or start a business – and to rise as far as their talents and potential can take them.

This new Britain of enterprise for all cannot be built on inadequate investment, low skills, boardroom complacency, workplace resistance to change, or on cartels or restrictive practices from whatever quarter they arise. Instead the British economy will do best when enterprise is – and is seen to be – open to all.

So, first, we are improving our tax regime to reward enterprise and entrepreneurship – sending a message to the enterprising, the innovative and the dynamic: that if you are starting up or growing a business we are on your side.

. . .

Second, to help innovative and growing companies attract the best talent, the Enterprise Management Incentive scheme now includes all businesses with assets of up to £30 million. And, for those needing skills from abroad, we will continue to expand and improve the Highly Skilled Migrants programme and create a special unit to help small businesses.

Third, the small businesses of today are the big businesses of the future. And the chance to start a business should not depend on your background, or contacts, or just luck. In every area of Britain I want the enterprising to go as far as their talents and potential can take them: championing a wider and deeper enterprise culture in our country; understanding that wealth creation is vitally important to a Britain of opportunity and security not just for some but for all – and it is therefore right to do more to encourage people to start their own businesses.

So to help start-up companies access the finance that they need, the Small Firm Loan Guarantee Scheme will be extended to cover businesses with a turnover of up to £3 million a year, in a wider range of sectors, benefiting 400,000 businesses in all. To cut form-filling and red tape we are expanding the flat-rate VAT scheme so that 650,000 firms will no longer have to report on each VAT transaction, and we will now consult small businesses on how we can extend and improve the scheme further. And, following the exemption for 200,000 firms of the requirement for a statutory audit, we will also consult next year on the same deregulation for medium-sized firms.

Finally, because the rate of business creation in our high-unemploy-ment communities is one-sixth of our prosperous areas, we know that we must also do more to create new incentives for greater private-sector engagement in those areas. We should see inner cities and old industrial areas not as no-go areas for business or simply 'problem' areas but as areas of opportunity: new markets where businesses can thrive because of the competitive advantages they often offer – with strategic locations, untapped resources, a high density of local pur-chasing power and the potential of their workforce. So to remove the barriers preventing firms from starting up and growing in our most deprived communities, we are designating 2,000 new enterprise areas where we encourage economic activity by cutting the cost of starting up, employing, training, managing the payroll – and with the new Community Investment Tax Credit giving new incentives for invest-ment I hope that government and business can work together to bring investment, jobs and prosperity to areas that prosperity has still by-passed.

And while we have done a lot to make businessmen and -women role models for young people, we have a long way to go and I hope you will join us in our attempts to, by 2006, give every pupil the opportunity of five days' enterprise education, encourage business creation in every area and make successful business leaders role models in every community.

Creating a wider and deeper enterprise culture is not a task for government alone – success also depends on the innovation, crea-tivity and involvement of entrepreneurs like yourselves across the country:

- the leadership and vision you demonstrate;
- the growth and innovation you achieve;
- the new technology that you develop;
- the exceptional financial returns you deliver;
- the new markets you identify and create; and
- the needs of consumers that you meet.

By disseminating the lessons learnt from the most successful busi-nesses – your skills, your innovations, your achievements – through-out the business community, we can go further and help inspire the business leaders of the future.

So I urge each and every one of you to spread your expertise and experience to others – to continue to work in your communities, with young people, with schools and colleges, to become business mentors – role models for the next generation of entrepreneurs. In this way, working together, I know we can tap the immense skill and entrepreneurial talent that exists in Britain to the benefit of us all. Congratulations again on your success – you represent the very best of British business.

Rightly proud of the success of the UK economy, the Chancellor has been anxious to draw this experience to the attention of European neighbours, and to reform the approach and processes in the European Union. The fullest exposition of this approach is given in the speech made by the Chancellor to the Centre for European Reform at Church House, London, on 10 March 2003. Entitled 'The Road to Full Employment: Economic Reforms for a More Flexible and Dynamic Britain and Europe', the speech took place just before the Iraq conflict, and in the wake of 9/11, and is influenced by this timing. None the less the speech focuses on changes required to the economies of countries in the EU so as to bring about modern ways of achieving high and stable levels of growth and employment. In particular the Chancellor focuses on the role of governments in the modern world, setting out three areas of concern: the need for stability, because investment will flow most to those countries that are the most stable, and ever more rapidly away from those that risk stability; the need to create the best environment for high-quality investment – through policies for education, research and development, and infrastructure; and how enhancing productivity and competitiveness in a more open economy demands a new flexibility in labour, capital and product markets, and a commitment to root out inflexibilities, at both a national and increasingly a regional level.

This is an important speech, not just because of the message it sends to Europe, but because it encapsulates many of the macro-economic and micro-economic policies which have been employed by the Treasury during the first two terms of this government. However, it goes further than this, giving a social-inclusion context for much of the economic thinking. The Chancellor is fond of quoting a maxim coined by John Smith QC MP, the leader of the Labour Party 1992–4, that economic efficiency and social justice are two sides of the same coin. This speech is a good exposition of how this maxim and the related 'prudence for a purpose' maxim of Gordon Brown have been implemented under the Labour government since 1997.

If the last decade of the twentieth century will go down as the decade that ended the Cold War, the first decade of the twenty-first century will be remembered as the time when nations had to adjust to both the opportunities and insecurities of globalisation. A generation that has grown up free of the horror and pain of world wars, survived the uneasy truce of the Cold War, dared to hope that the fall of the Berlin Wall would mean a halt to the proliferation of weapons of mass destruction, is now having to confront the proliferation of chemical, biological and, often, nuclear weapons in the hands of terrorists and failed states.

. . .

This new era of globalisation brings insecurities as well as opportunities; so too in economic policy insecurities and opportunities arise together and challenge us to devise modern ways of achieving our traditional economic objective: high and stable levels of growth and employment.

Globalisation means that there is hardly a good we produce here in Britain that is not subject to intense competition from at home and abroad, not just competition from traditional competitors in the advanced industrial economies but competition from emerging market economies, not least in Asia and the east of Europe – competition which is itself a spur to growth and prosperity.

Twenty years ago, even ten years ago, it was just about possible – if costly and wrong – for countries to shelter their industries and sectors, protecting them from global competition. But today there is no safe haven, no easy escape from global competition without putting at risk long-term stability, growth and employment.

Some say governments are powerless facing these new global forces, that they cannot any longer play their part in achieving the old objectives: high and stable levels of growth and employment. I believe the opposite to be true. Globalisation has rightly limited the scope of government and in the modern, open, more fiercely competitive global economy governments cannot use the old levers to achieve their objectives. They cannot easily impose exchange controls, trade off inflation for growth, resort to old-style protection-ism, competitive devaluations or costly state aids – the policy of subsidies in one country – without undermining their long-term goal of high and stable levels of growth and employment. But it is because in a more open global economy countries pay such a heavy price, not least in long-term investment, for getting the big decisions wrong that I believe governments are even more important today to the attain-ment of high levels of growth and employment.

Because investment will flow most to those countries that are the most stable, and ever more rapidly away from those that risk stability, there is an even greater premium than before on governments running a stable and successful monetary and fiscal regime to achieve high and stable levels of growth and employment. That is why we attached so much importance to the first decision our government made – to make the Bank of England independent – and why, with low inflation, low interest rates and low debt, our stability makes us a far stronger economy today.

Globalisation also describes a world whose very mobility of capital and openness to competition is ushering in a restructuring of industry and services across continents. And while emerging-market countries are ready to attract low-value-added, low-investment and low-skilled work, we have to compete on ever higher levels of skill and technology rather than ever lower levels of poverty pay. So countries that make the right forward-looking decisions to create the best environment for high-quality investment – through policies for education, research and development, and infrastructure – will be better placed to achieve high and stable levels of growth and employ-ment. It is for this reason that in our recent Spending Review we decided to match new resources to major reforms in education, science and innovation.

But because high levels of productivity growth are essential to high levels of growth and employment, there is a third essential element that distinguishes the successful high-employment, high-growth economies from the least successful – and it is also one where governments can also make a difference. And it is this I want to talk about today both for Britain and for the Euro area: how enhancing productivity and competitiveness in a more open econ-omy demands a new flexibility in labour, capital and product mar-kets.

A few weeks ago I urged Labour to reverse traditional, often hostile, attitudes to markets and recognise the need to strengthen markets in important areas. And today I want to set out how Britain proposes to lead the way in labour-, product- and capital-market reform and how in this process of market liberalisation we can make progress with European economic reform. Some still argue that when global competition is challenging every industry and almost every service, the state should replace markets or, as difficult, seek to second-guess them through a corporatist policy of supporting national champions. But competition at home is not only essential for competitiveness at home and abroad; if we are to make the most of the potential of open trade and the European single market, we will need greater flexibility as we respond to new technologies, and adjust to changes in consumer demand. Indeed in a single-currency area where the old flexibilities to adjust exchange rates and interest rates are no longer available at a national level, labour-, product- and capital-market flexibilities are even more essential. Adjusting to shocks without putting at risk high and stable levels of growth and employment demands even greater market flexibility.

America's experience as a large and mature monetary union demonstrates the importance of sufficient flexibility to ensure that monetary union works well. In monetary unions, whatever their size, local economies need to respond to shocks and there is a premium on effective internal market-adjustment mechanisms. In the USA competitive pressures are strong, ensuring that prices respond quickly and efficiently. With risk-sharing diversified across a broad and deep capital market they can limit the impact of shocks. And a high level of product- and capital-market flexibility complemented by a high level of labour flexibility has helped sustain high levels of employment and growth.

In the past, supporters of full employment have not been in the habit of thinking of flexibility as a route to full employment. And supporters of greater flexibility in our economy have seldom described its benefits as the attainment of full employment. Yet today flexible economies are also the economies with higher employment. And I want to demonstrate how in the new world of global competition it is by creating a more flexible and dynamic economy in which firms and individuals respond to the challenges of change that we will best achieve our historic goals for full employment.

Britain and Europe have, of course, long since moved from the old assumption that there is a long-term trade-off between inflation and growth and employment. But, in a world where business must respond quickly and people must adapt to change, Europe has too often been unwilling to go beyond old assumptions that the labour-, capital- and product-market flexibility necessary for productivity is the enemy of social justice.

Yet the road to full employment starts with monetary and fiscal stability, is built on investing in skills and responsibility in the workplace, and demands attention to enterprise, competition and employability as necessary means of achieving high productivity. And this road to full employment in Britain depends on achieving economic reform not just in Britain but in Europe too. In the past the Labour Party – like the rest of Europe – has not been very good at facing up to issues relating to flexibility. Indeed flexibility has often been a term of abuse, derided as the antithesis of fairness, as the race to the bottom, as poverty pay – and it is often suggested that flexibility is a synonym for exploitation. Yet flexibility is, in reality, the ability to respond to change with speed. Changes in a marketplace include the impact of innovation and changing technology, changing consumer preferences and the changing need for particular skills.

Failure to respond to these changes by companies and by individuals leads to an unproductive use and wasteful allocation of resources in the economy and thus huge costs in lost output, jobs and prosperity. So in an open and far more rapidly changing global trading economy, flexibility – the ability to respond quickly – is not an option. It is a necessary precondition of success. Without firms prepared to innovate and adjust, economies become sclerotic. Without the capacity to develop the new skills needed, countries will simply be left behind. Indeed there are just two modern routes to achieving high levels of growth and employment – flexibility without fairness, which leaves people helpless in face of change, or flexibility with fairness, where governments and firms equip people to cope with change and tackle the insecurities that surround it. The issue of the best modern policies for fairness is one I will address in detail in a later speech.

But it is right both to create flexible markets and to equip people to master change – through investment in skills and training, through the best transitional help for people moving between jobs, and – as I hope to demonstrate – through the operation of a minimum wage and a tax-credit system.

And flexible markets and active labour-market policies are not incompatible opposites but can be essential allies of each other as we seek high levels of growth and employment. So the issue is not one of abandoning fairness but of achieving the right kind of flexibility. And what people should oppose is not governments that insist on flexibility but governments that fail to insist on matching that flexibility with fairness.

In other words, we should recognise that, with the right kind of flexibility in British and European labour, capital and product markets, economic efficiency and employment opportunity for all can advance together. So our goal – enterprise and fairness in a dynamic, flexible economy that delivers full employment and prosperity for all – demands that we match policies for stability, employment and fairness with flexible labour, capital and product markets.

Since 1997 we have, in pursuit of this:

- made our competition authorities independent and opened up product markets;
- revamped the physical planning system;
- encouraged our capital markets by cutting Capital Gains Tax and introducing new incentives for venture capital;
- encouraged enterprise with lower tax rates for small businesses;
- offered new incentives and resources to encourage greater investment, skills, and innovation; and
- devoted time and energy to promoting economic liberalisation in Europe.

At the same time as we have created a more flexible economy we have advanced fairness with the introduction of the National Minimum Wage, the Working Families Tax Credit and Jobcentre Plus – an employment service that offers personal help to people moving into and between jobs – reforms not at the expense of greater flexibility but consistent with greater flexibility.

But we can still go much further in product-, capital- and labour-market reform in Britain and in Europe to make our economy more flexible. When I argue for flexible product, capital and labour markets I want open well-informed markets that ensure capital flows to productive uses so that the price mechanism works to balance demand and supply and labour and capital are used efficiently. So flexibility in product, capital and labour markets means that instead of being suspicious of competition, we should embrace it, recognising that without it vested interests accumulate. Instead of tolerating monopoly or cartels which were never in the public interest, or appeasing special interests, we should systematically extend competition – forcing producers to be efficient, extending the choices available to consumers and opening up opportunity for the ambitious and the risk-takers.

To back up independence for the Competition Commission and the new proactive role of the OFT, we will take action where investigations reveal challenges that have to be met and demand that the same rigorous pro-competition policies are applied to the public sector as well as the private sector. As the DTI Secretary of State is showing: the old days of the 'sponsorship' department are over, freeing up resources to enhance the DTI's role in promoting competition and enabling markets to work better.

And it is right to demand the same liberalisation throughout Europe to make the single market work. Britain has learnt much from the steps taken in the European Union, before and after the Lisbon agenda, that promote liberalisation and economic reform. And we have supported wholeheartedly the attempt to restrict the wasteful use of state aids that prevents markets functioning well. Yet while in 1988 Cecchini estimated that single-market liberalisation would add 4.5 per cent to Europe's GDP, cut prices by 6 per cent and increase employment by 1.75 million, many of the gains have yet to materialise. The way forward is mutual recognition of national practices not harmonised regulations; and tax competition not tax harmonisation.

So we support:

- a more proactive EU competition regime furthering a strong and independent competition policy for Europe;
- investigations into particular European markets and sectors to drive up competition and prevent British firms from being excluded from European markets, from energy and telecommunications to agriculture;

- faster progress on the reform of airport slot allocation and liberalisation of postal services; and
- support for private-finance initiatives in Europe.

And Britain remains at the forefront of countries supporting the European Commission's demands for tougher state-aid rules to prevent unwarranted subsidies for loss-making industries and at the European Economic Reform Summit we will continue to push for a more aggressive approach to tackling unfair competition and state failure. In the UK we are removing the last of the permanent, ongoing subsidies – thus removing aids which have no market justification. But while it is right to remove state aids which distort the single market, it is also right to reform state aids to target market failures which need correction.

It took Britain more than a year to secure European permission to create regional venture-capital funds for localities desperately in need of strong local capital markets that work for small businesses. And it has taken months more for permission to abolish stamp duty for business-property purchases in areas urgently in need of local property markets that work and the new businesses and jobs that can ensue.

Here again, as I said in a speech on markets a few weeks ago, the case for state intervention is not to extend the role of the state but, by tackling market failure, to help make markets work better: instead of thinking the state must take over responsibility where markets deliver insufficient investment and short-termism in innovation, skills and environmental protection, we must enable markets to work better and for the long term.

An effective competition policy helps new and small businesses enter markets and prevents them being held back or penalised by large vested interests. And instead of being suspicious of enterprise and entrepreneurs, Labour should celebrate them – encouraging, incentivising and rewarding them, hence our reduction in Capital Gains Tax (from 40 pence to 10 pence) and our small-business tax reforms (from 23 pence to 19 pence and the lower rate from 10 pence to zero).

With their recommendations on small-business banking, the competition authorities have tried to cut the cost of investing for small businesses. The next stage is to help small and medium-sized businesses get fair access to public-sector procurement. Opening up markets to new suppliers intensifies competition as well as encouraging innovation. That is why we have asked the Office of Government Commerce to identify what more can be done to increase competition in markets where government has substantial purchasing power and to enable small businesses to compete for government contracts and deliver value for money.

I have said that instead of maximising regulation to restrict the scope of markets, we should systematically pinpoint regulation that does not serve the public interest and can be reduced. So as I examine measures for the Budget we will continue the process of cutting the cost and burden to small businesses of starting up, investing and growing, especially in areas of high unemployment. And as the government strengthens our assessments of the impact of regulation on small firms which have included examinations of the retail and chemical sectors we will also look at transport, pesticides, food and drink processing, and the collection of statistical data.

Because 40 per cent of new regulations originate in the EU, the European Economic Reform Summit this month should call for the same rigorous assault on unnecessary regulation throughout the European Union: an agreement to examine all new directives for their impact as well as taking stock of existing EU directives.

Achieving greater flexibility not just in product markets but in capital markets is essential for high levels of growth, and as we press ahead with the Cruickshank, Myners, Sandler and Higgs reforms and build on our cuts in Capital Gains Tax we should continue to examine where local capital markets have had least success, and continue to cut the barriers to entry faced by small businesses and to open up venture-capital markets in our regions.

State-aid rules – and thus the treatment of early-stage research – should be reformed to help Europe bridge the gap between our research and development performance and that of Japan and the USA. With the R&D tax credit we are trying to cut the cost of investing in innovative research, but state-aid rules should make it easier to address the market failures that obstruct research and innovation in its early and pre-commercial stages.

Capital markets can and must help us manage risk more efficiently, between sectors, over time and across national boundaries. While America has achieved a high degree of diversification across state borders, investment in Europe remains fragmented on national lines and there is a need to remove barriers to diversification of investments across borders, for example in pension and mutual funds.

So we will support the European Financial Services Action Plan as it improves mutual recognition of financial-services providers in insurance, banking and capital markets. It is also true that competition between trading systems in capital markets is vital to improve efficiency and reduce dealing spreads, and so cut the cost of capital and raise the returns from investment. And where EU regulation such as the proposed new Investment Services Directive threatens to weaken rather than strengthen competition we will fight to change it.

And instead of the old protectionism we must embrace open markets and thus free trade. Efforts to improve the flexibility of product and capital markets should not stop at the EU's borders. Greater openness to global trade and investment creates new opportunities for European producers and consumers, and strengthens the incentives for reform. A more flexible and dynamic Europe would, in turn, play a leading role in breaking down barriers to trade and investment in the rest of the world – a virtuous circle of reform and openness, leading to a stronger and more resilient economy from which the EU, and the global economy, would benefit. So we must drive forward the Doha agenda and also do more to strengthen the trading links between the EU and USA. Deepening what is already the world's largest trade and investment relationship would do much to stimulate flexibility and reform in Europe.

By looking for market solutions to market failures, we move beyond the old centrally imposed industrial policies – the corporatist policy of picking winners – in favour of a new regionally driven focus on local enterprise, local skills and local innovation. For it is not just how national economies adjust that matters but how local and regional economies and their markets adjust and respond that will determine whether full employment can be achieved in each region and on a sustainable basis. And that requires us to move beyond not only the first generation of regional policy that was centrally delivered first aid but the second generation of regional policy, which was London and then Brussels imposing centrally set rules focusing on incentives for incoming investors.

Today, in the third generation of regional policy, the focus is, rightly, moving from centrally administered subsidies to locally led incentives that encourage local skills, innovation and investment and boost the indigenous sources of regional economic growth. And to achieve this we also move from the old idea that regional policy is just the work of one or two departments. In the new regional policy for a more flexible economy each department must step up the pace of reform and devolution:

- from centrally administered R&D policies to the encouragement of local technology transfer between universities and companies and the development of regional clusters of specialisms;
- from a national 'one size fits all' approach to skills to devolving 90 per cent of the learning and skills Budget, so that we can promote regional excellence;
- from centrally run housing and transport policies to greater regional coordination . . . offering greater flexibility in response; and
- from centrally administered small-business polices to more local discretion starting with, in the East and West Midlands and the North-West, the small-business Budget locally administered with the Regional Development Agencies.

Because small-business creation is so important to the success of local economies it makes sense to examine why the rates of small-business creation vary so much between localities and regions and what we can do about it. In the UK just 5 per cent of adults think of starting a business; in the United States it is 11 per cent – so we have a long way to go. And there are also large variations in the rates of business creation between areas of the UK, with ten times the number of firm start-ups in the best-performing areas of the UK than in the worst performing.

So to remove the barriers preventing firms from starting up and growing in our most deprived communities, we have designated 2,000 new enterprise areas – where we encourage economic activity by cutting the cost of starting up, investing, employing, training, managing the payroll. Here we are bringing together industry, planning, employment and social-security policies to tackle local property-market, capital-market and labour-market failures – hence the new community investment-tax relief, the relaxation of planning regulations, the abolition of stamp duty, the engagement of the New Deal – government and business working together to bring investment, jobs and prosperity to areas that prosperity has still bypassed.

It makes sense for Europe to help this process forward. And while, as I argued last week, structural funds will inevitably be concentrated on the poorer regions of central and eastern Europe, more prosperous countries with large regional inequalities should be given the freedom to tackle capital-, labour- and product-market failures through a reform of state-aid legislation.

And we need to extend our approach of encouraging regional and local initiatives from R&D, skills, small-business, transport and housing policies to the critical area of employment and welfare policy. Because we seek local and regional labour markets that match labour demand and supply efficiently and help us meet our aim of full employment, the Work and Pensions Secretary, is focusing on how regional- and local-employment and social-security policies can help our labour markets get people back to work more quickly and help people move more easily from the old jobs that are becoming redundant to the new jobs that can give them greater security.

So while the preconditions for full employment are national stability, employability and an environment for investment and high productivity, the achievement of full employment and high levels of growth and prosperity depends upon regions and localities becoming better equipped to adapt to change. In particular, when there are negative economic shocks, it is all the more important that the economy can adjust and ensure that temporary output and job losses are minimised and do not become more permanent. And while it is true that in recent years in the United Kingdom earnings growth has been consistent with the inflation target, and what is called the NAIRU (non-accelerating inflation rate of unemployment) has fallen, it is still the case that UK labour-market flexibility – while greater than much of Europe – is lower than in the USA.

A dynamic economy needs adaptable and flexible labour markets where there is:

- first, mobility – a willingness to be more mobile, and firms and a labour market that support the ability to do so;
- second, what economists call functional flexibility – the skills to meet new and different challenges;

- third, employment flexibility – the ability of firms and individuals to adjust working patterns to new challenges; and
- fourth, at a local level the ability of our employment and wage systems to respond more quickly to shocks and imbalances between supply and demand.

And to meet the challenges of a global economy we have, in each of these areas, much further to go. While the rate of job turnover in Britain is higher than the seven years per job in the Euro area but lower than in America – five years against four years – it is also true that there is far less geographical mobility in response to change in Britain and in Europe than in the USA.

While around 25 per cent of the UK's workforce have degree-level skills, the UK, with 8 million men and women with low or no skills, 20 per cent of 18–24-year-olds, has a long way to go. While nearly 25 per cent of British employees work part-time compared with less than 15 per cent in the Euro area, and while working outside the five days a week is common in Britain – 13 per cent working on a Sunday compared to 11 per cent in the EU and as low as 4 per cent in some countries – adjusting to the global economic challenge will require firms and individuals to be more flexible. Indeed it is because our aim is not just achieving but sustaining full employment in our regions that we need not only stability but this flexibility to respond to shocks. And this is more important than ever in a single-currency area, with the US experience demonstrating labour mobility and wage flexibility to be critical to the success of their single currency.

In the American single-currency area geographical mobility, which can help tackle skill shortages and help people find new opportunities, is twice the level of Britain and Europe today. It is often argued that mobility will be greater:

- the more flexible the housing market;
- the easier it is to commute; and
- the easier it is to attract economic migrants to high-demand areas.

Britain has a smaller privately rented sector than most countries. And the Deputy Prime Minister is examining how we can encourage more flexibility for those in social housing through initiatives such as choice-based letting and the new housing and mobility scheme to help tenants relocate to access employment. And because we also need to ensure we are building sufficient housing in areas of high employment, the Deputy Prime Minister has also set out ambitious plans to deliver a step change in housing provision and expand assistance for key workers to enable them to rent as well as buy in high-demand housing areas. Around 3.8 million tenants currently rely on housing benefit for help with their rent, but delays in processing new applications after a claimant returns to employment can lead to rent arrears and debt, dissuading some people from moving into work. So because housing benefit can constrain mobility, affecting an individual's ability to move into jobs and move between localities, the Work and Pensions Secretary is piloting major reforms in housing-benefit administration and incentives that make it easier for the unemployed to return to work. The current Housing Benefit Pathfinders Scheme offers a flat-rate payment in the private rented sector and it makes sense to pursue the pilot of a flat-rate payment based on household circumstances and location.

International migration can help tackle skill shortages and aid adjustment to shocks. Migration into the UK through the work-permits system has risen from 50,000 in 1997 to 170,000 this year and is projected to rise to 200,000 by 2004. And while tackling illegal immigration, the Home Secretary and I have been considering further extensions to the successful work-permit system for legal migration.

The more skilled men and women there are, and the more they are willing to develop new skills, the more flexible and productive the economy is likely to be. And the more globalisation opens up the world economy to fierce competition across continents the more competitive advantage countries like Britain will gain from a higher level of skills. Yet despite our successes at university and college level, skills – particularly in basic and intermediate qualifications – are Britain's Achilles heel, the most worrying inflexibility of all within our labour market. And we are learning a great deal from successful industrial-training policies in other parts of Europe.

So the Education Secretary is right to forge a new partnership between government, employee and employer with a view to expanding our skills and making labour markets work more flexibly. Here, as elsewhere, a partnership between employers and workforces is the best means of combining flexibility with fairness. Building on the Union Learning Fund and other innovative partnerships, I believe we can do more to encourage and help trades unions expand their role in training and education. The increased registration for the University for Industry (providing courses for over 700,000 people already), the high levels of young people undertaking modern apprenticeships (now over 220,000 a year) and the success of the new Employer Training Pilots prove that the issue is not an unwillingness to get new qualifications and skills but the availability of training at the right time, price and standards.

So we are expanding the Employer Training Pilots now operating in six areas to around a quarter of the country – offering incentives for firms to give their staff paid time off to train towards basic skills and NVQ Level 2 qualifications. And a major shake-up in skills training will be announced this summer. From April, we are piloting devolved pooled budgets for adult learning in four areas of the country – providing greater incentives to employers and individuals to develop their skills, reducing bureaucracy and strengthening the regional and local dimension in skills development. Looking to the workforce of the future we are not only investing heavily to raise standards in schools but, from September next year, rolling out Educational Maintenance Allowances in England – providing young people from poorer families with up to £1,500 a year to encourage them to stay on at school and get the qualifications they need. And we have set up the National Modern Apprenticeship Taskforce, which will look at how to increase the opportunities for young people to participate in Modern Apprenticeships and how to engage employers more fully in the programme.

More flexible patterns of employment can remove unnecessary inflexibilities and enable more men and women to balance work and family and other responsibilities. And it is important to look at new ways of ensuring that firms have the flexible working patterns they need and families have the flexible arrangements they need. So the government is not only looking carefully at employment regulation, but also at how we can empower mothers in particular to secure the benefits of more flexible working arrangements.

So we will resist inflexible barriers being introduced into directives like the European Working Time Directive and we will support flexible interpretations of existing rules and remove unnecessary regulations and restrictions.

In recent years attitudes to part-time work have changed. Companies have found flexible working patterns help them be more productive. Families have found that flexible working arrangements help them balance work and family responsibilities.

So most people who work part-time today do so not because there are no full-time jobs available but out of choice. So while temporary employment is half the European Union average, 6 per cent compared with 13 per cent in the EU, 25 per cent of our total employment is part-time and employees already work far more flexible hours than most EU countries.

One reason is our tax-credit system and the Childcare Tax Credit. And we continue to seek ways of making it easier and less costly for employees to balance their work and family responsibilities and for businesses to recruit.

That is why building on:

- our rise, from April, in maternity pay to £100 a week;
- the extension in paid maternity leave to twenty-six weeks;
- the first ever paternity and adoption pay;
- a new right for parents of young or disabled children to request flexible working; and
- the first ever National Childcare Strategy . . .

. . . we will consider further reforms: new tax and national-insurance incentives to expand employer-supported child care; paying Childcare Credit for approved home child care by carers who are not already childminders; and increased flexibility in parental time off, including giving fathers time off to attend ante-natal appointments.

Lone parents genuinely worry that without flexible working patterns they will end up neglecting their children and fear that the price of employment may make it difficult to discharge family responsibilities. To ensure the balance is better, the Childcare and Child Tax Credits are not only making work pay for the single parent – £10 an hour for a part-time job – but ensuring that a decent income does not require them to work excessive hours damaging to their family life.

And because employers recognise these anxieties, a new employer taskforce is now examining how, among other measures, working patterns can be more flexible and childcare provision better to suit the needs of lone parents. With a national discussion of how we help lone parents balance work and family responsibilities, we can offer companies a smart solution to their employment needs, help thousands of lone parents move out of poverty from welfare into work, and reach our target of 70 per cent of lone parents in employment. And similar initiatives will also be forthcoming for men and women who have previously lost out in the old economy – such as the ethnic minorities – but who, by more flexible recruitment patterns, could gain in a new economy where we should see diversity as a source of strength.

While there are more than 900,000 men and women over fifty now in work compared with 1997, more flexible recruitment patterns could make it easier for older workers to move between jobs and tomorrow the Work and Pensions Secretary will host a summit of employers aimed at more flexible recruitment incentives for firms to take on the 1 million disabled men and women who want to work to find suitable employment.

To reduce unemployment and to achieve full employment we must not only focus on the needs of particular groups of the unemployed but also focus on regional and local flexibilities and so tackle the regional and local variations in unemployment rates, in skills, in the ability to create new jobs and generate new businesses. And here we are able to learn from the success of active labour-market policies especially in the Nordic countries and the low-unemployment countries of the European Union.

Without the New Deal, youth long-term unemployment would be twice as high and today inflows to Jobseekers Allowance are at their lowest since records began in 1967. Unemployment in the UK is 5.1 per cent compared to 6 per cent in the US and 8.5 per cent in the Euro area.

But after six years of a national programme I am more convinced than ever that if we are to get more of the long-term unemployed back to work, and more successfully match vacancies to jobs, a full-employment strategy now demands regional and local flexibility as well as a national framework of incentives and sanctions. And this is needed too to increase the New Deal's ability both to respond in the event of a local or regional shock and to help the unemployed move into work more rapidly.

Today vacancies – 2.5 million notified at Jobcentres every year, 5 million overall – are still at historically high levels in almost every region and nation of the UK. And in relatively low-skilled trades like in hotels and catering 350,000 vacancies were reported last year. Often large numbers of vacancies exist side by side with large numbers of unemployed in adjacent communities. Tottenham, for example, has some of Britain's worst long-term male unemployment among its 5,000 unemployed while neighbouring districts have seen nearly 90,000 vacancies in the last nine months, with many more in the wider London economy.

So it makes sense for Jobcentres to develop programmes more sensitive to, and tailor-made for, local and regional conditions and to have greater flexibility and discretion to move people quickly the into work, to stop too many long-term unemployed falling through the net, and to tackle shocks when they arise. So we should consider extending the areas of job search for the newly unemployed and as we combine flexibility with help for people coping with change we are prepared to help with initial transport costs where appropriate.

And while in France nearly 40 per cent of unemployed have been unemployed for more than a year, in Germany more than 50 per cent, in Italy more than 60 per cent, Britain's 27 per cent compares unfavourably with 6 per cent in the USA so, with our Step Up and other programmes that require the long-term unemployed to take jobs on offer, we will consider an even greater emphasis on responsibilities as well as opportunities in moving the long-term unemployed back to work.

In the global economy it has been easier in the past for nations to respond to shocks when wages are either highly centralised at a national level or highly decentralised at a local level. In Britain only 5 per cent of private-sector workplaces are covered by multi-employer collective-bargaining arrangements – and many have profit-related pay schemes, helping to make pay more responsive to the economic cycle. Wage-setting tends to be local, annual and normally at a plant or workplace level.

But a willingness to be flexible in both the private and the public sectors can be matched with a guarantee of fairness. Indeed as the government has implemented its reforms to the tax and benefit system, two of the critical guarantees that have been put in place for people in work are the minimum wage and the Working and Child Tax Credits. Critics of the minimum wage have argued that it reduces the flexibility of the labour market by inhibiting the workings of the price mechanism, with the potential to create stronger wage growth throughout the economy and reduce employment. But research suggests that the minimum wage has not led to increased unemployment or inflationary earnings growth across the economy. Adjusted through regular reviews by the Low Pay Commission, who consider the effect on pay, employment and competitiveness, wages can still respond effectively to labour-market changes and there is no reason why the minimum wage cannot continue to be uprated and rise this year.

But an even stronger guarantee of fairness at work is the tax credits which provide not only an even more generous floor but work to sustain incomes up the earnings scale:

- while the minimum wage today is £147 for a 35-hour week, the minimum for a family with two children – through tax credits – is a net £275, almost twice as much;
- the minimum for a couple in work without children is £183 and for a single adult over twenty-five is £154;
- a single parent working sixteen hours is guaranteed £179, the equivalent of £10.10 an hour after taxes;

compared with a minimum wage of £4.20 an hour. It is the guarantee provided by tax credits on top of the minimum wage – not just a minimal safety net but support right up the income scale – which makes it possible for regional and local wage flexibility to operate without undermining basic fairness. And this guarantee would matter even more in circumstances where, as happens in the United States single-currency area, real wages may have to adjust in response to a shock. Because of the tax credits, a fall in wages of £1 impacts to the tune of 30p on the earner – just one-third – with the generous Child Tax Credit making the same true for incomes extended up the income scale.

So what are the next steps?

First, we need to do more to help the newly unemployed and the long-term unemployed back into work and help our labour market work better and more rapidly.

Second, we need to take forward our tax-credit reforms which match flexibility with fairness.

Thirdly, all key public-sector workers in London receive some form of London premium. There are London arrangements for teachers, nurses and policemen, with officers in the Metropolitan Police receiving free travel in the London area. And there are attempts at special housing-cost arrangements for public-sector workers with 10,000 key workers helped through the Starter Homes Initiative. Yet while professionals have benefited from London weighting and other arrangements it is clear that many lower-paid workers have been at risk of losing out. A more considered approach to local and regional conditions that pays attention to the needs of recruitment and retention makes sense. Reliable, timely regional prices and cost-of-living data can help inform the debate. So the review of regional information and the wider examination of statistics by Chris Allsop will help us address some of these issues, providing greater impetus to our objective of promoting economic growth in all regions and reducing the persistent gap in growth rates between the richest and poorest areas of our country.

But evidence so far suggests that the tax and benefit reforms introduced since 1997 have already improved the flexibility of the UK labour market. The unemployment trap – the trap that made it not worth while for unemployed men and women to take a job – has been addressed, work now pays more than benefits, and the reforms have extended support for families with children up the income scale, ensuring not only that work pays but that more people are protected from the impact of economic shocks.

So by examining the challenges ahead, we open up a rich reform and modernisation agenda for our product, capital and labour markets, an agenda of economic reform not just for the future of Britain but for the future of Europe. And policies for flexibility need not be implemented at the expense of fairness but can move forward together, indeed in support of each other, in ways that ensure that genuine concerns in Britain and in Europe about the importance of social cohesion are not swept aside or forgotten but rather recognised and addressed in ways consistent with the realities of today's global economy and of tomorrow's.

And we have shown today that greater flexibility in both Britain and Europe is good for Britain and Europe. We have learnt from Europe's emphasis on skills, on the social foundations of markets, and on social cohesion. And through the Luxembourg employment initiative and then the Lisbon economic-reform agenda we continue to learn from each other. But we also learnt – and this is an important message especially for trade unionists committed to full employment – that to achieve full employment in Europe we have to learn from the best of American flexibilities and sweep aside the worst of European inflexibilities. Indeed, in the future, achieving a full-employment economy will need much of the flexibility of America applied to much of Europe. And I have suggested a programme of economic reform not just in Britain but in Europe – a programme upon which I will elaborate in greater detail in my Budget and beyond.

In its history – from our Industrial Revolution through Empire – Britain has stood out: a beacon to the rest of the world as a land of enterprise – of invention, of commerce, of creativity – and of fairness.

As we prepare for the world upturn and to meet the long-term challenges of globalisation, Britain has a unique opportunity to be, once again, a beacon to the world, advancing enterprise and fairness together – a dynamic vibrant economy that is the first economy in the new era of globalisation to match flexibility with fairness and, in doing so, attain the high levels of growth and employment that are the best route to prosperity for all.

On 2 December 2005, the Chancellor opened the Advancing Enterprise Conference in London, and gave a *tour d'horizon* of the current range of policies in place, as he says, to ensure that 'Britain is made for globalisation and globalisation is made for Britain'. He stresses the framework for stability put in place in 1997, and which has turned Britain from a stop-go economy into one of the world's most stable economic environments. And he rehearses many of the achievements in the supply side of the economy, arguing for a Britain that is a leader in the world's fastest-growing, most wealth-creating sectors at the cutting edge of global advance – in capital markets and financial services; in science and innovation; in creativity and enterprise; in skills and education. A Britain that is the preferred international marketplace not just for European companies but also for growing Chinese, Indian and other companies, and the location of choice for the headquarters of multinational companies.

2005 has seen the doubling of oil prices, the threat of the recurrence of global inflation, and the shift of almost 1 million manufacturing jobs from Europe, Japan and America to Asia. And the starting point of this conference today is that each of us – companies, governments, individuals – are having to respond to the scale, speed and scope of a transformed global economy. And it is my pleasure and privilege to thank all British businesses represented here today for your leadership of the economy, and in challenging times your resolve, your courage to change and your determination to do what is best for enterprise and best for Britain. And let me also welcome distinguished guests here today from every continent, joining our dialogue which I hope will lead to a consensus and in time to a shared economic purpose that can make globalisation work best for Britain.

And in visiting, as I have done this year, many of our trading partners internationally and companies large and small domestically – and I see many of you here now – I know that our country's economic future depends on how we work together. This, our third enterprise conference, is a concrete expression of our partnership. I believe we have listened to, and learnt from, the debate at the previous two conferences, tried to forge a shared agenda and acted to take it forward. You told us that if we are to confront the challenges of globalisation, we needed to tackle the issue of regulation. So earlier this year, we accepted in full the recommendations of the Hampton and Arculus reports to cut red tape. You told us that if we are to lead in the high-tech value-added industries of the future, our ambition must be to become world class in science, hence our ten-year framework for science which sets out a step change for research and development across the UK and I want to say more about this today. And you told us that if we are to attract the best companies and be world class, we can never settle for being second best but instead have to be world leaders in education and skills.

So today's conference matters because what you think and tell us will continue to be critical in ensuring we focus on the right issues and pursue the right goals. Like you I want a Britain that is a leader in the world's fastest-growing, most wealth-creating sectors at the cutting edge of global advance – in capital markets and financial services; in science and innovation; in creativity and enterprise; in skills and education.

More than ever, as we have discovered, in one of the most challenging years for the global economy, the foundation for growth is economic stability. We know that in a global economy investment flows to the stable economies and away from the volatile. So when I present my Pre-Budget Report on Monday, I will show how Britain has taken long-term decisions on monetary and fiscal policy and moved from being one of the stop–go economies of the world to one of the most stable. Under our monetary and fiscal regime we will maintain low inflation, low public debt and a long-term commitment to strong fiscal discipline. And nothing we do will endanger that position.

Upon our foundation of stability, Britain can become the location of choice and the place to do business. Take financial services and capital markets: today Britain exports twice as much in business services as we import and four times as much in financial services. And I want to congratulate businesses here on their drive, global competitiveness and innovation which have made the City of London alongside New York the leading financial centres of the world – London, the world's largest foreign-exchange market, the largest foreign-equity market, the largest bond market – London's success born not out of serving a large domestic economy, but on winning the lion's share of international business.

I want us to build on our advantages – your talent for innovation, the critical mass of skills now in London, our openness to the world, including our deepening links with China and India, a unique combination of language, time zone and a legal system that makes English law the law of choice for international contracts. And now the determination of the Financial Services Authority to extend their risk-based approach of financial regulation that is both a light touch and a limited touch. All strengths that we wish to develop so that we become the preferred international marketplace not just for European companies but also for growing Chinese, Indian and other companies and the multinational headquarters of choice.

To meet our next ambition, to become world leaders in science, we cannot rest upon our heritage of scientific invention and achievement: we must build upon it, at all times looking to convert our scientific genius into commercial success. Today a higher share of our growth is delivered by science-based innovations than in any other industrial nation, including the USA, and Britain has a higher share of inward investment in research and development than any of our major competitors. Our ten-year framework for science – a public–private partnership between government and business – is already leading to £2.5 billion more science investment. Just as the Victorians built great entrepreneurial cities, so too for a new age, business and government are developing science and technology cities where universities, research institutes and high-tech companies come together to create clusters of creative activity. British universities already lead the world in medical research – pioneering some of the most remarkable breakthroughs of the past half century from the discovery of the Y-chromosome to DNA-profiling to the mapping of one-third of the human genome.

British pharmaceutical and biomedical companies already lead the world in applied research – contributing £3.7 billion to our exports. And our National Health Service has, over the last fifty years, pioneered some of the great medical breakthroughs: the world's first ever test-tube baby; magnetic resonance imaging, the MRI that allows early detection and treatment of potentially life-threatening diseases; the first combined liver and bone-marrow transplants.

How much stronger we will become from what I can announce today – thanks to the work of Sir David Cooksey – a strengthened clinical-research partnership linking our universities, our pharmaceutical and biomedical companies and our NHS.

In advance of the Secretary for Health announcing the new research-and-development strategy for the NHS in January – I can announce the establishment of a new National Institute for Health Research in the NHS, which will comprise around ten major centres of excellence, initially, 250 clinical academic fellowships and 100 clinical lectureships a year. A new IT network will make the unparalleled data base of the NHS available to improve our understanding of health so that in future Britain will be the premier location for developing new drugs and treatments and testing and tracking them. And as a result of this new partnership, our major pharmaceutical and biomedical companies are today announcing that they expect to make further investment in medical R&D in Britain of up to £500 million, rising to an additional £1 billion.

Britain should also be the world's number-one centre for genetic and stem-cell research, building on our world-leading regulatory regime. I can today also announce we are taking forward a new public–private partnership to invest in pre-commercial aspects of stem-cell research and to coordinate future research.

And in support of this, the Medical Research Council is today announcing an extra £50 million in total – including £40 million for basic stem-cell research and clinical trials and nearly £10 million for consolidating the UK stem-cell bank.

And because of the importance of a strong and clear regime of intellectual-property law to the location and development of companies in the UK, I am asking Andrew Gowers, former editor of the *Financial Times*, to consult with business and advise us on any updating of the law necessary.

Our inventiveness ranges beyond science and medicine. Today the dynamism of British business is leading the world in many of the most modern and creative industries. Our creative industries from digital electronics and communications to film, design and fashion – once only 1 per cent of our economy – now contribute 8 per cent. In the last eight years Britain's knowledge-intensive sector has grown twice as fast as the overall economy – highlighting the extraordinary creative talent Britain possesses. The opportunity now is to build on this extraordinary promise and ensure Britain becomes the world leader in creative industries. And the challenge is not just to encourage creative industries, but to encourage all industries to be creative. Today, Sir George Cox is publishing his report on creative industries and I can announce we will take forward his recommendations.

Sir Terence Conran and Lord Foster have agreed to work with him, the London Development Agency, and creative-industries business leaders to develop a new Creativity and Innovation Centre in London as a national hub of international stature that will be a showcase for British design. At the same time we will create a network of centres across the country, a centre in every region that will also nurture emerging talent.

At each stage we must maximise our flexibility and minimise the barriers – from over-regulation to under-investment – that hold business back.

- On planning, we should make our planning laws, more flexible and more responsive.
- On competition, we will maintain the stability of the new competition regime.
- On tax, we will continue to ensure we provide rewards for success and incentives for investment.

- On regulation, we will apply our risk-based approach across the board, review all European regulations, and I call on Europe to apply a competitiveness test to existing as well as proposed new rules.
- And on transport, where we all know we are still paying the price for decades of under-investment, we are doubling investment and will work with you on the basis of the Eddington Review of long-term needs to agree future priorities and how the public and private sectors can work together to deliver them.

But to become world leaders in any sector, we must be world leaders in education. All of us know that as global restructuring moves mass production to other areas Britain's future success will be founded upon high levels of skills. Britain is today undertaking the first stage of an audit of Britain's skills needs to 2020 – and I thank Lord Leitch, who is here this morning, for this work. And after the publication of the conclusion next week, a national debate will lead to decisions about our vocational-training goals for the future. I want business to join the debate – and today Sir Terry Leahy will lead a discussion on our educational priorities. And at all times whether it be schools, colleges or universities I assure you that we will insist that investment must be matched by reform.

I turn to trade. For Britain, the pioneer of free trade, the English Channel has never been a moat but a highway for commerce; the oceans around us never cutting British enterprise off but providing the route to markets in every continent of the world. And we have always stood against protectionism and in favour of open trade. In the next few days an opportunity presents itself which may not come again for ten or perhaps even twenty years – negotiations on world trade in Hong Kong.

In our view the trade round could bring wide-scale benefits to all economies, developed and developing, and contribute to the economic-reform agenda. As recently acknowledged by the Secretary-General of the WTO, Pascal Lamy, at the heart of the discussion is the future of agriculture protectionism.

On that, Britain has long argued that we need to have a long-term view of agricultural policy in our own countries. The paper which the International Development Secretary and I have published today contributes to the debate already under way on how to achieve a sustainable future for agriculture and helps answer those who have asked what the UK government means when it calls for further CAP reform. And it is because we believe that, through reform, there can be progress on trade, we continue to argue for an ambitious and balanced outcome to the Hong Kong meetings. Countries now being urged to move on services and non-market access may be prepared to make progress if there is willingness to take steps on agriculture. And it is this we must discuss internationally in the next few days.

So, for Britain's long-term future, the foundation is stability. The priority to encourage enterprise is to invest in science research and the creative industries, maximise flexibility and open up trade. At every point building the best-educated, most highly skilled workforce in the world. Beyond this conference I want to continue to encourage business to define what is needed for Britain to become more competitive and more enterprising and I invite you to help us do this. And if we work together then I believe we shall prove that Britain is made for globalisation and globalisation is made for Britain.

3

ADVANCING THE PUBLIC INTEREST

The public interest is an important but also an elusive concept. Its definition itself is the subject of political debate. Gordon Brown's position in this debate is clear: 'opportunity and security for all'. Accepting this notion the question remains how this interest can best be served, and here the Labour leader and long-serving Chancellor of the Exchequer has given his own reply.

It is in two parts. One is insistence that there must be a common floor on which all citizens stand. Gordon Brown does not refer to the idea of basic income guarantees but his concern with poverty, notably child poverty, and with the belief that work must pay, has led him to a number of measures which are stepping stones to a secure income for all: the minimum wage, welfare-to-work measures, tax credits at least for working families are elements of what may be described as a policy of citizenship.

This is of crucial importance, but the other part of Gordon Brown's route to the public interest has become his personal trademark. He respects the history of both the political left and the right. The state has a role in correcting serious market failures, and markets have a role in remedying state failures. But in order to avoid the costly errors of repeated pendulum swings from one to the other, a more stable approach has to be developed. It consists in giving each, government and business, the state and the market, its place, but above all in developing new forms of partnerships between the two which provide stability and flexibility at the same time.

Gordon Brown's original contribution to Britain's long-term prosperity but also to the politics of socio-economic progress generally, lies in imaginative combinations of historically separate institutions and approaches. Arms-length public institutions are one method, the Bank of England being the first example. At the other end, what in his James Meade Lecture he calls, 'binding in the private sector into long-term relationships with the public sector', has the same purpose. PFI, the Private Finance Initiative, is an example, as are PPPs, Public Private Partnerships of many kinds. One point to be added here is Gordon Brown's deep interest in the Third Sector, and in partnerships between public, private and philanthropic institutions (PPPs as it were) which include a 'public-interest test' for the latter.

Some may prefer a greater liberal emphasis on the independence of non-state actors, others may find it easier to rely on the benevolence of the state. There can be no doubt, however, that Gordon Brown has introduced a wide range of alternatives into our understanding of the public sphere, and more, that he has practised what he preached. His speeches on the public interest demonstrate his achievement but also stimulate further debate.

Lord Ralf Dahrendorf

What is the Treasury for? What is the proper role of government in modern society? How and in what ways should the public and private sectors advance the public interest? From the earliest days in government, Gordon Brown has devoted a number of speeches to these important questions.

In a speech to the Treasury staff in October 1997 the Chancellor set out what he saw as the government's overall mission, and in so doing raised some issues about the role of the state in advancing the public interest. In particular he refers to his belief that, when devising economic policy in the past, Britain has not had a sense of common purpose. In his view the divisions between public and private sector, between state and market, between capital and labour, management and workers, have destroyed all attempts to build prosperity and full employment. The Chancellor makes it clear that a main task for the new government is to leave behind these debates and divisions, and to establish a new common purpose. And he sets out the changes in the way he sees the Treasury operating in future.

The Chancellor develops the different role that he intends the Treasury to take compared to the Conservative governments in the period 1979–1992, in the Mais Lecture, given in October 1999. The speech starts with a reminder that the first act of the incoming government was not in fact Bank of England independence, but setting the Treasury the objective of achieving high and stable levels of growth and employment for the nation. This was a direct reference to a 1944 White Paper, which first set out these objectives. And as the Chancellor points out, the government of that time was clear that if full employment was to be sustained there were other conditions which had to be in place as well: stability, employability, productivity and individual responsibility. In other words, this was a task for the whole of government, not just the Treasury. Contrary to Nigel Lawson's distinction between the roles of macro-economic and micro-economic policy as set out in his 1984 Mais Lecture, Gordon Brown argues that the role of a macro-economic policy is not simply to bear down on inflation but rather, by creating a platform of stability, to promote growth and employment; and that an active supply-side policy is necessary not only to improve productivity and employment, but to make it possible to sustain low inflation alongside high and stable levels of growth and employment.

In the James Meade Memoral Lecture, given in May 2000, the Chancellor returns to the question of what should be the economic and social goals for the UK. He also uses the speech to review the progress made after three years in office, and to outline the next steps. But in addition to these points, the Chancellor extends an argument, touched on in earlier speeches, that in a modern economy, efficiency and equality, far from being incompatible, are necessary allies. But to achieve these desirable outcomes it is necessary to define a new relationship between individuals, markets and government. Indeed the Chancellor makes the point that not only does the new Labour government accept that there is a public interest in growth, employment, fairness and the provision of the best public services, but it also understands that this public interest can best be advanced by the public sector ceasing to be controller or owner, and becoming a partner, catalyst, sponsor, or co-ordinator. A government that empowers rather than directs.

In an important speech to the Social Market Foundation in February 2003, entitled 'A Modern Agenda for Prosperity and Social Reform', the Chancellor has set out his most thoroughgoing appreciation of the issue about how to determine the respective roles of the public and private sectors in advancing the public interest. In addition to redefining the public interest, there are extended sections on the role of government in relation to the creation and operation of markets; definitions of where markets should not be permitted; and thoughts about how best to harness the creativity and innovation of the private sector in provision of public services. When this speech was published by the SMF in May 2004, the Chancellor made a short address at the launch updating some of the arguments he had used the previous year. In particular, the Chancellor tries to resolve the dilemma posed in the last speech – that the government's three goals for public services (greater personalisation, higher efficiency and increased equity) were mutually incompatible, by arguing that public funding and largely public provision cannot only be equitable and efficient but can provide personalised services as well.

In a speech to Treasury staff on 15 October 1997, the Chancellor set out what he saw as the government's overall mission, and in so doing suggested that over the last fifty years, divisions between public and private sector, between state and market, between capital and labour, management and workers have destroyed all attempts to build prosperity and full employment. The Chancellor makes it clear that a main task for the new government is to leave behind these debates and divisions, and to establish a new common purporse. And he sets out the way he sees the Treasury operating in future: more international than it has been in the past, because the international stage is more important to every country's economic policy; more strategic, because the objectives can only be realised in cooperation with other departments; and more policy-oriented, because the scale and scope of the policy changes envisaged by the Chancellor and his team are so great.

. . .

What I want to suggest to you today is that all the changes that we have started in motion look forward to a new view of both the Treasury and economic policy and the way the Treasury relates to other departments, and our country to the rest of the world, in the years to come. In other words, the changes all add to a new role for the Treasury in a changing world.

Now, of course, the Treasury – formed in 1250; the first Budget 500 years later; the first time we had economic responsibilities officially designated, fifty years ago in 1947 – the Treasury has always had to change to respond to new events while retaining its professionalism, its discipline, its commitment to public service. But taken together, the changes that we are talking about add up to a new role for the Treasury as we approach a new century. And a new task for government in a modern, international economy.

Because what has changed, particularly in these last twenty years, is first of all decision-making on economic policy and markets. Indeed, what were national decisions are now international and global and that is irreversible.

What has changed also is that the waves of change in industry, in technology, in innovation which have been true of our industrial history for 200 years, are ever more rapid, ever more intensive, ever more essential to the workings of a modern economy. And, of course, there are new pressures, environment, demographic. And the challenge really is how we can equip ourselves as a nation for all the difficulties and all the challenges of the modern world. And it is to meet these challenges that I believe that the Treasury is adopting a new role as we approach this new century.

In the past, in economic policy Britain has not had the sense of common purpose, in my view, that is absolutely necessary. We have had divisions between public and private sector, between state and market, between capital and labour, management and workers. And I believe that the first thing we are doing is setting behind us all these differences of the past; these sterile, old-fashioned debates and divisions that held the country back, and establishing a new and common purpose for us all. But it is more than that. It is the Treasury preparing itself for a new role in economic policy. Because as markets become more international and as decision-making becomes quite different from what it was fifty years ago, and as the institutions that were set up particularly after the Second World War, the Welfare State, the tax and benefit systems that emerged from that, the employment policies, the fine-tuning of the economy, all these things have to be reassessed as we approach the new world.

From 1945 to 1975 there was what you might call the dominance of macro-economic policy. With fine-tuning being the catchword about what the Treasury did, to the exclusion, to some extent in all the government departments, of what you might call involvement in the supply side of the economy or what some people call micro-economic policy.

In the next twenty years, there was also a period of macro-economic dominance where the aim was to control inflation rather than directly to deal with the issues of growth and employment; where the role of government was seen as getting out of the supply side and into deregulation.

Now I think as we approach the new century, in this global economy, we're beginning to see that macro-economic policy is necessary and it must be got right, and that is why the new rules governing the Bank of England are so important. It is necessary, but it's not sufficient – we must look at all the barriers to growth; whether they be institutional, or the lack of competition in markets, in our welfare system, in the tax and benefits system, in all these areas where barriers to growth can affect employment opportunity, can affect the prosperity of this country.

And therefore I see the next few years as macro- and micro-economic policy working together: a new attention to the supply side of the economy, or what you might call barriers to growth; a new interest in the reform of the Welfare State to make possible greater opportunities for people; reform of the tax and benefit system for work incentives, and to give people the opportunities to rise in their careers and make the best of them; reform of markets so that they are more competitive and we can create more jobs and opportunities; and in this way achieve what has always been the aim of government policy since 1945, high and sustainable levels of growth and employment.

And how then does it work in practice? It means, of course, that when we look at the tax system, it is not simply a matter of only raising revenues, it is a matter of how our tax policies affect the ability to work, the employment opportunity, the chances for growth in the economy.

When you look at public expenditure, it's not simply how we can control public expenditure, although as you all know that remains very important to me and to the Chief Secretary, but also how the decisions we make about priorities in public expenditure can affect the growth rate of the economy, the opportunities for employment, fairness throughout our society.

And when we look at competition policy, and this is the importance of the growth unit we set up, the question is how we can remove all these barriers to growth that have prevented the British economy having the highest sustainable levels of growth over time.

When we look at our international policy in Europe, it is not simply how we play our part as a member state of the European Union; but how we could persuade Europe to move further and faster towards more competitiveness in the economy, more growth, and therefore more employment opportunity.

Keynes said that politics was about the survival of the unfittest, and he may have been referring to politicians like us. But I hazard to suggest that if Keynes had been here today, he would say that these are the great challenges of economic policy in the future.

We have got to get the macro-economic policy right. And that is why I think the decision we made about the Bank of England to create a long-term framework for monetary policy is absolutely right. We have got also to have the right fiscal framework for public expenditure, in particular for public borrowing – and we have set down the five-year deficit-reduction plan. But all the areas of activities in the Treasury – macro-policy, micro-policy – can be seen by all of us now as being directed towards achieving our mission, which is high and sustainable levels of growth and employment in the economy.

And I would like people to think that we are all working towards this common goal, which is shared irrespective of political party, right throughout the country. But there are new ways of achieving it as we approach a new century in an international economy. And when we look at the different things that we are doing, I like people to think that we are contributing to a common effort to achieve prosperity and opportunity for our country. And that means some changes. It means that the relationship between the Treasury and other departments is different.

I've studied the history of the Treasury, as someone who studied history, and the Treasury's role is often seen as stopping departments doing things. And that is absolutely right when it is wrong things that they are doing. But we must also see our role as encouraging departments, other departments, to do the right things; of driving them towards measures that will increase growth and increase employment. It also means a different role for the Treasury: a new role in communicating with these departments and the outside world to show that we are proactive and not simply trying to halt some of the spending decisions for the sake of it when we have these wider purposes as part of our remit.

It means a new role for the Budget itself. I've often thought that the old view of the Budget – a yearly statement where you divide up the national cake between different groups in your society, you give something to someone and then you take something away from someone else – is something that is now out of date. The new role of the Budget, in my view, is how as a nation together we can meet these challenges of the global economy and therefore in a Budget you will be as likely to announce decisions about the future of your Welfare State as about the future of public spending and tax revenues.

It means a new role for us internationally. Because it seems to me that Britain is now in a very strong position – because of the reforms that have been made in Britain – to put a message to Europe about reform in Europe itself. And we are also in a strong position to talk to the international world about international coordination, not least in the solving of the problems of world debt.

So if you sum up the role I see for the Treasury in the future: it is more international than it has been in the past, because the international stage is more important to every country's economic policy. And so naturally we are going to be more outward-looking and more international.

It is more strategic, therefore, than people have seen it in the past, because we are talking about strategic objectives that can be realised only in relation to other departments as well as our own, and not by us acting on our own. It is more policy-oriented, because we are talking about big policy changes in our country to make our economy more prosperous and to give more opportunities to many people who have been excluded from opportunities. And, for example, we are interested, as you would expect us to be, on how our Welfare to Work programme can yield new opportunities for the long-term unemployed, for young people and so on. And we are interested in our public-spending review as to how we can get new priorities for public spending throughout our country that can help improve the fabric of the nation.

And, of course, we are more interested and attentive to communication and how other departments can listen to and respond to our message; how we can persuade them to do that as well as persuade the outside world that we have new objectives and new aims to achieve.

And I hope that in these remarks I have summed up what I think most people will agree is that common-sense purpose for a Treasury looking towards the next ten, the next twenty years: a global economy where the task of government is simply this: to equip our companies, our industries, ourselves as individuals and our families for all the tasks that will face us in achieving prosperity and opportunity for all.

On 27 May 1999, the Chancellor gave the 30th Anniversary Lecture to the Institute of Fiscal Studies. Entitled 'Modernising the British Economy – The New Mission for the Treasury', this takes the 1944 White Paper as its starting point, and then is used by the Chancellor to set out the long-term challenges for modern government and the Treasury – a long-term commitment to stability; to raising the trend growth rate; to delivering employment opportunity for all; and, by tackling child poverty, ensuring everyone has the chance to realise their potential. Some of the arguments and detail are technical and deal with the minutiae of the debate at that time, but the argument is worth seeing in full, if only because it shows, once more, the Chancellor's desire that the Treasury should not just be a Department of Finance, but also the partner of other Departments dealing strategically with the provision of opportunity for the many, not the few.

. . .

When we came into government, we faced the prospect of another inflationary spiral, de-railing the British economy: what would have been yet one more damaging episode in the repeated cycles of boom and bust that have marked British macro-economic policy management in the last thirty years.

In these circumstances, the first thing that the Treasury had to do was to get inflation and the public finances under control and break decisively with the short-termist, secretive and unstable record of macro-economic policy-making of the past two decades by setting a credible framework.

We took early action to put in place a framework for economic stability – not only making the Bank of England independent but putting in place a new long-term monetary framework based on clear rules and open procedures. And as a result of the decisions that we took, inflation has been brought down to historically low levels.

We also took the same tough action to tackle the fiscal deficit which we inherited: not just cutting public borrowing in our first two years by £31 billion, but also putting in place a long-term fiscal framework, underpinned by legislation, with clear rules that, over the cycle, there is a current budget balance and prudent levels of debt.

This platform of stability is founded on clear rules: first, setting out long-term policy objectives; second, the certainty and predictability of well-understood procedures for monetary and fiscal policy; and third, on an openness that keeps markets properly informed and ensures that objectives and institutions are seen to be credible.

We have also brought stability to our relations with Europe. For the first time we are committed in principle to economic and monetary union. We are working with our European partners to make sure EMU is a success. The UK has also been working with our international partners to help create the conditions for stability, prosperity and poverty reduction throughout the world.

Some said, when on our first weekend in office we gave responsibility for interest-rate decisions to the Bank of England, that the Chancellor and the Treasury would have nothing to do. But I was clear then that we were only putting in place the foundations that would provide a platform of stability from which we could build to achieve our objectives of high and stable levels of growth and employment. In other words stability is a necessary precondition to deliver our objectives for growth and employment, but it is not sufficient. An economy cannot fly on only one wing.

Indeed the experience of the last twenty years shows that simply trying to control inflation alone without tackling the underlying causes of sluggish productivity growth and inflationary pressure has proven to deliver neither stability nor the high and stable levels of growth and employment that we set as our central objective on coming into government.

So let me turn to raising our long-term growth rate. Some people argue that governments cannot affect the trend growth rate of the British economy. I reject this pessimistic view. Our task as a government is to raise the sustainable trend rate of growth of our economy from the low level we inherited. That is our ambition and in the next decade we will achieve it in new ways.

Fifty years of our economic history from 1945 was marred by a succession of sterile and self-defeating conflicts between state and market, managements and workforce, public and private sectors. We need a new national purpose based on an end to short-termism and an understanding of the need to take a long-term view:

- government – by ensuring lasting stability and removing the barriers to growth;
- industry – by investing for the long-term; and
- the financial community by refusing to resort to the short-termism and stop–go attitudes which have bedevilled us since the war.

So our analysis suggests that we must combine our strategy for stability with major structural reforms of our product, capital and labour markets.

One measure of productivity is output per worker. On this basis, when we came into government, we inherited an economy with a productivity gap approaching 40 per cent with the United States and 20 per cent with France and Germany, and a trend rate of growth which meant that a substantial productivity gap was set to remain.

Alternatively you can measure productivity as output per hour worked rather than on the basis of output per worker. Because a UK worker works fewer hours than in the United States but more than in Europe, we do better against the US, but even worse against Europe. However, there is still a considerable gap with the US of about 25 per cent.

The IFS have suggested that we should measure productivity as total factor productivity, a measure which strips out the contribution from capital and labour intensity. On this basis the UK's productivity gap narrows to 10–20 per cent compared to the US and to Europe. Although this is a useful measure it does not reflect the chronic under-investment in physical capital in this country over decades. It is that low level of investment that has led to lower levels of labour productivity.

In every year since at least 1960, the UK has invested a lower share of GDP than the OECD average and capital stock per hour is much lower in the UK than for our competitors – 31 per cent higher in the US, 36 per cent higher in France, 55 per cent higher in Germany. Raising productivity per worker in the UK requires a period of sustained high investment so that we can close the gap in capital stock per worker with our competitors.

Of course, how the extra investment is used, its effectiveness, is just as important as the volume of investment, which is why the productivity agenda is so important. So I do not believe that any of us – analysts, employers, employees, politicians – can wish away the productivity challenge that Britain faces. While thirty years ago governments responded to the productivity challenge with top down plans, and tax incentives and grants primarily for physical investment, today it is more complex – involving the modernisation of capital and product markets, the encouragement of innovation and an enterprise culture open to all, and the building of a modern skills base.

First, we moved decisively in our first two Budgets to encourage new businesses with a cut in the small companies' tax from 23p to 20p in the pound. To encourage start-ups we have introduced a new 10p rate of Corporation Tax for small companies and a new 10p rate of income tax which will help the self-employed. And to encourage growth we have provided 40 per cent investment incentives for small businesses and medium-sized businesses; provided additional support for venture capital; and reformed the Capital Gains Tax system with a long-term rate of 10 per cent to promote and reward long-term business investment.

Recent work by the OECD has highlighted the problems which small businesses face in raising finance where they have little track record. As part of this reform of capital markets the challenge for Britain is to create a stronger venture-capital industry and to make sure there is enough venture capital for high-risk, early-stage and start-up companies.

Some argue that the Capital-Gains Tax system is too blunt an instrument to encourage long-term investment by individuals. They also argue that companies and investors will not respond to tax incentives to encourage investment. But these are often the same analysts who are quick to point out the power of incentives in our tax system to tax avoidance. Our shared task is to ensure we put in place incentives to encourage long-term improvements to productivity not short-term tax avoidance. We are putting in place measures to encourage investment in early-stage, high-technology companies, through a new £20 million venture-capital challenge run jointly with the private sector; and will be introducing incentives to promote corporate venturing. And next year we will introduce a new Enterprise Management Incentive measure to provide help where it is most needed to smaller companies with potential for rapid growth which are seeking to recruit or retain key personnel by offering equity remuneration. So the scheme will allow tax relief for incentives of up to £100,000.

But we need to give all who create wealth a greater stake in the wealth they create. There is clear evidence that giving people a genuine stake in their company's future delivers real improvements in performance and productivity. One study from the US has shown that in 73 per cent of cases, firms significantly improved their performance in the five years after establishing an employee share-ownership scheme. And, on average, these firms increased sales and employment by 5 per cent more than similar firms without schemes. In this country, the value of employee share ownership is widely agreed.

We are introducing a new programme of shares for all, in which employees will be able, for the first time, to buy shares in their own companies from their pre-tax income. Every employer will be able to match, tax-free, what each employee buys. The only condition is that the scheme must be offered across the company's entire workforce.

Second, we need to do more to turn scientific inventions in Britain into jobs for Britain by honouring the spirit of invention, facilitating the exploitation of invention and encouraging the commercialisation of invention. Higher productivity in part depends on inventions which are created in Britain being developed and manufactured in Britain. The seedbed is basic science so we are investing an extra £1.4 billion in basic scientific research. And we are putting in place a new R&D tax credit to encourage small-business investment in R&D. Work by the OECD suggests that R&D investment contributes to productivity growth, and tax credits will encourage more R&D investment by the private sector. We expect the R&D tax credit to benefit over 3,000 companies and help support at least £700 million of R&D spending. Our University Challenge Fund is designed to help turn British inventions into businesses here, and the new British Institutes of Enterprise will provide management skills and advice on commercial expectations to ensure the innovations that are developed in the UK are turned into products manufactured in the UK, creating good paying jobs in the UK.

Third, the sharpest spur to innovation, efficiency and improvement is competition. Work by Steve Nickell at the Centre for Economic Performance indicates the positive effect of competition on productivity. It is competition which drives companies to invest in people and equipment, to match the best in management and marketing and to innovate in process and products. This requires reform of our product markets – tackling vested interests, exposing management to international best practice and bringing down unnecessary market barriers to new entrants and new ideas. So the Secretary for Industry is now proposing as fundamental a long-term reform of competition policy as we have achieved for monetary policy – a new long-term framework with clear objectives and rules, free of political interference. We have rewritten this country's outdated framework of competition law. We have given the Office of Fair

Trading new powers and new money to police anti-competitive practices which damage businesses and consumers alike. This is one of the most important legislative reforms of this parliament. Now we will be consulting on the next stage, withdrawing ministers from the decision process on merger cases.

And we have launched a major independent review of competition in our banking sector in which Don Cruickshank is working with the banks to examine the obstacles to firms getting the finance they need to start and to grow.

We have made progress on a number of areas but there is more to be done. With the help of Lord Haskins we are considering ways of reducing the impact of regulation on productivity and growth; we are looking at improving the efficiency of the planning process; at meeting ambitious targets for electronic commerce to help make the UK the best place to trade electronically by the end of this parliament; establishing Regional Development Agencies; and considering how urban policy can improve economic competitiveness in our towns and cities.

The drive to improve productivity is an ongoing task which the Treasury has a responsibility to help meet, including through the work of the new Cabinet Committee on Productivity at which cabinet ministers from a range of key government departments are represented. We are also continually looking at ways to improve public-sector productivity including through public–private partnerships and in public-sector procurement. We have set tough targets for outputs from every department in our public-service agreements. And we are learning from the Public Services Productivity Panel – a new advisory committee of outside experts from the private sector; leading businessmen and -women, bringing into the public sector expertise of managing change in large complex organisations.

In Europe too we need to pursue a strategy of structural reform: reforming labour markets to create jobs; reforming product and capital markets to raise investment and build dynamic economies. We welcome the initiative for an Employment and Economic Reform Pact of EU countries to further European commitment to create the conditions for high and sustainable levels of employment and growth.

To those who say the government's approach to productivity is piecemeal, I would respond that nobody is claiming there are simple solutions, silver bullets. None of the economists and business people I have spoken to have suggested there are. This is not a challenge which can be met by one Budget alone, or one single new act of parliament can meet and beat. It is a long-term challenge for every department and for all of us working together.

Achieving the 1944 aims in the new global economy and changed labour market also requires an employment policy that equips people to succeed by being adaptable, flexible and educated. Our aims are high and stable levels of growth and high and stable levels of employment. The key insight of the 1990s is that the modernisation of the economy can be achieved only by spreading opportunity more widely in employment, earning power and education. Some argue that the only role for government is further deregulation of the labour market – that we can never strike the right balance between minimum standards and open markets. They argue instead for a deregulated labour market underpinned by a minimalist Welfare State which acts only as a safety net. Others have argued that tax and benefit reform cannot improve the working of the labour market and expand opportunity, and argue instead for more regulation at work and for a more generous – but unreformed – Welfare State which still only compensates people for poverty and lack of opportunity.

We must be more ambitious and tackle the underlying causes of deprivation. Our approach is to build a new and modernised Welfare State around principles – that, in addition to its traditional and necessary function of giving security to those who cannot work, for those who can work, the Welfare State should promote work, make work pay and give people the skills they need to get better jobs.

The modernisation of our approach to the Welfare State, which we argued for in Opposition and have been implementing in government, is necessary because of the transformation of the labour market in the preceding two decades: women are now working in far greater numbers than ever before. The return to skills in today's labour market is qualitatively greater than ever before and, correspondingly, the penalty for lack of skills greater. It is a measure of the challenge we face that nearly 50 per cent of people with no qualifications are either unemployed or outside the labour market. The labour market is characterised by part-time working and self-employment as never before. And we face a problem of structural unemployment – large sections of the population excluded from work – as never before.

When we came into office, four and a half million adults lived in households where nobody worked, double the level of twenty years ago. Nearly one in five children were growing up in households where no one was working, twice the rate of France and four times the rate of Germany. And the reason that this issue of worklessness poses a particular challenge for this government is that it is now the primary cause of poverty in Britain today. Whilst twenty years ago, it was pensioners who made up the largest section of those in poverty, today it is those living in workless, working-age households. And two-thirds of working-age households on persistently low incomes have nobody in work, with eight out of ten having no full-time work.

The best form of welfare for these groups is work. Simply compensating people for their poverty through benefits is not enough; the task must be to deal with the causes of poverty. We must give people the chance to work, if they can. Indeed, the Treasury paper we published earlier this year, 'Tackling Poverty and Extending Opportunity', shows that over the period 1991–5, 80 per cent of the bottom quintile who moved into work moved out of the bottom income group. And our strategy has been to tackle the barriers that people face to getting into work – the lack of work opportunity, the unemployment and poverty traps, the lack of necessary skills. And our measures must recognise that different groups have different needs – lone parents, less than 50 per cent of whom are in work; young people, among whom the unemployment rate was 13 per cent at the time of the election, approaching double the rate for the population as a whole; partners of the unemployed, only half as likely to move back into work as those with partners in work; the long-term sick and disabled, 1 million of whom are without work but say they want to work; and the over-fifties, among whom nearly 30 per cent of men are either unemployed or inactive.

First, providing opportunities to work. Unemployment when young is more likely to mean persistent periods of unemployment when older. On average, men who before the age of twenty-three have been unemployed for twelve months or more will in the following decade spend fifteen times more time out of work than those who were never unemployed. Research now shows that while people without skills are more likely to become unemployed, long-term unemployment also erodes people's skills and employability.

Once long-term unemployment is entrenched, it requires much more than traditional demand management to solve it.

By increasing the effective supply of labour – the pool of employees and skills able to compete for work in the economy – we can increase the sustainable level of employment, consistent with low inflation. So I do not accept that there are a fixed number of jobs in the economy and micro-economic policies have no effect on this. Since we came into government, employment has risen by well over 400,000, unemployment has fallen substantially on both the claimant count and the ILO measure and record numbers of people are moving out of economic inactivity. But our aim is to deliver employment opportunity for all – the modern definition of full employment. If we are to maximise the effective supply of labour, it is clear that labour-market programmes must be oriented to getting people back into work before they lose touch with the labour market – matching new opportunities with new responsibilities for the unemployed to take up the opportunities.

Matching rights with responsibilities is at the heart of the New Deal programme. And it is why we have made our biggest investment in the New Deal for young people. And while it is early to come to firm conclusions about the scale of the New Deal's success, I think it is clear that it is showing very encouraging results. Already over a quarter of a million young people have joined the New Deal and over 95,000 have found jobs – the vast majority, sustained jobs. A further 64,000 are gaining valuable experience on New Deal options. And 47,000 employers have signed up to the New Deal. Since the election, long-term youth unemployment has halved.

One of the most important innovations of the New Deal, in my view, is the system of personal advisers – so that every individual is designated an adviser with the knowledge and skills to advise them on what work options are open to them. We have extended this approach to the long-term sick and disabled, partners of the unemployed, lone parents and soon, to the over-fifties. Furthermore, with the single work-focused gateway, 'ONE', we are moving towards a situation where nobody who signs on for benefit will simply be written off, without advice and support about how they can get back into work.

Second, making work pay. When this government came to power, with no minimum wage in place and the tax and benefits system unreformed, many of those without work faced an unemployment trap, where work paid less than benefits, and the low-paid in work faced a poverty trap which meant that they faced marginal tax and benefit rates of 80, 90 or even over 100 per cent. Now there are some who argue that improving work incentives at the bottom end of the labour market will not make a difference to the number of people moving into work. This fails to appreciate the new dynamism which is developing in the modern labour market – there are now over 3 million moves every year from unemployment or inactivity into employment. The Canadian self-sufficiency project examined the effects of a time-limited in-work payment for lone parents and suggested that it doubled the likelihood that they would move into full-time work. In addition, new research by Gregg, Johnson and Reed coordinated by the Institute of Fiscal Studies examines the actual employment decisions made by 12,000 people over a fifteen-month period. It suggests that every £10 increase in the return-to-work payment increases the likelihood of moving into work by around two percentage points for women and half that for men. The evidence is increasingly that incentives do matter especially at the low-income level of the labour market. That is why, just as we have ruled out penal tax rates at the top of the labour market, we are taking action to make work pay and tackle poverty traps at the bottom.

As the foundation of this strategy, we have introduced the National Minimum Wage. Because we are determined that this commitment to making work pay is consistent with our central objective of high employment, the minimum wage has been set at a sensible level which will not damage employment. And it is right that the youth minimum is set at a prudent level, thereby ensuring that our New Deal strategy is not put at risk. But our commitment to making work pay and to high levels of employment can only be met by combining a sensible and prudent minimum wage with a generous and fair system of in-work support. The old tax system set a personal allowance that failed to ensure that work paid, and also made thousands pay tax even as they claimed benefits. Our goal for the new tax system is that those who work will be guaranteed a minimum income, and by step-by-step integration of tax and in-work benefits this minimum income will be paid through targeted tax cuts and tax credits. No one who is in work should, in future, have to go to the benefits office to receive a living income. There will be some who say that the use of the tax system in this way disturbs the aim of a simplified tax system. Let me take this view head-on. The problem with the old tax system was not simply that it was complex. It was characterised by reliefs and subsidies not based on or justified by clear aims and objectives. We have acted to remove reliefs in the personal and corporate tax system which although no longer justified had remained for too long. Whether it be taking the decision to end Mortgage Interest Relief and Married Couple's Allowance, or Advance Corporation Tax or introducing a Climate Change Levy, I believe that people will look back at the first Budgets of this government as a period when major tax reform was enacted.

I believe that the tax system is about more than simply raising revenue in the simplest way; it must also help us to work towards our wider goals – of encouraging work as well as promoting enterprise and supporting families. That is why we are introducing measures to support those in work. From October of this year, the Working Families Tax Credit will mean that every working family with some-one working full-time will be guaranteed a minimum income of £200 a week, more than £10,000 a year. No net income tax will be paid until earnings reach £235 a week. The building blocks of this new system are therefore the minimum wage, which sets a rate below which no employer can pay, and building on this a Working Families Tax Credit which, even this year, delivers an hourly income of £6 an hour or more. For those receiving this Minimum Income Guarantee through the wage packet, the rewards from work will be far clearer than ever before, the duplication of receiving benefits and at the same time paying tax will be eradicated and the damaging polarisa-tion between taxpayers and benefit claimants will be removed.

The next step is to extend the principle of the WFTC. Of course, barriers to work across the workforce are different for different groups – for families with children, those without children, older workers and single people. Our long-term aim is an employment tax credit, paid through the wage packet, which would be available to households without children as well as households with children. As a first step in the Budget, we began the move towards an employment credit with a Minimum Income Guarantee for over-fifties returning to work. Nearly 30 per cent of men over fifty are outside the labour force, twice as many as twenty years ago. For those unemployed for six months or more, we will create a new employment credit which will guarantee a minimum income of £9,000 a year, for their first year back in full-time work, at least £170 a week.

So to make work pay we have introduced the minimum wage and a new system of in-work tax credits. We have also reduced taxes to reward work and encourage job creation: the new 10p starting rate of tax; reform of employees' national insurance to eliminate the perverse entry fee and align the starting point for national insurance with that of income tax; and reforms to employers' national insurance to help create entry-level jobs. This is a radical and long-overdue streamlining of the income-tax and national-insurance systems. It will halve the income-tax bills for nearly 1.5 million low-paid workers, take 900,000 people out of national insurance and tax altogether and remove substantial distortions in the labour market. And we have cut the numbers facing marginal deduction rates of over 70 per cent by two-thirds. A further step in this better deal for work is to include help with housing costs, not just help with rent but also help for homeowners going back to work. Taking a job should not put people in danger of losing their homes. And the government will be producing a Green Paper on Housing later in the year.

Third, opportunities for skills. We recognise that bringing out the best in people – by policies that ensure opportunities for skills – is the best route to prosperity in the modern world. That is why we are committed to widening opportunities in education and training: higher standards in our schools and lifelong learning. And in order to raise staying-on rates at schools and colleges, we are piloting Educational Maintenance Allowances, which are available at a higher level to those who need them most, thereby enabling us to more effectively target resources. About 80 per cent of people in employment today will still be in the workforce in ten years' time. And yet only a fraction of today's workforce are upgrading their skills – while their skills are all the time becoming obsolete. It is because experience shows that training while in work is more valuable than training while waiting for work that we are emphasising the starter job, getting back to work quickly and encouraging people to work their way up the skills ladder. Our proposals for Individual Learning Accounts and a University for Industry recognise the new reality that not only should people upgrade their skills throughout life but they should be encouraged to take responsibility for doing so.

Our aim is not just to deliver high and stable levels of growth and employment today but for the future. We must recognise that our economy can never reach its full potential unless everyone in our country has the opportunity to develop their talents to the full. Children are, rightly, the responsibility of the families in which they grow up. But they are more than this – invest in our children and we invest in the future of our country. We say – indeed, we all agree – that every child should have the best possible start in life. And this government sees it as a national goal. This is why Tony Blair has said we will abolish child poverty over twenty years.

It is not enough to tackle absolute poverty and simply prevent destitution. We should do more. It is not fair that children should be disadvantaged from the start of their lives because of who their parents are, what school they go to and where they live. Ensuring each child has a good start in life takes more than just money but cannot be done without money. We must ensure that children grow up in surroundings which enable their needs to be met. So government must play its part by using its system of child support to tackle the disadvantages that come from low incomes and poor parental support. The truth about Britain today is that millions of children are born into poverty. The facts of child poverty in Britain in 1997 are that: over 4 million children – more than a third of all children – live in low income families. And very many of them will remain poor for a large part of their childhood – up to a quarter of all children are persistently in low-income families. The problems of poverty and deprivation start with the very young. Babies born to fathers in social-class five are more likely to be low birth-weight. And low birth-weight is a key fact in a child's subsequent development and opportunity. Furthermore, poor children are less likely to get qualifications and to stay on at school. They start to fall behind their better-off peers from a very young age – the evidence shows that class differences in educational development are apparent by twenty-two months. Recent research commissioned by the Smith Institute shows that class background had as strong an impact on the academic achievement of children born in 1970 – and reaching adulthood in the late 1980s – as those born in 1958. The son of an educated professional father on average achieved qualifications two and a half levels higher than the son of an unskilled father who left school at sixteen. And the results for the 1970 generation are roughly the same as for 1958.

All of us have a part to play in a partnership to tackle child poverty and help all our children fulfil their potential and we are determined to tackle that vicious cycle of poverty, inadequate opportunities, and low aspirations. The evidence on child poverty shows the need for early intervention to give very young children the best start in life and it shows the need not only for financial support but for proper support services to help families.

So we are investing £540 million over the next three years in the new Sure Start programme providing integrated services for children under four and their families to promote the child's physical, intellectual, social and emotional development. On the birth of a child we know that parents face particularly heavy financial burdens, so in the Budget I announced a new Sure Start maternity grant at double the rate of the old maternity payment, benefiting around 250,000 families. And to encourage good health care at an early age the additional amount is linked to contact with a health-care professional. And in both of the last two Budgets – alongside our commitment to getting people into work and making work pay – we have also taken steps to increase direct financial support for children, provided through the benefits and tax system.

Our approach is based on two principles: we must substantially increase support for families with children and we must do so in the fairest way. As our manifesto promised, Child Benefit itself will remain as it is, paid to all mothers, and rising annually with inflation. As a recognition of its role, we have raised the level of universal Child Benefit from £11.05 a week for the first child to £14.40 today and £15 from next April.

The new Children's Tax Credit, replacing the Married Couple's Allowance, will provide more help for families when they need it most – when they are bringing up children. But because of our commitment that substantial extra resources for children should be allocated in a fair way, the Children's Tax Credit will be tapered for higher-rate taxpayers. And with the Children's Tax Credit added to Child Benefit, families who were receiving £11 a week in 1997 for their first child will, by April 2001, be receiving £23 a week: £1,200 a year.

Finally, for the poorest families in work and out of work, we are substantially increasing the rates of support for all children under eleven. When we came to office, parents on income support received £8 a week less for a child under eleven than a child over eleven. But there is no justification for this differential, particularly as families with younger children are more likely to live in poverty. So, with the measures we have taken in successive Budgets, from next April the under-eleven rate will have been raised to the level for 11–16-year-olds, an increase in support of over £400 a year for each child under eleven for all families on income support. The maximum support for the first child will be £40 a week: £2,000 a year for families when they need it most.

Our measures so far lift one and a quarter million people out of poverty – 700,000 of them children. Taking all our reforms together – Working Families Tax Credit, Children's Tax Credit, rises in Child Benefit and other tax changes – a family on £13,000 a year will gain up to £50 a week, £2,500 a year.

However, building upon the foundation of universal Child Benefit, we want to and will go further in improving child support and tackling child poverty. We are examining, for the longer term, the case for integrating the new Children's Tax Credit with the child premia in income support and the Working Families Tax Credit – an integrated child credit. This could allow families' entitlement to income-related child payments to be assessed and paid on a common basis. A single seamless system, without disruptions in financial support, would provide a secure income for families with children in their transition from welfare to work. Such an integrated credit, for those in and out of work, could be paid to the main carer, complemented by an employment tax credit paid through the wage packet to working households.

Again as I said before, our approach is based on two principles: we must substantially increase support for families with children and we must do so in the fairest way. Where we pay families an income-related benefit for children, it makes sense to take into account the circumstances of the family when we provide the support. In all our reforms we will honour the important principles of independent taxation: that we will never allow the wife or partner to be regarded as the chattel as was the case until the late 1980s; everyone should be treated equally in the tax system and everyone should have the right to their own personal allowance whatever their household status. Child poverty is unacceptable and these measures show our determination to help all our children fulfil their potential.

I said three years ago that a new Treasury under Labour would take its responsibility for the modernisation of Britain seriously. That it would be the guardian of the public finances and the guarantor of monetary stability, but that a Labour Treasury would need to be not just a ministry of finance, but also a ministry working with other departments to deliver long-term economic and social renewal. To achieve this, it needed to be innovative rather than obstructive; open rather than secretive; creating new ideas and not stifling them. Above all, that we would underpin our economic policy with a proper understanding of the challenges of the global economy and the modern relevance of our values by putting a radical commitment to equality of opportunity at the centre of our mission. Fulfilling the 1944 White Paper aims of growth and employment and doing so to the benefit of all our citizens.

The Chancellor develops the different role that he intends the Treasury to take in the Mais Lecture, given on 19 October 1999. The speech starts with a reminder that the first act of the incoming government was not in fact Bank of England independence, but setting the Treasury the objective of achieving high and stable levels of growth and employment for the nation. This was a direct reference to a 1944 White Paper which first set out these objectives. And as the Chancellor points out, the government of that time was clear that if full employment was to be sustained there were other conditions which had to be in place as well: stability, employability, productivity and individual responsibility. In other words this was a task for the whole of government, not just the Treasury. Contrary to Nigel Lawson's distinction between the roles of macro-economic and micro-economic policy as set out in his 1984 Mais Lecture, Gordon Brown argues that the role of a macro-economic policy is not simply to bear down on inflation but rather, by creating a platform of stability, to promote growth and employment; and that an active supply-side policy is necessary not only to improve productivity and employment, but to make it possible to sustain low inflation alongside high and stable levels of growth and employment. He concludes that while the shared economic purpose of 1944 broke down in fifty years of endless and sterile divisions between capital and labour, between state and market and between public and private sectors, denying Britain the national direction it needed, these issues are now at the heart of government policy.

My first words from the Treasury, as I became Chancellor and announced the independence of the Bank of England, were to reaffirm, for this government, our commitment to the goal first set out in 1944 of high and stable levels of growth and employment.

Now in this Mais Lecture – which has been, from time to time, a platform for politicians of all parties to reflect, to analyse and – as is the case with us politicians – often to get things wrong, I will seek to detail the conditions in our times under which the high ideals and public purpose contained in this economic goal of 1944 can be achieved.

Full employment – defined in 1944 as 'high and stable levels of employment' – was a reality for the twenty years after the Second World War. But rising unemployment in the 1970s was followed in the 1980s by unemployment rising to above 3 million, beyond its peak in the 1930s. As recently as 1997, 20 per cent of working-age households – one in five – had no one in work.

Some believe that full employment can be restored only by a return to macro-economic fine-tuning. Others believe that in the new more open economy governments cannot hope to meet the 1944 objectives. I reject both the dogma of insisting on old ways and the defeatism of abandoning the objectives.

So since 1997 the new government has been putting in place a new framework to deliver the objectives of high and stable levels of growth and employment. And as I said in New York last month there are four conditions which must all be met – and met together – if we are to deliver in our generation those objectives of 1944:

- first: stability – a pro-active monetary policy and prudent fiscal policy to deliver the necessary platform of stability;
- second: employability – a strengthening of the programme to move the unemployed from welfare to work;
- third: productivity – a commitment to high-quality long-term investment in science and innovation, new technology and skills;
- fourth: responsibility – avoiding short-termism in pay and wage-bargaining across the private and public sectors, and building a shared sense of national purpose.

I will show that these conditions – requirements for stability, employ-ability, productivity and responsibility – are and have always been the necessary conditions for full employment. The first condition, stability, is needed to ensure a sustainable high demand for labour. The second, employability, promotes a sustainable high supply of labour. The third, raising productivity, provides a sustainable basis for rising living standards. And the fourth, responsibility in bargaining, ensures a sustainable basis for combining full employment with low inflation.

I will show that the failure to meet these conditions led to persistently high unemployment in Britain in recent decades. And I will demonstrate how, by putting these conditions in place, we are restoring the goal of full employment for the next century.

If we start with that famous 1944 White Paper, we see that the government of the time was clear that if full employment was to be sustained all these conditions – stability, employability, productivity and responsibility – had to be in place. While the 1944 White Paper asserted the need for active macro-economic policy – to balance supply and demand – it also recognised there was no long-run gain by trading lower unemployment for higher inflation. Indeed, the 1944 White Paper included an explicit requirement for stability. And I quote: 'action taken by the government to maintain expenditure will be fruitless unless wages and prices are kept reasonably stable. This is of vital importance to any employment policy.'

As important for future generations was the White Paper's recognition that macro-economic action was a necessary but not sufficient condition for full employment and that policies for stability had to be accompanied by policies for employability, productivity and responsibility, not least in pay.

The 1944 White Paper stated that 'it would be a disaster if the intention of the government to maintain total expenditure were interpreted as exonerating the citizen from the duty of fending for himself and resulted in a weakening of personal enterprise'. It required that 'every individual must exercise to the full his own initiative in adapting himself to changing circumstances . . . [the government] will also seek to prevent mobility of labour being impeded . . . Workers must be ready and able to move freely between one occupation and another.'

And the 1944 vision was explicit about responsibility in pay, saying: 'if we are to operate with success a policy for maintaining a high and stable level of employment, it will be essential that employers and workers should exercise moderation in wages matters'.

So while that White Paper is remembered for its commitment to pro-active monetary and fiscal policy, it should also be remembered for its emphasis on employability, productivity and responsibility, not least in pay. And the evidence suggests that it was the accumulating failure – cycle by cycle – to meet not just one but all four of these conditions together that led to the rise of unemployment from the late 1960s onwards.

The 1945 government was resolved that Britain never would return to the unemployment of the 1930s. Indeed over the first two decades it seemed that it was possible to sustain both low inflation and low unemployment, a period many have called a golden age for the British economy. But we all now accept that a more detailed historical examination reveals that successive governments left unaddressed underlying long-term weaknesses. Once price and capital controls were dismantled, these weaknesses began to be revealed in low productivity and recurrent balance-of-payments difficulties. Governments repeatedly attempted to address these problems – through policies to enhance employability, productivity and responsibility. Indeed, the theme of the 1960s was a productivity revolution to be achieved through national planning; of the seventies, a social contract which would responsibly resolve distributional conflicts; of the eighties, deregulation which would 'set the economy free'.

Supply-side action to improve productivity included the NEDC, the national plan, regional plans, the IRC, and later the NEB – all attempts to harness new technology to the productivity challenge and secure high growth. Supply-side action to enhance employability in the labour market ranged from selective employment taxes to trade-union reforms. But the swift succession of improvisations to control pay – which ranged from guiding lights and pay pauses, to latterly 'severe restraint' and the social contract – showed just how elusive was the shared purpose necessary for pay responsibility to work. In their desire to maintain the 1944 objectives, even as supply-side action failed, governments resorted to attempting to control the economic cycle through doses of reflation.

And every time the economy grew, from the fifties onwards, a familiar pattern of events unfolded – a pattern we characterise as the British disease of stop–go – rising consumption unsupported by sufficient investment, growing bottlenecks and balance-of-payments problems as the sterling fixed exchange-rate link came under pressure – and then monetary and fiscal retrenchment as growth in the economy had to be reined back. Unemployment around 300,000 in the mid-fifties rose to over half a million in the late sixties and 1 million by the late seventies, and with hindsight we can conclude that at no time in this period was Britain meeting all the conditions judged in 1944 to be necessary for full employment.

- Despite the promise of stability, no credible institutional arrangements were put in place to deliver that stability;
- Despite talk of rights and responsibilities in the labour market, no serious reform of the Welfare State was instituted, even though – from the late 1960s onwards – growing global competition and new technologies were transforming our labour markets;
- Despite repeated expressions of concern about our productivity gap, no long-term strategy for tackling it ever succeeded;
- While pay restraint was a central issue for most of the period, the initiatives that were introduced to ensure pay responsibility were invariably short-term and were not underpinned by a broadly based consensus that resolved the difficult issues.

Each time governments sought to restore the shared, long-term purpose of 1945, they found it more – not less – difficult and attempts to do so descended into a mixture of exhortation – like the 'I'm backing Britain' campaign – and a British version of corporatism – vested interests cooking up compromises in smoke-filled rooms in London, far removed from the workplaces where such agreements would have to be sustained. The national consensus – which Mr Wilson sought around his national plan, Mr Heath sought around low inflation, Mr Callaghan sought around the social contract – broke down in a series of divisive conflicts – state versus market, capital versus labour, public versus private.

And the more governments failed on pay, productivity and industrial relations, the more they fell back on short-term fine-tuning in a doomed attempt to square the circle and deliver higher living standards and jobs despite sluggish productivity growth: problems massively compounded by the collapse of the Bretton Woods system of fixed exchange rates and the 1973 oil shock. So the golden age gave way to the era of boom and bust. With each successive cycle, a clear pattern developed. Unsustainable growth, leading to stagnation, and cycle by cycle to ever higher levels of inflation and unemployment. Inflation rising from 3 per cent in the late fifties to 9 per cent in the early seventies and more than 20 per cent by 1975; unemployment ratcheted up every cycle and doubling over the period.

What began in 1944 as a comprehensive long-term strategy for growth and employment built on a commitment to stability, employability, productivity and responsibility had by the seventies descended into short-termism and rising unemployment. Quite simply governments could not deliver growth and employment through a macro-policy designed to exploit a supposed short-term trade-off between higher inflation and lower unemployment. A crude version of the 1944 policy – using macro policy to expand demand and micro policy to control inflation – simply could not work. And it was this insight that the 1979 Conservative government seized upon with what they termed a medium-term financial strategy to return Britain to economic stability.

But the Conservatives went further than simply arguing that fine-tuning was the problem. For them the very idea that dynamic economies required active governments was the problem. As they stated, their policies reflected a neo-liberal view of the state:

- first, the application of rigid monetary targets to control inflation – choosing in succession £M3, £M1, then £M0; then, when they failed, shadowing the Deutschmark; then the Exchange Rate Mechanism as the chosen instrument for monetary control;
- second, a belief in deregulation as the key to employability – in the absence of an active labour-market policy or an active, reformed Welfare State;
- third, as the route to higher productivity, again deregulation alone in capital and product markets – a philosophy of 'the best government as the least government';
- fourth, an explicit rejection of consensus.

The clearest intellectual statement of the new position was Nigel Lawson's Mais Lecture in 1984. Its central thesis was that the proper role of macro-economic and micro-economic policy 'is precisely the opposite of that assigned to it by the conventional post-war wisdom'.

The conquest of inflation, not the pursuit of unemployment, should be the objective of macro-economic policy. The creation of conditions conducive to growth and employment, not the suppression of price rises, should be the objective of micro-economic policy. On one point, arguing against a crude version of the 1944 policy of using macro policy to expand demand and micro policy to control inflation, he drew the right lesson from the failures of previous decades. But far from tackling the boom–bust cycle endemic to the British economy, the early 1980s and nineties saw two of the deepest recessions since 1945. And even at the peak of growth in 1988, unemployment was still over 2 million, before it rose again to 3 million in 1993. As the late-eighties boom showed, the government of the day eventually relapsed into the very short-termism they had come into government to reverse. Just as the fine-tuners had in the 1970s given way to the monetarists, so now monetarism lapsed into fine-tuning.

By 1997 there were strong inflationary pressures in the system. Consumer spending was growing at an unsustainable rate and inflation was set to rise sharply above target; there was a large structural deficit in the public finances. Public-sector net borrowing stood at £28 billion. By the mid-1990s, the British economy was set to repeat the familiar cycle of stop–go that had been seen over the past twenty years. So against a background of mounting uncertainty and then instability in the global economy, the new government set about establishing a new economic framework to achieve the four conditions for high and stable levels of growth and employment – to promote new policies for stability, employability, productivity and responsibility. We started by recognising we had to achieve these 1944 objectives in a radically different context – integrated global capital markets, greater international competition, and a premium on skills and innovation as the key to competitive advantage.

The first condition is a platform of economic stability built around explicit objectives for low and stable inflation and sound public finances – in our case an inflation target and a golden rule – along with a commitment to openness and transparency.

The new post-monetarist economics is built upon four propositions:

- because there is no long-term trade-off between inflation and unemployment, demand management alone cannot deliver high and stable levels of employment;

- in an open economy rigid monetary rules that assume a fixed relationship between money and inflation do not produce reliable targets for policy;
- the discretion necessary for effective economic policy is possible only within an institutional framework that commands market credibility and public trust;
- that credibility depends upon clearly defined long-term policy objectives, maximum openness and transparency, and clear and accountable divisions of responsibility.

Let me review each proposition one by one. A few decades ago many economists believed that tolerating higher inflation would allow higher long-term growth and employment. Indeed, for a time after 1945, it did – as I have said – appear possible to fine-tune in this way – to trade a little more inflation for a little less unemployment – exploiting what economists call the Phillips curve. But the immediate post-war period presented a very special case – an economy recovering from war that was experiencing rapid growth within a rigid system of price and capital controls. We now know that even at this time fine-tuning merely suppressed inflationary pressures by causing balance-of-payments deficits. And by the 1960s and 1970s, when governments tried to lower unemployment by stimulating demand, they faced not only balance-of-payments crises but stagflation as both inflation and unemployment rose together.

Milton Friedman argued in his 1968 American Economic Association Presidential Lecture that the long-term effect of trying to buy less unemployment with more inflation is simply to ratchet up both. And here in Britain conclusive evidence for this proposition came in the 1980s experience of high inflation and high unemployment occurring together. So, because there is no long-term trade-off between inflation and unemployment, demand management alone cannot deliver high and stable levels of employment. Friedman was right in this part of his diagnosis: we have to reject short-termist dashes for growth. But the experience of these years also points to the solution. Because there is no long-term trade-off between inflation and unemployment, delivering full employment requires a focus on not just one but on all the levers of economic policy.

The second proposition in the new post-monetarist economics is that applying rigid monetary targets in a world of open and liberalised financial markets cannot secure stability. Here experience shows that while Friedman's diagnosis was right his prescription was wrong. Fixed intermediate monetary targets assume a stable demand for money and therefore a predictable relationship between money and inflation. But since the 1970s, global capital flows, financial deregulation and changing technology have brought such volatility in the demand for money that across the world fixed monetary regimes have proved unworkable. So why, even as monetary targets failed, did the British government persist in pursuing them? Why even as they failed was their answer more of the same? The answer is that they felt the only way to be credible was by tying themselves to fixed monetary rules. And when one target failed they chose not to question the idea of intermediate targeting but to find a new variable to target, hence the bewildering succession of monetary targets from £M3 to £M0; then shadowing the Deutschmark; then the Exchange Rate Mechanism as the chosen instrument for monetary control. As with fine-tuning, the rigid application of fixed monetary targets was based on the experience of sheltered national economies and on apparently stable and predictable relationships which have broken down in modern liberalised global markets. And yet the more they failed, the more policy-makers felt they had to tie their hands, first by adding even more monetary targets and then by switching to exchange-rate targets. But having staked their anti-inflationary credentials on following these rules, the government – and the economy – paid a heavy price. The price was recession, unemployment – and increasing public mistrust in the capacity of British institutions to deliver the goals they set.

What conclusion can be drawn from all this? Governments are in theory free to run the economy as they see fit. They have, in theory, unfettered discretion. And it is not only the fact that they have this unfettered discretion but the suspicion they might abuse it that leads to market distrust and thus to higher long-term interest rates. That is why governments have sought to limit their discretion through rules. The monetarist error was to tie policy to flawed intermediate policy rules governing the relationship between money demand and inflation. But the alternative should not be a return to discretion without rules, to a crude version of fine-tuning. The answer is not no rules, but the right rules. The post-monetarist path to stability requires the discipline of a long-term institutional framework.

So my second proposition – that in a world of open capital markets fixed monetary targets buy neither credibility nor stability – leads directly to my third. The third proposition is that in this open economy the discretion necessary for effective economic policy is possible only within a framework that commands market credibility and public trust.

Let me explain what I mean when I talk of the new monetary discipline: in the new open economy subject to instantaneous and massive flows of capital, the penalties for failure are ever more heavy and the rewards for success are even greater. Governments which lack credibility – which are pursuing policies which are not seen to be sustainable – are punished not only more swiftly than in the past but more severely and at a greater cost to their future credibility. The British experience of the 1990s is a case in point. It shows that once targets are breached it is hard to rebuild credibility by setting new targets. Credibility, once lost, is hard to regain. The economy then pays the price in higher long-term interest rates and slower growth.

On the other hand governments which pursue, and are judged by the markets to be pursuing, sound monetary and fiscal policies, can attract inflows of investment capital more quickly, in greater volume and at a lower cost than even ten years ago. The gain is even greater than that. If governments are judged to be pursuing sound long-term policies, then they will also be trusted to do what is essential – to respond flexibly to the unexpected economic events that inevitably arise in an increasingly integrated but more volatile global economy. So in the era of global capital markets, it is only within a credible framework that governments will command the trust they need to exercise the flexibility they require.

This leads to my fourth proposition – a credible framework means working within clearly defined long-term policy objectives, maximum openness and transparency, and clear and accountable divisions of responsibility. It is essential that governments set objectives that are clearly defined and against which their performance can be judged. That is why we have introduced clear fiscal rules, defined explicitly for the economic cycle. That is why, also, we have a clearly defined inflation target.

Let me say why it is so important that our inflation target is a symmetrical target. Just as there is no gain in attempting to trade higher inflation for higher employment, so there is no advantage in aiming for ever lower inflation if it is at the expense of growth and jobs. If the target was not symmetric – for example, if in the UK case it was 2.5 per cent or less, rather than 2.5 per cent – policy-makers might have an incentive to reduce inflation well below target at the cost of output and jobs. Instead a symmetrical target means that deviations below target are treated in the same way as deviations above the target.

But, to be credible, the monetary and fiscal framework must also be open, transparent and accountable. The greater the degree of secrecy the greater the suspicion that the truth is being obscured and the books cooked. But the greater the degree of transparency – the more information that is published on why decisions are made and the more the safeguards against the manipulation of information – the less likely is it that investors will be suspicious of the government's intentions.

That openness needs to be underpinned by accountability and responsibility. So public trust can be built only on a foundation of credible institutions, clear objectives, and a proper institutional framework. The flaw in Conservative economic policy was not just the failure of monetary targets. It was that the 'medium-term financial strategy' had no credible foundation – it was neither consistent in objectives, nor transparent in its operation, nor underpinned by credible institutional reforms. Failure led, after 1992, to some reform. The inflation target was an important step forward. But it was ambiguously defined and it was not underpinned by anything other than an improvised and still highly personalised institutional framework. Minutes of meetings between the Bank of England and the Chancellor were published, but they could not allay the suspicion that policy was being manipulated for political ends. In fact despite the then government's commitment to an inflation target of 2.5 per cent or less, financial market expectations of inflation ten years ahead were not 2.5 per cent or less but 4.3 per cent in April 1997, and never below 4 per cent for the whole period. Long-term interest rates remained 1.7 per cent higher in Britain than in Germany.

This has changed significantly in the last two years: long-term inflation expectations have fallen from 4.3 per cent to 2.4 per cent, a figure consistent with the government's inflation target; the differential between British and German long-term interest rates has fallen from 1.7 per cent, to just 0.2 percentage points. I believe the explanation for this improvement lies in the immediate and decisive steps that our new government took in May 1997 – to set clear monetary and fiscal objectives; to put in place orderly procedures, including a new division of responsibility between the Treasury and an independent central bank; and to insist on the maximum openness and transparency.

Contrary to Nigel Lawson's distinction between the roles of macro-economic and micro-economic policy as set out in his 1984 lecture, we recognise that the role of a macro-economic policy is not simply to bear down on inflation but, by creating a platform of stability, to promote growth and employment; and that an active supply-side policy is necessary not only to improve productivity and employment, but to make it possible to sustain low inflation alongside high and stable levels of growth and employment. In other words, macro-economic and micro-economic policy are both essential – working together – to growth and employment.

In short we have sought to learn the lessons of the post-war years and build a new platform of stability. Making the Bank of England independent was and is only one of the institutional reforms that form our new post-monetarist approach to economic policy. First, clear long-term policy objectives:

- a pre-announced and symmetrical inflation target; and
- strict fiscal rules to ensure sustainable public finances.

Second, well-understood procedural rules:

- a clear remit for the Monetary Policy Committee of the Bank of England to meet the inflation target set by government supported by the open-letter system and the code for fiscal stability; and
- effective coordination between fiscal and monetary policy – including the presence of the Treasury representative at the Monetary Policy Committee meetings.

Third, openness and transparency to keep markets properly informed, ensuring that institutions, objectives and the means of achieving the objectives are seen to be credible:

- publication of the minutes and votes of Monetary Policy Committee meetings; and
- transparency in fiscal policy, including the independent auditing of key fiscal assumptions.

It is the same search for stability in an open economy that has led to European Monetary Union. And at the global level, the same lessons are being learnt. In Washington last month, the IMF agreed a new framework of codes and standards, new economic disciplines for openness and transparency to be accepted and implemented by all countries which participate in the international financial system. These codes and standards – including fiscal, financial and monetary policy – will require that countries set out clear long-term objectives, put in place proper procedures, and promote the openness and transparency necessary to keep markets informed.

With the reforms we have already made in Britain, I believe that we have now – for the first time in this generation – a sound and credible platform for long-term stability for the British economy. We will not make the old mistake of relaxing our fiscal discipline the moment the economy starts to grow. The same tough grip will continue. The Monetary Policy Committee will be, and must continue to be, vigilant and forward-looking in its decisions, as we build a culture of low inflation that delivers stability and steady growth. We will not repeat the mistake of the late eighties. Those who today are arguing that economic stability comes by opposing necessary changes in interest rates and by avoiding the tough decisions necessary to meet the inflation target would risk returning to the boom and bust of the past. We can achieve high and stable levels of employment and meet our inflation target. Indeed we will not achieve and sustain full employment for the long-term by failing to meet our inflation target.

This credible platform of stability, built from the solid foundations I have just described, allows people to plan and invest for the long-term. This is our first condition for full employment.

The second condition for full employment is an active labour-market policy matching rights and responsibilities. The idea of a fixed natural rate of unemployment consistent with stable inflation was discredited by the evidence of the 1980s. For even when the economy was growing at an unsustainable pace – above 5 per cent in 1988 – in all regions of the country there were high levels of vacancies, including vacancies for the unskilled; alongside high unemployment. How did this happen? Part of the explanation was the 'scarring' effect on skills and employability inflicted by the deep and long recession of the eighties; partly also the mismatch between the skills and expectations of redundant manufacturing workers – and the new jobs in service industries; partly the failure to reform the Welfare State, especially its unemployment and poverty traps which, for many, meant work did not pay.

So there was a rise in what, in the 1980s, economists termed 'the non-accelerating inflation rate of unemployment' or the NAIRU. Whether measured by the relationship between wage inflation and unemployment – as Phillips stressed in the 1950s – or vacancies and unemployment as Beveridge had highlighted in the 1940s – Britain had clearly seen a dramatic structural deterioration in the UK labour market. The same level of wage pressure or vacancies existed alongside much higher levels of unemployment than in the past.

So the new government has taken a decisively different approach to employment policy over the past two years, aimed at reducing the NAIRU. All our reforms are designed for the modern dynamic labour market, now being transformed by the new information technologies. We recognise that people will have to change jobs more often, that skills are at a premium and that reform was needed in the 1980s to create more flexibility. The New Deal which offers opportunities to work but demands obligations to do so is the first comprehensive approach to long-term unemployment. Designed to re-engage the unemployed with the labour market, it addresses both the scarring effect of unemployment and the mismatch between jobs and skills. The Working Families Tax Credit and associated reforms that integrate tax and benefit are, for the first time, making work pay more than benefits; and our educational reforms including lifelong learning, the University for Industry, Individual Learning Accounts and our Computers for All initiative will tackle skill deficiencies.

The last two years have brought record levels of employment and sharp falls in youth and long-term unemployment – early signs that our policies are having an impact. But with still 1.2 million claimant unemployed and others excluded from the labour market – even at a time when there are around 1 million vacancies spread throughout all areas of the country – there is much more to do. The Working Families Tax Credit is now being extended to new Employment

Credits for the disabled and for those over fifty. And as the New Deal extends its scope from the under-25s to the long-term unemployed, opportunities to work and obligations to work will be extended together. The more our welfare-to-work reforms allow the long-term unemployed to re-enter the active labour market, the more it will be possible to reduce unemployment without increasing inflationary pressures. And the more our tax and benefit reforms remove unnecessary barriers to work, and the more our structural reforms promote the skills for work, the more it is possible to envisage long-term increases in employment, without the fuelling of inflationary pressures.

Next our third condition: only with rising productivity can we meet people's long-term expectations for rising standards of living without causing inflation or unemployment. It is important to be clear about the relationship between productivity, employment and living standards. Low productivity can exist side by side with low unemployment if people accept that living standards are not going to rise – as happened to the United States in the 1980s. But rising productivity can exist side by side with high unemployment if we pay ourselves more than the economy can afford. If people demand short-term rewards which cannot be justified by economy-wide productivity growth, the result is first inflation and then the loss of jobs. That has been the historic British problem – repeated bouts of wage inflation unmatched by productivity growth, leading in the end to higher unemployment. Indeed between 1950 and 1996 productivity growth in Britain was only 2.6 per cent a year compared to 3.7 per cent and 3.9 per cent in France and Germany.

But if we can now achieve rising productivity, bridging the gap with our competitors, high levels of employment and rising living standards can go together. Britain cannot assume that the new information technologies will automatically bring the higher productivity growth now seen in the United States. So we must work through a new agenda that involves a shared national effort to raise our game. Policies to encourage higher productivity will be the theme of the government's Pre-Budget Report on the 9th of November. While thirty years ago governments responded to the productivity challenge with top-down plans, and grant aid primarily for physical investment, today the productivity agenda is more complex and more challenging. So we are developing new and radical policies for the modernisation of capital and product markets, the encouragement of innovation and an enterprise culture open to all, as well as the building of a modern skills base.

I come now to our fourth and final condition for full employment – responsibility, not least in pay, and by responsibility I mean, as I have stressed throughout this lecture, a willingness to put the long term above the short term, a willingness to build a shared common purpose. To succeed we must all be long-termists now.

The reality of the more complex and flexible labour markets of Britain today is that pay decisions are dictated not by the few in smoke-filled rooms but made by millions of employees and employers across the country. And the more that we are all persuaded to take a long-term view of what the economy can afford, the more jobs we will create, the more we can keep inflation under control so interest rates can be as low as possible. The Bank of England has to meet an inflation target of 2.5 per cent. The target has to be met. Unacceptably high wage rises will not therefore lead to higher inflation but higher interest rates. It is in no one's interest if today's pay rise threatens to become tomorrow's mortgage rise. The worst form of short-termism would be to pay ourselves more today at the cost of higher interest rates tomorrow, fewer jobs the next year and lower living standards in the years to come. So wage responsibility – to rescue a useful phrase from its old woeful context – is a price worth paying to achieve jobs now and prosperity in the long term. It is moderation for a purpose. But responsibility means not just responsibility in pay but building a shared commitment to achieve all the conditions necessary for full employment – in other words, to work together as a country to promote stability, employability and higher productivity too.

It is undeniable that the shared economic purpose of 1945 broke down in fifty years of endless and sterile divisions between capital and labour, between state and market and between public and private sectors, denying Britain the national direction it needed. Britain and the British people can now move beyond these outdated conflicts. Building a consensus around the need for stability, employability, productivity and responsibility we can define anew a shared economic purpose for our country. The conditions for full employment can all be met. And the surest way is that the whole country is determined to meet them.

The James Meade Memorial Lecture, given on 8 May 2000, finds the Chancellor returning to the question of what should be the economic and social goals for the UK, and reaffirming the long-term strategy being pursued to implement them. He also uses the speech to review the progress made after three years in office, and to outline the next steps. But the speech is interesting for another reason: it allows the Chancellor to extend an argument, touched on in earlier speeches, that in a modern economy efficiency and equality, far from being incompatible, are necessary allies. But to achieve these desirable outcomes, it is necessary to define a new relationship between individuals, markets and the government.

The distinguished British Nobel Prize winner, James Meade, argued that if we want to achieve high growth without inflation, we need full employment as it is not only efficient but fair; and we need high-quality public services, especially in health and education, as the key to security and equal opportunity for all. However, the Chancellor extends this point, arguing that while the new Labour government is committed to tackling the substantial problems of economic inefficiency and social injustice inherited in May 1997, it recognises that if it is to do so it requires us to arrive at a better understanding of the duties of citizenship and the role and limits of government. And in approaching this new under-standing the Chancellor makes the new point that not only does the new Labour government, in direct opposition to the views of the right-wing parties, accept that there is a public interest in growth, employment, fairness and the best public services, but also that it understands that this public interest can best be advanced not by allowing the public sector to become a vested interest. In many cases the preferred option may be for the public sector ceasing to be controller or owner and becoming a partner, catalyst, sponsor, or coordinator: a government that empowers rather than directs.

. . .

To achieve our objectives in a new economy that simultaneously offers greater opportunity and yet threatens greater insecurity, we require a fresh understanding of the rights and responsibilities of the citizen and the reach and role of government.

For only with a credible and radical view of citizenship as respon-sible citizenship, and a new view of the state as the enabling state, can we fulfil our historic mission as a government: building a Britain where there is security and opportunity, not just for the privileged few but for all.

Such objectives were, in my view, at the centre of James Meade's work, which we honour with this lecture this evening. His life's work was to show that in a modern economy efficiency and equality, far from being incompatible, were necessary allies. To achieve these, he sought a modern and fair relationship between individuals, markets and government. Like us, he wanted to achieve high growth without inflation; he led the way in seeing full employment as efficient and fair; and he saw the best – not just the most basic – public services, especially in health and education, as the key to security and equal opportunity for all. The precondition – of high employment, higher living standards and strong public services – is economic stability. And it is by building on a platform of stability and by meeting our national economic goals that we can realise security and equal opportunity not just for those born to privilege but for all:

- our prosperity goal – in place of our historic under-performance against other countries, a faster rise in productivity than our competitors, as we close the productivity gap;
- our full employment goal – in contrast to years of high unemployment, that we have employment opportunity for all, a higher percentage of people in work than ever before;
- our education goal – instead of lagging behind other countries and suffering huge disparities in our educational attainments, we ensure educational opportunity for all, aiming for 50 per cent of people going into higher education for the first time in our history, and as close as possible to 100 per cent of young people with computer skills;
- our anti-poverty goal – in contrast to the rise in inequality and poverty seen over recent decades, that we ensure every child has the best start in life as we halve child poverty in ten years and end it within twenty; and in addition
- the public services goal. Instead of our inheritance, inadequate public services which failed to guarantee opportunity or security for all, we invest for the future in strong public services there when people need them.

Not only the scale of our ambitions for the coming decade but Britain's legacy of economic under-performance, social division and rising inequality required us in 1997 to reject the short-term, quick fix in favour of a consistent, long-term strategy. So we have never pretended that Britain's problems could be solved overnight, or that they could be resolved without the need for tough decisions. Indeed, we will not waiver and must remain single-minded in focusing on our long-term challenges: whether it is reforming labour, capital and product markets to bridge the productivity gap or modernising delivery of public services to achieve our health, education, and anti-poverty goals.

The last few decades teach us to reject the short-termism of flawed quick fixes – policy lurches in face of short-term difficulties – rather than taking the tough decisions to achieve our long-term economic and social aims. It is not by populist quick fixes or gesture politics but by maintaining stability and seeing through long-term modernisation and principled reforms that we will achieve our goals for full employ-ment, prosperity and social justice. And we recognise most of all – and this is my theme tonight – that our goals cannot be achieved by the old methods of old left or old right.

Indeed, fundamentally, they require a new, modern understand-ing of the duties of citizenship and the role and limits of govern-ment. We reject the old left command-and-control view of government which mistakenly equated public ownership and a public bureaucracy with the public interest, argued that full em-ployment could be achieved simply by old-style demand manage-ment, and suggests that the only answer to poverty is compensating the poor for their situation rather than tackling the underlying causes.

This old and misguided view of the state – irrelevant for a global economy – was accompanied by a failure to place sufficient emphasis on personal responsibility. I believe instead that our determination to combat social and economic injustice should be matched, not by insisting on rights without responsibilities, but by asserting the responsibility of the individual. So an out-of-date view of the relation-ship between individual and state led in the eighties to the right-wing attack on collective provision: their exclusive reliance on markets, their rejection as evil of any kind of state intervention, and the crude dogma of a self-interested individualism which denied there was such a thing as a society. For the right, the best government is the least government. Yet abandoning established responsibilities of government – saying that there is nothing government can do – did not improve our productivity performance, but instead led to more people out of work and a cycle of poor skills, worklessness and deprivation.

That has been the legacy of absentee government and it was to, step by step, tackle these problems of economic inefficiency and social injustice that a new government was needed and given a mandate in 1997. That was – and remains – our task, a strong economy and a fairer society, but to do so we require a better understanding of the duties of citizenship and the role and limits of government. I believe that as advocates of economic and social renewal, we should reclaim both the ethic of personal responsibility as we stress obligations as well as opportunities, and affirm the ethic of fairness, as we root out economic injustice.

Take our goal of full employment. We know it cannot be achieved by the old right ways – of leaving it wholly to market forces – nor by the old left methods – simply by pulling the macro-economic levers without tackling underlying structural weaknesses, not least the need for rights and responsibilities in the labour market. And just as we support, in the New Deal, new opportunities for employment but new obligations to seize them, so too elsewhere we support responsibilities accompanying rights:

- new opportunities for already an extra 100,000 higher-education students, but in our new system of student finance new obligations to contribute when earnings are higher;
- new help for mothers – a £300 maternity grant in the year their babies are born, but a new responsibility that health checks for the baby are met;
- new help for teenagers – with educational-maintenance allowances available in return for staying on at school and seeking higher qualifications;
- new help for adult learning, a break from the old system of levies or simply doing nothing, with an Individual Learning Account for initially 1 million adults to which government contributes but the individual contributes too.

And with the growth of personal responsibility, we seek the growth of corporate responsibility too:

- new opportunities in the financial-service industries but in return a new requirement from financial-services companies for openness and transparency;
- for the environment, new incentives for heavy energy users matched by a responsibility, in the climate-change levy, to deliver environmental improvements; and
- in the global economy, a new responsibility on governments to be transparent, to be accountable and to agree a dialogue and partnership with the private sector – and in return greater responsibilities on the private sector to contribute to crisis prevention and crisis resolution.

So whether it be individual or corporate responsibility, our call is for a responsible citizenship. And we understand what the right fails to acknowledge, that there is a public interest in growth, employment, fairness and the best public services, but understand too that this public interest can best be advanced not by allowing the public sector to become a vested interest, but often by the public sector ceasing to be controller or owner and becoming partner, catalyst, sponsor, coordinator: action that empowers rather than directs. So our call is not for big government but better government, what we might call an enabling state.

And underlying all this is our understanding of the changed world in which we live – a period of great technological advance and opportunity, but also a period of unprecedented restructuring and insecurity – and the reform this necessitates in the relationships between individuals, markets, and government. More than ever, we need to help equip people to cope with the insecurities that ever faster change brings. More than ever, we need to remove the old barriers and let everyone move ahead.

In the new economy where capital and companies are mobile, we must ensure that we offer the right environment and help for business to succeed in every part of Britain, and ensure that we have the right competitive environment, the key to competitiveness abroad. So in the new economy, the role for government is neither to obstruct change nor to passively abdicate responsibility for managing the consequences of change that affect working people, but instead equip people and companies to meet and master change. So it is on this basis – an enabling government encouraging responsible citizenship in pursuit of opportunity and security for all – that we will continue to take the tough long-term decisions on the side of Britain's hard-working majority – in the Spending Review, in drawing up the next election manifesto and beyond.

The first objective national governments must have, in a global marketplace, is to maximise economic stability. We have learnt that monetary and fiscal stability is a necessary precondition for national economic success. For in a global economy, funds will flow to those countries whose policies inspire confidence. And investors punish mistakes more quickly and more severely than in the past. Both the old Keynesian fine-tuning, and the rigid application of fixed monetary targets, were policies designed for sheltered national economies and based on apparently stable and predictable relationships which have now broken down in our modern, liberalised and global capital markets.

So our policy has been to set for a global economy a new long-term framework for monetary and fiscal policy that can command new confidence. Its essence is that long-term, open and transparent decision-making procedures which command credibility provide a better route to stability than fixed monetary or exchange-rate rules. That is why, when we came into power in Britain in May 1997, we put in place a radically different monetary framework based on imposing consistent rules – the symmetrical inflation target; settled and well-understood procedures – with Bank of England independence; and openness and transparency; side by side with this and as important, a radically improved fiscal discipline with, again, clear and consistent rules – the golden rule for public spending; well-understood procedures – our fiscal responsibility legislation; and here, too, a new openness and transparency. Already we are seeing the rewards of creating Bank of England independence and new fiscal rules.

And it is because we sought to learn from the political mistakes of the last forty years that this government will maintain its prudent and tough approach. So we must all be determined not to make the old British mistake of paying ourselves too much today at the cost of higher interest rates and fewer jobs tomorrow. I understand the great difficulties that the current fall in the Euro is causing for British industry, particularly in manufacturing. Such a Euro–Sterling exchange rate cannot be justified by any view of long-term economic fundamentals. But manufacturers who have suffered from the old boom and bust – and the short-term policy lurches which all too often went wrong – would also reject a return to the short-term quick fix which would put at risk the long-term stability which is the foundation for steady growth, investment and job creation.

Stability is a necessary precondition to deliver our objectives for growth and employment, but it is not sufficient. An economy cannot fly on only one wing. Supply-side or micro-economic reform is also essential to raising our productivity. Some people argue that governments working with business cannot improve the productivity levels of the economy. I reject this pessimistic view. Of course it is businesses that create wealth, and managers and workforces that create jobs and higher output, but governments must ensure that the environment within which wealth is created is one that favours competition, not monopoly or vested interests, and that the economy has properly functioning labour, capital and product markets. And fifty years of economic history from 1945 – marred by a succession of sterile and self-defeating conflicts between state and market, managements and workforces, public and private sectors – taught us the need for national economic purpose, for an end to short-termism and the need for all – industry, the financial community, and government – to take a long-term view:

- industry, by investing for the long term;
- the financial community, by refusing to resort to the short-termism and stop–go attitudes which have bedevilled us since the war; and
- government, by not only ensuring lasting stability but taking seriously its responsibilities to remove the barriers to productivity and growth.

So while thirty years ago, governments responded to the productivity challenge with top-down plans, and tax incentives and grants primarily for physical investment, today it is a more complex role for government – the encouragement of competition, the modernisation of capital and labour markets, and the encouragement of innovation and an enterprise culture open to all, so that British industry – manufacturing and services – can close our productivity gap and deliver higher profits, investment, employment and growth. First, we are removing the tax barriers to enterprise and creating in Britain the best tax environment for business investment – we have cut small companies' tax from 23p to 20p, introduced a new 10p rate of Corporation Tax for small companies, and radical reforms to Capital Gains Tax. While for a decade capital gains have been taxed at 40 per cent or above, they will now be taxed at 10 per cent for investments of four years or more.

Second, new incentives to encourage and reward the inventor and the innovator – we are investing an extra £1.4 billion in basic scientific research, and have put in place a new R&D tax credit; our University Challenge Fund is providing finance to commercialise inventions; and to transfer technology from the science lab to the marketplace, we have new Institutes of Enterprise. And these measures are of special importance to manufacturing, which will secure the biggest benefit from permanent capital allowances, the new R&D tax credit, the 100 per cent allowance for introducing new technology; and the regional funds and the doubling of Modern Apprenticeships.

Third, because we recognise the sharpest spur to innovation, efficiency and improvement is competition, we are removing the barriers to competition. We have rewritten this country's outdated framework of competition law. We have given the Office of Fair Trading new powers and new money to police anti-competitive practices which damage businesses and consumers alike. And now we will be consulting on the next stage, withdrawing ministers from the decision process on merger cases.

Our productivity push will be stepped up in the coming year. We will build on the measures we have already introduced with further reforms and incentives for the modernisation of our capital markets, product markets and labour markets. These will be set out in detail in this November's Pre-Budget Report. We are examining how we can further promote the best competitive environment for industry and consumers alike. For the professions, the Office of Fair Trading is now working through a detailed remit to examine how best to ensure that the rules of professional bodies do not unnecessarily restrict or distort competition. For banking, having accepted the main Cruick-shank recommendations, we will legislate to ensure the UK payments system is open to new competition.

In our capital markets, we must ensure there are no barriers to competition and innovation, that there are no unnecessary constraints restricting investment decisions, and that investors have every opportunity and encouragement to back dynamic small and growing companies in manufacturing and services in all our regions. Not City and industry working against each other, nor the old battles between private and public sector, but City, industry and government together playing their part in promoting industrial growth. That is why, following the Cruickshank report, I have asked Paul Myners to head a review of institutional investment to cover all these issues. Institutional investors have a vital role to play, controlling around 45 per cent of quoted equity investments and Mr Myners will report back to me in time for action in the next Budget.

In this way we are removing the old barriers of under-investment and neglect that for too long have held our regions back. Working with the new Regional Development Agencies and the Small Business Service, our aim is balanced economic development across all the regions and nations of the United Kingdom – a modern regional policy supporting local innovation, more investment and improved infrastructure. Having launched a network of regional venture-capital investment funds – with a target of £1 billion – the Deputy Prime Minister and I will, in the Comprehensive Spending Review, announce further measures to strengthen the work of the Regional Development Agencies. I want Britain to be a world leader in enterprise – and by moving from a Britain where enterprise was confined to a closed circle of the few to a Britain where enterprise is open to all, I want, as this week we launch the National Enterprise Campaign, the opportunities and benefits of enterprise to be shared by all regions and all people. I believe government, business leaders, and local communities can now work together to achieve this aim.

When the government came to power in 1997, we put the restoration of the work ethic at the centre of our social and economic policy. Our aim, for the next decade, employment opportunity for all with a higher proportion of people in employment than ever before. To help achieve this, we are building a new and modernised Welfare State, one that in addition to its traditional and necessary function of giving security to those who cannot work, promotes work, makes work pay and gives people the skills they need to get better jobs. In the last twenty years, unemployment has been the primary cause of poverty in Britain today.

Simply compensating people for their poverty through benefits is not enough; the task must be to deal with the causes of poverty. And the best form of welfare is work. So we have put in place a long-term strategy to help those sections of the population excluded for too long:

- the young unemployed;
- the long-term unemployed;
- lone parents; and
- the disabled who can work.

Already over 400,000 young people have joined the New Deal and almost 200,000 have found jobs – the vast majority, sustained jobs. A further 120,000 have gained valuable experience on New Deal options. And over 70,000 employers have signed up to the New Deal. Since the election, long-term youth unemployment has halved. And because we have succeeded in this parliament in removing the old barriers to employing the young, from April next year we will extend the opportunities and the obligations of the New Deal to the long-term adult unemployed – with four options of work, work-based training, work experience including in the voluntary sector, and self-employment. But no fifth option, no staying at home on benefit doing nothing.

The relationship we are forging between rights and responsibilities is firmly rooted in both economic opportunity and individual responsibility. Instead of being left to draw benefit at a Social Security office, the unemployed who are able to work will sign up to seek work, with the long-term unemployed offered the help of a personal employment adviser. In Britain, unlike any other comparable countries, unemployment among lone parents is over 50 per cent. Starting nationally from next April, lone parents with children over five will attend work-focused interviews to find out about the new choices on offer: the choice to train for work with a new cash payment of £15 a week on top of benefits for training; the choice of a few hours' work a week, with the first £20 of earnings allowed with no reduction in benefit; the choice of part-time work with a guaranteed £155 for sixteen hours of work, or the choice of full-time work on a guaranteed £214 a week; and on every rung of this ladder of opportunity there will be help with child care.

Our aim is to create a ladder of opportunity with government on the side of working people as they seek and find jobs, and in many cases consider self-employment and starting a business. And to sustain our goal of full employment, government needs to ensure work pays. When this government came to power, with no minimum wage in place and the tax and benefits system unreformed, many of those without work faced an unemployment trap, where work paid less than benefits, and the low-paid in work faced a poverty trap which meant that they faced marginal tax and benefit rates of 80, 90 or even over 100 per cent. To tackle this, we needed to combine a sensible and prudent minimum wage with a generous and fair system of in-work support. And all the measures we have introduced – the 10p tax rate, the 22p basic rate, reform of National Insurance, the Children's Tax Credit and the most important innovation, the Working Families Tax Credit, are the building blocks of this strategy.

Already, over 1 million people are receiving the Working Families Tax Credit, which means that every working family with someone working full-time is guaranteed a minimum income of over £200 a week today, and £214 a week from April next year. And, as a result of all these measures, the family on half average earnings will be £2,600 a year better off in real terms in 2001 compared to 1997 – a rise in living standards of 20 per cent this year alone – the biggest improvement in living standards for a generation.

So while the old tax system simply set a personal allowance that failed to ensure that work paid, and also made thousands pay tax even as they claimed benefits, we are putting in place a new more progressive system that encourages and rewards work. Instead of a tax system that has rates from 40 per cent to 0 per cent, we now have a tax and benefits system with rates from 40 per cent to 10 per cent and then to as low as –200 per cent at earnings of around £60 a week – for every pound people earn, up to £2 paid in WFTC. Our next step is to extend the principle of the WFTC. Of course, barriers to work across the workforce are different for different groups – for families with children, those without children, older workers and single people.

From 2003, we will introduce an employment tax credit, paid through the wage packet, available to households without children as well as households with children. As a first step, we began this April with an employment credit with a Minimum Income Guarantee for over-fifties returning to work.

Full employment is not just about the right to work, but, where there are jobs, the responsibility and the requirement to work. So, as we extend opportunities to those who are out of work, we will extend the responsibility to take up the work on offer. The informal or hidden economy is now draining billions of pounds in fraudulent benefit claims and unpaid taxes.

This loss of revenues, this incidence of fraud, this waste of resources, cannot be allowed to continue and especially when there are jobs that benefit claimants could take. That is why we are implementing the report of Lord Grabiner QC. I can confirm we will legislate to tackle benefit fraud and we will take powers in the Finance Bill for a new statutory offence of fraudulent tax evasion. This will enable the Inland Revenue to prosecute in the magistrates' court those who evade their responsibilities.

New opportunities matched by responsibilities are also at the heart of our education policy too. By the end of the coming decade, our goal is not the old 10 per cent of the sixties, or 20 per cent of the eighties, but more than 50 per cent of young people entering higher education. In addition to the investment in higher standards in schools, colleges and universities, let me emphasise that we make equal opportunity count by the creation for lifelong learning of Individual Learning Accounts and the University for Industry and the extension of educational-maintenance allowances of up to £40 a week in our highest-unemployment communities. Higher rates of staying on in education are our aim and in return for young people pursuing higher qualifications, we provide new cash support: once again the enabling state; in schools, encouraging and rewarding effort.

Our goal is that every child has the best possible start in life – ending child poverty in twenty years and halving it in ten years. And it is because the scale of the injustice over the last twenty years was so great that we have already taken action to lift 1.2 million children out of poverty and are investing in a new Sure Start programme to give the youngest children in the poorest areas a far better start in life. In the Child Poverty Action Group lecture next week, I will set out new measures to fight the war against child poverty, showing how we plan to tackle social injustice and extend opportunity in new ways. First, we recognise the war against child poverty cannot be won by government and parents alone. It depends on engaging the voluntary community and charitable sector and in both our Sure Start programmes and the Children's Fund we will devolve power from the national and local government to community-based organisations. And second, we match new opportunities with new responsibilities – new help for mothers when their babies are born, but a new responsibility that vital health checks for children are undertaken.

Just as we have a long-term strategy to tackle child poverty and have made a start, so too pensioner poverty. As a result of the measures introduced since 1997, we will be spending £6.5 billion more over the parliament, supporting pensioners. We are spending more than we would have spent if we had simply restored the earnings link. And we are spending it in a fairer way – helping the poorest most. As I said in the Budget, based on forecast rates of inflation, we expect the basic state pension rise in April 2001 to be over £2 for single pensioners and over £3 for couples. All pensioners benefit from the new winter fuel allowance – raised to £150 for the coming winter – and measures like free TV licences for the over-75s and the new Minimum Income Guarantee have helped the poorest pensioners the most. So our first priority was to tackle pensioner poverty. And, taking these measures together, 1 million pensioners will be up to £20 a week better off since 1997.

The next stage is to ensure that pensioners are not penalised for their thrift, and therefore to do more for pensioners with modest occupational pensions and small savings. And, later in the year, the Secretary of Pensions will be consulting on a measure for the next parliament – the new pensioners credit. This will do more for those with modest occupational pensions and savings, who should not be penalised for having worked hard all their lives and saved for their retirement.

In all these initiatives to meet our productivity, employment, education and anti-poverty goals, our approach is driven by a desire to match opportunity and security and it is underpinned by reform. This approach is at the heart of this year's spending review as we build public services that make people more secure, something that is even more important in today's world of rapid economic uncertainty and change. In the last spending review, we recognised that to achieve these objectives both the role of government and the management of spending and investment has to change, as we broke from the annual cycle that was short-termist and wasteful. In this review we extend these reforms further, matching new investment with further modernisation. With our focus on results, we are breaking down the old incrementalism that concentrated on inputs and not results.

With our commitment to crosscutting reviews and decisions to target public spending on our priority policy areas, we are breaking down the crude departmentalism that led to duplication and waste. With the doubling of public investment, we are breaking from the old focus on consumption alone, as instead we seek to equip Britain for the future. And with our public–private partnerships extended, we are ending the old public–private split.

This prudent approach is to ensure that department by department we implement our commitment to extending opportunity for all, investing in our future and creating a fairer Britain. Already we have shown our commitment to the NHS with the largest ever sustained increase in NHS funding and the intensive review of the NHS which the Prime Minister is leading. I am convinced that, with tough decisions, we can also meet our priorities not just in health but in our other key priorities, including additional money for education, criminal justice, transport and tackling social exclusion, in return for reform.

So we are determined to stay the course of reform and modernisation to achieve these ends. The way forward is through an enabling government which encourages responsible citizenship and aims for security and equal opportunities for all – the key to lasting change in our country and a stronger fairer Britain.

In an important speech to the Social Market Foundation on 3 February 2003, entitled 'A Modern Agenda for Prosperity and Social Reform', the Chancellor has set out his most thoroughgoing appreciation of how to determine the respective roles of the public and private sectors in advancing the public interest. In particular there is an attempt to define what the public interest is – policies which create a Britain where there is opportunity and security not just for some but for all and the equity, efficiency and diversity necessary to achieve it. There are extended sections on the role of government in relation to the creation and operation of markets; definitions of where markets should not be permitted; and thoughts about how best to harness the creativity and innovation of the private sector in provision of public services. The speech marks a major advance on the arguments deployed so far in this debate. As the Chancellor says, it is time to face up to fundamental questions that cannot be sidestepped about the role and limits of government and markets – questions, in fact, about the respective responsibilities of individuals, markets and communities, including the role of the state. He notes that in almost every area of current policy controversy – the future of the private-finance initiative, of health care, of universities, of industrial policy, of the European economic-reform agenda, of public services generally – the question is, at root, both what is the best relationship between individuals, markets and government to advance the public interest; and also whether it is possible to set aside, and move beyond, the old sterile and debilitating conflicts of the past.

The Chancellor states the issue with great clarity: how can we renegotiate the relationship between markets and government? His view is that agreeing on where markets have an enhanced role and where market failure has to be addressed is absolutely central to the next stage of the new Labour project. To hold on to old, discredited dogmas about what should remain in the public sector and how the public sector operates, or to confuse the public interest with producer interests, makes no sense for a reforming party and, as technologies and aspirations change, would lead to sclerosis and make it impossible to achieve the government's goals. His plea is that the party 'must not adhere to failed means, lest it fails to achieve enduring ends'. Equally, to fail to put the case for a reformed public sector, where the case is strong, not only leads directly to the allegation that new Labour merely imitates old Conservatism, but also makes it impossible to achieve the efficient and equitable outcomes that the government is seeking. As long as it can be alleged that there is no clarity as to where the market requires an enhanced role (in which the government enables markets to work better by tackling market failure), and where markets have no role at all, then the impression may be given that the only kind of reform that is valuable is a form of privatisation. If so, new Labour will have failed to advance the case for a renewed and reformed public realm for the coming decades.

Since 1997, our government's central objective, the heart of our vision for a prosperous Britain, has been to promote opportunity and security for all. Our first priority was to address our country's chronic long-term failures in macro-economic policy. And in government we had the strength to take difficult decisions, including to freeze public spending for two years, as we constructed a new monetary and fiscal regime. But a sound macro-economic framework is a necessary but not sufficient condition to achieve, in what is an increasingly competitive global economy, a Britain where there is opportunity and security not just for some but for all.

So successive Budgets have sought to promote, on the one hand, competition, innovation, and the enterprise economy, and on the other hand, the New Deal, tax credits and public-service reform as the routes to an efficient and fair Britain in which individuals can realise their potential. Achieving these objectives demands the courage to push forward with all the radical long-term reforms necessary to enhance productivity and to improve public services, and, as we do so, we must have the strength to face up to fundamental questions that cannot be sidestepped about the role and limits of government and markets – questions, in fact, about the respective responsibilities of individuals, for markets and communities, including the role of the state.

Indeed, in almost every area of current controversy – the future of the private-finance initiative, of health care, of universities, of industrial policy, of the European economic-reform agenda, of public services generally – the question is, at root, what is the best relationship between individuals, markets and government to advance the public interest and whether it is possible to set aside, and indeed move beyond, the old sterile and debilitating conflicts of the past.

Take the health service. The essential question in a world of advancing technology, expensive drugs and treatments, and rising expectations, is whether efficiency, equity and responsiveness to the patient are best delivered through a public health-care system or whether, as with commodities generally, market arrangements, such as the hospital selling and the patient buying, are the best route to advancing the public interest.

Take higher education. Our universities operate in an increasingly global marketplace and at the same time their excellence depends upon drawing upon the widest pool of talent – making change inevitable and necessary. And one of the central questions round the world is the extent to which universities should become, in effect, the seller, setting their own price for their service, and the prospective graduate the buyer of higher education at the going rate, whether through an upfront or deferred system of payment, and what are the consequences for equity and efficiency as well as choice of such arrangements.

Take the private-finance initiative. The argument is whether, at a time of unprecedented need for investment in our public infrastructure, for example in hospitals and schools, the private sector can provide the benefits of efficiency and value for money to promote what most agree is the public interest: schooling and health care free for all at the point of need.

Take industrial policy. The essential question is whether, when global competition is challenging every industry, the state should replace market forces where they fail – the old Labour policy; whether the state should refuse to intervene at all even in the face of market failure – the old Tory *laissez-faire*; whether we should second-guess the market through a corporatist policy of supporting national champions – a policy I also reject; or whether, as I would propose, the best industrial policy for success in a global economy is to help markets work better.

Or take European economic reform. The question is how far, in a world where business must respond quickly and people must adapt to change, Europe is willing to go beyond old assumptions that flexibility is the enemy of social justice and recognise that the right kind of flexibility in European labour, capital and product markets can advance not only economic efficiency but also social cohesion.

In each area the questions are, at root, whether the public interest – that is opportunity and security for all – and the equity, efficiency and diversity necessary to achieve it, is best advanced by more or less reliance on markets or through substituting a degree of public control or ownership for the market and whether, even when there is public-sector provision, there can be contestability. Every modern generation – since Adam Smith counterposed the invisible hand of the market to the helping hand of government – has had to resolve this question for its time: what are the respective spheres for individuals, markets and communities, including the state, in achieving opportunity and security for their citizens. In the United States in the 1930s the New Deal – and in Britain in the 1940s, in a different way, nationalisation and the Welfare State – established new paradigms. Whole areas traditionally left to markets became regulated or owned by the state in the avowed interests of efficiency and equity.

In the 1960s and 1970s Labour's story could be summed up by the story of the breakdown of that relationship as – in the way Anthony Crosland predicted – old forms of collectivism were seen to fail. And, when Labour refused to update our conception of the respective roles of markets and state, and take on vested interests, the government also failed.

In the 1980s there was an attempt – some of it largely successful, as in utilities, and some of it unsuccessful, as in health – to withdraw the state from areas where previously the public interest was seen to be equated with public ownership. But by 1997 major questions about the relationships between individuals, markets and communities, including the role of the state, remained unanswered. On the other hand, it is also true that in every single post-war decade – on both sides of the political spectrum – the centralised state was wrongly seen to be the main, and sometimes the sole, expression of community, often usurping the case for localities and neighbourhoods taking more responsibility for the decisions that affect their lives.

The question I want to focus specifically on today is how, for a new decade in which globalisation and technology are challenging traditional assumptions anyway, we renegotiate the relationship between markets and government. Agreeing on where markets have an enhanced role and where market failure has to be addressed is, in my view, absolutely central to the next stage of the new Labour project. To hold to old discredited dogmas about what should remain in the public sector and how the public sector operates, or to confuse the public interest with producer interests, makes no sense for a reforming party and, as technologies and aspirations change, would lead to sclerosis and make it impossible to obtain our enduring goals. We must not adhere to failed means lest we fail to achieve enduring ends. Equally, to fail to put the case for a reformed public sector where the case is strong not only leads directly to the allegation from our opponents that new Labour merely imitates old Conservatism but also makes it impossible to achieve the efficient and equitable outcomes we seek.

As long as it can be alleged that there is no clarity as to where the market requires an enhanced role, where we should enable markets to work better by tackling market failure, and where markets have no role at all, an uncertain trumpet sounds and we risk giving the impression that the only kind of reform that is valuable is a form of privatisation and we fail to advance – as we should – the case for a renewed and reformed public realm for the coming decades

By stating our vision clearly, however, we can bring to an end the sterile and self-defeating argument over PFI where producer interests have often been wrongly presented as the public interest; move forward from what has been a debate insufficiently explicit on the role of public and private providers in some of our public services; and, most of all, open up a broad and challenging agenda for prosperity and social reform. In the last parliament we overturned old Labour shibboleths, rejected an old-style Keynesian assumption that there was a trade-off between inflation and growth, and, in making the Bank of England independent and applying fresh rules, procedures and systems of accountability in a new monetary and fiscal regime, sought to make Labour the party of stability and economic competence.

Now we need to affirm a yet more radical break with Labour's past – and in this parliament go further. By drawing the proper distinction between those areas where markets require an enhanced role; where, by tackling market failure, we can enable markets to work better; and where markets cannot deliver opportunity and security for all, we can, with confidence, make new Labour the party not just of social justice but of markets, competition and enterprise and show that advancing enterprise and fairness together best equips our country to succeed in the global economy.

I have said that the respective role of markets and the public sector has been the underlying, even if sometimes the unspoken, divide at the heart of British political arguments for nearly a century. But let us be clear at the outset where there is at least consensus. Left and right have always agreed that there is a sphere of relationships – which encompasses family, faith and civic society – that should never be reduced to transactions, either buying and selling, or to diktat, state command and control. In his recent Dimbleby Lecture on the market state the new Archbishop of Canterbury, and in his recent book *The Dignity of Difference* the Chief Rabbi, Dr Jonathan Sacks – profound and influential thinkers who have led the debate – tell us that while there are areas where the market is legitimate, there are areas where to impose market transactions in human relationships is to go beyond the bounds of what is acceptable, indeed where to do so corrodes the very virtues which markets rely upon for success.

Markets, they would suggest, may be the best way of constructing exchanges, and thus providing many goods and services, but are not good ways of structuring human relationships. They also argue that while, generally, markets are good at creating wealth they are less good at guaranteeing fairness and opportunity for all – and certainly not normally good at dealing with their social consequences. And they conclude that many of the choices we make cannot be made through markets alone and to have faith in markets cannot justify us sidestepping fundamental moral questions. Quite simply it is an unacceptable market fundamentalism that leaves markets to take care of all their consequences.

The political philosopher Walzer talks of blocked exchanges – some things that are not and should not be for sale and are off limits. In the same way, the economist Okun has said that the market needs a place and the market needs to be kept in place. Everyone but an economist, he says, knows without asking why money shouldn't buy some things.

But that agreement between left and right extends beyond a proper distinction between the sphere of relationships and that of transactions and recognition of what Michael Sandel calls 'the moral limits of markets'. Both left and right generally agree also that markets are best seen as a means and not an ends. Of course some on the right have argued that because market exchanges are freely entered into, markets define freedom; and the left have often slipped into arguing that because markets cannot cope with their social consequences, they are a threat to equality, liberty and the realisation of human potential; but both left and right say that for them markets or the public sector are means not ends.

There should indeed be a legitimate debate between left and right about values and the stress we place on opportunity and equity, while safeguarding the importance of liberty. But the debate between left and right need not be any longer a debate about whether there should be a market-based economy or not.

But beyond this consensus, it is the respective role of markets and the public sector that has been the greatest dividing line between left and right. For the left historically it has been a matter of dogma to define the public interest – opportunity and security for all – as diminishing the sphere of markets; and for the right it has been historically a matter of ideology to expand the role of markets.

Why? Because for the left markets are too often seen as leading to inequality, insecurity and injustice. In this view, enterprise is the enemy of fairness, and the interests of social justice are fundamentally opposed to the interests of a competitive economy. The left's remedy has therefore been seen to lie in relegating the impact and scope of the market – through greater public ownership, regulation and state intervention. Indeed for nearly a century the left in Britain wrongly equated the public interest with public ownership and at times came near to redefining one means – public ownership – as a sole end in itself.

For the right, on the other hand, it is the absence rather than the prevalence of markets that is to blame. This benign, neo-liberal view of markets sees them as sufficient to produce a combination of liberty, equality, efficiency and prosperity. And so as Professor Michael Barber records of a conversation with a Treasury official during the 1980s: 'It doesn't really matter what the issue is,' the civil servant said, 'we know that the question we have to ask is, "How do we create a market?"' – the prescription on every occasion: deregulation, marketisation and the withdrawal of the state.

So for the left opportunity and security for all is prejudiced by reliance on markets. For the right opportunity and security for those who deserve it is only possible by greater reliance on markets. These views – too much market on the one hand, too little market on the other – have defined the terrain of political debate in Britain and elsewhere in the post-war period.

Yet for all their differences both views reflect the same doctrinaire approach to the question of the role of markets. Whether markets are seen as the cause or the solution to inequality of opportunity and insecurity, they have been seen by the left and right as universally so – the vices and virtues of markets applying everywhere or nowhere. The result is that neither left nor right has been able to contribute to a considered view, and therefore a viable policy agenda, for where markets can serve the public interest and where they cannot.

So we start from a failure on the part of the left: that the left has too often failed to admit not just that, in order to promote productivity, we need markets but also that we should normally tackle market failure not by abolishing markets but by strengthening markets and enabling them to work better. But we also start from a failure of the right: the right's failure to understand that there are some areas where markets are not appropriate and where market failure can only be dealt with through public action.

So the argument that is often put as public versus private, or markets versus state, does not reflect the complexity of the challenges we face: that markets are part of advancing the public interest and the left are wrong to say they are not; but also that markets are not always in the public interest and the right is wrong to automatically equate the imposition of markets with the public interest. The challenge for new Labour is, while remaining true to our values and goals, to have the courage to affirm that markets are a means of advancing the public interest; to strengthen markets where they work and to tackle market failures to enable markets to work better. And instead of the left's old, often knee-jerk, anti-market sentiment, to assert with confidence that promoting the market economy helps us achieve our goals of a stronger economy and a fairer society.

So in this speech I want to achieve three purposes. First, to show how a progressive government seeking a strong economy and fair society should not only support but positively enhance markets in the public interest. Second, applying that same public-interest test, to recognise that there are limits to markets – not only where, as a matter of morality, we have always accepted they have no place, but also in those areas as a matter of practicality where they do not and cannot be made to work, and hence where we should support public provision as the more equitable, efficient and responsive solution. Third, to set out how we can avoid the trap of simply replacing market failure with state failure and, applying the same public-interest test, achieve equity, efficiency and diversity by reforming and modernising the public realm for the decades ahead, in parti-cular through devolution, transparency and accountability.

First, advancing markets where they are in the public interest. In 1994, after Tony Blair led the abolition of Clause Four of the party's constitution, our first decision, which I announced two days after, was to revamp Labour's competition policy. We did so because we recognised that competition – not the absence of it – was essential not just to an efficient economy but also to a fair society. Indeed in a break from a hundred years of Labour history I said that the public interest required a pro-competition policy that would deliver effi-ciency, choice and lower consumer prices. Some asked us why we were extending markets when all around us we see the failures of the market economy. I argued that where there was insufficient competition our aim should be to enable markets to work better.

I said then too that we needed not just a new pro-competition policy but also a new industrial policy whose aim was not to second-guess, relegate or replace markets but to enable markets to work better. People asked me why I proposed this when it was clear that in Britain short-termism and low investment were glaring examples of chronic market failure. My opponents within Labour argued that the last thing we should do was to extend markets. The best industrial policy, they said, was the old one: as markets fail, to replace markets with state action – national investment banks, national enterprise boards; import controls to protect big companies; even nationalisation of financial institutions. But I said that markets here failed because special interests were undermining their dynamism. Here again the new industrial policy should be to enable markets to work better and successfully extend them and harness the initiative, creativity, innovation and coordination which can come from the decentralisation and dynamism of properly functioning markets – that is, where there is:

- first – if not perfect information – fair and accurate information possessed by the consumer;
- second – if not perfect competition – fair competition between many suppliers with low barriers to entry and producers who are not monopolists with the power to dictate prices; and
- third, with mobility, capital and labour, like consumers, free to go elsewhere.

And it is ever more important that markets are strengthened. While twenty years ago, even ten years ago, it was just about possible – if costly and wrong – to protect and insulate companies, sectors or whole economies from global competition, there is now no longer any safe haven from the inefficiency and uncompetitiveness of the past. With hardly a good or service not subject to intense global competition it is not only unwise but impossible to shelter our goods and services markets by subsidies or by other forms of protectionism without long-term damage. Indeed, competitiveness abroad is best served by competition at home so in the modern global economy stronger markets become more and more necessary.

So our new approach leads to fundamental changes in direction from the old policy approach. Instead of being suspicious of competition, we should embrace it, recognising that without it vested interests accumulate, and, instead of tolerating monopoly or cartels which were never in the public interest, or appeasing special interests, we should systematically extend competition – forcing producers to be efficient, extending the choices available to consumers and opening up opportunity for the ambitious and the risk-takers. Instead of being lukewarm about free trade, free trade not protectionism is essential to opportunity and security for all, and instead of the old protectionism we advocate open markets. Instead of being suspicious of enterprise and entrepreneurs, we should celebrate an entrepreneurial culture – encouraging, incentivising and rewarding the dynamic and enthusing more people from all backgrounds and all areas to start up businesses – here again enabling markets to work better and strengthening the private economy. Instead of thinking the state must take over responsibility where markets deliver insufficient investment and short-termism in innovation, skills and environmental protection, we must enable markets to work better and for the long term – here again the case for state intervention is not to extend the role of the state but wherever possible to tackle market failure and help make markets work better. Instead of the old centralisation that characterised industrial policy – promoting 'national champions' or 'picking winners' or offering subsidies to loss-makers – our industrial policy should reject special privileges for anyone – embracing a level playing field for all – and should aim to deliver higher growth and jobs in every region with a new decentralising regional policy that addresses market failures in skills and innovation closer to home at the local level. Instead of extending regulation unnecessarily to restrict the scope of markets, we should systematically pinpoint services where regulation does not serve the public interest and can be reduced. Instead of thinking of employment policy as maintaining people in old jobs even when technological and other change is inevitable, it is by combining flexibility – helping people move from one job to another – with active intervention to provide skills, information and income support that is the best route to full employment. And instead of viewing flexibility as the enemy of social cohesion, we should recognise that the right kind of flexibility in European labour, capital and product markets is becoming even more essential for competitiveness and that while government does have a role to play in easing the transition for those affected by change, it should not involve itself in resisting change.

So what are the next steps in the economic-reform agenda that will shape our Budget decisions this spring and help us towards higher productivity and thus towards a Britain of opportunity and security for all?

First, in testing times for every national economy it is ever more important to pursue policies for monetary and fiscal stability. The recent volatility in global stock markets – with US markets (S&P 500) now down 44 per cent since their peak, UK markets (FTSE 100) down 49 per cent, France (CAC 40) down 58 per cent and Germany (DAX) down 66 per cent – has demonstrated once again that no country can insulate itself from the ups and downs of the world economy. I understand the concerns that uncertainty causes for investors and consumers alike. Indeed it is because we have always understood that monetary and fiscal regimes must work well in challenging times as well as good times that – with tough decisions in 1997 on deficit and debt reduction, including a two-year freeze on spending in the late 1990s – we sought to ensure that Britain is better placed than we have been in the past to deal with economic challenges and ongoing risks.

And at all times we will have the strength to take the tough decisions. Instead of being, as in previous downturns, first into recession and last out, the country that normally suffers most, Britain has continued to grow in every quarter over the past six years while other major economies have been in recession. The true test of economic policy is whether it can cope with difficult as well as good times and I am confident that tested in adversity our system will demonstrate its credibility and resilience. With our fundamentals sound, and debt low, we have met our fiscal rules, are meeting our fiscal rules and will continue to meet our fiscal rules. And with interest rates, inflation and unemployment at record lows, this is indeed the right time, building on that underlying stability, to push ahead with competition, enterprise and productivity reforms in our economy so that in an increasingly competitive and uncertain world we can secure higher levels of long-term growth.

So, secondly, in every product and almost every service we must do more to open up competition. Having already in the past six years gone a long way:

- independence for the competition authorities;
- as Dr Irwin Stelzer proposed, trust-busting incentives and criminal penalties for those engaging in cartels;
- giving the Office of Fair Trading a proactive role in investigating markets;
- dealing with a range of professions where regulation has been an excuse for vested interests and exclusions from entry; and,
- in the EU, demanding improvements to the functioning of the single market . . .

. . . we have a long way still to go.

The independent Office of Fair Trading is currently investigating the markets in liability insurance, private dentistry, estate agents, taxis, and doorstep selling. It has reported on many industries, including most recently the market for prescription drugs, recommending reforms that expose them to the bracing winds of competition. We look forward to tough pro-competition decisions and for them to continue to scrutinise areas where we expect them to do more. But the competition test should apply to the public sector as well as the private sector. And I hope that the OFT will use to the full their new powers to investigate all those areas where not just the private sector but the public sector through regulation or its actions unjustifiably restricts competition.

This month we will publish our progress report on European economic reform with detailed proposals, based on the pro-market principles I have set down, for further labour, product and capital-market deregulation, for a new approach to state aids, for support for private finance initiatives in Europe, for action to prevent British firms from being excluded from European markets from energy and telecommunications to agriculture, and for extending the principles of a strong, proactive and independent competition regime to the EU. And we will progressively seek to tackle barriers to a fully open trading and commercial relationship between Europe and America – strengthening joint arrangements to tackle competition issues.

Third, we must take far more seriously the need for urgent progress in the post-Doha trade discussions. And in the case of Europe, sooner or later Europe's leaders must come together to tackle, at root, agricultural protectionism, which imposes enormous costs on taxpayers, consumers and the world's poorest people.

Fourth, around one-third of our country's productivity gains come from new entrants challenging and then replacing existing companies so the Budget will continue our work of removing barriers to business success – the government on the side of small business:

- helping to cut the cost of starting, investing, hiring and training;
- continuing our reforms of the business tax regime for enterprise and entrepreneurs and capital gains;
- opening up public procurement to small firms and
- moving forward with measures to encourage the entrepreneurial culture.

Fifth, where markets by themselves cannot deliver the long-term returns from investing in skills and new technologies, and cannot safeguard the environment for the long term, it is right to act.

- So where firms, large or small, cannot themselves make the large investments needed in basic research, it is right for government to attempt to safeguard their intellectual-property rights more fully and to share the costs.
- And it is right to build on the new employer-skills pilots and to forge a new partnership between government, employee and employer with a view to making labour markets work more flexibly.
- Where there are barriers to the unemployed getting back to work, it is right to extend both the opportunities and the compulsion of the New Deal, ensuring labour markets are more flexible as we tackle the social and economic causes of unemployment.
- Where capital markets are short-termist and fail in the long term we should press ahead with the Cruickshank, Myners and Sandler reforms and be prepared to build on our Capital Gains Tax reforms (short-term rates at 40p to long-term rates at 10p) to encourage the long-term view.
- And our approach to the environment must not only be to prevent environmental damage but to offer incentives to invest in environment-friendly technologies.

Sixth, this emphasis on market solutions to market failures – and rejection of old-style centrally imposed industrial policies – demands a new regionally based policy focusing on local enterprise, skills and innovation. And our new regional-policy consultation document urging greater devolution of powers from the European Commission will be published shortly. We are removing the last of the permanent, ongoing subsidies for operating costs in coal, shipbuilding and steel and as the DTI Secretary of State, is showing, the old days of the 'sponsorship' department are over, freeing up resources to enhance the DTI's role in promoting competition and enabling markets to work better.

The measures for competition, trade, enterprise, science and skills, and regions take us along the road towards a Britain of opportunity and security for all. They mean a more efficient economy that delivers more opportunity. But the extent to which we go further and ensure opportunity and security for all depends upon a further set of political choices. Let me give a few examples.

For a party that does not care about opportunity for all, need be at best agnostic on those excluded from it. But for a party for whom equity matters a central element of a pro-competition policy is to remove all the old barriers that prevent new entrants, and – integral to a skills and education policy – draw on the talents of not just some but the widest range of people and their potential. In both cases the most equitable solution is also likely to be the most efficient.

A party unconcerned about equity would be agnostic about the need for regional policy or be against it. I have suggested that an effective regional policy is economically efficient but those who are most concerned about divisions between regions and the inequalities that result will wish to demonstrate that balanced economic growth is not only in the interests of the least prosperous regions but in the interests of regions where prosperity can bring congestion, over-crowding and overheating.

Too often, in Britain, unlike America, opportunities to start a business have seemed accessible mainly to a closed circle of the privileged so those of us who believe in opportunity for all will wish to go furthest in promoting enterprise for all. In the poorest areas in Britain, where only one business is created for every six in the wealthier areas, and where not only family savings but also bank capital at the right price is often unavailable even where men and women show initiative and dynamism, our whole approach must radically change. Enabling markets to work better for the enterprising demands that we remove the old barriers to enterprise that discriminate against lower-income groups and hard-hit unemployment black spots where the enterprise culture is already weakest and open up wider access to capital, management expertise, telecommunications and financial advice: active intervention to widen economic opportunities irrespective of background. So in tackling these market failures – especially failures in the availability of information and the mobility of capital – a new agenda opens up that helps markets work better and delivers opportunity for all. It is our answer to those who allege that we can only pursue equity at the cost of efficiency, a demonstration that equity and efficiency need not be enemies but can be allies in the attainment of opportunity and security for all. Here social justice – equality of opportunity and fairness of outcomes – not bought at the cost of a successful economy but as part of achieving such a success – a point I made when I gave the Smith Lecture six years ago, an agenda that must continue to be at the centre of our thinking and policy-making.

I have sought to show that markets can sometimes fail. We also know that public services can fail, too. The experience of telephones, gas, electricity and water was of public-sector monopolies created to guarantee supply of service but which had become, over time, not an empowerment for the consumer but a restriction of their choices. In opposition, Labour had to come to terms with and accept the privatisation of telecoms. We saw that with the right framework – regulation only where necessary and light touch wherever possible – we could create the conditions in which markets could work in the public interest and deliver choice, efficiency and a fair deal for consumers. Too often the Tory approach was pro-privatisation but not pro-competition – to privatise without liberalising or regulating in conditions where private vested interests replaced public vested interests and denied the consumer choice, thus undermining the public interest.

Our insight was to see that the Tory solution was a private-sector solution at the expense of markets and, in the end, of the public interest. In this and other areas we knew that if we could ensure competition, proper flows of information and mobility of labour and capital – and thus help markets work better – then the consumer would gain from the efficiencies that would result and the extension of choice achieved, and that, over time, the regulation necessary to

ensure security of supply for all could be diminished. But interestingly the Tory solution was to equate support for private sector and
private business with support for markets. They adopted a pro-
private-sector policy which replaced public-sector monopolies with
private-sector monopolies and failed to develop a pro-market policy
where there was genuine competition, the possibility of new entrants
and proper flow of information to, and choice for, consumers.
Indeed when they privatised they often failed to put in place the
conditions for effective markets. Instead they privatised rather than
liberalised and the old monopolies returned this time but in the
private sector.

It has been for new Labour to insist in opposition and in government that utility reform must promote a market economy (and not
just a privatised economy) and that we liberalise where possible and
regulate where necessary so that the needs of the consumer are best
advanced. So while some on the left still say we should be anti-market
and renationalise, in these areas our values can best be advanced
through markets working in the public interest. So this is our
approach to utilities:

- We are opening up to greater competition utilities like water
  and postal services;
- As markets fully develop we will withdraw unnecessary regulation while never putting at risk opportunity and security for all;
- We will ensure that the new consumer watchdogs now in place –
  for example, Postwatch, Energywatch and Water Voice – represent and empower consumers effectively; and that regulators
  make regulatory impact assessments, including effects on competition – standard practice for all significant new proposals;
- And we will press in Europe for the same liberalisation for
  energy and utility services: at all times our approach shaped
  by our view that the public interest can best be guaranteed with
  market means of delivery through the price mechanism.

And we cannot either hold to old ideas about what should be in the
public sector when there is no justification for it. This demands we
look at services to consumers where traditionally the public sector has
been used and where markets are seen to have failed – but where, in
future, markets, with their dynamism, capacity for innovation and

enhancement of choice, can better respond to new technology and rising aspirations. Already we have proposed a shareholder executive bringing together all government shareholdings. And we have insisted on all government assets being publicly accounted for. And where there is no justification for them being in the public sector – indeed where the answer to market failure has wrongly been seen to be public ownership – we must be honest with ourselves – as with a range of industries and services already from the government's shares in privatised companies and from QinetiQ to the Tote – about the changes necessary when the public interest is best advanced not by government ownership but by markets.

Enhancing markets will mean reducing government. But – as I suggested in a series of articles and speeches last autumn and as the Chief Economic Adviser to the Treasury also argued in his New Localism pamphlet last year – we must also have the courage to recognise where markets do not work. Our clear and robust defence of markets must be combined with a clear and robust recognition of their limits. Let me explain.

For most consumer goods, markets adjust to preferences and thus to demand and supply on a continuous basis. But what about situations where this not only does not happen but the market failures cannot be corrected through market-based government intervention to make the price mechanism work? What of situations where there are clear externalities and clear social costs that cannot, even with the use of economic instruments, be fully captured by the price mechanism? What of situations also where there are multiple distortions in the price and supply disciplines and where even the removal of one distortion to create a purer market may turn a second-best outcome into a third-best outcome?

Take health care – the successful delivery of which has proved to be a mammoth challenge in every modern industrial country. The economics of health care are complicated and difficult. No sensible person pretends to have all of the answers to all of the complex, interrelated and excruciatingly difficult policy problems that rapidly rising demand, expectations and costs create. The only thing that is certain is that, as technologies change and needs change too, changes will follow in health-care delivery, now and for the foreseeable future. But those of us in positions of responsibility cannot afford the luxury of inaction: we have to come up with the best system we can devise and be prepared to adapt it in the light of changing technology and the rapidly changing needs of our citizens. The modern model for the British NHS – as set down by the government and the Secretary of State for Health – embodies not just clear national clinical and access standards but clear accountability, local delivery of services, independent inspection, patient choice, and contestability to drive efficiency and reward innovation. The free-market position which would – on the proposals of the Conservative Health Spokesman – lead us to privatised hospitals and some system of vouchers and extra payments for treatments – starts by viewing health care as akin to a commodity to be bought and sold like any other through the price mechanism. But in health care we know that the consumer is not sovereign: use of health care is unpredictable and can never be planned by the consumer in the way that, for example, weekly food consumption can.

So we know:

- that the ordinary market simply cannot function and because nobody can be sure whether they need medicinal treatment and if so when and what, individuals, families and entire societies will seek to insure themselves against the eventuality of being ill;
- that in every society, this uncertainty leads to the pooling of risks; and
- that the question is – on efficiency grounds – what is the best insurance system for sharing these risks?

A year ago when the government examined the funding of health care we concluded that, with uncertainty about risk, insurers often have poor information on which to base their risk assessment of the customer; that as a result of these uncertainties – and, with many citizens considered too high a risk, too expensive and therefore excluded – there are serious inefficiencies in private pricing and purchasing. Indeed in the United States some insurance policies are now thought to have a 40 per cent loading simply to cover the administrative costs involved in risk-profiling and billing, and today premiums average around $100 a week, are rising by 13 per cent a year, and even then often exclude high-cost treatments. Forty-one million Americans are uninsured.

And in my Social Market Foundation lecture a year ago I argued that on efficiency and equity grounds private insurance policies that by definition rely for their viability on ifs, buts and small print and can cover only some of the people some of the time should not be preferred against policies that can cover all of the people all of the time. But I also argued on efficiency as well as equity grounds that the case for such a comprehensive national insurance policy was greater now than in 1948 when the scientific and technological limitations of medicine were such that high-cost interventions were rare or very rare – there was no chemotherapy for cancer, cardiac surgery was in its infancy, intensive care barely existed, hip and knee replacement were almost unknown.

I argued that today the standard of technology and treatment is such that, unlike 1948, some illnesses or injuries could cost £20,000, £50,000 or even £100,000 to treat and cure and I suggested that because the costs of treatment and of drugs are now much higher than ever, and the risks to family finances much greater than ever – not just for poorer families but for comfortably-off families up the income scale – therefore the need for comprehensive insurance cover of health care is much stronger than ever.

But the very same reasoning which leads us to the case for the public funding of health care on efficiency as well as equity grounds also leads us to the case for public provision of health care. Let me explain.

The market for health care is dominated by the combination of, on the one hand, chronically imperfect and asymmetric information, and the potentially catastrophic and irreversible outcome of health-care decisions based on that information and, on the other, the necessity of local clusters of medical and surgical specialisms. This means that while in a conventional well-functioning market the price set by the producer is the most efficient, in health not only is the consumer not sovereign but a free market in health care will not produce the most efficient price for its services or a fair deal for its consumer. Take the asymmetry of information between the consumer as patient – who may, for example, be unknowingly ill, poorly informed of available treatments, reliant on others to understand the diagnosis, uncertain about the effectiveness of different medical interventions and thus is not sovereign – and the producer. With the consumer unable – as in a conventional market – to seek out the best product at the lowest price, and information gaps that cannot –

even over the long term – be satisfactorily bridged, the results of a market failure for the patient can be long term, catastrophic and irreversible. So even if there are risks of state failure, there is a clear market failure.

But market failures do not only exist because of asymmetry of information and the irreversibility of decisions but because local emergency hospitals are – in large part – clusters of essential medical and surgical specialities and have characteristics that make them akin to natural local monopolies:

- 50 per cent of admissions, 75 per cent of hospital beds taken up by emergency, urgent or maternity cases – non-elective cases where patients are generally unable to shop around;
- the need for guaranteed security of supply which means that, generally, a local hospital could not be allowed to go out of business;
- the need also for clusters of mutually reinforcing specialities (trauma, pathology and emergency medicine, for example);
- a high volume of work to guarantee quality of service;
- the economies of scale and scope, making it difficult to tackle these market failures by market solutions; and
- as the US system has also demonstrated, it is also difficult for private-sector contracts to anticipate and specify the range of essential characteristics we demand of a health care system.

So the many market failures in health care, if taken individually, challenge the adequacy of markets to provide efficient market solutions. But what could happen when these market failures – the asymmetry of information between consumer and producer, clusters of local specialisms, and the difficulty of contracting – combine with a policy that puts profit maximisation by hospitals at the centre of health care? It is then that the consumer, the patient, would be at greatest risk of being overcharged, given inappropriate treatments for financial rather than medical reasons, offered care not on the basis of clinical need but on the basis of ability to pay, with some paying for care they do not need and others being unable to afford care they do need – as a two-tier health-care system developed.

One response would be to regulate a private health-care market, as we do in the case of utilities which are privately owned but independently regulated. But let us list what, in Britain, a private-sector health-care regulator would have to do to fully safeguard the public interest. It would fall to a regulator:

- to control entry to the market by setting, specifying and policing basic standards for quality, workforce, facilities, governance and customer service;
- to maintain an inspection regime to protect patients by ensuring these standards were met;
- to step in when inadequate service was provided;
- to ensure security of supply and training provision;
- to police the market to guard against abuse, monopoly pricing and unfair competition;
- to adjudicate in disputes;
- to ensure that information supplied to patients and consumers is honest and accurate; and
- it would fall to a commissioner to attempt to specify every aspect of the service it purchases in a contract.

It is hardly surprising that in every advanced private health-care system in the world clinical-negligence litigation is a great and growing problem; complaints of bureaucracy, legion; attempts by insurers to standardise entitlements and restrict choice, controversial; huge government subsidy, reluctantly seen as essential; and allegations of two-tier care, divisive. Conventionally, regulation copes best in situations where we are insisting on minimum standards. But when there is an explicit undertaking that medical treatment must be given at the highest level to every patient based on health need and not ability to pay, then one is led to the conclusion that, even if that task of market regulation could be practically accomplished, public provision is likely to achieve more at less cost to efficiency and without putting at risk the gains from the ethic of public service where, at its best, dedicated public servants put duty, obligation and service before profit or personal reward.

So equality of access can best by guaranteed not just by public funding of health care but by public provision. The case for non-market solutions for education and other public services can also be made and there is a debate that will continue about what equality of access means for the coming generation; but my point today is that we can make the case on efficiency as well as equity grounds that market failures in health care, as in some other services, are not easily subject to market solutions.

So in health:

- price signals don't always work;
- the consumer is not sovereign;
- there is potential abuse of monopoly power;
- it is hard to write and enforce contracts;
- it is difficult to let a hospital go bust;
- we risk supplier-induced demand.

And having made the case for the limits of markets in health care for both finance and provision, I do not accept:

- that the future lies in a wholly centralised service;
- that we should rule out contestability or a role for the private sector in the future; and
- that we need devalue or ignore the important issue of greater consumer choice.

Even in a world where health care is not organised on market principles with consumers paying for their care, it is in the public interest to have devolution from the centre and to champion decentralised means of delivery. This includes contestability between providers on the basis of cost and efficiency. And the Secretary of State for Health is matching the record increases in investment with further far-reaching reforms:

- devolution with multi-year budgets for primary care and hospital trusts;
- more payment by results;
- NHS foundation hospitals with greater management flexibility;
- increased choice for patients through booked appointments and using NHS Direct and walk-in centres; and
- to ensure that the money invested yields the best results, independent audit, independent inspection, and independent scrutiny of local and national provision.

Reforms that are essential not only to promote contestability but to decentralise control to where it can be exercised most effectively in the interests of citizens and patients. And where the private sector can add to, not undermine, NHS capacity and challenge current practices by introducing innovative working methods, it has a proper role to play – as it always has – in the National Health Service. But it must not be able, when there are, for example, overall capacity constraints, to exploit private power to the detriment of efficiency and equity . . . which is why the areas where the Health Secretary is introducing a greater role for the private sector are not those areas where complex medical conditions and uncertain needs make it virtually impossible to capture them in the small print of contracts but those areas where the private sector can contract with the NHS for routine procedures, where we can write clear accountable contracts to deliver NHS clinical standards, where private capacity does not simply replace NHS capacity and where we ensure that patients are given treatment solely on clinical need. Indeed, the case I have made and experience elsewhere leads us to conclude that if we were to go down the road of introducing markets wholesale into British health care we would be paying a very heavy price in efficiency and equity and be unable to deliver a Britain of opportunity and security for all.

And because we are clear about the limits as well as the uses of markets in health care, we can now put the debate about PFI in its proper context. In my view the Private Finance Initiative is in the public interest. It must be right that government seeks to secure, over the long term, the most cost-effective infrastructure for our public services. PFI enables us to do this by binding the private sector into open and accountable long-term relationships with the public sector aimed at securing a proper sharing of risk and access to private-service managerial expertise and innovative ideas to secure better public services. The public sector has always drawn on the expertise and experience of the private sector. But, whereas in the public procurement of the past, private companies built and then walked away, PFI seeks to ensure that the companies involved are held transparently accountable for design faults, construction flaws, over-runs and long-term maintenance so that value for money is achieved.

Those who say that PFI is privatisation have got it wrong because, while the private sector is rightly helping in public-service delivery, the public interest is paramount. PFI is thus quite distinct from privatisation – where, for example, in privatised health or education it would be the market and the price mechanism, not the public (sector), that defined and provided the service directly to those customers that can afford it and thus where the public sector can end up sacrificing both fairness and efficiency in the delivery of these core services. But under PFI the public sector can harness the efficiency that can come from contestability and the private sector in pursuit of better-quality public services and, throughout, retains control of the services it runs, enabling these services to be comprehensive, efficient, universal. So there should be no principled objection against PFI expanding into new areas where the public sector can procure a defined product adequately and at no risk to its integrity and where the private sector has a core skill the public sector can benefit and learn from – as in the provision of employment and training services, the renovation of schools and colleges, major projects of urban regeneration and social housing, and the management of prisons. And in each of these areas we can show that the use of private contractors is not at the expense of the public interest or need be at the expense of terms and conditions of employees but, if we can secure greater efficiency in the provision of the service, it is one means by which the public interest is advanced.

And this leads to my third theme. Even when a market is inappropriate, old command-and-control systems of management are not the way forward but, instead, we are seeking and should seek – in the NHS and other public services – a decentralised, not centralised, means of delivery compatible with equity and efficiency.

It is the assumption that the only alternative to command and control is a market means of public-service delivery that has obscured the real challenge in health care and other public services – the challenge to develop decentralised non-market means of delivery that do not have to rely on the price mechanism to balance supply and demand. Indeed it is only by developing decentralised non-market models for public provision that respond to people's needs, extend choice and are equitable and efficient that we will show to those who assert that whatever the market failure the state failure will always be greater that a publicly funded and provided service can deliver efficiency, equity and be responsive to the consumer.

This opens up a challenging agenda for modernisation and re-form: more radical devolution of responsibilities from Whitehall as we give the role of Whitehall a sharper focus; greater attention to the conditions favouring a new localism in delivery, with greater trans-parency, proper audit and new incentives. It demands an honest appraisal of the ethic of public service which, at its best, is public servants seeking to make a difference and, at its worst, just the defence of vested interests. In this new world we need to ask about the next steps in matching responsibility and reward in the civil service as we encourage professionals who welcome accountability and whose ethic is about maximising the difference they make; and we will need a better appreciation of the important role local, voluntary and charitable community organisations can play in future delivery. Our approach to public services has been to move away from the old system of controls:

- from a narrow centralism that dominated public-expenditure control from the days of the Plowden Report to devolution to regions, localities and communities;
- from a focus on inputs and process to a focus on outputs and results;
- from annual and incremental spending decisions that ignored investment needs to long-term, usually three-year, allocations based on proper policy analysis of consumption and investment requirements;
- from a crude departmentalism that put the consumers' needs second to how, by breaking down departmental boundaries, consumer needs can best be met; and
- from *ad hoc* policy initiatives and postcode lotteries that failed to meet public expectations for lower waiting times, better exam results and, generally, better service to national targets set in public-service agreements within which local authorities, hospi-tals, departments and others have the incentive to innovate and the discretion to do so.

The four principles of public-service delivery set down by Tony Blair correctly require a balance to be struck between national standards and local autonomy. And our long-term objective has always been to match the attainment of ambitious national standards with the promotion of local autonomy so we can achieve efficiency, equity and choice. Far from targets being a tool for centralisation, the modern company has lean headquarters that set clear targets, set the incentives and rewards, provide the freedom for local managers to deliver and then they collect the information so that results can be monitored and assessed; and so too in the public sector. Where objectives are clear, well-defined targets can provide direction; where expectations are properly shaped, they provide the necessary ambition; where people can see and assess the impact of policy, and where national standards are achieved and can be seen to be achieved, targets can make for the consistency, accountability, equity and flexibility to meet local needs that the traditional delivery of public services has often seemed to lack. Without targets providing that necessary focus and discipline for achieving change, recent public-service improvements – from literacy and numeracy performance in the primary school to waiting times and cancer- and heart-care improvements in the NHS – could simply not have been achieved. And there is thus a critical role for targets, now and in the future, in shaping expectations of what can be delivered on what timescale and avoiding the trap of low ambition on the one hand and – when faced with decades of chronic investment – over-promising on the other.

We know that national targets work best when they are matched by a framework of devolution, accountability and participation – empowering public servants with the freedom and flexibility to make a difference: first, to tailor services to reflect local needs and preferences; second, to develop innovative approaches to service delivery and raise standards; and third to enable – as we should – a bonfire of the old input, interventionist, departmentalist controls over front-line public-service managers – which is too often what they still find frustrating. And so it is right to consider greater local autonomy, and its corollary, greater local democratic oversight.

What then are the next steps as we prepare for our next spending review and as targets are achieved and national standards established? One way forward is that local communities should have the freedom to agree for each service their own local performance standards – choosing their own performance indicators and monitoring both the national and local performance indicators with, as a backstop, last resort, national powers to step back in. Accountability would be enhanced with local and national performance indicators published and tracked, and – as pioneered in New York – the local community expecting their local managers to continuously monitor and learn from their performance.

Further reforms flow from such improvements: greater flexibility for local pay and conditions of service; the reduction of ring-fenced budgeting; the reform of both inspectorates and monitoring regimes to recognise the benefits of local discretion; work with service providers and user groups on performance indicators to help community groups and local residents, especially in poor areas, build their capacity to hold local services to account. So the accountability of local services providers to patients, parents and local communities would be improved through greater transparency and a deeper democracy, tailoring services to needs and choices expressed both individually and collectively.

But we have also to get the balance right between responsiveness to choice and efficiency – and equity. Local autonomy without national standards may lead to increased inequality between people and regions and the return of the postcode lotteries. And the view we take on the appropriate balance between efficiency, diversity and equity will be shaped by the values we hold. The modern challenge is to move beyond old assumptions under which equity was seen to go hand in hand with uniformity; or diversity appeared to lead inevitably to inequality. Instead we should seek the maximum amount of diversity consistent with equity. Indeed we are, in my view, already developing non-market and non-command-and-control mechanisms for service delivery and championing diversity by devolving further and faster to local government, the regions and the voluntary sector, and I want to suggest next steps here too.

In local government with clear and concise information about each council's performance across its local services, with inspection regimes now more proportionate and with interventions concentrated on the small number of failing councils, the Deputy Prime Minister has moved us far from the destructive centralism – the universal capping, inflexible borrowing, the Poll Tax – of the 1980s and early 1990s. As we move forward we propose more freedoms and flexibilities – a 75 per cent cut in the number of plans; reduced ring-fencing; local PSA agreements that give localities more discretion; more targeted and thus more limited inspection; and more freedom with a fairer prudential regime for borrowing; greater freedom to trade; more scope to use self-generated income, including the freedom to benefit from new rates income from the growth of new businesses – freedoms and flexibilities that reflect a government that enables and empowers rather than directs and controls.

And in return for reform and results, and as an incentive to all the rest, the best-performing localities will soon have even more freedoms and flexibilities:

- the removal of both revenue and capital ring-fencing;
- the withdrawal of reserve powers over capping;
- sixty plans reduced to just two required – the best-value performance plan and a community plan; and
- a three-year holiday from inspection.

Freedom and flexibility matter just as much as we innovate with a new regional policy with its emphasis on indigenous sources of economic strength and thus a philosophy that requires genuine devolution of power from the centre. There has been more devolution to English regions in the last few years than in the preceding one hundred years and this localism involves the freedom to determine local needs in regional-development-agency budgets worth £2 billion a year and in economic development, regeneration, tourism, planning, and – from April in selected pilots – the management of skills, training and business support. Soon 90 per cent of the £7-billion-a-year learning and skills budget, 50 per cent of the small-business-services budget and the vast majority of housing capital investment will be devolved to the freedom and flexibility of local decision-making as we pioneer non-centralist means of delivering these services.

The financial freedoms and flexibilities are matched by greater accountability through the role of regional chambers and, for those who in time choose to have them, elected regional assemblies. And having, in the NHS, already devolved 75 per cent of health budgets to primary-care trusts, we have also established strategic health authorities. And there is already discussion of democratic arrangements in these areas too. There is greater freedom and flexibility, too, for charities, voluntary and community organisations as they take a bigger role in the delivery of services.

At the heart of each of the new services we have played a part in developing – Sure Start for the under-fours, the Children's Fund, IT learning centres, Healthy Living Centres, the New Deal for jobs, the New Deal for Communities, as well as the Safer Communities Initiative, Communities Against Drugs, the Futurebuilders programme and Gift Aid – is a genuine break with the recent past: services, once centrally funded and organised, can and should now be led, organised and delivered by voluntary, charitable and community organisations.

This new direction – this agenda for prosperity and social reform – moves us forward from the era of an old Britain weakened by 'the man in Whitehall knows best' towards a new Britain strengthened by local centres awash with initiative, energy and dynamism. And the next steps should include not just further reform of local government but reform in the civil service as we map out the full implications of extending choice, equity and efficiency in individual public services.

Of course in each decade the relationship between individuals, markets and communities will evolve as technology and rising expectations challenge each generation's vision of what is possible and best. But I am suggesting today that, today and in the future, in the large areas of the economy I have highlighted, our mission must be relentless: to strengthen markets to maximise efficiency. And, in those areas where market failures are chronic, I am suggesting that we step up our efforts to pioneer more decentralised systems of public-service delivery. This agenda I propose – one where we advance enterprise and fairness together – not only meets the contemporary challenges of competitiveness and equity but is, in my view, wholly in tune with British traditions and enduring British values. Indeed, this agenda for prosperity and reform is the modern means of applying enduring British values.

For centuries Britishness has been rightly defined to the world as a profound belief in liberty and in the spirit of enterprise, combined with a deep civic pride that has emphasised the importance of what Orwell called decency: fair play and equity. It is this long-standing commitment to both enterprise and fairness which has shaped our past that now should define not only our economic policy but Britain's modern mission as a nation. Some continents are defined to the world as beacons of enterprise but at the cost of fairness; others as beacons of fairness or social cohesion at the cost of efficiency. In our time, Britain can be a beacon for a world where enterprise and fairness march forward together. It is this very British idea and patriotic purpose, and its enormous potential for shaping our country's future prosperity, which should give us the strength to make all the tough and demanding reforms now necessary to create a Britain of opportunity and security for all.

When the Social Market Foundation published this speech on 18 May 2004, the Chancellor spoke at the launch, making some additional remarks on this topic, and taking forward some of the themes in the original. In particular he deals with the issue of personalisation of public services, trying to resolve what some perceived as a dilemma posed in the last speech – that the government's three goals for public services (greater personalisation, higher efficiency, and increased equity) were mutually incompatible. In this speech, the Chancellor argues that achieving equality of opportunity is a fundamental goal in a progressive society, and hence that each person has an equal entitlement not just to high standards of service, but to as equal a chance as another of developing themselves and their potential to the fullest. Because people begin from different starting places, in different circumstances and with different needs, public services need to be personalised in terms of their resources and range of provision. Achieving this vision of personalised public services – meeting the individual needs of all our citizens – requires continuing reform in the way we deliver public services. And this vision is not of personalised services just for the few, for those who can afford to buy them in the market. It is for all. The Chancellor therefore concludes that personalisation is not opposed to equity; it is at the very core of what equity means. Achieving the goal of equality of opportunity – enabling each person to achieve their own potential to the fullest – requires a tailored approach that takes into account each person's unique circumstances.

In the original speech I argued for a new clarity on one of the oldest and most important issues in political economy: the role and limits of the state and markets. I argued that markets are in the public interest, while not to be automatically equated with it, and that we should be advancing market disciplines across the economy – promoting greater competition, open trade, entrepreneurship and flexibility in labour and capital markets.

I said that where there are market failures we should work to make markets perform better – as in skills and training, in science and research and development, in financial markets, in regional policy and to tackle environmental damage.

And I suggested that where there are systemic problems with the operation of markets that cannot easily be corrected, such as in health care and other public services, the challenge is to develop efficient and equitable but non-centralist means of public provision.

Since that speech we have already announced major changes in policy that were prefigured or anticipated by the arguments of the speech. We have removed the last permanent industrial subsidies in coal, steel and shipbuilding. We have announced the sale of UK government privatised shareholdings. From a platform of an increased National Minimum Wage and tax credits, we have promoted regional and local pay flexibility. We have announced new deregulatory initiatives for the administration of small companies in, for example, VAT and audit. We have agreed a four-presidency deregulation initiative for the EU, with the aim of putting every regulation to the competitiveness test. We have proposed a further round of European economic reform – liberalising product, capital and labour markets. We have proposed how the European Union can reform its state-aid regime – abolishing wasteful state aids but also making sure the rules do not prevent measures which help make markets work better. We have implemented our new competition and enterprise regime and the OFT and Competition Commission have a new work programme with investigations into market conditions in areas from pharmacies and doorstep selling to estate agents and the professions. And we have invested substantially more in the areas where if government does not act, voluntary, private or other agencies cannot be relied on to do so – in schools, adult learning, universities, colleges, health and infrastructure.

And in adult learning we are seeking a new partnership between government, employers and employees. In health and the public services the programme of reform is proceeding faster than ever, and that reform will go on and on.

Tony Blair and I are working closely on both our spending round and the five-year departmental plans for the future: radical plans for investment matched by reform which we and the Cabinet are also working through together, reform plans that we will outline in the next few weeks, reforms on the basis of which Tony Blair will map out the road ahead.

And working with John Reid in the field of health care, we are recognising just how much more progress on the reform agenda we can make.

Last year I argued for more devolution, more local accountability, more flexibility and more choice – more diversity of supply – in the delivery of services. But advances we are making now allow us to go even further.

Take information available to the patient. In my speech last year I pointed out that professional and care relationships suffer from information asymmetries – information asymmetries that made the typical market model of service provision difficult to work in every health-care system, including in America as well as Britain. Whereas in a market there is always a temptation for the supplier to exploit information asymmetries, in public services we must attempt to face up to them in the interests of patient power. So increasingly we will empower patients.

In addition to producing better information for patients through star ratings, putting waiting times and other information on the NHS.UK website, we are piloting expert support for patients in exercising choice over their care. In our coronary and heart disease choice pilots, for example, specialist nurse 'patient care advisors' are being provided to help patients. And we are now planning to roll out choice at referral, where PCTs and GPs will provide advice and support either directly to patients or with the help of voluntary organisations. We are also providing more information, particularly in primary care and for patients with chronic conditions where patients increasingly have considerable knowledge of their condition.

Addressing these asymmetries – putting patients and users of other public services at the heart of the delivery of those services – is a crucial aspect of the government's desire to achieve a wider aim: to make public services more personal to the needs of the user.

Personalisation means opening up wherever possible a greater range of options to the service user and I believe it will serve us well to consider the future of the public services in this way: making public services responsive to the particular needs of their users so that his or her needs are better met:

- for the NHS patient, the opportunity to book an appointment time, to see their own electronic records, to choose a hospital;
- for the school pupil, allowing the individual to learn at his or her own pace and style;
- for the elderly or disabled person, the chance to design for themselves and then obtain the right package of care options;
- for the young person on the New Deal, access to an adviser who can provide help tailored to the particular circumstances of the individual and the employment conditions of the area;
- for the parent, a range of flexible childcare services and financial support to choose from;
- for the local community, the opportunity to discuss and influence community safety strategies and environmental improvements.

And in this way the work of the doctor, the nurse, the teacher and the provider focus more on the individual needs of the patient, pupil and user than ever before; public services can be shown to be superior to privately provided services in these areas; and a new model of non-centralised non-market public-service delivery can evolve – devolved, accountable, flexible, with the user in the driving seat.

For too long in the past chronic underinvestment made many resigned to the poor performance of too many public services, standardised and uniform services starved as they were of resources and of long-term direction and hope. But today we can see a new vision ahead of us – where instead of standardised and uniform services, public services meet people's diverse needs, in ways personal to those who depend upon them.

As Amartya Sen has famously argued, equality rooted in an equal respect and concern for our citizens demands not just greater equality of resources but also equal capability to function and develop their potential. Such capability can be developed through a new approach to public services – one that maximises responsiveness and flexibility to provide services that empower the individual to flourish and one that engages individuals themselves to be active partners in achieving these results.

Because achieving equality of opportunity is a fundamental goal in a progressive society, I believe each person has an equal entitlement not just to high standards of service, but to as equal a chance as another of developing themselves and their potential to the fullest. Because people begin from different starting places, in different circumstances and with different needs, public services need to be personalised in terms of their resources and range of provision.

Achieving this vision of personalised public services – meeting the individual needs of all our citizens – requires continuing reform in the way we deliver public services. This is the process on which the government has embarked and on which we continue to push ahead, as we shall show in the spending review in the summer.

And this vision is not of personalised services just for the few, for those who can afford to buy them in the market. It is for all. For personalisation is not opposed to equity; it is at the very core of what equity means. Achieving the goal of equality of opportunity – enabling each person to achieve their own potential to the fullest – requires a tailored approach that takes into account each person's unique circumstances.

When I gave the speech to the SMF last year, some people said that the government's three goals for public services – greater personalisation, higher efficiency, and increased equity – were mutually incompatible. They said that we faced a dilemma:

- that if public services were to be efficient, they had to be inequitable, because only market mechanisms, which depend on ability to pay, can achieve efficiency; and
- that if services are to be equitable and universally available to all, then they cannot be personalised, but must inevitably be uniform, inflexible and standardised.

Yet, in my speech and now pamphlet, I showed how not just equity but efficiency is better served through a publicly funded and publicly provided NHS than a private market.

But now I believe we can go further than this. We can show that public funding and largely public provision cannot only be equitable and efficient but can provide personalised services as well.

4

DELIVERING LOCAL
PUBLIC SERVICES

'All politics,' said Tip O'Neill, 'is local.' It is there that the energies are, where problems are best understood and solved, where individuals not otherwise politically engaged can be enlisted in the service of others. The neighbourhood, the parish, the congregation, the youth club are where people experience directly and immediately the power of working together to achieve what none of us can do alone. They are where the virtues of community are born and sustained among people we know, in the midst of whom we live. Community is society with a human face.

Throughout much of the twentieth century, political interest lay elsewhere, in the nation and its two great institutions: the state and the market. The pendulum swing between right and left lay between the two, the left favouring the state, the right, the market. Yet despite the best efforts of governments of either orientation, intractable problems remained: concentrations of urban blight, poverty, educational underachievement, deprivation and other social pathologies. Noting this, people began to ask whether there might not be something missing in this entire way of conceiving the political.

Seeking wisdom in the past, they began re-reading the great thinkers of the eighteenth and nineteenth centuries: Edmund Burke, Thomas Jefferson, Alexis de Tocqueville, John Stuart Mill. There they discovered a surprising emphasis on the local – long derided for most of the twentieth century as small-minded and parochial compared to the gleaming schemes of government action that alone seemed to offer hope of social transformation. They were struck by Burke's emphasis on the 'little platoons' where loyalties and responsibilities were formed, and by de Tocqueville's 'habits of association' which he believed to be the safeguard of democratic freedom and the antidote to individualism.

This led to an enthralling debate, mostly in the United States, about what was called in some circles 'civil society', in others 'communitarianism'. There were great landmarks on the way. First came Peter Berger and Richard John

Neuhaus's 1977 pamphlet To Empower People, *with its emphasis on 'mediating structures' – families and communities – larger than the individual but smaller than the state. This was followed by Michael Sandel's* Liberalism and the Limits of Justice *(1982) and Robert Bellah's* Habits of the Heart *(1985), both critical of the shallowness of a politics of atomic individuals without attachments or a sense of belonging. More practically, there was Osborne and Gaebler's* Reinventing Government *(1992), with its powerful examples of how individuals and local networks sometimes brought about change in ways no government could.*

The political vision that emerged was as much about neighbourhood as nation, responsibilities as rights, local involvement as government action. It was an activist politics, recognising that one of the best ways of creating change is to empower those most immediately affected by it. In my own work on the subject, The Politics of Hope, *I spoke about altruism not just self-interest as a force in politics, and drew a distinction between the social contract that creates a state and a social covenant that sustains a society.*

The Chancellor has had a deep interest in this entire debate. He has read the books, engaged with the ideas, thought through ways of translating them into policy, tested them in practice, and set them in the context of a highly articulated political vision. He has understood how empowering localities creates active citizens with a strong sense of the common good. He has seen the transformative energies that communities and voluntary associations can generate. He knows that politics involves not only people trusting politicians, but also politicians trusting people to solve their own problems, while giving them access to resources that only a government can provide.

These speeches testify to a politics of high ideals, in which there is more to citizenship than self-interest: there is also service to others. They bespeak an all too rarely articulated truth: that what matters in politics is not only what we achieve through it, but also what we become by it.

Sir Jonathan Sacks

One is struck when reading Gordon Brown's speeches by both the passion and the clarity of purpose which drive his political commitment.

In an age when electoral choice is so often portrayed as just one more decision a consumer makes, it is refreshing indeed to see the social democratic vision for opportunity and security for all so eloquently expressed.

What makes these speeches all the more powerful is the fact that as Chancellor of the Exchequer, Gordon Brown has put his ideas into action. The result is a Britain where so many more people are employed and have hope for the future for their families.

In this chapter on public services, Gordon Brown first makes the overwhelming case for preserving the National Health Service and the means by which it has been funded. He argues powerfully that, far from the NHS being a dinosaur from another age, it stands up very well against other Western nations' health systems as comprehensive, equitable and accessible.

Gordon Brown accepts that in the twenty-first century citizens are looking for services which are personalised, but argues that that together with efficiency and equity can be achieved through the NHS.

I agree : there is no reason why a public health system cannot meet all three objectives well. The same vision drives my government in New Zealand to fund the public health service so that all our citizens' reasonable health needs can be met within it, and so that any consideration of seeking private care is a personal choice for those with the means to do it rather than an imperative for those needing essential treatment.

It is good to see the vision of Aneurin Bevan invoked in these speeches. In New Zealand we recognise him as one of a remarkable generation of Labour leaders who created a new Britain in the immediate post-war era. Their simple commitment to fulfilling the potential and guaranteeing the security of every citizen had a transformational effect of Britain, in particularly in opening up opportunity through education to working-class children in an unprecedented way.

Even so, and despite the sterling efforts of Britain's subsequent Labour Governments in the 1960s and 1970s, Labour elected in 1997 still had work to do – at home and abroad.

In the past nine years, Labour has not only run a strong, job rich economy and invested heavily in public services in Britain; it has also put its philosophy into action through its overseas development assistance, with Chancellor Gordon Brown being a driving force behind that commitment.

Speeches like those in this chapter and through the book enable us to see the policies Gordon Brown supports, promotes, and funds within the context of their strong philosophical base. There is a clear logic behind and coherence about his programme. Gordon Brown believes there is a purpose in politics, and that purpose has motivated him to give the best years of his life to the noble cause of the betterment of the people of Britain.

Twelve thousand miles away in New Zealand, I as Labour Prime Minister read Gordon Brown's speeches with considerable interest, and believe that they resonate not only in our country which has been influenced so much by British political traditions, but also throughout the social democratic family world wide.

Helen Clark

A consistent theme in many of the Chancellor's speeches is a determination to devolve power for service delivery to local communities. Whether it is in the speeches on Britishness, on how best to advance the public interest, or more recently in his speeches on liberty, responsibility and fairness, there is a consistency of approach which is at odds with the allegations made by his political opponents that he is an instinctive centraliser. His belief is that effective service delivery for families and communities cannot come from central command and control but requires local initiative matched by local accountability. Instead of people looking to Whitehall for solutions, people should take more control of the decisions that most affect them – a real devolution of power to local communities and neighbourhoods, faith and voluntary groups and local centres of initiative, across all regions and communities. This is 'double devolution' – power being shed not only from Whitehall to local government; but also from local government to neighbourhoods.

The relatively few speeches the Chancellor has given in this field are interesting for the way they show how the argument has developed. After the general election in May 1997, many people in local government felt that the new government would quickly restore them to their former position in the body politic. The long years of the Thatcher and Major administrations had seen funding cut, and new market disciplines introduced. Boundaries and organisational changes had been introduced which broke many historic links with communities. New quangos had been created, taking powers that had previously been the preserve of local government. And many regulations and restrictions had been placed on the ability of local government to deliver core services.

The early speeches are couched in what might be termed a 'partnership' approach: the speeches broadly assume that the relationship between central and local government will revert to that which existed pre-1979 – a partnership between central strategic overview, and local delivery of services by local government. However, over the years, there has been a shift in thinking. The first occurs in parallel with the Treasury's support for the establishment of the Regional Development Agencies at the end of the first term and at the beginning of the second term. This exposes a concern that local government is not doing enough to support the government's aim of full employment and rising prosperity in all areas of the country. In speeches in this phase, broadly referred to as the 'new localism', the Chancellor outlines a role for local government in economic development, education, children's services and in social services, and commits the government to devolving powers to ensure that this can happen. 'New localism' occurs where there is flexibility and resources in return for reform and delivery – local authorities however are still at the heart of public services, albeit with greater operational and financial freedoms, and more accountable to the communities whose needs they serve.

But in later speeches, the Chancellor goes further, calling in effect for 'double devolution': a new era of active citizenship within an enabling state; a renewal of civic society where the rights to decent services and the responsibilities of citizenship go together; where personalisation of services improves the quality of our public services for the many and not just the few who can afford to pay extra for them; and where voluntary agencies and faith groups (which have always been such a feature of Britain) work together with neighbourhood-level elected bodies to ensure that none are left behind. He says: 'many social problems once addressed only by the state gaining more power can be solved today only by the state giving much of its power back to the people'. And he specifically mentions the need to engage with voluntary and faith organisations in the drive to devolve more power from government into the hands of local communities: matching local devolution with agreed national goals so that local innovation can be encouraged without putting at risk a shared commitment to the highest-quality public services available not just to the few but for all.

In his Hugo Young Memorial Lecture (December 2005), reproduced in full in Chapter 9, the Chancellor suggests that 'our long-held commitment to liberty demands . . . that we break up any centralised institutions that are too remote and insensitive, devolving and decentralising power, encouraging structures and initiatives so that the power so devolved brings real self-government to communities'. His view is that we need to make local accountability work by reinvigorating the democratically elected mechanisms of local government as well as exploring a new pluralism in our politics: 'searching for not just consensus but for a shared sense of national purpose, seeking new ways of involving people in shaping the decisions that affect them – from citizens' juries to local citizen forums – where the evidence is that participation does not just enthuse those directly involved, but makes the public generally feel more engaged'. In this speech he refers to the way the interplay of liberty for all, responsibility by all, and fairness to all have led to the Britain of thousands of voluntary associations; the Britain of mutual societies, craft unions, insurance and friendly societies and cooperatives; the Britain of churches and faith groups, the Britain of municipal provision from libraries to parks and the Britain of public service – mutuality, cooperation, civic associations and social responsibility. And in his British Council speech in July 2004 he welcomes an idea that the Chief Rabbi, Sir Jonathan Sacks, has written about, in which he talks of British society and citizenship not in terms of a contract between people that, in legalistic ways, defines our rights narrowly on the basis of self-interest, but a British 'covenant' of rights and responsibilities born out of shared values which can inspire us to neighbourliness and service to others. The Chancellor argues that this analysis helps to explain why in Britain today 'responsibility by all' means corporate social responsibility expected of business; the obligations accepted by the unemployed to seek work; the challenge to residents in poor neighbourhoods to break from a dependency culture; and local initiative and mutual responsibility coming alive in new areas of community life from child care to drug rehabilitation to the tremendous contribution made by our hospices. A demonstration, if one were needed, of the strength of the foundations on which a new polity of local governance could be erected, one which utilises to the fullest extent the rich British tradition of voluntary organisations, local democracy and civic life.

And the speech by the Chancellor at the National Council for Voluntary Organisations' Annual Conference on 18 February 2004 develops this theme of partnership in the delivery of public services. The speech reaffirms the government's determination to devolve funding and power to deliver public services, but it also confirms that the government feels that the voluntary and charitable sectors (often referred to as 'the third sector') are now ready to partner local councils and neighbourhood organisations so as to better serve our communities. While warning that the third sector must never be seen as a cut-price alternative to statutory provision, or seen as a way of ducking the responsibilities of families or society, or seen as a second-class alternative to state provision it is now recognised that even when the public interest is established it is often better for it not to be guaranteed by a public-sector organisation but by those who on the ground can advance the public interest better. He continues: 'governments should have the humility to recognise that voluntary organisations can provide solutions that governments cannot offer'.

A good example of the Chancellor's speeches on local government in the first term is the speech to the Local Government Association on 23 July 1997. In this the Chancellor pays tribute to local-government leaders, and the contribution they can make to a fair and decent society across the UK, and then outlines what he calls a 'new partnership opportunity', based on a recognition of the importance of locally elected government, trust, mutual understanding, devolution, democracy, and partnership. He also draws a distinction with the previous administration, making the point that, under new Labour, public service is once again welcomed, and esteemed.

. . .

You represent the democratic leadership of our cities towns and communities across England and Wales: and I want to begin by acknowledging and indeed congratulating you for the work you undertake, the hours you give up, the service you offer, the good you do and the difference you make in building stronger communities – making the very idea of community work in practice – and to say that it is because all of us here – government ministers and councillors – have a common purpose, have shared ideals, and are in politics for the service of the communities we represent, that I can come here to Manchester today on behalf of a new government to say to all of you:

- nearly twenty years of conflict between local and central government are now over;
- a new era of partnership has begun;
- a working partnership, not just on words but on action together;
- a partnership based on the knowledge that whenever we walk down the street, collect our kids from school, turn to the emergency services, or look for help for the weak and the frail we are using locally provided services;

- a partnership based on the recognition that these vital services should be delivered locally, to meet local needs, and are provided by locally elected people.

And in future I assure you they will be delivered with the support rather than the hostility of central government.

Over the last two difficult decades, it is in local government most of all that the values every community in this country holds to be important – fairness, justice, opportunity for all – have been applied in practice. And just as I am proud of the local authority that I represent – Fife in Scotland – and what we have achieved, so too I am proud that round the country even in the most difficult of times you have pioneered new approaches to providing services, new approaches locally from which we in national government can now learn.

So it is time for a new partnership. Not a partnership of words we each speak, but of actions we take together:

- a partnership grounded in the maximum devolution of power. That is why this week the government has published White Papers on Devolution in Scotland and Wales, and will introduce Regional Development Agencies;
- a partnership grounded also in power for local communities – the people themselves – built on dialogue and communication between local and central government and a partnership that is focused on meeting the challenges of the future;
- in place of mistrust there should be trust, in place of centralisation there should be devolution, in place of unelected quangos elected democracy.

. . .

A partnership based on one simple truth. That we are not isolated individuals out on our own, in endless competition vying with and struggling against each other. We are citizens striving together for common goals; with our shared needs, mutual interests and linked destinies. It is a Britain in which each of us depends upon each other. It is a Britain where we succeed as a nation or we do not succeed at all. It is a Britain where when we advance we will advance together. It is a Britain where public service is again welcomed, and esteemed. And it is a Britain of compassion where by the strong helping the weak it makes us all stronger.

There was an American poet who said in poetry what I think we all believe: in fact we depend on each other, he said. And society works not because of the invisible hand but because of the visible hands of men and women helping each other: home helps, teachers, local-authority workers, policemen, care assistants, volunteers, neighbours, local-authority and public-service workers working together.

In this way we all depend upon each other. It is the hands of others, he said, who grow the food we eat, who sew the clothes we wear, who build the houses we inhabit; the hands of others who tend us when we are sick, who lift us up when we fall. It is the hands of others who bring us into the world, the hands of others who lower us into the grave.

And that recognition of our interdependence encapsulates Britain at its best today. Millions of people working in their own local communities for a better society, who know that we each depend upon each other.

At the Convention of Scottish Local Authorities conference on 26 March 1999, the Chancellor repeated much of the 'partnership' theme given above, and reaffirmed the centrality of the services traditionally associated with local government and stressed the need for local delivery. In addition he argued that there was an opportunity for local government to do more to support employment and support working people, as well as helping to create 'a just society, where the strong help the weak and we all grow stronger as a result of that partnership'.

. . .

I want to talk today about the long journey upon which national government and local authorities are embarked in partnership together. About the shared values that underlie all we do and will sustain and inspire us on that journey. About the stages in this journey when difficult decisions have to be made. And about the goals and targets we must set.

For ours is a journey with a purpose: to build a Scotland where there is opportunity for all, where everyone has a contribution to make. For a stable Scotland, built on the sure foundation of the economic and political stability that is essential in the new global economy if we are to secure higher levels of investment and growth. For a dynamic Scotland that breaks with the old sterile conflicts of the past, encourages enterprise and entrepreneurship in Scotland and allows inventiveness and creativity to flourish. The next stage of our journey is a Scotland at work and not on welfare, where the rights and responsibilities of the Scottish New Deal remove dependency and provide opportunity. And that will require also an educated Scotland that not only matches our traditional belief in the liberating force of education, and also recognises that higher educational standards are now the essential means to higher productivity and higher growth.

The evidence in the Treasury paper we publish next week is that poverty and worklessness go together. So our priority is to have more men and women in work. And I believe this has always been a priority is Scotland. Call it the Keir Hardy slogan, which was 'work for all'; full employment; call it high and stable levels of growth and employment; opportunity for all; the right to work. The demand for work has been the constant, indeed the central, demand of one hundred years of Scottish history. Since we came to government we have been clear how we can meet this demand – building on the foundation of a stable economy we need more opportunities for work, we must ensure that work pays, we must equip everyone with the skills for work.

And as we look now to the future let us remember not just the challenges ahead but the inspiration that comes from the achievements of the pioneers of public service. We remember this month those who created the National Health Service. And also those who saw beyond the here and now, who took the shame out of need when they created modern social services, educational opportunity for all, public services in transport, housing and environmental protection. And whose hopes, whose vision, whose ideals inspired a whole generation to greater public service. Men and women prepared to modernise, to reform, to change, to tear up old ideas and adopt new ones. They developed a shared vision that remains our vision today: a vision of a just society in which everyone – and not just a few – has a chance to fulfil their potential, in which even in times of hardship people strove to help each other. A shared vision of a society in which by the strong helping the weak it made us all stronger.

Never let us lose that ambition for our country and for the communities which we serve. We must never lose the ambition that we can scale new heights, meet new needs, tackle deep-rooted injustices, and work together for a better stronger society; that shared ambition that social justice and economic progress can go hand in hand, and that in our Scotland everyone has a part to play. That is the vision I put before you today. That is our aim. That is now our task. That, if we work together, will be our achievement.

The first speech to deal with the 'new localism' policy comes in the Chancellor's speech to the LGA General Assembly on 19 December 2001. This is an important speech which not only goes some way to explaining why so little had been done with local government in the first term, but it also sets out a programme for future work. The speech begins in similar vein to earlier speeches in this area, in particular stressing the shared vision between central and local government. But it then opens up new territory. The government wants all sectors of society to get behind the overall aim of full employment and rising prosperity in all areas of the country. The Chancellor goes on to outline a role for local government in economic development, education, children's services and in social services, and commits the government to devolving powers to ensure that this can happen, in return for responsibilities expected of local government to serve their communities, and to radically reform public services for which they are responsible so that they are more responsive to client needs, and lead locally. He also promises new freedoms to innovate and to experiment, with wider powers to trade and to partner with the public, private and voluntary sectors (which he thinks need to be given a much bigger part in the 'new localism' agenda).

. . .

I am here today to celebrate the importance of our strengthening partnership, a modern partnership between central and local government without which neither of us will be able to deliver the stronger economy and better services the British people have demanded of us.

It is a partnership not of convenience but a partnership of principle because, whenever we walk down the street, collect our kids from school, turn to the emergency services, or look for help for the weak and the frail, we know we all depend upon locally provided services.

It is a partnership of principle because every day millions of acts of service by dedicated public servants – inspired not just by individual commitment but by a higher ideal of duty and obligation – shape the ethos of public service in our country.

And our partnership – local and central government working together – is strengthened by an equally important belief we share in common: whatever people said in the past we know that Whitehall does not know best, and we know that effective service delivery for families and communities cannot come from central command and control but requires local initiative and accountability.

For all the time I have been involved in politics I have believed in devolving power, so that those who are affected by the decisions are close to and can hold accountable those who make the decisions – and our aim must always be the maximum devolution of power possible: government encouraging not stifling local action, local people making local decisions about local needs.

And our strengthened partnership today in 2001 is built on something equally fundamental: on our commitment to advance shared goals, to ensure opportunity and prosperity not just for some in our country but for all.

. . .

Our first task in 1997, and the foundation of all we do, was to create a national framework for stability, for sound public finances and for employment growth.

And the difficult decisions we took then – to make the Bank of England independent, to rein in spending, to cut debt, to put up interest rates – are the platform not just for low inflation and 1.2 million more in jobs but also for the largest sustained growth in investment in our public services for fifty years with:

- growth in spending of 4 per cent on average this year, next year and the year after;
- public investment almost doubling year on year this year, and rising to three times its 1996–7 level by 2003–4;
- £10 billion a year saved from debt and low unemployment now invested in health, education and our public services;

- and as we started putting in place this new national economic framework we also began putting in place the building blocks that allow us to devolve power *and* responsibility.

In the first parliament we created a devolved legislature in Scotland, Wales and Northern Ireland, restored city-wide local government to London, and created Regional Development Agencies. And at the beginning of this year the Deputy Prime Minister and I set out our plans for a new generation of regional policies – strengthening, within the regions, the essential building blocks of self-generating growth, the capacity to innovate, invest, build skills and match the unemployed to jobs available; offering the Regional Development Agencies new freedoms and flexibilities and in return demanding strenuous targets be met in skills, innovation, business creation, new technology and employment: a new regional policy – locally sensitive and locally delivered, through local management decisions.

And just as we made a start with regional policy in the last parliament, we also made a start in devolving power to local government, moving away from the destructive centralism characteristic of the years marked by universal capping, Compulsory Competitive Tendering and the Poll Tax. So in the past few years we have:

- boosted financial support for councils, through real-terms increases in revenue and in capital expenditure for four years in a row;
- replaced the bureaucracy of CCT with the duty of best value, enabling councils to develop their own methods of service delivery rather than being constrained by the requirement to cut costs at all cost;
- improved the transparency and efficiency of local leadership through provision for new constitutions for local government, following local consultation;
- expanded the capacities of local government by introducing statutory community strategies, and a new power to promote community well-being through coordination and partnership with other local actors, via local strategic partnerships and the neighbourhood-renewal fund;

showing our approach is a belief in local government not local administration.

In the first parliament, to support our national public-service agreements we developed local public-service agreements. And as I said to the Labour party conference in February this year, over the next two years the number of local PSAs matching resources to outcome targets signed with local authorities is rising from 20 earlier this year to 150 by 2003 – which we will match with further steps towards greater flexibility: flexibility and resources in return for reform. These are only the first steps in expanding our partnership and we are now ready to do more to achieve our goals of full employment, higher quality of public services, and an end to child and pensioner poverty – combining more flexibility and more resources in return for more reform and better results.

And as set out in the White Paper last week, we are:

- abolishing the council-tax benefit subsidy limitation scheme and providing greater freedom for all councils to decide council-tax discounts and exemptions;
- making councils themselves responsible for deciding how much they can prudently borrow; providing greater freedom for councils to invest;
- removing unnecessary bureaucracy as well as targeting a reduction of 50 per cent in the numbers of plans and strategies that government requires councils to produce;
- providing councils with wider powers to deliver services to others and to work in partnership;
- restricting ring-fencing to cases which are genuine high priorities for government and where we cannot achieve our policy goal by specifying outcome targets;
- and high-performing councils will receive extra freedoms to lead the way to further service improvements, including the ending of reserve powers over capping, as a first step towards our long-term goal of dispensing with the power to cap altogether; further reductions in ring-fencing of revenue from central government, and of support for capital investment; more freedom to use income collected locally from fines and charges; extra exemptions from the plan requirements of central government, and more discretion over best-value programmes; and a much lighter-touch inspection regime.

Reforms that will significantly expand the freedoms and flexibilities available to local government. Our approach is to devolve power *and* responsibility so that these freedoms will be accompanied by greater accountability to local communities. That is why alongside devolution of power we will introduce a new comprehensive performance framework – providing clear and concise information about councils' performance, enabling us to make our inspection regimes more proportionate, to target support where it is most needed, and to identify the small minority of failing councils in need of tough remedial action.

A democratic framework for devolving power to modern local authorities based on new rights and new responsibilities – the power you need to improve your performance – the responsibility expected of you to serve your communities. And in this parliament we are ready to go even further to enable local people to do more to make local decisions about meeting local needs. Already the option of congestion charging is now available and being implemented in London. I believe that we should be prepared to consider further radical options to ensure devolution of power and responsibility go hand in hand so that the public can get the best possible services. And once we have carried out further analysis, we shall establish a high-level working group involving ministers and senior figures from local government to look at all aspects of the balance of funding, reviewing the evidence and looking at reform options.

So let me set out how – through local and national government working together, building on the new freedoms and flexibilities the White Paper has put in place – we can rise to today's challenges and meet our shared goals.

First, employment: I could talk about the 1 million jobs we have created, but I am more anxious about the 1 million men and women still left out, still unemployed – and as local councillors I hope you will want to play a bigger role in the next steps to help the newly redundant get back into work quickly and expand the New Deal to assist those hard to employ. This means following the innovative example of councils such as Brighton and Bristol, councils that have tailored supplementary employment programmes to complement the New Deal. Last month the Work and Pensions Secretary announced twenty special projects to test whether guaranteed jobs for the long-term unemployed could get more people permanently off the dole. It is a new opportunity – a guaranteed job – but there is also a new obligation to take it up. And as we learn from these successes, I hope we can work together to make long-term unemployment a thing of the past, and make possible full employment in every region and every community.

Second, the economy and enterprise: everyone knows that the sources of growth in every local economy are local innovation, local skills, and local enterprise. More jobs of the future will come from small businesses growing in each of your areas than from large inward investment projects. So together we must remove the barriers that prevent local firms starting up, growing bigger, getting investment in capital, finding export markets and training skilled staff. That is why together in every local area we must bring about a revolution in education, skills and training.

As long as prosperity bypasses a single community or a single family our work is not yet done. And it is why together we must concentrate on lifting up the high-unemployment areas that for too long have been left behind and why we have introduced – and I hope you can encourage local economic activity to benefit from –

- a cut in VAT on residential property conversions to 5 per cent;
- 100 per cent first-year capital allowances for bringing empty flats over shops back into the residential market;
- legislation for an accelerated tax relief set at 150 per cent for cleaning up contaminated land;
- the abolition of stamp duty for property transactions up to £150,000 so that in 2,000 wards across the country the buying of property and bringing land back into use will be tax free; and
- legislation in the Budget for a new tax credit for local-community investment.

We want to see a dynamic, enterprising public sector at all levels. And that is why we will give you new freedoms to innovate and to experiment, with wider powers to trade in public, private and voluntary sectors, as well as allowing councils to introduce Business Improvements Districts. And just as we have released borrowing restrictions on local airports, I am prepared to consider how within the new prudential borrowing regime we can engender more freedoms for local government consistent with macro-stability and our fiscal rules.

Third, ensuring every child has the best possible start in life: you have been responsible for pioneering the development of child care in the most difficult of circumstances. Since 1997 we have learnt from your successes and it is thanks to you as councils that we can have nursery education with places for all four-year-olds – and soon all three-year-olds. And thanks to your imagination and commitment we now have a national childcare strategy to ensure affordable, accessible and quality child care in every neighbourhood, creating by 2004 new childcare places for 1.6 million children. Child poverty is a scar on the soul of Britain, and we must work together – local and national government – to make sure that we give each and every child the best possible start in life – and that no child is left behind.

Our first task as a government was to boost the income of all families with children, with the greatest help for those in greatest need. And that is why since 1997 we have increased Child Benefit to £15.50 for the first child so that, combined with our other tax and benefit reforms, our poorest families are now better off by £1,700 a year on average – money to all children. And having already lifted more than 1 million children out of poverty, we will introduce the Child Tax Credit as well as work towards taking the second million out of poverty – moving closer to eradicating poverty completely.

Our second task is to match higher incomes for these families with better services. I welcome the LGA's commitment in this area. And I hope that we can work together to develop imaginative ways of delivering these services for the communities you represent, building on the innovative examples set by councils such as Sunderland, whose local PSA is providing an active citizenship plan for its children and young adults, or Darlington, which has created a one-stop shop delivering an integrated service for all children in need – demonstrating to us all what pioneering local government is able to do.

In the new economy, which depends on knowledge, innovation, on mobilising the talents of all – getting the best out of everyone – it is essential to develop all the potential of our children. And it has been a tragedy of wasted potential for our country that there are thousands of young people with talent and ability still denied the chance to make the most of themselves. That is why in the four years up to 2003 the real-terms growth in education spending will be more than 5 per cent a year and we will in the new spending round make education a priority.

And in the past five years we have worked with you to put in place the framework for addressing the needs of our nation's children, with local government directly engaged in:

- Sure Start for under-fives;
- The Children's Fund, now rolled out across forty areas, for 5–13-year-olds;
- Connexions for 13–19-year-olds;
- 'Quality Protects' for all children in need;
- and professional learning mentors.

Programmes with a new partnership between local government and voluntary organisations to support all our children and identify those who are showing signs of difficulties – providing them and their families with the support they need to overcome personal and social problems.

Fourth, pensioners: pensioner poverty is a reproach to us all. And just as we are working to eliminate child poverty – so too we must act now to ensure that pensioners are able to enjoy a higher standard of living. So we are building on the basic state pension – cash increases which boost the incomes of all pensioners – with the Minimum Income Guarantee – targeting extra financial support on the poorest pensioners. We have also set aside new funds to ensure that, from 2003, pensioners whose hard work has secured a small occupational pension or modest savings will be rewarded through the new Pension Credit by extra money, not penalised – as in the past – by losing their benefits – ensuring that pensioners enjoy a share in the rising prosperity of our country. But we must match higher incomes for pensioners with improved community services – both for pensioners in care and those living in housing which needs to be maintained to a higher standard. We have made a commitment to make decent all social housing by 2010 and have already invested £7.3 billion in local-authority housing. Our task is to match resources with reform in social services and housing. And to help local authorities to be more flexible and innovative, we are:

- providing local authorities with increased freedoms in the way they deliver social services as their performance improves;

- investing £460m in high-performing local authorities to set up companies to manage their housing stock, leaving them free to think more creatively about the housing strategies they wish to pursue; and
- extending the prudential borrowing freedoms to housing expenditure, allowing local authorities to choose the best way to invest in their housing.

And in the forthcoming spending review we will do more.

Finally, fifth: I turn to our shared commitment to public services as a whole. For twenty years at least your job as local authorities had been to protect public services against those who wanted to dismantle them. Our task together now is different. It is to move from the old narrow agenda of the years of self-protection – when many argued that saving the service had to come first – to the positive task of building, investing, reforming and modernising. In the public services we are employing more – 140,000 more in jobs, investing £8 billion more, and with private-sector investment of £4.4 billion – making public investment go even further.

There is a new debate in this country – not just about the future financing of our public services, including our health service, but about more than finance – about the future of our public services. And those of us who believe passionately in the public services must be the most determined to modernise and reform so that public services can best serve the public. Just as schools exist for schoolchildren, the NHS exists for patients; public services exist not for the public servant but for the public who are served. And our aim must be that every classroom has the best teacher, every school the best staff, every operating theatre the best doctors and staff, every police station the best policemen and -women – that every public service has the best public servants.

Just as we cannot serve the public if investment is low, staffing poor and conditions unacceptable, we cannot serve them either if service is poor, if performance is faulty, if the atmosphere is confrontational. Those of us who believe in the public services must learn from both the public and the private sectors and revitalise our public services from the inside or others will seek to dismantle them from the outside. We will maintain our £180 billion ten-year plan to modernise our transport infrastructure – a doubling of transport investment.

And we will continue our programme of public–private partnerships. Whether it be in the London underground or in the building of new hospitals, I am convinced that instead of the old sterile divide which pitted public against private, we do best when public and private sectors work together to enhance investment in our transport and infrastructure.

And we should aim for higher productivity in our public services, backing management as well as employee training. And I can tell you that we are supporting the National College for School Leadership and the Leadership Centre for the NHS, devoted to doing more to improving the quality of public-service management. In Britain we rightly pride ourselves on our ethos of public service – an ethos across all areas of the country and across all political persuasions – and a tradition of distinguished public service in Britain that runs deep in our history – a tradition for which people from all over the world rightly look to Britain. All of us can tell our own story about the importance of that ethos of the public service – not just about the past but about the present. For me, every opportunity I have had – the best schooling, the best chance at university, the best health care when ill – every opportunity I have enjoyed owes its origin to the decisions the British people made to open up opportunity, and ensure there are decent public services. Just as good teachers have an extraordinary power to make a difference to people's lives – so too we know nurses and doctors who every day can make the difference between life and death – social workers who can transform hopelessness into hope – home helps and care assistants who for the frailest and the weakest make public service the mark of civility – street orderlies and ancillaries who show by their commitment why public service is about improving the quality of life. And if you've ever been involved in an emergency remember the calm unflappable skill, the professionalism, and offering self-sacrifice of all our public services.

It shows we are not simply self-interested individuals isolated or sufficient unto ourselves but men and women who share the pain of others, a belief in something bigger than ourselves, and who – to paraphrase Robert Kennedy – see pain and seek to heal it; see suffering and seek to triumph over it; see injustice and seek to overcome it.

Each time a good is done it sends out a message that duty, obligation and service are at the heart of a country that believes there is such thing as a society. And it is from these acts of selfless dedication inspired by a higher ideal of duty and obligation that not just the ethos of public service is shaped but the very character of our country. And just as under this government an NHS will be modernised for the coming generation as a national health service free at the point of need – so too public services will be reformed for the coming generation as locally managed public services there to serve the public. If by our actions you or I, each of us, could lift just one child out of poverty, give one young person a chance of training and a job, give one more person suffering from pain the chance of the help they deserve, give one more classroom the books and computers it needs, secure for one more pensioner a greater measure of dignity and decency in retirement, then we are doing something not just for ourselves but for our communities.

But if working together, national and local government, we can be at the service of whole communities, we can do far more – giving every child the best start in life, creating a Britain where there is employment opportunity for all, offering security for the elderly in retirement, building, from the foundation of economic stability, public services we can all be proud of; working together in our partnership of principle.

This is our shared challenge and – working together in partnership – that can be our achievement.

A speech given by the Chancellor in Hull on 11 October 2002, entitled 'Empowering Local Centres of Initiative, is a good summary of much of the argument so far. In addition the Chancellor uses the opportunity to define 'new localism' for the first time. But the key announcement foreshadows the drive to double devolution: a proper strategic division of responsibilities is to be introduced, on the basis that 'the man in Whitehall does not know best', and on the basis that effective service delivery for families and communities cannot come from central command and control but requires local initiative matched by local accountability. Instead of people looking to Whitehall for solutions, people will themselves take more control of the decisions that most affect them – a real devolution of power to voluntary groups and local centres of initiative, across all regions and communities.

. . .

The first generation of regional policy, before the war, was essentially ambulance work getting help to high-unemployment areas. The second generation in the 1960s and 1970s was based on large capital and tax incentives delivered by the then Department of Industry, almost certainly opposed by the Treasury. It was inflexible but it was also top-down. And it did not work.

The new approach to regional economic policy, wholeheartedly promoted by the Treasury, is based on two principles. It aims to strengthen the long-term building blocks of growth, innovation, skills and the development of enterprise by exploiting the indigenous strengths in each region and city. And it is bottom-up not top-down, with national government enabling powerful regional and local initiatives to work by providing the necessary flexibility and resources.

. . .

So to build a long-term and strategic partnership between central and local government, and to deliver improved public services, this government has begun to reverse the trend towards ever greater centralisation. We have:

- boosted financial support for councils, through real-terms increases in revenue and in capital expenditure for four years in a row;
- matched devolution with greater accountability and with new constitutions for local government following local consultation;
- recognised the key role of local government by introducing statutory community strategies, supported by a new power to promote community well-being through coordination and partnership with other local actors;
- introduced local public-service agreements with councils, which link resources and greater flexibilities to stretching outcome targets for both national and local priorities. By this time next year we will have concluded local PSAs with virtually all upper-tier authorities. And in 2004 we will launch a new round of local PSAs that will boost partnership working and local innovation still further.

These are important measures, but they are only the first steps in developing this new partnership. We must now be ready to do more to achieve our goals. The White Paper last December set out our vision of local authorities as strong community leaders responsible for high-quality public services. And we have made good progress since then in developing further reforms that will let councils make more decisions for themselves free from central control. So we are introducing a range of new financial freedoms – new powers for local authorities to trade, retain fines, develop new services and decide council-tax exemptions and discounts – allowing responsible councils to innovate and respond to local needs.

We are making councils themselves responsible for deciding how much they can prudently borrow, providing greater freedom for councils to invest in local services. We are removing unnecessary red tape and bureaucracy and will cut the numbers of plans and strategies that the government requires councils to produce by 50 per cent. We are developing a more coordinated and proportionate inspection regime to generate real performance improvements for all local authorities. And we are restricting ring-fencing of central grants to cases which are genuine high priorities for government and where we cannot achieve our policy goal by specifying outcome targets.

But with freedom comes responsibility and the need for greater accountability to local communities. That is why the Treasury has worked with the Deputy Prime Minister to introduce a new comprehensive performance assessment – for the first time providing clear and concise information about each council's performance across a range of local services. The assessment will enable us to make our inspection regimes more proportionate, to target support where it is most needed, and to identify the small minority of failing councils in need of tough remedial action. And to encourage all councils to deliver the best public services, high-performing councils will receive substantial extra freedoms to enable further service improvements. Our best local authorities will see a dramatic reduction in the amount of their funding that is ring-fenced, plan requirements reduced to the absolute minimum and inspection cut by around 50 per cent. We will also withdraw reserve powers over capping, as a first step towards dispensing with the power to cap altogether.

This is our vision of a modern partnership between central and local government – a new localism where there are flexibility and resources in return for reform and delivery – local authorities at the heart of public services, equipped with the freedom they need, and accountable to the communities whose needs they serve. This is the shape of a government that enables and empowers rather than directs and controls. Many social problems once addressed only by the state gaining more power can be solved today only by the state giving much of its power back to the people. And this is why there is renewed interest in voluntary organisations – devolving more power from government altogether, and into the hands of local communities. It is because we are committed to matching local devolution with agreed national goals that we can encourage local innovation without putting at risk our shared commitment to the highest-quality public services available not just to the few but for all.

A few illustrations will show how Britain is changing. With Sure Start – new local partnerships to run services for the under-fives – we break new ground. For the first time, services for the under-fours not only involve private, voluntary and charitable organisations, but can be run through and by them – not implementing a standardised central plan, but reflecting the needs of local communities and families. And this is just one of the new social initiatives at the heart of a new relationship now being forged between individual, community and state. Our children's policy is evolving not just through better financial support for mothers and fathers, balancing work and family responsibilities, but with a national and local network of Children's Funds, seed-corn finance to enable and empower local community, charitable and voluntary action groups to meet children's needs.

Through the New Deal, we are working in ever closer partnerships with third-sector organisations; our Healthy Living Centres bring together public, private and voluntary sectors; we have introduced new Computer Learning Centres run not centrally but locally as we work to ensure that no one is excluded from the computer revolution – even more not being run by government agencies but by community organisations and partnerships. And of course voluntary action extends to community economic regeneration. Today the Phoenix Fund is pioneering new community finance initiatives and the boards of New Deal for Communities have strong voluntary and community-sector involvement. The whole purpose of Communities Against Drugs, and the Safer Communities Initiative, is to engage voluntary, community and local organisations at the centre of the war against drugs and crime.

What do all these initiatives have in common? In the not-so-distant past, each of these public efforts would have been initiated, planned and run by the state. Today, instead, they are the domain of local leaders, local and community organisations, private-sector leaders working in partnership for the public good. In Britain today there is not one centre of initiative but many centres of local initiative ready to flourish in all parts of the country. So in the provision of these services the old days of 'the man in Whitehall knowing best' is and should be over: men and women in thousands of communities round the country – the mother in the playgroup, the local volunteers in Sure Start, parents in the fight against drugs – know much better. So instead of people looking to Whitehall for solutions in locality after locality, more and more people will themselves take more control of the decisions that most affect them – a devolution of power, an empowerment of local centres of initiative that is now ready to spread across regions, local government and communities, large and small.

The government's approach to localism empowers people – bringing public, voluntary and private sectors together, encouraging innovation to deliver our shared goals of high-quality public services for all. Others appear to be simply advocating privatisation under another name – public services taken over by private companies with the best provision guaranteed just for the few not the many. Instead, for us, a new era – an age of active citizenship and an enabling state – is within our grasp. And at its core is a renewal of civic society where the rights to decent services and the responsibilities of citizenship go together.

. . .

The speech by the Chancellor at the National Council for Voluntary Organisations' Annual Conference on 18 February 2004 develops the theme of partnership in the delivery of public services. Entitled 'Civic Renewal in Britain', the speech reaffirms the government's determination to devolve funding and power to deliver public services, but it also confirms that the government feels that the voluntary and charitable sectors (often referred to as 'the third sector') are ready to partner local councils and neighbourhood organisations so as to better serve our communities. The speech also offers an apology for past mistakes and misjudgements about the third sector; an acceptance that the uniqueness of voluntary and community organisations has not always been recognised by government. The Chancellor feels that in the past some on the left wrongly saw the voluntary sector as a threat to the things that they believed only government should be doing; while others on the right misused the goodwill of a caring voluntary sector as an excuse to relieve government of its proper responsibilities. He feels that both failed to recognise the uniqueness and richness of the third sector, and in different ways had it completely wrong – and unfortunately as the political battle swung back and forth, voluntary organisations were too often caught in the middle.

In an important passage, the Chancellor argues that the third sector must never be seen as a cut-price alternative to statutory provision, or seen as a way of ducking the responsibilities of families or society. Nor should it be seen as a second-class alternative to state provision. For it is now recognised, for example in many Sure Start projects, that even when the public interest is established it is often better for it not to be guaranteed by a public-sector organisation but by those who on the ground can advance the public interest better. He continues: 'governments should have the humility to recognise that voluntary organisations can provide solutions that governments cannot offer. And it is because your independence as a voluntary sector is the essence of your existence, the reason you can serve, the explanation of why you can be so innovative, that you can make the difference that others cannot.'

. . .

My theme today is that of new challenges, new responses – civic renewal flourishing in a changing Britain. I know that a recent survey suggested the amount of time spent in Britain on unpaid activities fell from 2.3 billion hours in 1995 to 1.6 billion hours five years later – a drop of more than 30 per cent. So some suggested we have a caring deficit. But in fact a recent MORI poll showed that 59 per cent of 15–24-year-olds want to know more about how to get involved in their communities. I believe we have a goodwill mountain just waiting to be tapped.

I want today to set out why I believe in the independence and strength of a thriving voluntary and community sector in Britain both now and in the future – a strength and independence that we all should and do value. And in setting out my views I want to discuss

with you how for the future we can help strengthen that independence and vitality by complementing the measures we are taking and
will continue to take to incentivise the giving of money with measures
to incentivise the giving of time.

. . .

Now, the community I grew up in – even though it was one made
famous as the birthplace of the theorist of the free market Adam
Smith – revolved not only around the home but the church, the
youth club, the rugby team, the local tennis club, the scouts and boys'
brigades, the Royal National Lifeboat Institution, the St John's and St
Andrew's Ambulance Society . . . community not in any sense as
some forced coming-together, some sentimental togetherness for the
sake of appearances, but out of a largely unquestioned conviction
that we could learn from each other and call on each other in times
of need, that we owed obligations to each other because our
neighbours were part also of what we all were: the idea of neighbourliness woven into the way we led our lives.

And while some people say you have only yourself or your family, I
saw every day how individuals were encouraged and strengthened,
made to feel they belonged and in turn contributed as part of an
intricate local network of trust, recognition and obligation, encom-
passing family, friends, school, church, hundreds of local associations
and voluntary organisations.

And while it is easy to romanticise about a Britain now gone, I
believe that there is indeed a golden thread which runs through
British history not just of the individual standing firm against tyranny
but also of common endeavour in villages, towns and cities – men and
women with shared needs and common purposes, united by a strong
sense of duty and a stronger sense of fair play.

And their efforts together produced not just a rich tradition of
voluntary organisations, local democracy and civic life but also a
uniquely British settlement that, from generation to generation, has
balanced the rights and responsibilities of individuals, communities
and state.

The British way has always been much more than self-interested
individualism. And this was always recognised, even by those philosophers associated with free-market ideas like Adam Smith and
Samuel Smiles. They knew that prosperity and improvement must
be founded on something more and something greater than harsh

organised selfishness: instead a sense of social obligation – often infused with religious values – and a broad moral commitment to civic improvement. And while it is true that voluntary organisations have risen and fallen over time, it is also true that, in our own time, new organisations from playgroups and mothers-and-toddlers' groups to pensioners or third-age groups and the hospice movement have grown to become vital threads in our national fabric.

And this is my idea of Britain today . . . not the individual on his or her own living in isolation 'sufficient unto himself' but the individual at home and at ease in society. And in this vision of society there is a sense of belonging that expands outwards as we grow from family to friends and neighbourhood; a sense of belonging that then ripples outwards again from work, school, church and community and eventually outwards to far beyond our home town and region to define our nation and country as a society.

Britain – because there is such a thing as society – as a community of communities. Tens of thousands of local neighbourhood civic associations, unions, charities, voluntary organisations. Each one unique and each one very special, not inward-looking or exclusive. A Britain energised by a million centres of neighbourliness and compassion that together embody that very British idea – civic society.

It is an idea that best defines a Britain that has always rejected absolutism and crude selfish individualism and always wanted to expand that space between state and markets. But it is not a sentimental attempt to hark back to the past nor a rejection of modernity but its practical fulfilment – a Britain where social change redefines community but does not abolish community. And it is an idea that Rabbi Jonathan Sacks captures best and most eloquently when he talks of British society, not in terms of a contract between people that defines our rights but a British covenant that sets out the shared values which can inspire us to neighbourliness and service to others.

And today civic society finds its greatest embodiment in the strength of your voluntary organisations – a genuine third sector established not for self or for profit but for mutual aid and, most often, to provide help and support for those in need.

We know from the theory and evidence on what is called 'social capital' that societies with strong voluntary sectors and civic-society institutions have lower crime, greater social cohesion and better-performing economies than those without. But we in government should be honest and humble, recognising that even as you play a vital role in delivering services because you are better than anyone at doing so, it is your independence that is the source of your strength. And let me explain why not just you but I, from not just history but everyday, on-the-ground experience of living in Britain, believe that to be the case.

For it is true that the uniqueness of voluntary and community organisations has not always been recognised by government. In the past let us be honest that some on the left wrongly saw the voluntary sector as a threat to the things that they believed only government should be doing; while others on the right misused the goodwill of a caring voluntary sector as an excuse to relieve government of its proper responsibilities. Both, failing to recognise the uniqueness and richness of the third sector, had it completely wrong. And yet unfortunately as the political battle swung back and forth, voluntary organisations were too often caught in the middle.

I hope the political establishment has learnt from these mistakes, from the conflicts and sterile battles for territory of the past. The voluntary sector must never be seen as a cut-price alternative to statutory provision, never seen as a way of ducking the responsibilities of families or society. Nor should it be seen as a second-class alternative to state provision. For it is now recognised that even when the public interest is established it is often better for it not to be guaranteed by a public-sector organisation but by those, quite simply, who on the ground can advance the public interest better. That is why today – with for example Sure Start – local voluntary organisations with their unique local knowledge not only provide the service but run many of the projects.

And governments should have the humility to recognise that voluntary organisations can provide solutions that governments cannot offer. That instead of – if I might put it this way – the man from Whitehall always knowing best, it is the woman from the WRVS or Sure Start or Community Service Volunteers or any of the NCVO organisations, that knows better. And it is because your independence as a voluntary sector is the essence of your existence, the reason you can serve, the explanation of why you can be so innovative, that you can make the difference that others cannot.

So I believe, with you, that the great strength of voluntary action –

and why we should value your independence – is your capacity for the individual and unique rather than the impersonal or standardised approach. Your emphasis on the individual need, aspiration and potential – and on a one-to-one, person-to-person approach, on being at the front line. As has so often been said, you do not rebuild communities from the top down. You can only rebuild one family, one street, one neighbourhood at a time; or as faith-based organisations, who are so important, often put it – one soul at a time. As one Jewish saying puts it: 'if you have saved one life, you are saving the world'.

And voluntary action, while often conducted through national organisations is, characteristically, local; volunteers and local-community workers, working on the ground, at the coal face, at the heart of local communities, far better positioned than ever a government official could be, both to see a problem and to define effective action. It is about being there.

John Dilulio – former head of the White House Office of Faith-based and Community Initiatives – quotes a conversation between Eugene Rivers, a minister in Boston, worried about his hold on a new generation of young people, and a local youth who has not only become a drug dealer but has a greater hold now over the young people. 'Why did we lose you?' asks the minister of the drug dealer. 'Why are we losing other kids now?' To which the drug dealer replies, 'I'm there, you're not. When the kids go to school, I'm there, you're not. When the boy goes for a loaf of bread . . . or just someone older to talk to or feel safe and strong around, I'm there, you're not. I'm there, you're not . . .'

In the face of drugs, crime, vandalism, social breakdown, voluntary and community organisations – there on the ground, one to one, person to person – really do matter and make the difference that others cannot.

And so too does the second great strength of voluntary action, your freedom to innovate. Long before government took notice, voluntary organisations saw wrongs that had to be righted. Indeed, it is because you innovate that societies most often change. And – often more so than the state – voluntary organisations can be flexible, can pilot, can experiment, can try things out, and can more easily move on.

And just as you did in the past with, for example, the settlement movement or the new campaigning organisations which sprung up in the 1960s, today you are pioneering in new directions: from the hospice movement to anti-AIDS campaigns, from environmental groups to the playgroup movement, from advocates for disabled people to the global coalition against the debt burden of developing countries.

. . .

I am conscious that when we talk of public-service delivery we have a further responsibility not just to ensure voluntary organisations can help – as they have done successfully with Sure Start – and to shape the services they run, but to build upon what I felt was a ground-breaking 2002 Cross Cutting Review on the role of the voluntary and community sector in service delivery – which, I can say, helped us in government, right across departments, understand much better the issues which voluntary-sector organisations face in public-service delivery.

And when you identified a fundamental problem – basic capacity needs in it, sustainable funding, financial management and skills, and the need for an 'infrastructure map' – we tried to respond. And from this summer, grants and loans will be available through the Futurebuilders fund to help build capability and I can tell you that, recognising that there are skill shortages in management and business planning, the Home Secretary is also finalising work with you on a new capacity and infrastructure framework, including funding to help improve skills, use of IT, performance management and governance in the sector. And I hope that as we discuss all the new challenges ahead, the same spirit and practice of partnership will flourish to the benefit of all.

My late father always said that each of us could make a difference. We could all leave, in his words, 'our mark for good or for ill'. He said that it was not IQ or intelligence or, for that matter, money that defined whether you made the best mark in your society. He believed in Martin Luther King's words, that everybody could be great because everyone can serve. So I certainly grew up influenced by the idea that one individual, however young, small, poor or weak, could make a difference.

Robert Kennedy put it best: 'Let no one be discouraged by the belief there is nothing one man, one woman can do against the enormous army of the world's ills, misery, ignorance, and violence,' he said. 'Few will have the greatness to bend history, but each of us can work to change a small portion of events. And in the total of all these acts will be written the history of a generation'.

Together, your organisations are ensuring not only that service remains an honourable tradition in Britain but that as

old person helps young person;
young helps old;
neighbour helps neighbour;
mentor helps mentored;
business helps community; and
voluntary organisations help, enable and empower
    individuals,

service can make us a stronger, more caring, more resilient society: a Britain with a strong and independent and forward-looking voluntary and community sector . . . a Britain true to its values . . . a Britain ready to face the future.

5

INTERNATIONAL
ACTION ON POVERTY

Gordon Brown is one of a small group of political leaders who first embraced the notion that our current generation has the power and the know-how to overcome world poverty. Over the past decade, he has used his influence to place the case for development firmly on the agenda of the developed world. He has been a source of innovation and ideas for new forms of international development cooperation. He has been a driving force in making things happen, showing how the international community can deliver on promises, from debt relief to the genuine scaling-up of development assistance. And he has done this at a make-or-break time for the Millennium Development Goals – and for the world's poor.

It goes without saying, therefore, that the speeches of Gordon Brown are vivid testimony to a rare combination of vision, commitment and action. He was among the first to champion the need for an additional $50 billion a year in overseas development assistance. He has fought tirelessly – and sometimes single-handedly – for debt relief, including on multilateral debt owed to international financial institutions. He was the first finance minister to back the Global Fund to Fight AIDS, Tuberculosis and Malaria. He championed the use of public guarantees to raise market finance for development. And he was instrumental in creating the pilot International Finance Facility (IFF) for immunisation.

A staunch but not uncritical ally of the United Nations, Gordon Brown is playing a leading role in my High-level Panel on UN System-wide Coherence, charged with exploring ways to make the UN family work more effectively around the world in the areas of development, humanitarian assistance and the environment. And through the UK's $15-billion commitment to ensure universal primary education by 2015, he is yet again demonstrating why it matters to men, women and children in poor countries that finance ministers in rich ones care about development. Because of him, more children are being

immunised, more families are escaping poverty and more people have access to
safe drinking water. In short, he has been a finance minister who has also
spoken and acted like a development minister, and all the world is richer for it.

Kofi Annan

In this chapter are collected the speeches delivered by the Chancellor in
his much-admired campaign to relieve world poverty through pursuit of
debt relief; enhanced economic activity through trade; and the establishment of an International Finance Facility. Using his position on the IMF
and the World Bank, and working with finance ministers in Europe, the
Commonwealth and the G8, with the international agencies and with the
UN, the Chancellor and the International Development Secretaries
(have worked tirelessly to achieve real progress in this area. The impact
of the measures so far introduced has been significant, and the approach
has been widely praised and supported across the political spectrum. It is
also an issue, perhaps more than any other, that has become associated
with Gordon Brown personally.

In his early speeches on this topic, the Chancellor roots his initiative
in a belief that we are not just self-interested individuals 'sufficient unto
ourselves, with no obligations to each other', but a community bound
together as citizens with shared needs, mutual responsibilities and
linked destinies. He argues that because we believe that 'we have
obligations beyond our front doors and garden gates, responsibilities
beyond the city wall, duties beyond our national borders, that we are
called on to feed the hungry, shelter the homeless and help the sick
whoever they are and wherever they are'. However, the argument for
action to relieve poverty has both an economic and a moral basis. Too
many poor countries are forced to spend millions on debt interest
payments, money which is then not available to invest in the young, the
sick, the undernourished and the poor, and that blocks economic
development. This unsustainable debt is a burden imposed from the
past on the present, and in those terms is morally indefensible, as it is
depriving millions of their chance of a future – preventing them
breaking out of the vicious cycle of poverty, illiteracy and disease –
and the advancement of economic opportunity.

By January 2000, in Oxfam's Gilbert Murray Memorial Lecture, the

Chancellor was developing a much more ambitious set of arguments, based on a new understanding of what makes for sustainable economic development – how to break out of the vicious circle of debt, poverty and economic decline, and create a virtuous circle of debt relief, poverty reduction and economic growth. His central thesis is that debt reduction and aid on their own are not enough: only when combined with the right economic and social policies can debt relief be the catalyst for the true release from poverty. The Chancellor argues that the experience of many countries is that growth is not sustainable if large sections of their communities live in extreme poverty, because an economy cannot respond adequately and in a flexible manner to market forces without the human capital, institutions and basic infrastructure necessary for growth. This means invoking what the Chancellor calls a

> new paradigm, the key elements of which are: a recognition of the critical role of the public sector as well as the private; the need for macro-economic stability; the vital need for the poorest countries to participate in the flow of capital, technology and ideas in the global economy but in a manner that benefits rather than harms them; and recognition that sustainable economic growth and social justice are totally interdependent.

The tragic events of 9/11 changed the way America looked at the world, and set in train many adjustments to international agreements and previous working assumptions. In a speech in Washington DC, in December 2001, the Chancellor blended some of his earlier thinking on international action on poverty to the values which he felt should dominate the dialogue in the future. His solution was to invoke a new 'Marshall Plan' for the developing countries. His speech starts by recalling that the original Marshall Plan was for 'investment for a purpose' – to rebuild Europe – and it involved a new alliance for prosperity between rich and poor countries that played a vital part in winning the peace. The plan involved the transfer of 1 per cent of the national income of the United States every year, for four years, from America to war-torn Europe – in total the equivalent in today's money of $75 billion. This was not just an act of charity, but a recognition that, 'like peace, prosperity was indivisible; that to be sustained it had to be shared; and that to achieve this goal would require a new public purpose and international action on a massive scale and [it] would not merely secure a working economy in the world' but, even more important, 'permit the emergence of political and social conditions in which free institutions can exist'. The Chancellor quotes George Marshall approvingly as one who had a unifying vision for a global fight, not against one country or one ideology, but against 'hunger, poverty, desperation and chaos'. And he points out that just as the urgent needs of Greece and Turkey provided the catalyst for the Marshall Plan, today's plans for global reconstruction are precipitated by a specific challenge – that of Afghanistan and the Middle East – where it is increasingly clear that national safety and global economic reconstruction are inextricably linked.

The Chancellor accepts that in the last fifty years the Marshall Plan's European model could not be applied wholesale to developing countries because neither the economic foundations nor the necessary open, transparent and accountable systems for managing the public sector were properly in place to prevent corruption and waste. And he argues that we also need new 'rules of the game' for the global economy. By this, he means we need to do more to ensure stability in a new world of ever more rapid financial flows. We know that capital is more likely to move to environments which are stable and least likely to stay in environments which are or become unstable. And such flows today are quicker than they have ever been before. So for every country, rich or poor, macro-economic stability is not an option but an essential precondition of economic success. Developing countries, which need capital most, are at the same time the most vulnerable to the judgements of global financial markets. And he proposes in the interests of stability – and of preventing crises in developing and emerging market countries – that we seek a new rules-based system – a reformed system of economic governance under which each country, rich and poor, adopts and operates agreed codes and standards for fiscal and monetary policy and for corporate governance.

So, a new Marshall Plan for developing countries would be, as in the 1940s, investment for a purpose, so that they can play their part in a peaceful world. It would have many components, and shared obligations. There would be obligations on developing countries: to end corruption, put in place stable economic policies, to invite investment, to meet their commitment to community ownership of their poverty-reduction strategies and to ensure resources go to fighting poverty, including education and health. Obligations on businesses: to engage with the development challenge and not to walk away, including participating in business-investment forums and playing their part in preventing and resolving economic crises. Obligations on the world community as a whole: to reform systems to ensure greater transparency and openness, to open up trade and the opportunities for faster development and to focus on priorities that meet the international development targets. And obligations on the richest governments: to tackling inequalities through a substantial and decisive transfer of resources, investment that will increase the capacity of the poorest countries.

In the CAFOD Pope Paul VI Memorial Lecture, in December 2004, the Chancellor used the opportunity to reflect on the moral case for action to relieve the poverty and suffering in the Third World, and to make a powerful case for action. This is a thoughtful and moving speech, which draws widely on moral and philosophical texts to make the point about the need to continue the work undertaken so successfully to date by the Make Poverty History campaign.

In early January 2005, the Chancellor gave a major speech on international development at the National Gallery of Scotland in the aftermath of the South-Asian tsunami. He drew attention to the way such natural tragedies link us: they show both our shared vulnerabilities and our linked destinies – an earthquake in one continent has left families devastated in every continent. And, as he says, 'humbled first by the power of nature, we have since been humbled by the power of humanity – the awesome power of nature to destroy; the extraordinary power of human compassion to build anew'. And we have witnessed not only an unprecedented demonstration of sympathy but also 'an unprecedented demonstration of generosity, with more people giving spontaneously than at any time and in any previous appeal'. The Chancellor argues passionately for the need for a doubling of effort in 2005 to deliver the Millennium Development Goals; he rehearses the case for a modern Marshall Plan; and then in a bravura passage spells out what the benefits would be of a properly funded International Finance Facility: frontloading investment in infrastructure, education and health systems, and economic development so that developing countries can benefit from access to markets; providing grants immediately to help ensure a sustainable exit from debt so that poor countries do not need to choose between emergency relief and long-term investment; making primary schooling for all a reality; and cutting infant mortality and maternal mortality through eliminating malaria and TB and treating millions more people who are suffering from HIV/AIDs.

In a speech entitled 'The Economics of Hope', given at the Church of Scotland General Assembly in May 1999, the Chancellor linked his call for action on poverty to the faith in which he was brought up, and to Scottish history.

. . .

I have chosen as my theme the Economics of Hope because we meet on the eve of the millennium, when we are all challenged to define our hopes and ambitions for the years to come.

And I am conscious that in speaking to you about the challenges of world poverty and international debt relief, which I consider to be the great moral issue of our decade, and in suggesting to you how together we can make progress on this issue in the millennium year, I am addressing the institution which has, across the world, done more than any other – by precept and by example – to make us aware of our duties to the neediest in the world – and of the sheer scale of human suffering: the 30,000 young children who will each day lose their fight for life because of diseases which can be prevented; the 200 million men and women in avoidable poverty whose lives today are ruined by hunger and the constant struggle to survive; the shamefully blighted existence of more than 1 billion of the world's people, almost a quarter of the world's population, today unnecessarily trapped in poverty as a consequence of their country's weakness and debt. To speak to you today about this, the greatest single cause of injustice and source of conflict across the earth, and to do so in Christian Aid week, is a responsibility that both humbles and challenges me.

And if I may add a very personal note – to come to this Assembly is for me, a son of the manse, a very special privilege. And to do so this year allows me to thank you for the warmth and the friendship and the support shown to my late father throughout his ministry. Today, of all days, I feel guided by his and your faith.

To few is given the privilege of addressing this Assembly; to even fewer politicians and – some would say – rightly so. For in our nation over the centuries this institution above all others has an honourable history of curbing the vanities and presumptions of political power, and has done so with the utmost propriety. Today, in the media and halls of power, we are often told of the economic and commercial links that now bind countries and markets together in an increasing global economy. But for far longer, indeed for centuries, the churches, with their worldwide mission, have affirmed and forged the links that bind us together, all of us, citizens and nations, rich and poor, in one moral universe.

I was brought up to revere the sacrifice of Mary Slessor, to marvel at the courage and the daring of David Livingstone, and at the integrity and dedication of Eric Liddell, and to give thanks for the Christian inspiration of all those missionaries who took the injunction of the Bible literally, as they went forth into all the world. Indeed, when the history of the crusade to help the world's poor is written, one of its finest chapters will detail and honour the commitment of all denominations of churches in Britain, from the missionary work we celebrate today, to the human chain that encircled Birmingham last year. Martin Luther King spoke of how we are each strands in an inescapable network of mutuality, together woven into a single garment of destiny. For it is our Christian teaching – the faith I was brought up in – that when some are poor, our whole society is impoverished; that when there is an injustice anywhere, it is a threat to justice everywhere; that what – as Dr King said – selfish men tear down, selfless men and women must build anew.

We Scots think of ourselves as a people with a love of justice, who value the human before the material; whom hard times, as William McIlvanney once wrote, have taught not selfishness but compassion. Who rose above and then blessed the bleakness of our circumstances by transforming hardship into a vision – a vision, he said, that all should be measured by the width of their humanity and the breadth of their compassion and not by the size of their wallet. Who, no matter what has happened to us, have tried to stay as big as that vision.

And I believe that this theme runs like a golden thread through Scottish history, from the Christian purpose of the first Book of Discipline in 1560, to the ideal of the Covenanted Nation embodied in the National Covenant of 1638, to the Westminster Confession of Faith of 1647, right through the Godly Commonwealth of Thomas Chalmers and right up to our own day: that we are not here as self-interested individuals sufficient unto ourselves, with no obligations to each other, but we are a community bound together as citizens with shared needs, mutual responsibilities and linked destinies; a community where I am indeed my brother's keeper and that belief in right relationships – or, as the Bible calls it, righteousness – as the foundation of a just society lies, I suggest, at the root of everything from the Kirk's centuries-long commitment to ensure a school in every parish, through to the welcome Scotland is giving today to the displaced and the homeless from Kosovo. It is precisely because we believe that we have obligations beyond our front doors and garden gates, responsibilities beyond the city wall, duties beyond our national borders, that we are called on to feed the hungry, shelter the homeless and help the sick whoever they are and wherever they are.

In two years as Chancellor, as I have visited Asia and Africa, I have seen much of both need and greed. I have had a new insight into the world as it is – and a glimpse also of the world as it can be, and I know we must help. In Asia I have seen young children who, because of poverty, are destined to fail even before their life's journey has begun – but my memory is not only of the pain I witnessed, but of the hope shining in their eyes, and I know we must help. I have been to Africa and seen the unemployment of Soweto, a whole generation of young people denied the chance to earn a better life, yet young men and women who yearn to believe that their new political freedom can finally bring them freedom from want, and I know we must help. And I have met and talked to finance ministers in Asia and Africa, from countries weighed down by the burdens of debt and the consequences of war, and seen hopes for reconstruction tragically dashed, as too many poor countries are forced to spend millions more in their debt interest payments than they are able to invest in the young, the sick, the undernourished and the poor.

Now debt relief is an economic issue, because a mountain of inherited and hitherto immovable debt stands in the way of economic development in Africa and elsewhere. But debt relief is also a moral issue: that unsustainable debt is a burden imposed from the past on the present, which is depriving millions of their chance of a future, preventing them breaking out of the vicious cycle of poverty, illiteracy and disease, preventing the investment in what is really necessary – the healing of the sick, the teaching of the children, and the advancement of economic opportunity for those denied it.

So this call for debt relief is a call to action to all men and women full of idealism irrespective of political party; a call to action to all, full of campaigning vigour irrespective of age; a call to all people of conviction and faith, irrespective of religious denomination. It is a call to action as new as the debt crisis, but it is as old as the call of Isaiah to 'undo the heavy burdens and let the oppressed go free'.

And I would suggest our first task is to cut the burden of unpayable debt, and do so by at least $50 billion in the year 2000. Our second task, to help pay for this, is for all of us to persuade world governments to sell IMF gold. Our third task is to convert debt relief into poverty relief by increasing aid for health, education and economic development. And our fourth task – the task for the millennium – is to demand responsibility not just of governments but of citizens – that in the year 2000 we dramatically increase our own giving to the neediest of the world.

And I am pleased that the Church of Scotland took part in the inter-church forum held in Downing Street to discuss how we make progress on debt relief. By 1997 not one country had achieved debt relief. By last month two – Uganda and Bolivia – had secured relief and nine more, including Tanzania and Mozambique, had joined the process to secure a place at the table for the next country, Guyana, and then for 15, 20, and then 30 and more by the end of the year 2000.

Now is the time to act. Take the tragedy of Guyana. One hundred million dollars is being spent this year on their debt repayments while they are able to spend only $43 million on education and $20 million on health. So without debt relief there will be no poverty relief. So as the millennium approaches, now is the time for us to persuade all rich countries to write off their aid loans. Now it is time for us to ensure that countries with reform programmes receive the benefit of debt relief immediately – and not to have to endure, as now, three more years of misery. Now it is time too for countries like Honduras and Nicaragua, so recently ravaged by natural disasters, to be guaranteed the debt relief they need. And as my colleague the Secretary for International Development has urged, now is the time for Albania and Macedonia, weighed down by the burden of debt and war, to be given special assistance to move from crisis to development. And now is the time to bring all these aims together in one ambitious but practical goal, agreed by world governments – that by the end of the year 2000, all the world's poorest countries will have a place at the table in a programme that will reduce debt by $50 billion, releasing money now spent on servicing debt to far better causes – the schools, hospitals and clinics and development programmes that need them.

To achieve all this will require us to implement a second international economic decision – the sale of at least a billion, and probably two billion dollars, of the world's gold reserves held by the International Monetary Fund. This is a hard decision for many governments hitherto opposed to the very idea of gold sales. But it is a decision we must now all take as a matter of both necessity and morality. So I would like you, as a church, to consider using your moral authority to join us in pressing on other governments the case for selling the gold currently stored by the IMF.

I have discussed this with fellow finance ministers round the world. I say here to you what I have said to them: 'when the poverty is so immediate, the need so urgent, the suffering so intense, we cannot – we must not – bury the hopes of a quarter of humanity in lifeless vaults of gold'.

We must empower all international economic institutions to reduce the burden of debt of the poorest countries. So now is the time also to urge the world's richest countries to complement resources for the IMF by also placing $1 billion in the World Bank debt-relief trust fund. And, because debt reduction, poverty reduction and economic progress must go together, the billions saved from debt payments must not be wasted on weapons or lost to corruption, but they must be invested in health, education and economic development.

John Kennedy once warned us that if a free society cannot help the many who are poor, it cannot save the few who are rich. And our goal, cutting in half the proportion of the world's population living in absolute poverty by 2015, demands sacrifice from us all. I believe that next year, as we wipe out billions of debt, at least $60 billion should go from rich countries to poor countries in international development aid; at least $60 billion from rich to poor countries devoted exclusively to peaceful progress, health, education and economic development. And to assure that progress, often in the face of corruption, we should agree – as a world community – and every nation should agree, on international minimum social standards: levels of health care, education, social protection that we pledge to support and determine that no country should ever fall below again.

And just as you rightly urge governments to give more, I hope that, as a church, you can also urge each and every citizen to give more. Let us together encourage our fellow citizens to mark the millennium in the best way, by making the year 2000 'the giving year'. Last March I had the honour, as Chancellor, to announce a special form of tax relief, Millennium Gift Aid: for every £100 that anyone donates to a Third World charity in 1999 and 2000, the government will add another £30 – to encourage and increase the giving of every individual and to realise in practice the economics of hope.

Just as a hundred years ago a handful of Scottish missionaries, supported by a willing and generous nation, achieved great things all over the world and far beyond their numbers, so too together all our gifts and efforts, individual and governmental, from all over our nation – even the smallest gifts – can reach out and make a huge difference. In the words of one American writer:

> 'I am only one but still I am one;
> I cannot do everything but I can do something;
> What I can do, I ought to do;
> And what I ought to do, by the grace of God I will do.

Our aim: millions more giving so that by the end of the year 2000 we, as a people, have given £1 billion more. And it is my hope today that together we can explain to the people of Scotland why in the millennium year this must be done. It is because, not only across our nation but also across our world, our fates and interests are bound together. Environmental disaster, poverty, famine and disease cannot simply be shut off in one part of our world and ignored by the rest. And as individuals and nations we are dependent upon each other for our sustenance and livelihood. Dr James Stockinger explained our mutual dependence when he said: 'It is the hands of others that grow the food we eat, sew the clothes we wear, build the homes we inhabit. It is the hands of others who tend us when we are sick and lift us up when we fall. It is the hands of others who bring us into this world and lower us into the grave.'

I have spoken this morning about the economics of hope and how together we can turn hope into reality, because I believe what should be done can be done, I believe that as a people, we can meet and master this challenge of debt redemption and thus celebrate the millennium as jubilee. We can meet and master the challenge of debt redemption because there are millions who know that now as never before, we in this generation have – within our power if we choose to use it – the means to eliminate abject poverty. We can meet and master this challenge because not just a few, but millions, feel, however distantly, the pain of all those in need. We can meet and master the challenge of debt redemption because across the world there are millions of people of conscience and of belief in something bigger than themselves – who want to realise that ancient dream that we become truly one moral universe, in which by the strong helping the weak, all of us become stronger.

So, as we leave behind us the twentieth century, let us leave behind in it the injustice of unpayable debt and avoidable poverty. Let us together go on a journey, out of the shadow of the mountains of debt and let us, inspired by the faith of our fathers, build that better world for our children that, for me, is the millennium challenge, a challenge worthy of the millennium – a challenge rooted in the faith of this church, a challenge we can and will surmount together.

In the Gilbert Murray Memorial Lecture delivered in January 2000, in Oxford, the Chancellor developed the goals for international action on poverty, setting them in a much more ambitious and wider context. He argues that if these goals are to be achieved, we need to move beyond the economic and social assumptions of the past two decades and develop a new understanding of what makes for sustainable economic development – how to break out of the vicious circle of debt, poverty and economic decline, and create a virtuous circle of debt relief, poverty reduction and economic growth. He goes on to argue that debt reduction and aid on their own are just not enough. Only when combined with the right economic and social policies which are essential to sustainable economic development can debt relief be the catalyst for the true release from poverty. However, as the speech makes clear, this is a major agenda of activity: it will involve substantial and continuing work with the international agencies, not just the World Bank and the IMF; negotiations with many countries rich and poor; and a new approach to treaty obligations and trade deals.

The fleshing-out of the link between economic growth and social justice is what makes this speech such a change from the earlier one. The Chancellor argues that the experience of many countries is that growth is not sustainable if large sections of their communities live in extreme poverty, because an economy cannot respond adequately and in a flexible manner to market forces without the human capital, institutions and basic infrastructure necessary for growth. But he also makes the point that the international context for the work is complex, time-consuming and fraught with the difficulties which affect diplomacy and international trade deals. Much has been achieved, and there is cause for celebration, but in a sanguine passage, the Chancellor reflects on how much more there remains to do. The Chancellor does not spare his audience the details of what has still to be done, as it is clear that this speech is, in some senses, a report on 'work in progress', but he also finds space to return to the link between economic and moral arguments. And in the conclusion, the Chancellor echoes the calls made by Oxfam and others for education: he reminds us that while universal primary education across the world is a basic human right for all children, it is also the absolute precondition for progress in development and in the reduction of poverty.

I am delighted you have invited me to be here with you in Oxford this evening; privileged to have been asked to deliver this lecture in honour of the late Gilbert Murray; and honoured to pay tribute to the world-wide contribution of a movement for change which, from modest beginnings in 1942 as the Oxford Committee for Famine Relief, has become a beacon of social idealism:

- championing Freedom from Hunger in the fifties and sixties;
- then the Hungry for Change campaign;
- its development and emergency work extended to more than seventy countries;
- now championing world-wide education for all.

Throughout – a force for justice in every continent and every country where injustice needs to give way to justice. Indeed, no British organisation has done more to make us aware of famine relief, of the sheer scale of human suffering, and our duties to the poorest.

. . .

If in 1999 the world's wealthiest governments finally woke up to the urgent need for debt relief in support of the poorest, this year 2000 we must set ourselves a new task: instead of the new vicious circle of debt, poverty and economic decline, we must seek to establish a new virtuous circle of debt relief, poverty reduction and economic development.

. . .

In implementing the high ideals and public purpose which characterised the creation of the IMF and World Bank, the founders put our world-wide mutual dependence very well. As the American Secretary of the Treasury said at the very start of the opening session of the Bretton Woods Conference in 1944:

> Prosperity like peace is indivisible. We cannot afford to have it scattered here or there amongst the fortunate or enjoy it at the expense of others . . .
> Prosperity has no fixed limits, it is not a finite substance to be diminished by division. On the contrary the more of it that other nations enjoy the more each nation will have for itself.

In short, prosperity, to be sustained, has to be shared. Prosperity and morality go hand in hand. The task we face today is as urgent, if not more than that faced by the founders of the IMF and World Bank more than half a century ago. As we embark on another wave of the technological revolution, we must resolve to include in the new opportunities the people and places that the world has too long forgotten. We must strive for a more global social inclusion. And our international goal, cutting in half the proportion of the world's population living in absolute poverty by 2015, demands a strategy under which debt relief and poverty relief can promote what is most important of all to the poorest countries – sustainable economic development.

To achieve our goals I suggest that we need to move beyond the economic and social assumptions of the past two decades and require a new understanding of what makes for sustainable economic development – how we break from the vicious circle of debt, poverty and economic decline and create a virtuous circle of debt relief, poverty reduction and economic growth. Those who argued that you could achieve growth and poverty reduction simply by cutting deficits, cutting spending or by introducing an appropriate exchange-rate policy have been proved wrong. But so have those who argued that we should provide debt relief and aid with no conditions. For debt reduction and aid on their own are just not enough. They could simply lead to millions of pounds flowing to prestige projects that do nothing to relieve poverty, or to corrupt regimes and to military excess that destroys rather than builds for a better future.

Only when combined with the right economic and social policies which are essential to sustainable economic development can debt relief be the catalyst for the true release from poverty. So what we need is a new approach that recognises the links that form the virtuous circle.

First, we need to deliver the enhanced debt relief. Second, we need to build the link between debt relief and poverty-reduction strategies. Third, we need to create the new conditions for economic development – stability and a recognition of the roles of the public and private sector – that will allow the participation of all poor countries in the global economy. And fourth, we recognise that, as at the heart of Oxfam's campaign, education for all is central. Because the creation and sustenance of human capital is both a means and an end for the virtuous circle of debt reduction, poverty alleviation and economic development.

You can understand from what I have said why I see debt relief as both an economic and moral issue – an economic issue, because a mountain of inherited and hitherto immovable debt stands in the way of economic development in Africa and elsewhere and their full inclusion in world society; a moral issue, because unsustainable debt is a burden imposed from the past on the present, which is depriving millions of their chance of a future, preventing them breaking out of the vicious cycle of poverty, illiteracy and disease, preventing the investment in what is really necessary – the healing of the sick, the teaching of the children, and the advancement of economic opportunity for those denied it.

The exhibition on the history of debt – 'In the Red' – that I have just opened at the Ashmolean Museum highlights both the destructive impact of unsustainable debt but also shows the occasions in history where governments have recognised the need to forgive debt. In 1997, when we came to power, only one country had passed its decision point in the Heavily Indebted Poor Countries Initiative. Indeed this time last year there was no G7 or governmental consensus for our call for deeper, wider and faster debt relief and how it would be delivered. But spurred on and encouraged by Oxfam and other NGOs, agreement was reached at the Cologne Summit in June on the principle of enhanced relief. And last autumn – at the annual meetings of the IMF and World Bank – agreement came on a new framework for financing that strategy. And we agreed a millennium target not just for new qualifying criteria for enhanced debt relief but for the numbers of countries gaining debt relief, and for the actual amount of debt which will be wiped out, cutting the debts of the world's poorest countries by $100 billion. And we resolved that when a decision is agreed, countries get the benefits of debt relief immediately, and do not have to wait three years – three more years of misery.

The challenge now is to implement this enhanced relief. Within a month, the first countries – Uganda, Bolivia and Mauritania – should start receiving funds from enhanced debt relief. By April, our target is to have decisions to enable around ten countries, including Tanzania, Mozambique and Benin, to receive relief. By the end of 2000, our target is to have more than twenty-five countries receiving debt relief.

It was crucial that we concentrated first on getting and funding the international agreement on multilateral debt relief. That is worth $100 billion and ensures that any additional unilateral relief benefits the poor countries and not other creditors. And I can say that Britain is the largest committed donor to the trust fund which finances the debt relief. And it was amongst the five countries that provided the additional $250 million since October 1999 which allowed the initiative to proceed. Having secured the international agreement and, critically, the agreement that money from debt relief must go to poverty relief, it was right for Britain to take an extra step, to eliminate the burden of all remaining bilateral debts owed to the government by the poorest nations that receive relief under the enhanced HIPC Initiative. And let me explain to this audience that I mean all the debts – those treated under the HIPC Initiative, known as pre-cut-off debt and also post-cut-off debt. And we will ensure that this relief is genuinely additional.

Just before Christmas – with David Bryer of Oxfam present at a seminar at No. 11 – I met the Ugandan Financial Secretary and he told me not only that we were right to insist that debt relief led to poverty relief but the additional 100 per cent relief would enable every primary-school child in Uganda to be educated in a classroom with a roof above their heads and halve the pupil/teacher ratio in Ugandan schools from the unacceptable 100:1 of today to 50:1 in three years' time. For me this is the test of effective debt relief – schools with enough classrooms; classrooms with enough teachers; and teachers and children with books to study with. That is not just a promise from the Ugandan government – it is a condition of all countries receiving debt relief simply because we want to ensure that the money saved in all these countries goes to education, health, and poverty reduction, not to corruption, bureaucracy or buying military arms.

So our pledge of 100 per cent debt relief is a pledge for a purpose. I hope it will encourage other creditor countries to follow this lead. The nominal amount of this additional debt relief from Britain is £640 million due over the next twenty years. This is in addition to the cost of writing off debt under the enhanced HIPC Initiative and our contributions to the World Bank Trust Fund and the IMF Trust Fund. It brings our debt-relief package, including past overseas-development assistance loans, to a total of £5 billion.

We have shown we are willing to go still further. For countries weighed down by the double burden of debt and recovering from the ravages of war, we have proposed special post-conflict assistance. For countries disfigured by natural disasters, like Honduras and Nicaragua last year, we and others have proposed new arrangements: the special three-year moratorium on debt interest to Paris Club Creditors, and a Trust Fund to meet debt service payments to international financial institutions. So in addition to the write-off of debt, we are prepared to take special action to tackle worsening economic and social conditions where we can.

I believe that the last year has seen a major and decisive shift in international policy towards the needs of our poorest countries and citizens. What you and other public-spirited organisations have demanded over long years of campaigning – a shift from 'structural adjustment' to 'sustainable development' – has been agreed as a principle. And before I discuss the significance of its detail let me just summarise the extent of the change.

When, at the annual meetings of the IMF and World Bank in September 1999, the Interim and Development Committees met jointly for the first time to discuss poverty questions, they agreed – also for the first time – that the development of anti-poverty policy and economic policy will in future go hand in hand. They agreed, for the first time, that civil society in the poorest countries will engage in and own their own poverty strategies. In other words, anti-poverty strategies that will not only be country-driven but community-driven – developed transparently with broad participation of civil society, key donors and regional institutions. But most of all they agreed for the first time that both economic and social strategies must be clearly linked to the international development goals of halving world poverty by 2015 with measurable indicators to monitor progress.

So the IMF and the World Bank are now charged to demonstrate how macro-economic reform, policies for sustainable development, and anti-poverty programmes can together bring less poverty and more growth. The key is the decision to transform the Enhanced Structural Adjustment Facility (ESAF) into the Poverty Reduction and Growth Facility (PRGF); for a joint framework for future IMF and World Bank concessional operations in low-income countries; and the primary vehicle for closer World Bank–IMF collaboration in IDA (International Development Association) and ESAF/PRGF countries. And we must meet the challenge for change in the culture and operations of the IMF and World Bank that this requires.

So our task from this year is to move from noble resolutions to detailed implementation, from agreement on change to delivering that change effectively. Effective delivery requires policy measures and action in three key areas:

- first, measures to build skills and capacity of individuals in the governments and civil society of these countries to implement and participate in the process;
- second, a partnership with Oxfam and other NGOs on the ground, in as many countries as possible, to provide support and objective monitoring; and last
- vigilance in ensuring that resources are not wasted on unproductive expenditure.

For the poverty-reduction strategies to be genuinely country-driven, and be developed transparently with the broad participation of civil society, many if not all of the countries receiving debt relief need to build the skills and capacity of their governments and society. I would therefore propose:

- first, an internationally coordinated technical-assistance programme of capacity-building for the delivery of poverty-reduction strategies in the countries that require it; and
- secondly, ensuring that all donor aid programmes in HIPCs and other poor countries, for whichever sector – health, education, infrastructure projects – provide support for and recognise the importance of capacity-building and skills transfer.

This would be one of the most worthwhile investments in empowering the poorest to build a better future for themselves. The International Development Secretary has already demonstrated Britain's commitment to capacity-building. For the last two years we have helped countries in delivering their programmes through advice, technical assistance, sponsorship of forums. For example:

- an HIPC capacity-building programme which enables secondment of experienced personnel from one HIPC country to another, recognising and sharing some of the unique skills and experience that can only be developed within countries that face these challenges every day;
- in Uganda, help with putting in place a framework for consultation with the poorest sectors of society, which will ensure Uganda's poverty-reduction strategy reflects the realities of poor people's lives;
- in Ghana and Malawi, support for the development of medium-term expenditure frameworks which look systematically at government resource allocations.

But Britain, other donors and the IMF and World Bank cannot work effectively alone. So we need a partnership with NGOs such as Oxfam who have a greater presence in the countries and often a keener insight into the daily challenges faced. You can provide vital assistance in creating a stronger civil society and providing an independent and objective monitor of progress – both of the results and of the integrity of the process. This is crucial particularly for the early cases that will come up in the next few months as they will set the examples of best practice. In order to make the best use of resources, I would urge that all the NGOs adopt countries to work with on implementing the poverty-reduction strategies.

And lastly, if anti-poverty strategies are to work and secure the resources they need, we need to be far more vigilant in ensuring that resources are not wasted in unproductive expenditure, particularly on destructive military purchases. This is not just an obligation on the part of the recipients of debt relief but also on the part of lenders and exporters of richer nations who benefit from this expenditure. We require a new resolve from poor countries to pursue anti-poverty strategies, to be more transparent, and as I will suggest, to follow certain codes and principles in macro-economic and social policy. These obligations require great effort and will on the part of the poorest nations. The least we can do from our position of wealth, is fulfil an obligation not to benefit from burdening these countries further. While we were pursuing agreement on the HIPC Initiative, Britain banned export credits for unproductive expenditure in the forty-one Highly Indebted Poor Countries for a two-year period and did so unilaterally. This ban has now expired. But the problems faced by these countries as we all know will take much longer to resolve. It is right that we announce today that Britain will, once again unilaterally, extend this ban to help ensure these countries are released from poverty.

But HIPCs are of course not the only poor countries in the world. There are others as poor and, while they do not have a historic debt burden, can ill afford to take on new burdens of commercial loans for unproductive expenditure. We will therefore also widen the ban to all countries defined by the World Bank as 'IDA only' – poor countries who can only borrow from the World Bank on highly concessional terms – currently a further twenty-two countries. Britain's export credits will only support productive enterprise that assists social and economic development and thus reduces poverty. Britain's ban will of course only fully achieve its aim if it is applied by all exporting countries. Just as our pledge to unilaterally write off all debts due from HIPCs was a pledge with a purpose – to call on others to follow – so is this pledge. I urge all countries to ban export credits for unproductive expenditure in all IDA-only countries and join us in banishing for ever the spectre of unproductive unpayable debt.

But if we are to break from the cycle of debt, poverty and decline, we must see the central importance of economic development – and the necessity of new approaches to securing it. We must restore to the heart of economic policy the high ideals and public purpose which made us seek for every country from 1945 the highest sustainable levels of growth and employment. Let us remind ourselves that in macro-economic policy our aim is not only to control inflation, important as that is, but, based on a platform of stability, to pursue policies for growth and employment for all countries which will increase living standards, including improved health and education. And let us remind ourselves that we seek equitable development which ensures all groups in society, not just those at the top, enjoy the fruits of development; we seek sustainable development which includes preserving natural resources and maintaining a healthy environment; and we seek democratic development in which citizens participate in making the decisions that affect their lives, and countries and communities have ownership of the policies. In the years to come we must build anew our understanding of the relationship between democracy, equality, environmental protection and growth.

In other words, we need to move beyond the Washington Consensus of the 1980s, a creature of its times which narrowed our growth and employment objectives. Which assumed that just by liberalising, deregulating, privatising and getting prices right, private markets would allocate resources efficiently for growth. This has proved inadequate for the insecurities and challenges of globalisation. We need to find a new 2000 paradigm. The new consensus cannot be a Washington Consensus, but as we have recognised in the poverty-reduction strategies, countries must claim ownership and make it a part of their national consensus.

Let me set out what the key elements of this new paradigm might be:

- first, it must recognise the critical role of the public sector as well as the private;
- second, macro-economic stability is an essential condition to growth and all countries need to follow clear policy codes and principles to ensure this;
- third, it is vital for their development that the poorest countries participate in the flow of capital, technology and ideas in the global economy but in a manner that benefits rather than harms them;

- and fourth, we need to recognise that sustainable economic growth and social justice are totally interdependent.

First, the new paradigm needs to recognise the role of governments and the public sector. The public sector is an investor in human capital and also in science, research and technology where benefits to society often outweigh benefits to individual entrepreneurs. But critically governments also have the role of ensuring the right macro-economic conditions, the right corruption-free institutional and regulatory framework, the right framework for competition, and a sound financial system to underpin growth, employment and equity. Without governments ensuring a robust financial system, effective competition and the protection of consumers, it is difficult to mobilise savings or allocate capital efficiently.

The original Washington Consensus grew in the context of highly regulated and protected financial systems in need of deregulation. But, as the Asian crisis has shown, it is but one thing to eliminate regulations that restrict competition. It is also necessary to create regulations to ensure competition – and proper prudential behaviour. The issue is not, as posed in the eighties, regulation versus deregulation: it is achieving the correct balance of regulation and deregulation to ensure financial systems work better. The new paradigm is not about how government can be pushed aside – but how the right kind of government can be an essential complement to markets.

Second, the new paradigm needs to recognise the importance of macro-economic stability. For every country, today's rich and today's poor, macro-economic stability is not an option but an essential precondition of economic success. Indeed, in the new global marketplace there is a new premium on economic stability. Any nation state operating in a global economy which relies on or seeks to achieve investment flows from round the world now knows that the punishment for getting things wrong is greater than ever, the rewards for getting it right better than ever. Good macro-economic policy includes, in my view, clear rules for monetary and fiscal policy that can allow for flexibility to respond to shocks; and a fiscal policy that allows automatic stabilisers to operate. I believe that the way forward is for each and every country, rich and poor, developed and developing, to adopt and apply codes of conduct or plans for stability in monetary, fiscal, corporate and also, critically, social policy, founded on agreed ground rules of the game which each country can adopt and apply.

That is why the UK pressed for and secured agreement that there should be internationally agreed codes for transparency in monetary and fiscal policy. Take the monetary-policy code for example, which was agreed at the annual IMF/World Bank meetings last year. It sets out that we should each announce our targets, identify responsibility for achieving these objectives, and for reporting and explaining monetary-policy decisions. The Code of Monetary Policy makes it clear that countries should provide a complete picture of usable central-bank reserves, including any forward liabilities, foreign-currency liabilities of the public sector and commercial banks, and indicators of the health of the financial sectors.

But these new principles need to go beyond public policy. In the corporate sector, for example, we also need an international standard of best practice in corporate governance, and for financial institutions and regulators. The OECD has now finalised its Code of Good Practice in Corporate Governance.

I think it is also true that the UK has taken the lead in pressing the IMF to develop the social dimension to its work in all countries. The IMF and World Bank need to ensure, and we need to monitor with international surveillance, that the burden of adjustment is not placed on the poor and most vulnerable. The Asian crisis demonstrated the devastating impact that economic shocks can have on the most vulnerable sections of society and highlighted the need to ensure adequate social provision. Building on the codes of good practice in fiscal policy, monetary policy and corporate governance, the UK has stressed the need to identify and disseminate principles and good practice in social policy. Following discussion at the Development Committee in April 1999, this work has been taken forward by the World Bank and the UN. In his statement to the Board of Governors of the Fund on 28 September 1999, the Managing Director of the Fund explicitly highlighted the vital relationship between growth and social development.

However, for many developing countries the poor quality of data on social spending, social indicators, and social-protection arrangements is a key constraint on effective policy design and implementation. Clearly we need a strengthened social-data standard. Let us not forget that when we talk of codes of conduct we are talking about the conditions in which international investment flows can benefit the poorest in the poor countries not about how they can benefit investors. Transparency will discourage waste, corruption and increase the accountability of governments to civil society. The transparency and clarity of these codes will help ensure that investors can differentiate between the performance of countries – hence prevent some of the indiscriminate contagion that we saw destabilise the international financial system eighteen months ago. And by building the confidence of investors they will prevent the exclusion and discrimination of investors against the poorest countries.

So the third element of the new paradigm is the recognition that in order to grow out of poverty, the poorest countries must participate fully in the global economic system, but under conditions in which they get their fair share of the benefits. Without access to the flows of technology, ideas and capital that are revolutionising our world, the poorest nations will be permanently excluded from the prospect of prosperity. To complete the virtuous circle of debt relief, poverty relief and economic development, our aim in 2000 must be to ensure greater private as well as public investment in Africa and the poorest developing countries and also their share of the benefits of trade. Now, there will be critics of globalisation who say that the poorest countries can never benefit. There is indeed a real debate about capital liberalisation. For it is true that without a proper framework for development, capital liberalisation can destabilise. Yet this is precisely why the codes of conduct are essential – codes which Britain has argued for so hard and which the international community has now accepted. If capital liberalisation happened without the right macro-economic policies and financial regulation, then short-term flows could destabilise that country. So we need measures to encourage the introduction of sound and transparent economic policies, good financial regulation and corporate behaviour – exactly what codes of conduct intend to offer and why codes of conduct are in the interests of the poorest countries as they seek to benefit from participating in the international economic system. Of course the precise terms for a country's capital-account liberalisation need to be scrutinised, and there is a great deal of work on relationships between private lenders and public-sector borrowers both in normal times and in times when crises arise. But the codes of conduct are the new building blocks for economic growth in developing countries.

But to ensure that poorer nations genuinely benefit from the global economic system, there are also obligations on the richer countries to create a fair playing field. I believe this, first, is in ensuring a more stable international financial system, particularly for weaker economies which can be easily destabilised. That is why Britain proposed last autumn bringing together the IMF, the World Bank and key regulatory authorities in a new permanent Committee for Global Financial Regulation charged with delivering the global objective of a stable financial system. The Financial Stability Forum has now been established. The forum's work will make cooperation between international institutions and national regulators a fact of international financial life. I believe in time it can become the world's early-warning system for regional and global financial-market risk.

The second obligation, I believe, is helping the least developed countries promote greater productive foreign direct investment. At present only 3 per cent of foreign direct investment goes to low-income countries and only 1 per cent goes to the Highly Indebted Poor Countries. Direct investment into productive enterprise should bring not just capital, but transfer skills and technology and encourage best international business practice. Where domestic capital markets are not well developed, it can also be a more stable flow of inward investment than portfolio investment in stock markets. We need to consider creating an effective forum for investment in Africa which would discuss the current barriers to investment perceived by potential investors, propose reforms and encourage business investors in the continent.

Thirdly, we have an obligation to recognise that growth and trade are the key to tackling poverty, and our approach to trade should be informed by a progressive internationalism. So the test for trade talks will be whether developing countries benefit. Social principles which we support are there to benefit the poorest countries. Any attempt by developed countries to erect new protectionism should be resisted. We must take further steps to increase market access for the least developed countries. The UK's proposal, for example, is for zero tariffs to be applied to all goods. Trade talks would achieve more if openness prevailed and this requires new ways of working by the international organisations as well as the individual countries. I believe there is now a strong case for looking at reforms to improve the accountability and operations of the WTO, just as we are working to improve the IMF and World Bank. It is vital to make progress in the WTO. This must be done in a way that reflects the needs and views of the developing countries, and enables them to participate fully in the discussions and have ownership of the final agreement.

Fourth and central to the new paradigm is the recognition that economic growth and social justice are totally interdependent. The experience of so many countries has shown that growth is not sustainable if large sections of their communities live in extreme poverty. Because even if market prices are correct, an economy cannot respond adequately and in a flexible manner to market forces without the human capital, institutions and basic infrastructure necessary for growth. Indeed one of the main reasons private investors in Africa quote for not investing in the continent is insufficient skilled labour. They are telling us that education and the creation of human capital are as important as controlling inflation.

So I come, last in a list of areas for action, to social investment, particularly in education. Not because it is the least important but because, as I hope I have made clear, it is the most important. The new approach I have outlined today rests on two central ideas:

- first, social justice is vital to economic progress; and
- second, economic reform requires the support, participation and trust of the populations. In other words, there should not just be country ownership but community ownership.

It is here that education, empowering people for their future, putting opportunity directly in their hands, is critical. Oxfam rightly calls education the single most powerful weapon against poverty. Children – as I have said before – are 20 per cent of the population, 100 per cent of our future. And instead of developing some of the potential of some of the people, future economic growth depends upon developing all of the potential of all. What we want for our own children, we want for all our children. Universal primary education across the world is a basic human right for all children. But equally significantly it is the absolute precondition for progress in development and reduction of poverty. Countries cannot develop properly if only élites are educated. So the development case for education, the case for investing in primary education, is unanswerable. It is essential to the creation of an economy which has the flexibility to respond to market forces; it helps people to become more productive, and to earn more income; it leads to improvements in health, nutrition and child mortality. People are able to transform their own lives and society, and they acquire the basic skills of literacy and numeracy, as well as the capacity to utilise knowledge and information.

Let us remember the commitments we have all made. Not just fifty years ago, when the Universal Declaration of Human Rights proclaimed free and compulsory education to be a basic human right. But successively, in international declarations:

- the 1990 World Conference on Education for All, which set the target of ensuring universal access to, and completion of, primary education by the year 2000;
- the 1990 World Summit for Children – signed by all but two of the world's governments, which reaffirmed the right to an education as a legally binding obligation;
- the 1995 World Summit for Social Development, which said that by 2005 we would achieve universal access to basic education and completion of primary education by at least 80 per cent of primary-school-age children, and close the gender gap in primary- and secondary-school education;
- the 1999 Convention on the Rights of the Child, which reaffirmed that we would reduce by half the number of people living in extreme poverty by 2015; have universal primary education before 2015; and gender equality in primary and secondary education by 2005.

But as we all know there have been too many grandiose statements, too little development and implementation. Nine hundred million people over the age of fifteen are illiterate – one sixth of the world's population. And today 130 million children do not attend primary school – 21 per cent of the primary-age population. Two-thirds of these are girls: a gross denial of their right to education and to develop their full potential. Especially when we know that women with as little as four years of education are more likely to choose to have smaller, healthier families. Understanding the web of issues, constraints and power relationships that affect the schooling of girls – within families, communities, schools, cultures and societies, and

within governments – is essential if practical solutions are to be
defined, shared and implemented.

We must work together, with the international organisations, other
governments and NGOs, to explore the strategies. And not only
raising enrolment levels but retaining children in school is critical
when we know that in South Asia, sub-Saharan Africa, Latin America
and the Caribbean only two-thirds of the children who start primary
school reach the fifth year of primary education. For the majority of
children from poor households, primary education is the one chance
they will have to acquire basic literacy, numeracy and some essential
life skills to enhance their chances of a sustainable livelihood.

And as we embark on an information revolution, we have at our
disposal new tools such as the internet and distance learning. We
have a chance this year to make education for all a strategy that
works. As you know there are important dates. There will be:

- the first ever meeting of education ministers from the G8
  countries;
- in April 2000, the education community from developing countries meets in Dakar to review progress on education for all in
  the 1990s;
- in November, the Commonwealth education ministers meet in
  Nova Scotia.

We are preparing now for these meetings. Our priorities will be to
increase the focus on universal primary education; to work with
developing countries to identify workable strategies; to seek a coordinated approach bringing together work at national and international level; and to continue to address factors constraining the
equal participation of girls and boys in schools. As Oxfam has said,
the old ways have failed, and we need to refocus the use of resources.

What then is the way forward to achieve the improvements in
education so urgently needed? There has been some progress. In
Uganda, spending on education has trebled in five years. Primary-
school enrolment is 90 per cent in Zimbabwe and Botswana. The
enrolment of girls remains low in Pakistan, but is high in Bangladesh.
So we must now spread best practice. First there needs to be a
sustained commitment by developing countries to education. For
example, the poverty-reduction strategies developed by Heavily In-

debted Poor Countries must, I believe, make education a central plank. That would put education at the heart of national and aid budgets and ensure transparent monitoring of delivery. Once again, ownership by the countries of the policy is the key to its success.

Second, we need to shift from the project-based to the sector-wide approach Oxfam has proposed. Educational, and indeed other, aid is too often used to support isolated projects. In Tanzania there are thirty donors, 1,000 projects, 2,000 aid missions. Greater coherence is needed. All aid and concessional lending from donors, World Bank and Regional Development Banks need to be based on the agreed poverty-reduction strategies and be coordinated under an agreed framework. This poses real challenges to both donors and recipients. For donors it means no special pleading for projects that 'fly their national flag'. For recipient countries it means strengthening their institutions so they can take the lead in coordinating and targeting the aid. These challenges are worth facing because it is the only way in which we can ensure the effective targeting of funds.

Third, we need to focus, as I have mentioned before, on tackling the skills shortages which limit economic growth. These skills shortages are at all levels of the economy – from high-level policy-analysis skills needed to drive forward development, to the practical skills needed to exploit new technologies. To meet this need we have established a major new programme of assistance and support. Over the next two financial years, £25 million will be available under the Department for International Development's Skills for Development Programme. This programme is designed to help countries stimulate the entrepreneurial skills essential for economic growth and to develop new approaches to skills development. Let me give one example of how the programme is working in practice – matching skills to work. In Chennai in India we have been supporting the 'Colleges Without Walls' programme – informal learning organisations which are working with the poor and unemployed to help them acquire the skills which have been identified by local employers. So far, 85 per cent of trainees have found work with local employers.

Lastly, I would like to emphasise that we must continue to provide more financial aid for education. The Department for International Development currently have commitments of £800 million to education, of which around three-quarters is for basic education. Of the total of £800 million, approximately £300 million has been com-

mitted since 1997, which represents a dramatic increase for this
sector. And we are on target to meet the Prime Minister's 1997
Denver commitment to increase by 50 per cent our aid to Africa for
primary education, primary health care, and sanitation by 2000. This
represents an extra £360 million of aid to Africa. We all recognise
that economic development and the escape from poverty requires
increased flows of aid from rich nations to underpin the development of human capital and basic infrastructure. In Britain's case, the
Department for International Development will receive over £1.5
billion extra in the Comprehensive Spending Review over three
years, taking its budget to more than £3 billion in 2001–2 – a real-
terms increase of 28 per cent.

The task we all face is awesome. Recent estimates show that for
Africa, where currently nearly 50 per cent of the population live
below $1 a day, growth rates in GDP/capita will need to reach some 6
per cent per year for the poverty target to be reached. Yet between
1990 and 1997 growth in GDP/capita in Africa was minus 0.7 per cent
per year. In 1999 the world's richest nations finally accepted their
obligations to the world's poorest peoples. But we can and must do
more. We need a world economy working for everyone everywhere.

Tom Paine's message of the 1780s is even more relevant as we begin a
new millennium: 'We have it in our power to begin the world anew.'
The task for 2000 will be to transform goodwill into monumental
change. Because no one can be happy living in an oasis of wealth where
there is a desert of poverty, I want ours to become the generation who
lifted the scar of poverty and hopelessness from the world's soul. And I
am optimistic. Why? Because not just a few, but millions feel, however
distantly, the pain of all those in need. Why optimism? Because across
the world there are millions of people of conscience and of belief in
something bigger than themselves. Why optimism? Because there are
millions more who know that now as never before, we in this generation have – within our power if we choose to use it – the means to
eliminate abject poverty; and who want to realise that ancient dream
that we become truly one moral universe, in which by the strong
helping the weak, all of us become stronger.

So ours is a call to action to all men and women full of idealism
irrespective of political party. A call to action to all full of campaigning vigour, irrespective of age. A call to all people of conviction and
faith, irrespective of religious denomination. A call to action as new

as the debt crisis, but as old as the call of Isaiah to 'undo the heavy burdens and let the oppressed go free'.

We will not reach our goal today or tomorrow. Perhaps not in this generation. But the quest for prosperity round the world is the greatest challenge and greatest moral imperative of our times. This is indeed an age of possibility as we chart the world of tomorrow. It is not a time to look backwards but to plan ahead. I want this generation to be remembered for seizing the opportunities not missing them, for making us masters of our destiny, not victims of fate. In this new age, I believe our generation can achieve a new way forward. Here in January 2000 we are all making a start on a journey of hope and renewal and we must and will complete our path.

The tragic events of 9/11 changed the way America looked at the world, and set in train many adjustments to international agreements and previous working assumptions. In a speech entitled 'A Modern Marshall Plan', given in Washington DC, on 17 December 2001, the Chancellor blended some of his earlier thinking on international action on poverty to the values which he felt should dominate the dialogue in the future. In particular, in saluting the courage of America and the bravery of its citizens, the Chancellor argued that while he had no doubt that America and her allies would win the war against terrorism (which he characterised as not so much a war for territory but a war for values) we also had to consider how to win the peace.

His speech starts by recalling that the original Marshall Plan was for 'investment for a purpose' – to rebuild Europe – and it involved a new alliance for prosperity between rich and poor countries that played a vital part in winning the peace. The plan involved the transfer of 1 per cent of the national income of the United States every year, for four years, from America to war-torn Europe – in total the equivalent in today's money of $75 billion. This was not an act of charity, but a recognition that, 'like peace, prosperity was indivisible; that to be sustained it had to be shared; and that to achieve this goal would require a new public purpose and international action on a massive scale . . . not merely to secure "a working economy in the world" but, even more important, "permit the emergence of political and social conditions in which free institutions can exist" '. The Chancellor quotes George Marshall approvingly as one who had a unifying vision for a global fight, not against one country or one ideology, but against 'hunger, poverty, desperation and chaos'. And he points out that just as the urgent needs of Greece and Turkey provided the catalyst for the Marshall Plan, today's plans for global reconstruction are precipitated by a specific challenge – that of Afghanistan and the Middle East – where it is increasingly clear that national safety and global economic reconstruction are inextricably linked.

Let me first on behalf of the entire UK government, which has been proud to be America's first and strongest ally from the first moment the planes struck the World Trade Center and the Pentagon, salute the courage of America in the face of tragedy; your bravery and resilience in the most testing of times. America has shown by the actions of all its people that while buildings can be destroyed, values are indestructible; while hearts are broken, hope is unbreakable; and while lives have ended, the cause of liberty never dies. The war that together we are fighting against terrorism – not as a war for territory but as a war for values – we will win. Of that I am confident. But the question I want to address today is how we will win the peace.

This is not the first time the world has faced this question – so fundamental and far-reaching. In the 1940s, after the greatest of wars, visionaries in America and elsewhere looked ahead to a new world and – in their day and for their times – built a new world order. And what they sought to create was not simply a new military and political settlement that guaranteed peace but also new rules and institutions for a new international economic and social order that would guarantee prosperity.

Coming to America from Europe, the beneficiary of that post-1945 American generosity, I can testify to the greatness of the achievement. Indeed such was its scale that one of the architects of the new order – Dean Acheson – recalled that he 'had been present at the Creation'. In the truest sense they fought on after victory. They understood that, tempting as it might be, a retreat into isolationism was neither possible nor desirable. And what they achieved as they fought their day's greatest evil – totalitarianism – is what we must seek to achieve as we fight today's greatest evil – terrorism.

I want to urge that together we form a new global alliance for prosperity that starts from the shared needs, common interests and linked destinies of developed and developing worlds working together. I want to describe how America's post-Second World War achievement in what we now call the Marshall Plan should be our inspiration in this post-Cold War world – not just for the reconstruction of Afghanistan but for the entire developing world.

The plan proposed by US Secretary of State George Marshall transferred 1 per cent of national income every year, for four years, from America to Europe – in total the equivalent in today's money of $75 billion – not as an act of charity, but as a frank recognition that, like peace, prosperity was indivisible; that to be sustained it had to be shared; and that to achieve this goal would require a new public purpose and international action on a massive scale. Marshall and his colleagues also understood that the challenge extended far wider than the war-torn countries and was about more than temporary aid; that by combining historic American compassion with enlightened self-interest not only did they advance the spread of prosperity but the spread of democracy too. Indeed by identifying undemocratic as well as unstable regimes as a problem – and the attainment of democratic reform as well as economic reform as a solution – the world could best move forward. This is what George Marshall meant when, in his great Harvard speech, he articulated his great, unifying vision for a global fight, not against one country or one ideology, but against 'hunger, poverty, desperation and chaos'. And this is why he proposed to transfer resources on such a scale: not merely to secure 'a working economy in the world' but, even more important, to 'permit the emergence of political and social conditions in which free institutions can exist'. These were George Marshall's fundamental aims in 1947, and his vision resonated across the decades that followed – defining the very character of the next half century, defining the very essence of global cooperation. And they ring with relevance in our own time too.

Just as the urgent needs of Greece and Turkey provided the catalyst for the Marshall Plan, today's plans for global reconstruction are precipitated by a specific challenge – that of Afghanistan and Pakistan. Like our predecessors, we understand that national safety and global reconstruction are inextricably linked. Like them we see the need for a new economic leadership – a comprehensive plan that goes beyond temporary relief to wholesale economic and social development. Like them we see the need for a new global economic and social order grounded in both rights and responsibilities accepted by all. Like theirs, our proposals call on the poorest countries themselves to rise to the challenge.

But while there are parallels between our time and fifty years ago no historical analogies can ever be exact. Far more so than in Marshall's time, our interdependence means that what happens to the poorest citizen in the poorest country can directly affect the richest citizen in the richest country. And while the Marshall Plan deserves an honoured place in our history its remedies cannot be blindly or rigidly applied to efforts to solve the challenges of today and the future. The Marshall Plan was constructed in a post-war world of distinct national economies in need of rebuilding. Our job is now, in a more interdependent world, to help build – for the first time – market economies for a wholly different environment of open not sheltered economies, international not national capital markets, and global not local competition. And fifty years on we not only see more clearly our interdependence but the gap between what technology enables us to do – abolish poverty – and the reality of 110 million children without schooling, 7 million avoidable child deaths each year and 1 billion of our fellow citizens in poverty.

It is for these reasons that the whole international community – the IMF, World Bank, the UN and each of our countries – has solemnly committed to the most ambitious development goals for 2015: to halve world poverty, cut child mortality by two-thirds and guarantee every child primary education. Our plan is this: developing countries must pursue corruption-free policies for stability, for opening up trade and for creating a favourable environment for investment. In return, we should be prepared to increase by $50 billion a year in the years to 2015 vitally needed funds to achieve these agreed Millennium Development Goals.

The development funding I propose is not aid in the traditional sense to compensate for poverty, but new investment in the future to address the causes of poverty. In the last fifty years the Marshall Plan's European model could not be applied wholesale to developing countries because neither the economic foundations nor the necessary open, transparent and accountable systems for managing the public sector were properly in place to prevent corruption and waste. And too often we saw development funding as short-term charity aid, charity for being poor, instead of for a higher and more substantial purpose – long-term investment tied to tackling the underlying roots of poverty and promoting sustainable growth.

Indeed the proposal I am making today will work only if we see development assistance in this light: more effective in-country use of funds to help countries invest and compete; the multinational pooling of budgets and the proper monitoring of their use to achieve the greatest cost-effectiveness of new investment; untying aid so maximising its efficiency in diminishing poverty; and development funding conditional on pursuing agreed goals for social and economic development. Indeed our proposals are designed to create the best environment for private investment to take off and flourish by increasing funds for investment in health and education – not typically areas in which private capital flows but areas in which public investment is necessary to create an environment in which private investment can flourish.

Our vision of the way forward – akin to Marshall's challenge to rich and poor countries alike – is that by each meeting their obligations for change all countries can benefit. For the poorest countries: new responsibilities – to pursue transparent corruption-free policies for stability and the attraction of private investment – and new opportunities – with access to increased trade and development supported by a transfer of resources from rich to poor for investment in health and education. For the richest countries: new responsibilities – to open our markets, to reform our international institutions and to transfer resources – and yet new opportunities too – increased trade and a globalisation that works in the public interest. In future no country genuinely committed to pro-stability, pro-trade and pro-investment policies should be denied the chance of progress through the lack of basic investment in education, health and the basic infrastructure for economic development.

And this is our answer to globalisation and to the critics of globalisation. Some critics say the issue is whether we should have globalisation or not. In fact, the issue is whether we manage globalisation well or badly, fairly or unfairly. Globalisation can be for the people or against the people. Poorly managed, globalisation can create a vicious circle of poverty, widening inequality and increasing resentment. Managed wisely it can lift millions out of deprivation and become the high road to a more just and inclusive global economy. Our answer to anti-globalisation campaigners – as I will demonstrate today – is that we shall not retreat from globalisation. Instead we will advance social justice on a global scale – and we will do so with greater global cooperation not less, and with stronger, not weaker, international institutions. We will best help the poor not by opting out or by cutting cooperation across the world, but by strengthening that cooperation, modernising our international rules and radically reforming the institutions of economic cooperation to meet the new challenges.

So what are the building blocks for putting this new alliance for prosperity in place? The first is the most basic: the pursuit by developing countries of corruption-free, pro-stability policies building their capacity to compete and improving the terms on which they participate in the global economy. Round the world the importance of monetary regimes that ensure low inflation is now well understood. There is a greater consensus now than ever before that there is no long-term trade-off between inflation and growth or unemployment and that without control of inflation long-term growth is impossible. But building from that basic understanding, we need to do more to ensure stability in a new world of ever more rapid financial flows. Developing countries who need capital most are at the same time the most vulnerable to the judgements of global financial markets. We know that capital is more likely to move to environments which are stable and least likely to stay in environments which are or become unstable. And such flows today are quicker than ever they have been before. So for every country, rich or poor, macro-economic stability is not an option but an essential precondition of economic success.

And I have become convinced that it is in the interests of stability – and of preventing crises in developing and emerging-market countries – that we seek a new rules-based system – a reformed system of economic governance under which each country, rich and poor, adopts and operates agreed codes and standards for fiscal and monetary policy and for corporate governance. Clear transparent procedures for monetary and fiscal decisions include presenting a full factual picture of the national accounts, usable central-bank reserves, foreign-currency borrowings, and indicators of the health of the financial sectors. Such openness – and a willingness to be monitored for it – would improve macro-economic stability, deter corruption, provide to markets the flow of specific country-by-country information necessary to engender greater investor confidence and reduce the likelihood of contagion. Operating such codes can also support countries along the way to liberalisation of their capital markets, offering them a route map to avoid destabilising and speculative inflows. Just as I believe that – over time – the implementation of codes and standards should be a condition for IMF and World Bank support, so too I believe that the international community should offer direct assistance, transitional help and – in some specific and difficult cases – compensation for the early implementation of such codes.

And where countries do operate transparent and effective policies, the IMF's contingent credit-line facility should play a far more proactive role in helping member countries strengthen their financial position, guard against contagion and thus avoid crises. So these codes are not incidental to the financial architecture for the new global economy: they *are* the financial architecture for the new global economy, as we move from a global economy which has simply let crises happen to one where we work to diminish their likelihood. Our capacity to prevent crises is enhanced not just by the operation of codes and standards – and the offer of proportionate help to countries who adopt them – but also by rigorous surveillance, effective international early-warning procedures and a more consistent engagement by the private sector. The new architecture must therefore involve an enhanced role and authority for the IMF, monitoring and reporting on the operation of codes and standards, and my proposal is that we make the IMF's surveillance and monitoring functions independent of the inter-governmental decisions about financial support for crisis resolution.

Alongside greater independence for the IMF, the capacity to prevent crises would be improved by expanding the work of the Financial Stability Forum – which brings together the combined expertise of the IMF and key regulatory authorities – as an international early-warning system to tackle national financial-sector problems which have international repercussions. Where governments discharge their responsibilities for transparency and subject themselves to surveillance, then commensurately increased responsibilities by the private sector should include a willingness to participate in ongoing dialogue with their host countries to identify problems early and develop cooperative solutions for restoring stability. Where crises do occur, better crisis-resolution procedures should involve private creditors, with improved arrangements for the use of standstills and more effective international bankruptcy procedures.

Open, transparent and accountable national policies, internationally monitored, are the foundation for monetary and fiscal stability. But to ensure the long-term investment necessary for growth and development we must do far more. Rich and poor countries must work together to make investment itself more attractive to both domestic and foreign lenders and find better ways for public and private sectors to cooperate to raise investment levels. Experience from the eighties onwards has moved us on from the assumption that just by liberalising, deregulating, privatising and simply getting prices right, growth and employment would inevitably follow – a set of assumptions that has proved inadequate to meet the emerging challenges of globalisation in for example Asia, where public investment has played a catalytic role in securing growth.

In the new paradigm low inflation and fiscal stability are necessary but not sufficient conditions for securing employment and growth. The new paradigm recognises other drivers of growth in:

- the pursuit of competition and not just privatisation;
- the importance of public as well as private investment not least in education; and
- the need for sound laws and proper financial supervision as well as liberalisation, including a route map sequencing the liberalisation of capital markets.

Indeed the country-owned poverty-reduction strategies – imaginatively led by Horst Köhler at the IMF and Jim Wolfensohn at the World Bank – are now correctly focusing on creating the right domestic conditions for investment and have highlighted the contribution of public investment to development in infrastructure, sound laws of contract and legal processes that deter corruption, and an educated and healthy workforce. The challenge is immense: while in the last decade foreign direct-investment flows across national boundaries, including to and between developing countries, have increased fourfold – dwarfing aid – the poorest and least developed countries languish under a double handicap – insufficient foreign investment and inadequate domestically generated savings, with the result that investment per head is in Africa less than $50 a year.

I believe that in return for developing countries implementing codes and standards, there can and should be a new engagement by business as reliable and long-term partners in economic development. Indeed where developing countries guarantee transparency and proper legal and financial systems that deter corruption, the developed world and business should work together to raise levels of investment. One way forward is joint investment forums. These councils would bring public and private sectors together, examine the current barriers to investment and discuss in the light of regional conditions how developing countries can secure higher levels of business investment and take the first steps in the international marketplace through intra-regional trade. And companies investing in developing countries should seek to answer one of the main fears of anti-globalisation campaigners: that where there is no cross-border corporate accountability, large companies can often seem more powerful than the elected governments of the countries in which they operate. One way forward is adopting the OECD international standards of best practice for corporate responsibility and advancing both the global compact – introduced by Kofi Annan in 1999 – and the global reporting initiative under which multinationals assess their impact on developing countries.

The third building block is progress on trade. We know that developing countries that are open and trade have seen faster growth rates than closed economies. Indeed it is a matter of record that in the last half century no country has managed to lift itself out of poverty without participating in the global economy. Full trade liberalisation could lift at least 300 million out of poverty by 2015. Even diminishing by 50 per cent protectionist tariffs in agriculture and in industrial goods and services would boost the world's yearly income by nearly $400 billion, a boost to growth of 1.4 per cent. And while developing countries would gain the most – an estimated $150 billion a year – all countries and regions stand to benefit.

That is why we strongly welcome the WTO agreement in Doha to launch a new trade round focused on development. And in the next phase we must take forward the agreements to open up trade in agriculture, build the capacity of developing countries to participate more effectively in the negotiations and open up greater access to medicines. Indeed all developed countries should offer access to all but military products from the least developed countries and by banning export credit guarantees for unproductive expenditure discourage and diminish the diversion to arms expenditure of resources needed for education and health. Progress on trade could be worth $150 billion a year to the poorest countries, three times the development aid they receive today. So in addition to policies for stability and investment, new policies for open trade are fundamental building blocks of the new alliance for progress.

But there cannot be a solution to the urgent problems of poverty the poorest countries face without a fourth reform: a substantial increase in development funds for investment in the very least developed countries. By insisting on dissociating aid from the award of contracts, gains to anti-poverty programmes can be as high as 25 per cent; more effective in-country use of aid can secure further resources for anti-poverty work; and better collaboration among donors – pooling of budgets, monitoring of their use to achieve economies of scale and hence greater cost-effectiveness and targeting of aid – can also maximise the efficiency of aid in diminishing poverty. Most of all we must move from providing short-term aid just to compensate for poverty to a higher and more sustainable purpose, that of aid as long-term investment to tackle the causes of poverty by promoting growth.

The Zedillo Report, whose authors included several prominent Americans, costed meeting the Millennium Development Goals at a total of $50 billion a year, including $20 billion for anti-poverty programmes and nearly $10 billion for education. To meet this challenge my proposal involves the creation of a new international-development trust fund which builds on the existing achievements of the World Bank and the IMF but goes further by seeking to address the sheer lack of investment from which the poorest countries suffer. From the fund, countries operating the poverty-reduction strategies can draw investment support and it might be overseen by a new joint implementation committee of the World Bank, IMF and, possibly, member countries. To minimise bureaucracy its resources should be distributed through the existing mechanisms used in the poverty-reduction strategies.

Because we must never return to the unsustainable burdens of debt of the eighties and nineties, the very poorest and most vulnerable countries should receive investment help for poverty reduction in the form primarily of grants to partner their soft IDA loans. All other low-income countries should be offered interest-free loans. Some beneficiaries will be countries with millions of poor but today classified as middle-income countries. Here assistance should be in the form of interest-reduced loans, conditional upon implementing agreed poverty-reduction strategies and reforms with a national monitoring process including civil society. In recent months proposals have been made for new and innovative ways to meet this funding gap – the Tobin Tax, arms tax, an airline-fuel tax, IMF special drawing rights. The European Commission is examining the Tobin Tax and we are open to investigating other proposals in addition to our suggested development fund.

But in today's world every international initiative relies ultimately on approval by national governments and their peoples. And it comes down, in the end, to the duties national governments – especially the richest national governments – recognise and are prepared to discharge. There are many proposals that have been put forward. We are open to a discussion of their effectiveness. But if we are to move with the urgency that the scale of today's suffering demands, we must each as national governments be bold and recognise the duties of the richest parts of the developed world to the poorest and least developed parts of the same world. Through richer countries making a long-term commitment of increased resources for development for, say, thirty years and with national governments offering a guarantee, either through callable reserves or appropriate collateral as security, it is possible to lever up these contributions to meet our target for extra funds now. In this way, each year $50 billion more could be available to the poorest countries for investing in economic development.

These proposals are challenging but they are achievable. The international community has already made a commitment to raising the level of overseas development assistance to 0.7 per cent of GDP. And in Britain since 1997 we have increased the aid budget of the Department for International Development to £3.6 billion – a 45 per cent increase by 2004. And we are committed to making substantial additional progress. Today I am challenging each country to accept their responsibility to play their part and to go further than they have been prepared to go in the past. And it is right that there now be a full debate in the IMF, World Bank and the United Nations as we prepare for next spring's Financing for Development Conference at Monterrey.

Marshall's plan was investment for a purpose for a Europe rebuilt. He summoned forth a new alliance for prosperity between rich and poor countries that, for his time, played a vital part in winning the peace. So too today – summoning up the spirit of Marshall – the new plan I suggest for developing countries is investment for a purpose, so that they can play their part in a peaceful world. By each meeting their obligations for change all can benefit. First, the obligations on developing countries: to end corruption, put in place stable economic policies, to invite investment, to meet their commitment to community ownership of their poverty-reduction strategies and to ensure resources go to fighting poverty, including education and health. Second, the obligations on business to engage with the development challenge and not to walk away, including participating in business investment forums and playing their part in preventing and resolving economic crises. Third, the obligations on the world community as a whole – international institutions – to reform systems to ensure greater transparency and openness, to open up trade and the opportunities for faster development and to focus on priorities that meet the international development targets. Fourth, the obligations on the richest governments to the poorest of the world – our commitment to tackling the inequalities through a substantial and decisive transfer of resources; not aid that entrenches dependency but investment that empowers development – investment money that is, in the truest sense of the word, increasing the capacity of the poorest countries. A $50-billion-a-year investment fund that invites applications for health, education and anti-poverty work will help build the capacity of the poorest countries to compete and engage; and is the high road to a more just and inclusive global economy.

Our answer to anti-globalisation protestors is that, in the spirit of Marshall, we shall not retreat from globalisation. Rather, we will advance social justice on a global scale, as today's global alliance for peace is transformed into tomorrow's global alliance for prosperity. Since September 11th, President Bush, your government, your armed forces and your people have led a great and global effort worthy of America's history and its ideals. With steadfast resolve we work together to win the war against terrorism. Now, in the great tradition of Truman, Marshall, and that earlier generation, let us also resolve to fight on after victory. Let us together seize our moment of opportunity to win the peace.

In the words of Victor Hugo:

> The future has many names
> For the weak it is unattainable
> For the fearful it is unknown
> For the bold it is opportunity

This can be our permanent memorial to those whose lives have been lost – that, in remembrance of them, we build the world anew. Let it be our generation that takes up the challenge and discharges our duty to remove the scar of poverty and hopelessness from the world's soul. Let it be our generation that shows those who suffer in the bleakest places of the world that we can light a candle of hope which, radiating outwards, can cut through the darkness and shame of injustice and emblazon across the world a message of confidence and faith in the future.

In December 2004, the Chancellor delivered CAFOD's Pope Paul VI Memorial Lecture, and used the opportunity to reflect on the moral case for action to relieve the poverty and suffering in the Third World. Starting with a fulsome acknowledgement of the contribution CAFOD had made within the world-wide movement of charities, faith groups and individuals committed to international action on poverty, the Chancellor puts forward three propositions which he believes underpin the case for international action:

> that our dependence upon each other should awaken our conscience to the needs not just of neighbours but of strangers; more than that, that our moral sense should impel us to act out of duty and not just self-interest; and that the claims of justice are not at odds with the liberties of each individual but a modern expression of them that ensures the dignity of all – and there is such a thing as a moral universe.

This speech has been published separately, so only a short extract is reproduced here – but is well worth reading in full.

I want to pay my personal tribute to the work of CAFOD over forty years and your leadership in achieving, by your determined campaigning, what many thought impossible – 100 per cent bilateral debt relief. You led a coalition whose voices rose to a resounding chorus that echoed outwards to the world from Birmingham, then from Cologne, then from Okinawa – a clarion call to action, speaking not for yourselves alone but for the hopes of the whole world. And you led a coalition that achieved more standing together for the needs of the poor in one short year than all the isolated acts of individual governments could have achieved in one hundred years.

Reminding us that as CAFOD campaigning for justice for the world's poor you have for forty years:

- changed the way we think about giving;
- deepened our commitment to serving others;
- demonstrated that duty and obligation are more powerful than selfishness or greed; and in doing so,
- brought the world closer together.

Now, it is the churches and faith groups that have, across the world, done more than any others – by precept and by example – to make us aware of the sheer scale of human suffering – and our duty to end it. Indeed, when the history of the crusade against global poverty is written, one of its first and finest chapters will detail the commitment of the churches in Britain to help the world's poor. And my theme tonight is what this generation working together, each and all of us, can do – that we are not powerless individuals but, acting together, have the power to shape history. And each of us, building on the individual causes we cherish – from work on debt relief to education, from fair trade to clean water, from blindness to TB, from AIDS to child vaccination – can together not only make progress for our direct concerns but also turn globalisation from a force that breeds insecurity to a force for justice on a global scale.

Today I want to sketch out for you a vision of a new deal that demands a new accountability from both rich and poor countries; a new compact between those to whom so much is given and those who have so little; more than a contract – which is after all one group tied by legal obligations to another – and nothing less than what the author of *The Politics of Hope* called a 'covenant' – the richest recognising out of duty and a deep moral sense of responsibility their obligations to the poorest of the world.

. . .

Martin Luther King spoke of the American Constitution as a 'promissory note'. And yet – for black Americans – the promise of equality for all had not been redeemed. He said that the cheque offering justice had been returned with 'insufficient funds' written on it. He said, 'we refuse to believe that the bank of justice is bankrupt'. And he said the time had come to 'cash this cheque which would give upon demand the riches of freedom and the security of justice'. And in this way he exposed the gap between promises and reality in racial equality in the USA at that time.

But in exactly the same way today's Millennium Development Goals – a commitment backed by a timetable – are now in danger of being downgraded from a pledge to just a possibility to just words. Yet another promissory note, yet another cheque marked 'insufficient funds'. And the danger we face today is that what began as the greatest bond between rich and poor for our times is at risk of ending as the greatest betrayal of the poor by the rich of all time. As a global community we are at risk of being remembered not for what we promised to do but for what we failed to deliver, another set of broken hopes that breaks the trust of the world's people in the world's governments.

And when we know the scale of suffering that has to be addressed, the problem is not that the promise was wrong, the pledge unrealistic, the commitments unnecessary but that we have been too slow in developing the means to honour, fulfil and deliver them. In the past when we as a global community failed to act we often blamed our ignorance – we said that we did not know. But now we cannot use ignorance to explain or excuse our inaction. We can see in front of our TV screens the ravaged faces of too many of the 30,000 children dying unnecessarily each day. We cannot blame our inaction on inadequate science – we know that a quarter of all child deaths can be prevented if children sleep beneath bed-nets costing only $4. We cannot defend our inaction, invoking a lack of medical cures – for we know that as many as half of all malaria deaths can be prevented if people have access to diagnosis and drugs that cost no more than twelve cents. The world already knows we know enough. But the world knows all too well that we have not done enough. Because what is lacking is will.

So if we are to make real progress we must – together from this meeting room this evening – and then from countless other centres of concern and endeavour – go out into this country and other countries and show people and politicians alike everywhere why it is morally and practically imperative that we not only declare but fight and win a war against poverty; why we must not only pass resolutions and make demands but move urgently to remove injustice; why lives in the poorest countries depend upon converting, in the richest countries, apathy to engagement, sympathy to campaigning, half-hearted concern to wholly committed action. In short we must share the inspiration we have of the power of the dream of a better world – and why it is now more urgent than ever that people everywhere are awakened to the duties we owe to people elsewhere whose hopes for life itself depend upon our help, duties not just to people who are neighbours but to people who are strangers. So that even when we know that our sense of empathy diminishes as we move outwards from the immediate, face-to-face, person-to-person relationships of family, outwards to neighbourhood to country to half a world away, we still feel and ought to feel however distantly the pain of others – and why it is right to believe in something bigger than ourselves, bigger even than our own community, as wide as the world itself.

It has been written that 'if we answer the question why we can handle the question how'. And this evening I am going to put forward three propositions:

- that our dependence upon each other should awaken our conscience to the needs not just of neighbours but of strangers;
- more than that, that our moral sense should impel us to act out of duty and not just self-interest; and
- that the claims of justice are not at odds with the liberties of each individual but a modern expression of them that ensures the dignity of all – and there is such a thing as a moral universe.

First, does not Martin Luther King show our responsibilities to strangers, to people we have never met and who will never know our names, when he describes each of us as 'strands in an inescapable network of mutuality, together woven into a single garment of destiny'? Indeed just as the industrialisation of the eighteenth century opened people up to a society which lay beyond family and

village and asked individuals who never met each other to understand the needs of all throughout their own country, so too the
globalisation we are witnessing asks us to open our minds to the
plight and the pain of millions we will never meet and are continents
away but upon whom, as a result of the international division of
labour, we depend upon for our food, our clothes, our livelihoods,
our security.

I recalled a poem in my Labour conference speech:

> It is the hands of others who grow the food we eat, who sew the
> clothes we wear, who build the houses we inhabit; it is the hands
> of others who tend us when we're sick and lift us up when we fall;
> it is the hands of others who bring us into the world and who
> lower us into the earth.

When I talked of the hands of others, I meant our dependence upon
each other – the nurse, the builder, the farm worker, the seamstress –
not just in our own country but across the earth. We are in an era of
global interdependence, relying each upon the other – a world
society of shared needs, common interests, mutual responsibilities,
linked densities, our international solidarity. And since September
11th there is an even more immediate reason for emphasising our
interdependence and solidarity. Now more than ever we rely on each
other not just for our sustenance but for our safety and security.

Colin Powell, US Secretary of State, states:

> What poverty does do is breed frustration and resentment which
> ideological entrepreneurs can turn into support for terrorism in
> countries that lack the political rights, the institutions, necessary
> to guard the society from terrorists. Countries that are lacking
> basic freedoms. So we can't win the war on terrorism unless we
> get at the roots of poverty, which are social and political as well
> as economic in nature.

And President Bush said on the eve of the Financing for Development Conference in Monterrey:

> Poverty doesn't cause terrorism. Being poor doesn't make you a
> murderer. Most of the plotters of September 11th were raised in

comfort. Yet persistent poverty and oppression can lead to hopelessness and despair. And when governments fail to meet the most basic needs of their people, these failed states can become havens for terror. In Afghanistan, persistent poverty and war and chaos created conditions that allowed a terrorist regime to seize power. And in many other states around the world, poverty prevents governments from controlling their borders, policing their territory, and enforcing their laws. Development provides the resources to build hope and prosperity, and security.

So does not everything that we witness across the world today from discussing global trade to dealing with global terrorism symbolise just how closely and irrevocably bound together are the fortunes of the richest persons in the richest country to the fate of the poorest persons in the poorest country of the world even when they are strangers and have never met, and that an injury to one must be seen as an injury to all? But is not what impels us to act far more than this enlightened self-interest? Ought we not to take our case for a war against poverty to its next stage – from economics to morality, from enlightened self-interest that emphasises our dependence each upon the other to the true justice that summons us to do our duty – and to see that every death from hunger and disease is as if it is a death in the family? For is there not some impulse even greater than the recognition of our interdependence that moves human beings even in the most comfortable places to empathy and to anger at the injustice and inhumanity that blights the lives not just of neighbours but of strangers in so many places at so high a cost? Is it not something greater, more noble, more demanding than just our shared interests that propels us to demand action against deprivation and despair on behalf of strangers as well as neighbours – and is it not our shared values?

It is my belief that even if we are strangers in many ways, dispersed by geography, diverse because of race, differentiated by wealth and income, divided by partisan beliefs and ideology, even as we are different, diverse and often divided, we are not and we cannot be moral strangers for there is a shared moral sense common to us all:

Call it as Lincoln did – the better angels of our nature;
Call it as Winstanley did – the light in man;

Call it as Adam Smith did – the moral sentiment;

Call it benevolence, as the Victorians did; virtue; the claim of justice; doing one's duty.

Or call it as Pope Paul VI did – 'the good of each and all'.

It is precisely because we believe, in that moral sense, that we have obligations to others beyond our front doors and garden gates, responsibilities to others beyond the city wall, duties to others beyond our national borders as part of one moral universe – precisely because we have a sense of what is just and what is fair – that we are called to answer the hunger of the hungry, the needs of the needy, the suffering of the sick whoever and wherever they are, bound together by the duties we feel we owe each other. We cannot be fully human unless we care about the dignity of every human being.

Christians say: do to others what you would have them do to you.

Jews say: what is hateful to you, do not do to your fellow man.

Buddhists say: hurt not others in ways that you yourself would find hurtful.

Muslims say: no one of you is a believer until he desires for his brother that which he desires for himself.

Sikhs say: treat others as you would be treated yourself.

Hindus say: this is the sum of duty: do not do to others what would cause pain if done to you.

Faiths that reveal truths not to be found in economic textbooks or political theory – beliefs now held by people of all faiths and none – that emphasise our duty to strangers, our concern for the outsider, the hand of friendship across continents, that say I am my brother's keeper, that we don't only want injustice not to happen to us, we don't want injustice to happen to anyone. Indeed the golden rule runs through every great religion – what the Bible calls righteousness or what you and I might call justice – and the words of Gandhi reinforce this golden rule: 'Whenever you are in doubt apply the following test. Recall the face of the poorest and the weakest man whom you may have seen, and ask yourself if the step you contemplate is going to be of any use to him' . . . Then, he said, you will find your doubts melt away.

So we are not – morally – speaking in tongues. And while there are many voices from many parts and many places, expressed in many languages and many religious faiths, we can and must think of ourselves coming together as a resounding chorus singing the same tune – and as a choir achieving a harmony which can move the world. So our interdependence leads us to conclude that when some are poor, our whole society is impoverished. And our moral sense leads us to conclude, as we have been told, that when there is an injustice anywhere, it is a threat to justice everywhere.

But can we not also say – and this is my third point – that, even when we are talking about the needs of strangers, the claims of justice – that we should do our duty to ensure the dignity of every individual – are now more powerful than ever? It is because the dignity of the individual is at the heart of our concerns about human beings that those claims of justice are not – as many once argued – at odds with the requirement for liberty but are essential for the realisation of liberty in the modern world?

In her recent book Gertrude Himmelfaarb shows that, when the seventeenth and eighteenth centuries brought a revolt against outmoded forms of hierarchy, there was understandably a preoccupation not with justice or duty but with liberty. In 1789 'liberty' literally came before 'equality' and 'fraternity'. The call for freedom from outmoded forms of hierarchical obligations was then the only path to ending the power of absolute monarchs and repealing old mercantilist laws. But although the great Enlightenment philosophers marched under the banner of liberty, rightly wishing to prevent any ruler invading the freedom of the citizen, a closer reading of these writers shows that, for them, the march of individual freedoms did not release people from their obligations to their fellow citizens and fulfilling the duties they owed to each other. For them liberty was not at odds with justice or duty but liberty and duty advanced together.

One of the greatest tribunes of liberty, John Stuart Mill, stated categorically that 'there are many positive acts to the benefit of others which anyone may rightfully be obliged to perform'. And Rousseau wrote that 'as soon as men ceased to consider public service as the principal duty of citizens we may pronounce the state to be on the verge of ruin'. And as Adam Smith – often wrongly seen as the patron of free-market capitalism without a conscience – put it: the philosophy of 'all for ourselves and nothing for other people' was a 'vile maxim'. 'Perfection of human nature was to feel much for others and little for ourselves, to restrain our selfish and indulge benevolent affections'. And in that spirit, and as he died, Smith, not just the writer about the 'invisible hand' but about the 'helping hand', was writing a new chapter for his *Theory of Moral Sentiments* entitled 'On the Corruption of Our Moral Sentiments' which is occasioned by 'the disposition to admire the rich and great and to despise or neglect persons of poor and mean condition'. So the great apostle of freedom believed passionately in justice and in duty to others and saw no contradiction in saying so. And in our century this should be our focus. We should be asking not just what rights you can enforce on others but asking what duties we can discharge for others. Selbourne says duties without rights make people slaves but rights without duties make them strangers. Moral strangers demand rights without duties. Moral neighbours say that every time one person's dignity is diminished or taken away through no fault of their own it is an offence against justice. And if the dignity of a child or adult is diminished by poverty, or debt, or unfair trade, we are all diminished. Enlightened self-interest may lead us to propose a contract between rich and poor founded upon our mutual responsibilities because of our interdependence. But it is our strong sense of what is just that demands a covenant between rich and poor founded on our moral responsibility to each other – that even if it was not in our narrow self-interest to do so it would still be right for every citizen to do one's duty and meet the needs, and enhance the dignity, of strangers.

My father used to tell me we can all leave our mark for good or ill – and he quoted Martin Luther King saying everyone from the poorest to the richest can be great because everyone can serve. That all of us, no matter how weak or frail, or at times inadequate, can make a difference for good is emphasised by a story told by Chief Rabbi Jonathan Sacks writing of the film *About Schmidt*. Schmidt (played by Jack Nicholson) describes a futile life of family estrangement ending in an equally meaningless retirement, endured with an overriding sense of failure. In the film Schmidt says:

> I know we're all pretty small in the big scheme of things. What in the world is better because of me? I am weak and I am a failure, there's just no getting around it . . . soon I will die . . . maybe in

twenty years, maybe tomorrow, it doesn't matter . . . when everyone who knew me dies too, it will be as though I never even existed . . . what difference has my life made to anyone? None that I can think of . . . none at all.

But then he receives a letter from the teacher of a six-year-old in Tanzania whom in a small charitable gesture Schmidt has been paying for schooling and health care. The young boy cannot yet write, the teacher says, but he has sent Schmidt a drawing instead. It shows two little line figures, one large and one small, obviously the boy and Schmidt. And the drawing shows them holding hands together as the sun shines down upon their friendship. And so the film ends with Jack Nicholson's character slowly grasping that he has done one good deed in his life – for a stranger – a young child far away whom he has never met; the duty to others done by Schmidt giving his life meaning; proving that one generous act can redeem a life. So we do live in one interdependent world.

We are indeed part of one moral universe. Even the meanest of us possesses a moral sense. What really matters is the compassion we show to the weak. And you value your society not for its wealth and power over others but by how it can empower the poor and power-less. Now that moral sense may not be 'a strong beacon light radiating outward at all times to illuminate in sharp outline all it touches' as James Q. Wilson describes 'the moral sense' so brilliantly. Rather the moral sense is like 'a small candle flame flickering and spluttering in the strong winds of passion and power, greed and ideology'. As Wilson says, 'brought close to the heart and cupped in one's hand it dispels the darkness and warms the soul'. And even when it burns as a flicker it is still a flame and a flame that can never be extinguished.

So we do not wipe out the debt of the poorest countries simply because these debts are not easily paid. We do so because people weighed down by the burden of debts imposed by the last generation on this cannot even begin to build for the next generation. To insist on the payment of these debts offends human dignity – and is therefore unjust. What is morally wrong cannot be economically right. In the words of Isaiah – we must 'undo the heavy burdens and let the oppressed go free'.

In early January 2005, the Chancellor gave a major speech on international development at the National Gallery of Scotland. It was delivered in the aftermath of the South-Asian tsunami, which he describes as 'the biggest and most devastating earthquake the modern world has ever witnessed'. He drew attention to the way such natural tragedies link us: they show both our shared vulnerabilities and our linked destinies; an earthquake in one continent has left families devastated in every continent. And, as he says, 'humbled first by the power of nature, we have since been humbled by the power of humanity – the awesome power of nature to destroy; the extraordinary power of human compassion to build anew'. And we have witnessed not only an unprecedented demonstration of sympathy but also 'an unprecedented demonstration of generosity, with more people giving spontaneously than at any time and in any previous appeal'.

At the beginning of this speech, the Chancellor makes an announcement about writing off debt for Sri Lanka, and calls for the G7 nations to stand ready to consider options for further assistance at the finance ministers' meeting to be chaired by Britain at the beginning of February 2005. The Chancellor then reiterates many of the points made in earlier speeches about the need for a doubling of effort in 2005 to deliver the Millennium Development Goals; he rehearses the case for a modern Marshall Plan; and then in a bravura passage spells out what the benefits would be of a properly funded International Finance Facility: frontloading investment in infrastructure, education and health systems, and economic development so developing countries can benefit from access to markets; providing grants immediately to help ensure a sustainable exit from debt so that poor countries do not need to choose between emergency relief and long-term investment; making primary schooling for all a reality; and cutting infant mortality and maternal mortality through eliminating malaria and TB and treating millions more people who are suffering from HIV/AIDS.

When I delivered the CAFOD lecture a few weeks ago about the economic, social and moral case for us now seeing people we have never met and may never meet in other continents not as strangers but as neighbours, I argued that what impelled us to action where there is need was not just enlightened self-interest that recognises and acts upon our interdependence – our dependence each upon the other for our sustenance and our security – but, even more important, a belief in something bigger than ourselves: our shared moral sense that moves human beings even in the most comfortable places to sympathy and solidarity with fellow human beings even in far-away places in distress.

And the worldwide demonstration in the last few days not just of sympathy but of support shows that even if we are strangers, separated and dispersed by geography, even if diverse because of race, even if differentiated by wealth and income, even if divided by partisan beliefs and ideology – even as we are different, diverse and often divided – we are not and we cannot be moral strangers. We are one moral universe.

And the shared moral sense common to us all makes us recognise our duty to others. And it is this moral sense exhibited in the world-wide response to disaster that shows not only what can be done – in Britain alone, £76 million raised so far by the British public; after Gift Aid, almost £90 million – but also demonstrates what has now to be done – that we address the underlying causes of poverty. So while 2004 was a year which ended in the horror of a natural disaster, 2005 is a year that can start with the hope of human progress. 2005 is a year of challenge but also a year of opportunity when – from the foundation of hope – we can, I believe, see real change. A year which is also the year when the UK has special responsibilities as President of the G7 and European Union, a year in which we can tackle not just the terrible and tragic consequences of the tsunami – working together to forge a long-term plan for the reconstruction of Asia – but also forge a new 'Marshall Plan' for the entire developing world.

And let me say the urgency and scale of the agenda I am going to propose for debt relief, for new funds for development and for fair trade is now even more pressing given the tragic events of recent days. It is because I want a world that does not have to choose between emergency disaster relief and addressing the underlying causes of poverty and injustice – between advancing first aid and advancing fundamental change – that the proposals I am putting forward today to advance the interests of all the developing world will – the government believes – find support in all parts of the world. In just a few months time, just a few miles from here in Edinburgh, the G8 will meet in Gleneagles to discuss the most important issue of our generation – world poverty. This year is the year when world leaders will first gather here in Scotland and then in September at the United Nation's Millennium Summit to examine just how much we have to do together if we are to seriously address the scale of poverty round the world today. We meet because exactly five years ago in New York and in a historic declaration the world signed up to a shared commitment to right the greatest wrongs of our time, including:

- the promise that by 2015 every child would be at school;
- the promise that by 2015 avoidable infant deaths would be prevented;
- the promise that by 2015 poverty would be halved.

In other words promises that rich countries would work with the poor to right the great wrongs of our time. The Millennium Development Goals were not a casual commitment. Every world leader signed up. Every international body signed up. Almost every single country signed up; the world in unison accepting the challenge and agreeing the changes necessary to fulfil it – rights and responsibilities accepted by rich and poor alike.

But already, so close to the start of our journey to 2015, it is clear that our destination risks becoming out of reach, receding into the distance. The first commitment to be met is that by next year the gap between the chances for girls and boys in primary and secondary education would be closed. But we know already that not only are the vast majority – 60 per cent – of developing countries unlikely to meet the target but most of these are, on present trends, unlikely to achieve this gender equality for girls even by 2015. And we know one stark fact that underlines this failure: not only are 70 million girls and 40 million boys of school age not going to school today but today and every day until we act 30,000 children will suffer and 30,000 children will die from avoidable diseases. At best, on present progress in sub-Saharan Africa:

- primary education for all – the right to education so everyone can help themselves – will be delivered not in 2015 but 2130 – that is 115 years late;
- the halving of poverty – the right to prosper so each and every individual can fulfil their potential – not by 2015 but by 2150 – that is 135 years late; and

- the elimination of avoidable infant deaths – the right to a healthy life so all have the opportunity to make the most of their abilities – not by 2015 but by 2165 – that is 150 years late.

For decades Africa and the developing world have been told to be patient. To those who say Africa should remain patient, the reply now comes from Africa: 150 years is too long to be patient. One hundred and fifty years is too long to wait for justice. One hundred and fifty years is too long to wait when infants are dying while the rest of the world has the medicines to heal them. One hundred and fifty years is too long to wait when a promise should be redeemed, when the bond of trust should be honoured now, in this decade.

In 1948, with much of Europe still in a state of ruin, the American Secretary of State General Marshall proposed, for his generation, the most ambitious plan for social and economic reconstruction. Marshall's starting point was a strategic and military threat but he quickly understood the underlying problems were social and economic. Marshall's initial focus was the devastation wrought in one or two of the poorest countries but he rapidly realised his plan should be an offer to all poor countries in the neighbourhood. Marshall started with a narrow view of aid needed for an emergency but quickly came to the conclusion that his plan had to tackle the underlying causes of poverty and deprivation. Marshall's early thoughts were for small sums of money in emergency aid but very soon his searching analysis brought him to the conclusion that a historic offer of unprecedented sums of money was required. He announced that America would contribute an unparalleled 1 per cent of its national income. He said that his task was nothing less than to fight hunger, poverty, desperation and chaos. His Treasury Secretary argued that prosperity, like peace, was indivisible, that it could not be achieved in one country at the expense of others but had to be spread throughout the world and that prosperity to be sustained had to be shared. And Marshall's plan – and the unparalleled transfer of resources – not only made possible the reconstruction of Europe but the renewal of world trade and the generation of prosperity for both these continents.

And I believe today's profound challenges call, even in a different world, for a similar shared response: comprehensive, inclusive, an assault on the underlying causes of poverty, with unprecedented support on offer from the richest countries. I believe in 2005 we have a once-in-a-generation opportunity to deliver for our times a modern Marshall Plan for the developing world – a new deal between the richest countries and the poorest countries but one in which the developing countries are not supplicants but partners. And as we advance towards the G7 finance ministers' meeting next month and the heads-of-government meeting chaired by Tony Blair in July, our government calls on all countries to join with us in agreeing the three essential elements of a 2005 development plan for a new deal:

- first, that we take the final historic step in delivering full debt relief for the debt-burdened countries;
- second, that we deliver the first world-trade round in history that benefits the poorest countries and ensures they have the capacity to benefit from new trade; and
- third – alongside declaring timetables on increasing development aid to 0.7 per cent of national income – that we implement a new International Finance Facility to offer immediate, predictable, long-term aid for investment and development – building on commitments by individual governments, leveraging in additional funds from the international capital markets, raising an additional $50 billion a year each year for the next ten years, effectively doubling aid to halve poverty.

I make this proposal for a new deal between developed and developing countries because as we meet here today – at the start of 2005 – I am aware not only of the pressures for emergency aid but that the promises we all made five years ago will forever remain unfulfilled unless we act together and act now.

. . .

First, on debt relief, let us in 2005 make a historic offer that finally removes the burden of decades-old debts that today prevent the poorest countries ever escaping poverty and leading their own economic development. Whereas in 1997 just one country was going to receive debt relief, today 27 countries are benefiting with $70 billion of unpayable debt being written off, and 37 countries are now potentially eligible, up to $100 billion of debt relief now possible. And it is because of debt relief in Uganda that 4 million more children now go to primary school; because of debt relief in Tanzania that 31,000 new classrooms have been built, 18,000 new teachers re-

cruited and the goal of primary education for all will be achieved by
the end of 2005; because of debt relief in Mozambique that half a
million children are now being vaccinated against tetanus, whooping
cough and diphtheria. And it is partly because of debt relief that in
the past decade in developing countries, primary-school enrolments
have increased at twice the rate of the 1980s; the proportion of those
aged over fifteen who can read has risen from 67 per cent to 74 per
cent; life expectancy has increased from 53 years to 59 years; and
the number of people living in extreme poverty has fallen by 10 per
cent.

We do not wipe out the debt of the poorest countries simply
because these debts are not easily paid. We do so because people
weighed down by the burden of debts imposed by the last generation
on this cannot even begin to build for the next generation. To insist
on the payment of these debts is unjust – it offends human dignity.
What is morally wrong cannot be economically right. And when
many developing countries are still choosing between servicing their
debts and making the investments in health, education and infrastructure that would allow them to achieve the Millennium Development Goals, we know we must do more. That is why this year we
must make rapid progress and today I want to set out both the
principles to govern the next stage and the measures that can be
delivered. While we have achieved bilateral debt write-off, the fact is
that up to 80 per cent of the historic debt of some of the poorest
countries is owed to international institutions and a solution to the
debt tragedy now requires progress on debts owed not just to us but
owed to the World Bank, the IMF and the development banks.

So we propose, first, that this year the richest countries match
bilateral debt relief of 100 per cent with the bold act of offering 100
per cent multilateral debt relief – relief from the $80 billion of debt
owed to the IMF, the World Bank and the African Development
Bank; second, that the cancellation of debts owed to the International Monetary Fund should be financed by a detailed plan and
timetable and that we now agree to use IMF gold. Third, we propose
that countries make a unique declaration that they will repatriate
their share of the World Bank's and the African Development Bank's
debts to their own country. I can state that Britain will relieve those
countries still under the burden of this debt to these banks by
unilaterally paying our share – 10 per cent – of payments to the

World Bank and African Development Bank. And we will both deepen and widen our debt relief as we will pay our share on behalf not just of Heavily Indebted Poor Countries but – because their need is just as great – of all low-income countries, as long as they can ensure debt relief is used for poverty reduction. In the G7 finance ministers' meeting next month I will be asking other countries to contribute directly or to a World Bank Trust Fund. And I also ask the European Union, which deserves credit for more than €1.5 billion of debt relief so far, to match that generosity with deeper multilateral debt relief.

Alongside more debt relief, 2005 is the opportunity that may not easily return if missed to agree a progressive approach to trade. Economic development is the key to meeting the Millennium Development Goals and long-term prosperity. And no country has escaped poverty other than by participation in the international economy. Our task is and remains helping developing countries build the capacity – the monetary and fiscal policies, the infrastructure, the support for private investment – essential for their development. But we also know the damage that rich countries' protectionism has done and that the developed world spends as much subsidising agriculture in our own countries as the whole income of all the 689 million people in sub-Saharan Africa taken together. Fair trade is not simply about the financial benefits, it is also about empowerment and dignity – enabling people to stand on their own two feet and use trade as a springboard out of poverty. It is not enough to say, 'You're on your own, simply compete.' We have to say, 'We will help you build the capacity you need to trade'; not just opening the door but helping you gain the strength to cross the threshold.

So in 2005 we need to make urgent progress:

- first, we the richest countries agree to end the hypocrisy of developed-country protectionism by opening our markets, removing trade-distorting subsidies and, in particular, doing more to urgently tackle the scandal and waste of the Common Agricultural Policy – showing we believe in free and fair trade;
- second, while recognising that while bringing down unjust tariffs and barriers is important, agree that developing countries receive the support necessary to carefully design and sequence trade reform into their own poverty-reduction strategies. And

- third, we have to recognise that developing countries will need additional resources to build their economic capacity and the infrastructure they need to take advantage of trading opportunities – and to prevent their most vulnerable people from falling further into poverty as they become integrated into the global economy.

We know that after macro-economic stability, poor infrastructure, lack of transparency, legal problems, poor labour skills and low productivity are key risks and deterrents to both foreign and domestic investment. Nor do many countries have the elasticity of supply to react to international market signals. The World Bank estimates that giving twenty-four of the poorest countries total access to Western markets would have no impact on their economies as they would not have the capacity or infrastructure to make use of the opportunity. Even today, for twelve African countries less than 10 per cent of their roads are paved. Telecommunication costs are such that calls from the poorest countries to the USA are five times the costs of calls from a developed country. While water and sanitation underpin health and development, even today 40 billion working hours in Africa each year are used up to collect water. And while tariff costs are often highlighted, it is actually transport costs that often constitute a bigger burden of the cost of exporting. With freight and insurance costs representing 15 per cent of the total value of African exports it is difficult for them to be competitive. It is also a fact that the informal economy accounts for more than 50 per cent of national income in most poor countries and the International Labour Organisation estimates that in Africa 93 per cent of new jobs are in the informal sector.

So countries need investment in physical infrastructure, institutional capacity – from legal and financial systems to basic property rights and, at root, transparency that avoids corruption – physical infrastructure and, of course, investment in human capital to enable growth, investment, trade and therefore poverty reduction. And to secure investment in development we need funds for development. 2005 can be the year when we free nations from the burden of crippling and unpayable debts and remove unacceptable barriers to trade and private investment, but it is clear that we cannot solve the urgent problems of poverty and development around the world without a third step – a substantial increase in resources for development, for investment in the future. Making better use of existing aid – reordering priorities, untying aid and pooling funds internationally to release additional funds for the poorest countries – is essential to achieve both value for money and the improved outcomes we seek, but we face uncomfortable facts:

- that while ten years ago aid to Africa was $33 per person, today it has not risen but fallen to just $27;
- that when 80 million African children still do not go to school, all the public spending on education in sub-Saharan Africa taken together is still, per pupil, under $50 a year: less than $1 a week for schools, teachers, books and equipment; and
- that when in Africa 25 million people are infected with HIV/AIDS, with, in twenty-four countries, one in every ten children dying before the age of one, sub-Saharan Africa still devotes only $12 per person per year to public health, a fifth of 1 per cent that is spent on the health of each individual in the richest countries – which is why the everyday commonplace tragedy is of mothers struggling to save the life of their infant child and, in doing so, losing their own.

With the AIDS pandemic, average life expectancy in Africa is less than fifty. And today Ethiopia, the focus of Live Aid twenty years ago, has 70 million people but only 2,000 doctors. So it is clear that we are a long way short of the predictable, regular financing necessary to make the difference that is needed.

At the UN Monterrey Financing for Development Conference, donor countries pledged an additional $16 billion a year from 2006. For the UK's part, our level of official development assistance will increase to £6.4 billion – 0.47 per cent of our national income – by 2008. Beyond that we wish to maintain those rates of growth which, on this timetable, would lift the ODA ratio beyond 0.5 per cent after 2008 and to 0.7 per cent by 2013 – and over the next year we plan to ask other countries to join us and nine others in becoming countries which have either already reached 0.7 per cent or have set a timetable towards it. But we know that even if one or two of the G7 could overcome fiscal constraints and go to 0.7 per cent tomorrow, we will still not reach the scale of the resources needed to achieve the

Millennium Development Goals – at least $50 billion more a year – not in 2015 but now. And the truth is that the scale of the resources needed immediately to tackle disease, illiteracy and global poverty is far beyond what traditional funding can offer today.

That is why the UK government has put forward its proposal for stable, predictable, long-term funds frontloaded to tackle today's problems of poverty, disease and illiteracy through an International Finance Facility. And let me just explain what the IFF could achieve for the world's poor:

- the IFF is founded upon long-term, binding donor commitments from the richest countries like ourselves;
- it builds upon the additional $16 billion already pledged at Monterrey; and
- on the basis of these commitments and more, it leverages in additional money from the international capital markets to raise the amount of development aid for the years to 2015.

And let me tell you the significance and the scale of what I am proposing. With one bold stroke: to double development aid to halve poverty. Fifty billion dollars more in aid a year each year for the poorest countries. Think of what it could achieve:

- as many as half of all malaria deaths could be prevented if people had access to diagnosis and drugs that cost no more than twelve cents;
- a quarter of all child deaths could be prevented if children slept beneath bed-nets costing only $4 each;
- $3 more for each new mother could save up to 5 million lives over the next ten years;
- for an investment of $9 billion more a year we could build schools so that every child can get primary education;
- $10 – and preferably $20 – billion more a year could tackle TB and malaria, build health systems and address the tragedy of HIV/AIDS.

I believe the International Finance Facility has the following advantages. First, the IFF would urgently create the scale of funding necessary to invest simultaneously across sectors – providing humanitarian assistance as well as investment in education and health, trade capacity and economic development – so that instead of having to choose between first aid and tackling poverty, between health and education, between capacity-building in trade and tackling AIDS, the impact of extra resources in one area reinforces what is being done in others and has a lasting effect. Second, the IFF would provide a predictable flow of aid to developing countries so they no longer have to suffer from an up to 40 per cent variance in the amount of aid they receive from year to year, which prevents them from investing efficiently in health and education systems for the long term and tackling the causes of poverty rather than just the symptoms. Third, the IFF is designed to invest now to prevent problems later – to scale up development aid between now and 2015, enabling us to frontload aid so a critical mass can be deployed as investment now and over the next few years when it will have the most impact in achieving the Millennium Development Goals. Indeed, the fact is that unless we adopt the IFF or a similar mechanism immediately there is simply no other way of meeting the Millennium Development Goals in time.

The IFF is not only complementary to existing commitments to the 0.7 per cent target – allowing participating countries to take faster steps towards 0.7 per cent by increasing the resources available now – but can be implemented alongside continuing consideration of other proposals to provide financing in the longer term – including international taxes, special drawing rights and other forms of revenue-raising on a world-wide basis. I believe that the advantage of the International Finance Facility I have described is not just that it is a means of providing the necessary resources immediately and thus far faster than other initiatives, but also that we can move quickly with a committed group of countries – not moving at the pace of the slowest but tackling the problem head-on now with those that are prepared to sign up.

And so the practical benefits of the IFF are:

- we provide the support poor countries need straightaway – frontloading investment in infrastructure, education and health systems, and economic development so they can benefit from access to our markets;
- we provide grants immediately to help ensure a sustainable exit from debt so poor countries do not need to choose between emergency relief and long-term investment;

- we make primary schooling for all not just a distant dream but a practical reality – meeting these needs and rights now and not deferring them to an uncertain future; and
- we advance towards our global goals of cutting infant mortality and maternal mortality on schedule, eliminating malaria and TB and treating millions more people who are suffering from HIV/AIDS.

Let me give an illustration of what – because of the IFF model – could already be possible. The Global Alliance for Vaccines and Immunisation (GAVI) – who have immunised over the last five years not a few children but a total of 50 million children round the world – is interested in applying the principles of the IFF to the immunisation sector, with donors making long-term commitments that can be leveraged up via the international capital markets in order to front-load the funding available to tackle disease. If, by these means, GAVI could increase the funding for its immunisation programme by an additional $4 billion over the next ten years, then it would be possible that their work could save the lives of an additional 5 million people between now and 2015 and a further 5 million lives after 2015. And I praise Bill Gates and Bono for their far-sightedness – coming together to urge this week a financing proposal for making immunisation available to millions more.

So in one fund, with one initiative, we can glimpse the possibilities open to us if we act together. And there are other possibilities that could change the world. Let me say that with proper funds the medical breakthroughs now being achieved in developing a preventive vaccine for malaria could be matched by the far-sightedness of an advance-purchase scheme that could prevent the loss of more than 1 million lives a year because of this dread disease. Only £400 million a year is spent on research for a preventive vaccine for HIV/AIDS, despite the fact that 75 million are affected and 25 million have died. And as we examine what can be done to prevent as well as treat HIV/AIDS it is obvious that with proper funds there could be a similar bold initiative on research and development – to internationalise and advance the research and then to provide support for the development of preventive vaccines . . . once again showing the possibilities for the global fund for health and for building health capacity that the International Finance Facility we propose opens up for the world. And if what we achieve for health we could also achieve for schools, for debt relief, for the capacity to trade, for anti-poverty programmes, for economic development, think of the better world we can achieve.

So the aim of the International Finance Facility is to bridge the gap between promises and reality. Between hopes raised and hopes dashed. Between an opportunity seized and an opportunity squandered. And in the forthcoming G8 discussions we will ask all countries to join dozens of countries who have already given their backing to support and sign up to the IFF and we will be setting out a framework within which we can implement it.

2005 is therefore a once-in-a-generation opportunity. And when people ask whether it is possible to make a breakthrough, and say our proposals are too difficult, I say:

- people thought the original plans for the World Bank were the work of dreamers;
- people thought the Marshall Plan unattainable;
- even in 1997 when we came to power people thought debt relief was an impossible aspiration and yet we are wiping out $100 billion of debt; and
- people thought no more countries would sign up to a timetable for 0.7 per cent in overseas development aid and yet, this year alone, five countries have done so.

Each of us of course has our respective responsibilities, our very different duties, as politicians, aid organisations, individuals. But for all of us an even greater measure of the potential is that in 2000 first hundreds, then thousands, then millions of people first in one country then in one continent, then in all countries and in all continents, came together to demand debt relief and in doing so changed the world. And we can do this again. Even today that coalition is not just being reformed but growing in strength. And I pay tribute to all of you here today – aid workers, supporters, contributors, campaigners – who are fighting for great causes, standing for the highest ideals, often bearing huge burdens and bringing the greatest of hope to those in the greatest of needs.

A few months ago I quoted a century-old phrase, saying 'The arc of the moral universe is long but it does bend towards justice.' This was not an appeal to some iron law of history but to remind people in the words of a US president that 'The history of free peoples is never written by chance but by choice – that it is by our own actions that people of compassion and goodwill can and do change the world for good.'

Of course it is difficult – as we are witnessing in South-East Asia – and there are disappointments and set-backs in international development when progress is slow, but when we are stalled or set back in our development aims I am reminded of the words of the former head of the UN, Dag Hammarskjold, who said:

> When the morning's freshness had been replaced by the
>   weariness of midday . . .
> When the leg muscles quiver under the strain . . .
> When the climb seems endless . . .
> And suddenly nothing will go quite as you wish . . .
> It is then that you must not hesitate.

And if we do not hesitate but press on, if we do not allow set-backs to discourage us but let them challenge us to do even more on aid and trade and as a result are inspired to work and strive even harder – our determination not diminished but intensified – I believe that:

- with the scale of the challenge revealed in its starkest form this week and this month, summoning us to action;
- with the tsunami showing the capacity of people everywhere to unite in response;
- and with the growth, organisation and now clamour of public opinion calling for action now – 'the passion of compassion' – resonating here in Britain and reverberating across all countries; and
- with a determination among world leaders to be bold – shown by united global action over the Asian crisis

the arc of the moral universe, while indeed long, will bend towards justice in the months and years to come.

6

ENDING CHILD POVERTY

I met Gordon Brown for the first time in 2000, at a reception for the National Council for One Parent Families that was held at 11 Downing Street. I doubt that anybody without personal experience of lone parents' stigmatisation by the previous administration can imagine the slight air of unreality that hung over that gathering. One fellow lone mother muttered to me as she took a drink from a passing tray, 'Can you believe we're here?' I quite saw her point.

When I became a lone parent in 1993, following the break-up of my first marriage, the then government's view of 'single mothers' was that they cost the taxpayer far too much money (in spite of the fact that they were poorer as a group than pensioners). Though only 3 per cent of lone parents were under twenty years old, and 60 per cent of us had been married or cohabiting with a partner when we had our children, senior members of the Major administration stereotyped us as feckless teenagers who were 'married to the state' and whose children had been conceived as a means to secure a council flat. While these cowardly, rabble-rousing attacks did not help re-elect those who made them, they left their mark none the less: those of us struggling to bring up children on our own felt demoralised and alienated. Gordon Brown's invitation to hold a reception for lone parents in 11 Downing Street therefore sent a powerful message: poverty was a problem to be solved, not a well-merited punishment for failure to conform to some government-sanctioned ideal of family life.

Although (as you may have read somewhere) I no longer stand in personal need of financial help from the government, I watch every Budget with a view to how it would have improved my life between 1993 and 1997, when I lived in terror of the nappies running out before benefit day. Gordon Brown's Childcare Tax Credits and increases in maternity pay would have made a real difference to my family's life then, most importantly in enabling me to get back to work sooner.

Poverty is a bad place to live on your own, but the worst place on earth if you have a child with you. We will never know how much talent and ability has been stifled in poverty over the centuries, but we can be sure that we will continue to live with ill health, crime and addiction until we succeed in eradicating it from as many children's lives as possible. The same year that I met Gordon Brown, he made a speech (part of which is reproduced in this chapter) in which he expressed perfectly why the eradication of child poverty is surely the most important political goal: 'We must never forget that poverty – above all the poverty of children – disfigures not just the lives of the poor, but all our society.'

J.K. Rowling

Anyone who knows Gordon Brown well, or who came across him in his early days, knows of his deep-seated commitment to root out poverty and in particular to ensure that all our children are given the best chance of developing their potential. From the Anthony Crosland Memorial Lecture, in early 1997, to the latest speeches about the need to remove what he calls the scar of child poverty in Britain, there is a consistency of approach and a firmness of purpose which marks out the speeches collected in this chapter. And it is not surprising that he has used his position in the government and the Treasury to mount an impressive range of policies aimed at making Britain a fair society. Not only is there a determination to link the moral case for action against vested interests (which restrict the opportunity to get a good education, acquire skills, work and progress) but he continues to make the economic case. Squandering the potential of many of our people is not fair, but it also ignores the point that a country's human capital is most important to its economic prosperity. As he says, equal opportunity and economic prosperity go hand in hand, and that is why it is absolutely necessary to tackle child poverty and extend opportunity to all.

The discovery, on coming into government, that Britain had one of the highest rates of child poverty in the developed world was clearly a shock to many involved in the development of social policy. How could it be that the world's fourth-largest economy could permit a situation to exist whereby over 4 million children – more than a third of all children – lived in a poor family? The research showed that many of them would remain poor for a large part of their childhood – up to a quarter of all children were persistently poor. Most of the children living in poverty, 60 per cent, lived in a household where no one has a job. Overall in the UK, children – 20 per cent of all children – lived in a workless household. Each year around 100,000 children were born into families which were pushed into poverty by the birth of their child.

These figures and many more in the same vein were contained in a Treasury paper 'Tackling Poverty and Extending Opportunity', published in March 1999. The paper explains that the problems of poverty and deprivation start with the very young. Babies born to fathers in social-class five are more likely to be low birth-weight, with low birth-weight a key factor in a child's subsequent development and opportunity. More than one in five primary-school children in the UK are entitled to free school meals – and in more deprived areas the figures are higher – in Merseyside it is over a third. Poor children are less likely to get qualifications and to stay on at school. They start to fall behind their better-off peers from a very young age – the evidence shows that class differences in educational development are apparent by twenty-two months. And if they fall behind at school their future is bleak – almost half of all adults who left school without qualifications are without a job.

Other chancellors, faced with such overwhelming problems, might have been tempted to let colleagues in the spending departments take on this work, which because it spans so many government departments, and both central and local government, is a classic 'wicked' issue. But it is much to the Chancellor's credit that he has made delivering the Prime Minister's pledge to end child poverty in a generation one of the key drivers of his tenure of the Treasury. And he has been determined to reverse a situation which new Labour inherited in 1997, a country where 'a third of children were in poverty; and in which hundreds of thousands of children are born poor every year, and millions are growing up poor, destined to fail even before their life's journey had properly begun'.

A development of this approach is contained in the speech given by the Chancellor to the Child Poverty Action Group Child Poverty Conference on 15 May 2000. Entitled 'Our Children Are Our Future', the speech reviews the rationale for engagement with the issue of child poverty, and extends the argument both on moral and economic grounds. In particular the Chancellor makes the point that it is the duty of government to work not only for equality of opportunity but also for equity of outcome. For example, the Chancellor argues that in the new economy, which depends on knowledge, ingenuity and innovation, on mobilising the talents of all, it is essential to develop the potential of all. He also draws attention to the role of government in supporting families, and to the special support the government needs to provide to the poor and the workless. He suggests that these children are not just 'someone else's children and someone else's problem – they are the children of our country, the children of us all'. As he says: 'if we do not find it within ourselves to pay attention to them as young children today, they may force us to pay attention to them as troubled adults tomorrow'. And once we take the view that what matters on both moral and economic grounds is genuinely equal opportunities to realise potential, we are challenged not only to remove barriers of class, race, sex and other discrimination, but to positively shape and implement policies that will equalise opportunities for all. And in each case there must be a permanent duty on government not only to actively seek this objective, but to set our national economic goals to achieve this.

The Chancellor recalls that in 1942 Sir William Beveridge identified five evils – ignorance, squalor, want, idleness and disease – which a new Welfare State had to confront. However, in the view of the Chancellor, the government's goal today must be even more ambitious than the one Beveridge set, and must move forward from subsistence and minimum standards to modern policies for maximum opportunity and fulfilment. The Chancellor also raises the differences between left and right in this debate: he accepts that in the past the left accused the right of concentrating exclusively on individual responsibility and refusing to recognise social injustice. But in the past as the left called for social justice, the right were able to accuse the left of underestimating the importance of personal responsibility. Caricatured as advocating rights without responsibilities, the left were vulnerable to the attack of the right and their revolt against collective action, and unable to answer effectively the right's dogma that individuals – even children – should be left to their destiny, that the state should stand aside, and that there was 'no such thing as society'. Now, with an acceptance that individual responsibility matters within a responsible society the Chancellor argues that the way is open to draw support from the public as the government tackles the structural injustices that exist. The speech goes on to set out the principal strategies to tackle child poverty and it is noteworthy that these are not only comprehensive in scope but are now clearly multi-departmental and joined-up across government: a 'wicked' issue resolved.

In July 2004 the Chancellor gave the Joseph Rowntree Centenary Lecture, also entitled 'Our Children Are Our Future'. This is a *tour de force* piece covering the background and the philosophy underpinning all aspects of the action being taken by the government on child poverty. It is also a powerful argument for doing more to create equality of opportunity and equity of outcome for this crucial sector. And it is also a recognition that action at this level needs a new compact between the state and those who benefit from the measures. In the speech the Chancellor clearly endorses the radicalism of the approach being taken in Sure Start, under which services for the under-fives not only involve voluntary and charitable action at a local level – even more so than there has been in the past – but also the running of these local groups is being passed to community control, with hugely impressive benefits which the Chancellor clearly recognises. The speech is also noteworthy for its appraisal of what more needs to be done in this area. The Chancellor explains that (even) after seven years of government he is not less but more idealistic about what can be achieved. He wants Sure Start to be rolled out to all parts of the country, and building on this, perhaps even to tackle an even greater challenge – the poverty of aspiration amongst children and young people and their parents.

Some of Gordon Brown's early thinking surfaced in the Anthony Crosland Lecture given in February 1997. Strictly speaking, this falls outside the span of this book, but it is helpful to have an extract here, as it reflects the way the Chancellor bases his approach to equality of opportunity and equity of outcomes in the work of several of the great socialist writers and thinkers, including Adam Smith, Beveridge, Tawney and Crosland.

. . . .

The Future of Socialism was written at a time when equality was not under attack. Tony Crosland did not therefore feel the need to make the philosophical case for equality. Raymond Plant has suggested that, by failing to build an intellectual and a popular consensus for Croslandite social democracy, we allowed its collapse in the 1970s. And after twenty years in which new right ideology which has worshipped inequality has dominated the political landscape, it is now more important then ever that we argue the case for equality from first principles. Today, we argue for equality not just because of our belief in social justice but also because of our view of what is required for economic success. The starting point is a fundamental belief in the equal worth of every human being. We all have an equal claim to social consideration by virtue of being human. And if every person is to be regarded as of equal worth, all deserve to be given an equal chance in life to fulfil the potential with which they are born.

Crosland wrote of the importance of potential in *Socialism Now*. And in doing so he took issue with the old view – used to justify inequality in educational opportunity – that intelligence was a fixed quantity, something given in limited measure in the genetic make-up of the new-born child. Crosland was right. Intelligence cannot be reduced to a single number in an IQ test taken at the age of eleven. People cannot be ranked in a single hierarchy and talent cannot be regarded as fixed. So people should not be written off at 7, 11 or 14 or indeed at any time in their life. It is simply a denial of any belief in equality of opportunity if we assume that there is one type of intelligence, one means of assessing it, only one time when it should be assessed and just one chance of succeeding.

But we have still to act on the consequence of recognising these facts: that people have a richness of potential to be tapped, that their talents take many forms – skills in communication, language, and working with other people as well as analytical intelligence – that these talents can develop over a lifetime, and to get the best economy we need to get the best out of people's potential. And if we are to allow each person to develop that potential which exists within them, it is clear that we need to develop a more demanding view of equality of opportunity than a one-off equality of opportunity up till age sixteen.

So I believe that everyone should have the chance to bridge the gap between what they are and what they have it in themselves to become. But what is right on ethical grounds is, in the 1990s, good for the economy too. In our information-age economy, the most important resource of a firm or a country is not its raw materials, or a favourable geographical location, but the skills of the whole work-force. And so prosperity for a company or country can only be delivered if we get the best out of all people and that cannot happen without continuous and accessible equality of opportunity. Indeed I would suggest that Britain's economic weakness is not attributable to a neglect at the top of the educational pyramid, but it has arisen because we have given insufficient attention in education and employment policies to the latent and diverse potential of the population as a whole.

In the industrial age, the denial of opportunity offended many people but was not necessarily a barrier to the success of the economy. Today, in an economy where skills are the essential means of production, the denial of opportunity has become an unacceptable inefficiency, a barrier to prosperity. It used to be said in the fifties that what was good for General Motors was good for the American economy. I would say in the nineties that what's good for equality of opportunity is good for the British economy.

And once we take this view that what matters on ethical and economic grounds is the equal right to realise potential, we reject – as Anthony Crosland did – both an unrealisable equality of outcome and a narrow view of equality of opportunity. Indeed we reject equality of outcome not because it is too radical but because it is neither desirable nor feasible. Crosland himself wrote of 'the rent of ability', recognising that incentives for effort are essential in any economic system: greater incomes for some justified by the contribution they make to the society as a whole. Indeed I would go further: predetermined results imposed, as they would have to be, by a central authority and decided irrespective of work, effort or contribution to the community, is not a socialist dream but other people's nightmare of socialism. It denies humanity, rather than liberates it. It is to make people something they are not, rather than helping them to make the most of what they can be. What people resent about Britain today is not that some people who have worked hard have done well. What angers people is that millions are denied the opportunity to realise their potential and are powerless to do so. It is this inequality that must be addressed.

Just as we join Crosland in rejecting an unattainable equality of outcome, so we refuse to narrow our horizons to a limited view of equality of opportunity. There was an old idea of equality of opportunity in which it meant a single chance to get your foot on a narrow ladder, one opportunity at school till sixteen followed by an opportunity for 20 per cent to go into higher education. And for millions of people in Britain it has meant that if you missed that chance it was gone for ever. It is the equal opportunity only to become unequal: as Crosland wrote, 'only a few exceptional individuals hauled out of their class by society's talent scouts, can ever climb'. It is in the words of Tawney the invitation for all to come to dinner in the sure knowledge that circumstances would prevent most people from attending.

Whether done on the basis of birth or academic qualifications, the potential of all is clearly denied when we entrench the privilege of a few. So Crosland correctly concluded that a narrow equality of opportunity was not enough if we were to prevent the entrenchment of unjustifiable privilege, and sought a broader view of equality that complemented rather than conflicted with the importance he attached to personal liberty. He proposed what he called a democratic view of equality – one that sought to prevent the permanent entrenchment of privilege from whatever source it came. This more demanding view of equality of opportunity – democratic equality – had, as he said in *The Conservative Enemy*, 'revolutionary connotations'.

So what, in the 1990s, does this concept of democratic equality mean for me? First, it demands employment opportunity for all because work is central not just to economic prosperity for Britain but to individual fulfilment. And there must be a permanent duty on government to relentlessly pursue this objective. Secondly, we must as a society ensure not just one-off educational opportunity in childhood, but continuing and lifelong educational opportunity for all – second, third, and even fourth chances so that people are not written off if they fail at school and are not left behind by the pace of technological change. Thirdly, lifelong opportunity must be comprehensive, extending beyond education and employment, involving genuine access to culture and, most importantly, a redistribution of power that offers people real control over the decisions that affect their lives.

While Crosland did write about industrial democracy, he said less about the state or about an equal right to participate in the decisions that affect our lives. In the forties people accepted services handed down from the state – for example, housing. They now want to make their own choices over their own lives and rightly see themselves as decision-makers in their own right and they want a government that will enable them to make decisions for themselves and give them power over their lives. So the issue for socialists is not so much about what the state can do for you but about what the state can enable you to do for yourself. Political reform is central to this: it must enable people to have the chance to participate in decisions that affect them. This is about more than the concept of a classless society; it is about power and therefore about a truly democratic society.

So we should see our constitutional proposals – which range from abolishing the hereditary principle in the Lords to devolution of power and free information – as part of a programme that makes sense of people's aspirations by redistributing power from the state, or any other vested interest, to people themselves. Proponents of democratic equality must also – even in a global marketplace – address wealth and income inequalities. I believe that these inequalities can only be justified if they are in the interests of the least fortunate. Crosland took his stand against inequalities of social status and wealth. He viewed the question of income inequalities as of lesser importance, but he thought that great inequalities of wealth, and particularly inherited wealth, could not be justified as a source of enormous social and economic advantage. The abolition of Inheritance Tax and Capital Gains Tax to which the Conservatives are committed – unjustified by benefits to work, effort or the wider community – would bring huge benefits to a privileged few and so we oppose these Conservative proposals.

But Crosland also saw the distinction between the private ownership of property that simply furthered privilege and the private ownership of property that allowed people control over their lives. So he was ahead of his time on the left in wanting a more general diffusion of property among the entire population. Indeed, he was right to say in *The Conservative Enemy* that 'If the property is well distributed, a property-owning democracy is a socialist rather than a conservative ideal.' Democratic equality means we tackle unjustifiable inequalities, but it also, of course, presupposes a guaranteed minimum below which no one should fall. Our minimum standards must include a minimum wage, a tax and benefit system that helps people into work, the best possible level of health and social services for all, and the assurance of dignity and security for those who are retired or unable to work through infirmity.

Given what Gordon Brown was saying before the election it is not surprising that he has used his position in the government and the Treasury to mount an impressive range of policies aimed at making Britain a fair society. Not only is there a determination to link the moral case for action against vested interests (which restrict the opportunity to get a good education, acquire skills, work and progress) but he continues to make the economic case. Squandering the potential of many of our people is not fair, but it also ignores the point that a country's human capital is most important to its economic prosperity. As he says, equal opportunity and economic prosperity go hand in hand, and that is why it is necessary to tackle poverty and extend opportunity to all.

In the Adam Smith Lecture, given by the Chancellor in his home town of Kirkcaldy on 27 February 1998, he returned to the theme of unleashing the potential of all the people for both moral and economic reasons.

I am pleased tonight to give a lecture in memory of Adam Smith, a central figure in the Scottish Enlightenment, whose work is remembered in every continent where economics is today studied.

. . .

He was an influential man in his time and since, and we continue to look to Adam Smith today for, I think, three reasons:

First, Adam Smith looked at a world in flux and recognised the permanence of change in an industrial economy. More than anyone he saw, from Kirkcaldy, how the world was changing from a closed mercantile economy where entrenched interests were predominantly secure, to an open industrial economy which carried wholly new opportunities and totally new risks. And he saw that society must continuously reinvent itself to embrace that change.

. . .

This leads me to Adam Smith's second contribution to our thinking. Adam Smith believed not in economics – what Thomas Carlisle, another person who frequented Kirkcaldy, called the dismal science – he believed in political economy. He saw that markets were not god-given but our social and political institutions created the framework in which markets worked. His writing has been appropriated by the right as the study of the justification of unfettered markets. But this, in my view, is a misunderstanding of his work. He was a man who dedicated his life to trying to understand how society works and the part that can be played by government, political institutions and the law in ensuring that markets work effectively. In particular he recognised in his own day the need to break up vested interests, to tackle privilege head-on, to open up opportunities that challenge cliques, cabals, cartels and monopolies. Indeed we should recall his famous words that 'people of the same trade seldom meet together for merriment, or for conversation, but enter into a conspiracy against the public interest'. In other words, Smith knew that markets, while they worked in the public interest, did not automatically do so, and that the challenge of the economy was to ensure that while markets were to our benefit, they worked in the public interest, for the good of everyone.

But there is a third important contribution which arises from Adam Smith's study of political economy. He brought together ethics, economics and politics. Adam Smith recognised that economic growth depends on the behaviour of individuals: that we cannot separate our economic behaviour from our ethical behaviour and that ethical values must guide our approach to economic welfare. In Adam Smith's day the great cause was to free the individual from vested interests that were holding him or her back. So he called for an end to the closed mercantilist economy that denied opportunity. His aim was to create a society in which individuals could realise their talents free from the vested interests that denied them opportunities and held them back.

In our day I think the cause is even more ambitious: to enable every individual to realise their potential to the full. To enable every individual – from whatever background they come, whatever the circumstances of their birth, every individual – to realise their potential to the full and this is what I want to talk about this evening.

. . .

Adam Smith, I think, would have understood the importance of opportunity. He was the son of a single parent, born shortly after his father's death. He was brought up in relative poverty; he saw the poverty around him in Kirkcaldy and commented on it all the time. In his writings Adam Smith started from what he saw in Kirkcaldy, watching the local merchants under competitive pressure as trade began to open up with the rest of the world and the sufferings that resulted. And that is why he formulated the views that he did.

And I hope in a more modest way that the work that we are doing as a Labour government is learnt from what I saw in Kirkcaldy and what my colleagues saw when we were growing up. I first became aware of what was happening around me in the early sixties, when unemployment reappeared for the first time in a very big way since the 1930s; in the sixties in Kirkcaldy the demise of the linoleum, linen and textiles industries; and from the sixties onwards the failure of the

pits, the run-down of the central Fife coalfield, jobs were disappear-
ing in large numbers, emigration started again. But nothing I saw
then prepared me or any of us for the mass unemployment of the
1980s – if the thirties are remembered for men standing on street
corners with nowhere to go, the eighties are now remembered for
young people living in cardboard boxes – something we must never
allow to be repeated. So while I was brought up in Kirkcaldy, in a
town and in a country which believed in equality of opportunity –
what we sometimes in Scotland called the democratic intellect – the
idea that everyone, if they worked hard, and made the effort, could
realise their potential to the full – we found that real opportunity was
denied to thousands of people.

Today one working-age household in every five has no one in work
– that is 4 million households in Britain where no one is earning a
wage. And 40 per cent of our unemployed are long-term unemployed. Thirty per cent of our unemployed are young people. And in
some areas 50 per cent of young men are doing nothing and many
have not had real opportunity to obtain the skills for work. Now,
nobody I know can fail to feel compassion when you see a child whose
life you know is blighted by family poverty and unemployment, even
before that child's life journey has ever begun. There is no person I
know who thinks about things who does not feel anger welling up in
them when they see young people trained and motivated, yearning to
contribute to society, whose ambitions, indeed whose whole life is
crushed by the curse of unemployment. And I believe that no
community can ever be strong, no locality, no street or neighbourhood in any town can be free of division or social tension if we leave
unemployment without tackling it in the way that it is.

So far from assuming we have a society with opportunity for all, the
challenge we face is to create this in the changed economy of the
twenty-first century. And I believe that in the new global economy this
is more important than ever before. In the past economists could
dismiss a demand for equal opportunity as merely a call for social
justice. Now we are living in an economy that depends on employing
the talents of everyone and thus getting the best people and getting
the best out of people. Policies promoting equal opportunity are an
economic necessity.

Let me explain why. We are moving from an old industrial
economy based on mass production in purely national capital mar-

kets, to an economy characterised by global markets, instantaneous communications, new technology-driven, custom-built products, and an information, knowledge-based economy that depends on the skills and the adaptability of people. In the past our success depended on the raw materials we had – coal, oil or ore, or simply on the amounts of capital we could deploy. But now these can be bought from just about anywhere and our success depends instead on the quality of our one truly national resource, the quality of our human capital, the investment in their education and training and the cultivation of their talent and enterprise. And we used to hear what's good for General Motors, is good for America. In the 1990s, what's good in life is the equality of opportunity, bringing out the best in people is going to be good for the British economy.

So it is to meet the challenges of the new economy that this government sees it as its inescapable duty to advance equality of opportunity, the opportunity for everyone to contribute to economic success and to benefit from its rewards – and by that I mean employment, educational and economic opportunity for all, as well as the opportunity to participate in our democracy and have access to our cultural life. Some say that equality should mean equality of outcome, that we should impose on everyone the same outcomes irrespective of effort, merit or contribution to the community. But this kind of equality pays no regard to effort or desert and is thus indifferent to character. And because it pays little attention to individual choices, it describes, in the end, a state where opportunities are not provided but imposed.

And I think my friend the Scottish writer William McIlvanney put it best. He said that he rejected the equality of outcome that asks people to be something they are not. Instead he supported the equality that helps them to make the best of what they can be. That implies a vigorous pursuit of equal opportunity for all. On the other hand I would be criticised by the right who ignore equality but say we can stop simply at opportunity. They are not interested in extending opportunity but are content for those who already have it to have more. For them talk of opportunity for all becomes a defence of the status quo, even where privilege denies opportunity and holds people back. When they were in government they did nothing but stand aside as millions were denied a place at the table. It is a prescription for an underclass society with no-go areas as the powerful become more powerful and the privileged more privileged. I am clear that we cannot talk separately of equality and opportunity. We must strive for a society that gives everyone the chance to be all they can be.

So we must strive to create real equality of opportunity in our society, to break down the barriers to success that hold people back:

- equalising opportunity in employment where too many people are denied employment for months on end without being offered retraining or a job;
- equalising opportunity in education where people are left without the knowledge and skills they need to compete in the new economy;
- equalising opportunity in the economy: where we must strive to create the right conditions for business to compete on an equal basis, by attacking restrictive practices and by giving small business the chance to compete with big business;
- equalising opportunity in political and cultural life, where we need to create an open society with a participative democracy in which every citizen has a true stake in their community's decisions and everyone has access to our culture;
- education, skills and jobs for a modern economy.

The old deal, the deal I was brought up on in the fifties and sixties, was one chance in education, one chance in employment, one chance to get the right skills. Now school must not be the end of education but the beginning of a lifetime of learning. But the test for me of how we expand educational opportunity for all is, first of all, how we can extend the nursery education for those people who are very young, to all four-year-olds, and then all three-year-olds, and instead of spending millions on vouchers, we should spend the millions on places. I think, secondly, instead of investing money in the assisted-places scheme, we should invest that and more to raise standards in our schools – primary and secondary schools – ending a situation where so many of our children at eleven are unable to read or use mathematics properly. And thirdly, we have got to end the situation where far too many people leave school without qualifications, never return to education or are then capable of only an unskilled job and, of course, the difference in the school-leaving numbers between the poorest and richest in our areas is so high that you cannot ignore this problem without leaving huge problems in some of the most deprived communities.

And the government's ambition is that by the age of twenty-one, nearly everyone will have the equivalent of a Level-2 National Vocational Qualification; in other words, to provide opportunities for people to succeed at school and then opportunities for people to continue in education after school. And finally, as far as education opportunity is concerned, it seems to be absolutely essential that we extend the opportunity to learn to everyone through their working lives. And that is why we have published proposals for what we call the university for industry. To create a university which will allow, through new technology, computers, cable television and satellite, learning opportunities to be made available to people in their home as well as in their workplace, to extend to new courses outside universities, what the Open University did for people studying for second or first degrees, and to give people who have never had the chance of education in their lives the opportunity to study in the most amenable way from their home or in the workplace to gain the opportunities that they will need as they upgrade skills through their working lives.

For the agenda it seems to me, for equality of opportunity and education, is more opportunities to have a nursery-school education, high standards in primary and secondary schools, more people staying on or getting to college and getting qualifications as teenagers, and lifelong education for all. And it is in all these areas that we are seeking to make progress now. But of course the key to opportunity is not simply that people have qualifications, but have work in which they can use these qualifications. Now, we know that in the changing global economy no job is going to last a lifetime. Nobody can guarantee a job for life. A government can't just guarantee that people can stay in their last job. But what a government can do is help you get the next job. And I believe that in the modern world the proper way towards full employment, which is in my view a goal that ought to be pursued, is that a government should be able to give three guarantees.

They should give a guarantee that no young person will be unemployed without work or training for long periods of time in our society. And therefore they should do as we have done with the New Deal, make available options of training and education as well as of work experience and work itself for young people to get back into work or to get work for the first time so that there is never a period when young people are out of work for months on end. And I believe that the advances that employers are helping us make with the New Deal in this country is a path-breaking way of employers, government – local and national governments – operating together, voluntary organisations, indeed environmental organisations as well, so that we can make sure that every young person has opportunities either for work or for training and no one is rejected or left behind.

I think the second guarantee is that no adult should be unemployed for too many months without having the chance of a job or training. And what is tragic about Europe as a whole is that nearly 50 per cent of our unemployed are people who have been unemployed for more than a year. All the evidence is, the longer the people are unemployed, the more difficult it is for employers to be persuaded to accept them as workers and for them themselves to have the confidence that they can try new skills or get a job. And that is why, from July this year, every long-term unemployed person, who has not been employed for more than two years, will have with them a subsidy of £75 a week if employers take them on and I believe that this is only the first stage of measures that we have got to take to help people get back to work.

And the third guarantee, it seems to me, is that nobody should be left without help in their attempt to find a job if they lose a job; to minimise any gaps that exist between redundancy and people getting the next job. And that is why it is so important that advice and information of the link-up with employers, the advice about vacancies in particular, is made available in a way that people can take up opportunities. So in the modern world it seems to me that these are the right government guarantees and these are guarantees I believe we can fulfil. The guarantees that make it possible to say that nobody should be excluded from employment opportunities for long and that we are in a position to give people the right to work in a new world.

And I think these guarantees help us especially in dealing with the inequalities and opportunities that have affected women in employment. For many women the main barrier to getting a job is the lack of decent and affordable child care. In fact four out of five non-working mothers in the UK have said they would go out to work if they had the child care of their choice. We will put in place a national childcare strategy to help ensure that childcare provision matches the needs of a modern labour market. Through the New Deal for the young unemployed we are encouraging voluntary organisations to take on and train young people as childcare assistants. We believe that over a five-year period as many as 50,000 young people can be trained up. For families on low income we have provided help through changes to childcare disregard in Family Credit.

But an educational agenda for opportunity for all also depends on tackling the causes of child poverty. There are children who – because of poverty, deprivation and lack of opportunity – are destined to lose even before life's journey has begun and never to achieve their potential.

Adam Smith himself said: 'Poverty is extremely unfavourable to the rearing of children. The tender plant is produced, but in so cold a soil and so severe a climate, soon withers and dies.' So the government has set up a review of the provision of services to young children, looking at how some young children fall behind even before they reach school, and how better use of public resources can help. Thus far the New Deal has been about opportunity for individuals – providing work and training places, making work pay and reforming the welfare system. But we also need a New Deal for the communities, to tackle the cycle of deprivation and poverty.

The worst estates in Britain are the clearest evidence of the effects of lack of opportunity. Long spells of unemployment, low educational achievement and benefit dependency locks people in deprived areas into a cycle of poverty and lack of opportunity. We need to change the pattern where we are compensating people for their poverty rather than tackling the causes. For this reason I have been working with the Deputy Prime Minister and the Social Exclusion Unit to tackle the problems of the most disadvantaged neighbourhoods. Much work remains to be done. But the thinking is clear. We need an approach to the communities which extends economic opportunity rather than simply compensates people for their poverty.

And our approach will be on two fronts:

- first, a new initiative to extend economic opportunity in some of the worst areas of the country. Like the New Deal thus far it will be in partnership with business and with voluntary and community groups. Like the New Deal it will draw on the lessons of what works, and of best practice.

- Second, we must make existing public expenditure work more effectively to address poverty and deprivation at the local level – in all areas of the country.

But equality of opportunity must mean more than the opportunity to be an employee in employment. To release the full potential of the British economy requires fair access to capital so individuals are able to create a business or be self-employed and a fair chance for small business to compete with big business. The equality agenda requires that monopolies and cartels are prevented from dominating the marketplace and it requires a competition policy which means that capital markets and product markets are open to all.

Adam Smith was emphatic in his belief that markets cannot work in the public interest if vested interests are allowed to develop. I agree with him. I believe that Scotland and Britain are full of talent and creativity, something that has been manifest throughout our history: the creativity of Britain itself, from the first agricultural revolution to the pioneering work of Babbage and Turing that made possible the computer and information revolution; in science discoveries, from Newton to DNA and cloning; in engineering, from the steam engine to the TV; and in medicine, from penicillin to interferon; an inventiveness that has ranged right across medicine and science to the arts and music. Productivity in a nation like ours now depends as much on encouraging the innovation and creativity of inventors, managers and workforces as on investment in plant and machinery. Indeed the industries in which Britain is doing best today are exactly the creative talent-based industries – from pure science, computer software and communications to film, fashion design and music – where our ability and capacity to innovate is the source of wealth. To do that we must not only encourage new ideas, new entrepreneurs, and new talent but ensure they have the equal access to markets that they need to succeed.

Today in Britain the proportion of self-employed is well below parts of Europe. The survival rate of our small businesses is one of the worst in the G7. We need to take action to help small businesses to find a place in the market, to start up, to grow and become successful. Our aim is therefore:

- to tackle cartels and monopolies through a tough competition policy. We have already taken the first steps by introducing a Competition Bill which prohibits anti-competitive agreements and prevents abuses by companies with a dominant position in the market; and
- to help small businesses start up and grow. We have already made changes which have been welcomed by small businesses – cutting their rate of tax and temporarily increasing capital allowances to encourage them to invest now for future growth. We are providing, through the enhanced business-link network, access to advice and information, particularly for new technology and exports.

So the Budget on March 17th will be a Budget not just for work but for enterprise too, to encourage the enterprise of the many and not just the few. To help men and women create businesses, to help small businesses expand, to help high-technology industries to develop to bring out the enterprise in us all.

So there is an agenda, I believe, for a modern economy. To equalise what are essentially unequal opportunities at the moment. To give people new chances in education, employment and business. To give people the chance to flourish and prosper in a modern world.

. . .

A country which, having led the first industrial revolution but fallen back in the second, could lead again in the new information-age economy; a Britain where in education what every parent wants for their children, we aspire to – because of our belief in educational opportunity – for every child in the country. So starting from that challenging view of Britain prospering in a more open and dynamic economy that Adam Smith gave us from Kirkcaldy just over 200 years ago, we have yet again a vision of Britain prospering in the new economy. Everyone has new chances to realise their potential through employment and educational opportunities, the chance to bridge the gap between what they are and what they have it in themselves to become. Instead of just the invisible hand, the helping hand of ambitious communities determined to widen the circle of opportunity in our country. A vision of potential unleashed, aspirations fulfilled, the community improved in the spirit of the Scottish

Enlightenment but ever more challenging for our time. And for our time, a new generation, worth fighting for.

In a speech made on 29 March 1999 at the launch of a Treasury paper 'Tackling Poverty and Extending Opportunity', the Chancellor returned to the question of how best to support children born into poverty, and families who were workless, in the context of meeting the target of eliminating child poverty within twenty years.

Today I am launching a new analysis of the causes of the scale of poverty and inequality in the UK. Britain has become a society in which opportunity is concentrated in the hands of the few rather than the many. In the 1990s the opportunity to get a good education, acquire skills, work and progress too often depended on who your parents were, what school you went to, where you live and your age. This is incompatible with a fair society. But squandering the potential of many of our people is also bad economics in a world where a country's human capital is most important to its economic prosperity. Equal opportunity and economic prosperity go hand in hand. We are pledged to tackling poverty and extending opportunity to all.

The paper we are publishing today, which follows extensive analysis and research, paints a picture of child poverty that is bleak and a clear theme is the impact of lack of work in the family. Our emphasis on work is an integral part of the strategy for tackling one of the biggest problems we face. Today I want to focus attention on what, as a country, we can all do to tackle child poverty and help the two out of five children born into poverty in the UK today. Too many of our children are growing up in poverty, their life chances damaged by poverty. They are not making the best of their potential and, as often before, are being left behind. All of us have a part to play in a partnership to tackle child poverty and help all our children fulfil their potential and I want to outline a new strategy not just for addressing poverty and deprivation but for tackling the causes of child poverty – tackling that vicious cycle of unemployment, inadequate opportunities, and low aspirations.

Over 4 million children – more than a third of all children – live in a poor family. And very many of them will remain poor for a large part of their childhood – up to a quarter of all children are persistently poor. Most of the children living in poverty, 60 per cent, live in a household where no one has a job. Overall in the UK 20 per cent of all children live in a workless household. Each year around 100,000 children are born into families which are pushed into poverty by the birth of their child.

The problems of poverty and deprivation start with the very young. Babies born to fathers in social-class five are more likely to be low birth-weight – low birth-weight is a key fact in a child's subsequent development and opportunity. More than one in five primary-school children in the UK are entitled to free school meals – and in more deprived areas the figures are higher – in Merseyside it is over a third. And poor children are less likely to get qualifications and to stay on at school. They start to fall behind their better-off peers from a very young age – the evidence shows that class differences in educational development are apparent by twenty-two months. And if they fall behind at school their future is bleak – almost half of all adults who left school without qualifications are without a job.

So in 1997 we inherited a country where a third of children were in poverty; in which the evidence points to hundreds of thousands of children, born poor every year, and millions growing up poor, destined to fail even before their life's journey had properly begun. And we are putting in place a strategy to tackle the evil of child poverty throughout the United Kingdom. And to meet the target set by the Prime Minister to eliminate child poverty within twenty years. It is a strategy based on supporting work and on supporting families when they need it most. The evidence in the Treasury paper is that poverty and worklessness go together. So our priority is to have more men and women in work. Since we came to government we have been clear how we can meet this demand – building on the foundation of a stable economy we need more opportunities for work, we must ensure that work pays, we must equip everyone with the skills for work.

This is why the government established the New Deal: creating new opportunities for people without work. In the UK almost a quarter of a million young people are benefiting from the New Deal, more than 55,000 are in sustained jobs and 44,000 employers have signed up. We are also taking steps to make work pay. From next month Britain will have, for the first time, a National Minimum Wage. Almost

2 million people currently earn below the National Minimum Wage – two-thirds of them women. From next month their hourly wages will increase by an average of 30 per cent. And for families with children the government is introducing the new Working Families Tax Credit alongside our new 10p tax rate. From October 1999 families in work will be guaranteed a minimum income of £200 a week.

For many the opportunity to work depends on the opportunity to acquire new skills and we are committed to widening that opportunity – to learn, to train, to get qualifications. This is why we are investing an additional £19 billion in education over the next three years. We are continuing the expansion in higher and further education with a commitment to add over 700,000 extra students a year in further and higher education by 2002.

To help provide learning opportunities throughout people's lives the university for industry will connect people and businesses who want to improve their skills with the organisations and specialists who can offer them the courses required.

So our strategy to tackle child poverty is to support work and also to support families when they need it most. The evidence on child poverty shows the need for early intervention to give very young children the best start in life and it shows the need not only for financial support but for proper support services to help families. The Treasury paper confirms the findings of the cross-departmental review of young children in the Comprehensive Spending Review: the very earliest years of a child's life are critical. This is why we are investing £540 million over the next three years in the new Sure Start programme to help give very young children in our most deprived areas a better start in life so that when they start school they are ready to thrive. Sure Start will establish 250 local programmes in England by the end of the parliament, providing integrated services for children under four and their families, to promote the child's physical, intellectual, social and emotional development.

On the birth of a child we know that parents face particularly heavy financial burdens, so in the Budget I announced a new Sure Start maternity grant at double the rate of the old maternity payment, benefiting around 250,000 families. And to encourage good health care at an early age the additional amount is linked to contact with a health-care professional. We are putting in place measures to raise educational achievement levels for all children, to ensure that all children have the chance to fulfil their potential. And in the Budget I took steps to further increase financial support for children and make the tax system more fairly reflect the additional responsibilities faced by parents. We are increasing the rates of support for young children within the WFTC and income-related benefits by £5.75 over the next year. Further increases in Child Benefit will mean that by next year every mother will receive £15 a week for the first child and £10 for further children. And from April 2001 we are introducing a new Children's Tax Credit. It will be worth up to £416 a year for a family with children.

In total these measures represent an additional investment of £6 billion a year in financial support to children. By the end of this parliament we will have lifted one and a quarter million people out of poverty – 700,000 of them children. Families with children in the poorest fifth will be up to a thousand pounds a year better-off as a result of the measures I announced in my last two Budgets. By investing in education and introducing the Sure Start programme we will have the chance to break the cycle of disadvantage by which poor children become poor adults who then go on to give birth to poor children. This is only the start but it is the start of a strategy to tackle child poverty based on the evidence of the causes of poverty and focused on encouraging work and supporting families when they need it most.

A development of this approach is contained in the speech given by the Chancellor to the Child Poverty Action Group Child Poverty Conference on 15 May 2000. Entitled 'Our Children Are Our Future', the speech reviews the rationale for engagement with the issue of child poverty, and extends the argument both on moral and economic grounds. In particular the Chancellor makes the point that it is the duty of government to work both for equality of opportunity but also for equity of outcome. For example the Chancellor argues that in the new economy, which depends on knowledge, ingenuity and innovation, on mobilising the talents of all, it is essential to develop the potential of all. He also draws attention to the role of government in supporting families, and to the special support the government needs to provide to the poor and the workless. He suggests that these children are not just 'someone else's children and someone else's problem – they are the children of our country, the children of us all'. As he says: 'if we do not find it within ourselves to pay attention to them as young children today, they may force us to pay attention to them as troubled adults tomorrow'. And once we take the view that what matters on both moral and economic grounds is genuinely equal opportunities to realise potential, we are challenged not only to remove barriers of class, race, sex and other discrimination, but to positively shape and implement policies that will equalise opportunities for all. And in each case there must be a permanent duty on government not only to actively seek this objective, but to set our national economic goals to achieve this.

The Chancellor recalls that in 1942 Sir William Beveridge identified five evils – ignorance, squalor, want, idleness and disease – which a new Welfare State had to confront. However, in the view of the Chancellor, the government's goal today must be even more ambitious than the one Beveridge set, and must move forward from subsistence and minimum standards to modern policies for maximum opportunity and fulfilment. The Chancellor also raises the differences between left and right in this debate: he accepts that in the past the left accused the right of concentrating exclusively on individual responsibility and refusing to recognise social injustice. But in the past, as the left called for social justice, the right were able to accuse the left of underestimating the importance of personal responsibility. Caricatured as advocating rights without responsibilities, the left were vulnerable to the attack of the right and their revolt against collective action, and unable to answer effectively the right's dogma that individuals – even children – should be left to their destiny, that the state should stand aside, and that there was 'no such thing as society'. Now, with an acceptance that individual responsibility matters within a responsible society, the Chancellor argues that the way is open to draw support from the public as the government tackles the structural injustices that exist. The speech goes on to set out the principal strategies to tackle child poverty and it is noteworthy that these are not only comprehensive in scope but are now clearly multi-departmental and joined-up across government: a 'wicked' issue resolved.

Let me begin by paying tribute to the work of the Child Poverty Action Group: born thirty-five years ago as the Family Poverty Group out of anger and outrage about poverty; built by the dedicated commitment of volunteers who had a vision of the world not as it was but as it could be; now a nationwide crusade for justice for the poor, with an established and well-deserved reputation for advocacy and for authoritative research – that every day shines a spotlight on the needs and potential of our country's children.

So I want today at the outset to congratulate all of you – staff, members, supporters, campaigners – on your 35-year-long crusade to end the scourge and tragedy of child poverty in our society. You should take pride that your concern – child poverty – and your driving ambition – the eradication of child poverty – once written off as the goal of dreamers, for many years a call for justice unheard in a political wilderness – is the ambition not just of your organisation but now the ambition of this country's government.

Action on child poverty is the obligation this generation owes to the next: to millions of children who should not be growing up in poverty: children who because of poverty, deprivation and the lack of opportunity have been destined to fail even before their life's journey has begun, children for whom we know – unless we act – life will never be fair; children in deprived areas who need, deserve and must have a government on their side, a government committed to and fighting for social justice.

And we must never forget that poverty – above all, the poverty of children – disfigures not just the lives of the poor but all our society. Exactly one hundred years ago in 1900 the consequences of gross inequalities in childhood health were revealed by mass recruitment to the army for the Boer War. Today as we tackle global competition in the new economy, the glaring inequalities in educational opportunity and skills make it once again central to our national interest to tackle child poverty. Indeed in the new century economies that work for only the privileged few and not for everyone will ossify and their societies will become ever more divided and poor if they fail to encourage the latent potential of all their children. Our five-year-olds who will finish school after 2010 and graduate from university and college after 2015 will be our teachers, our doctors and our scientists, our employers and our workforces. The future of our country lies with the hopes and dreams of these children.

In the old economy of the past, of the industrial age, where brawn counted more than brain, we could get away with investing only in some of the potential of some of our children. But in the new economy, which depends on knowledge, ingenuity and innovation, on mobilising the talents of all – getting the best out of everyone – it is essential to develop all the potential of all of our children. In other words, policies for the good economy and the good society go together. We do well by doing good.

But we recognise that, for many children, that means special support, a government that fights on their behalf. We know that a child who grows up in a poor family is less likely to reach his or her full potential, less likely to stay on at school, or even attend school regularly, less likely to get qualifications and go to college, more likely to be trapped in the worst job or no job at all, more likely to reproduce the cycle of deprivation in childhood, exclusion in youth and disappointment that is lifelong. We need to understand that these children are not just someone else's children and someone else's problem – they are the children of our country, the children of us all. And if we do not find it within ourselves to pay attention to them as young children today, they may force us to pay attention to them as troubled adults tomorrow.

So it must be the government's objective to ensure that no child will go without help, that every child is included, that every child will have the chance to make the best of their lives, that we will never allow another generation of children to be discarded. That is why since we came into power we have been determined to do more to help those left behind. You would expect me as Chancellor to talk about money and I am happy to do that.

- Between 1997 and 2001, for the family with one child, Child Benefit will have risen by £4.45 – 26 per cent above inflation.
- For a low-paid working family with one child under 11, the maximum amount of financial support for children will have risen by £26.90 – 97 per cent above inflation.
- Many of our poorest families are now £50 a week better off.
- Our priority has been to do most for the children that need most.
- By next year, compared to 1997 we will be investing an additional £7,000 million a year in children's financial support
- The poorest 20 per cent of families receive not 20 per cent of that additional money but almost 50 per cent.
- As a result we have taken more than 1 million children out of poverty.

- The next step is to take the second million out of poverty. And this will be a commitment of our next election manifesto as we meet our goal of reducing child poverty by half in ten years and abolishing it in a generation.

So today I want to set out in detail our five-point plan, a plan based on:

- increased financial support;
- a national childcare strategy;
- new investment in education;
- special help in the poorest communities;

all guaranteed by a new alliance for children – local and national government working together with community and voluntary organisations with one common goal, the best possible start in life for every child.

Let me summarise the philosophy that inspires our work. Our starting point is a fundamental belief in the equal worth of every human being, and our duty to help each and every one develop their potential to the full: for all children and all adults – to help them bridge the gap between what they are and what they have it in themselves to become. And if we are to allow all as individuals to develop that potential which exists within them, it is clear that as a society we must develop a more generous view of equality of opportunity than the old idea of a one-off equality of opportunity up till age sixteen. Four years ago in the John Smith Lecture, and subsequently in the Crosland Lecture in 1997, I outlined our commitment to equality of opportunity and fairness of outcome, a new view of equality that must be more than the old idea of a single chance to get your foot on a narrow ladder, one opportunity at school till sixteen, followed by an opportunity for 20 per cent to go into higher education. And for millions of people in Britain it has meant that if you missed that chance it was gone for ever.

That was not equal opportunity, only the opportunity to become unequal: based on an old view that intelligence – or potential – was a fixed quantity, something given in limited measure in the genetic make-up of the new-born child. But neither potential nor intelligence can be reduced to a single number in an IQ test taken at the age of eleven. And we now know that people cannot be ranked in a single hierarchy, or their talent regarded as fixed. So people should not be written off at birth, 7, 11 or 16 or indeed at any time in their life. It is simply a denial of any belief in equality of opportunity if we assume that there is one type of intelligence, one means of assessing it, only one time when it should be assessed and only one chance of succeeding.

But we have still to act on the consequence of recognising these facts: that people have a richness and diversity of potential, that their talents take many forms – not just analytical intelligence but skills in communication, language, and working with other people – and that these talents can develop over a lifetime. So, as I set out in the Smith and Crosland Lectures, I favour a rich and expansive view of equality of opportunity – with a duty on government in education, in employment and in the economy as a whole to continuously and relentlessly promote opportunity not just for some of the people some of the time but opportunity for all of the people all of the time. And as I have already suggested, what is right on ethical grounds is good for the economy too. In the industrial age, the denial of opportunity offended many people but was not necessarily a barrier to the success of the economy.

Today, in an economy where skills are the essential means of production, the denial of opportunity has become an unacceptable inefficiency and brake on prosperity. In our information-age economy, the most important resource of a firm or a country is not its raw materials, or a favourable geographical location, but the skills, the talents and the potential of the whole workforce. Indeed what matters most in the new economy is not what a company has as assets in its balance sheet, its physical capital, but what assets it has in the talent in its workforce, its human capital. So even if we could not persuade some to support action against, for example, child poverty for reasons of social justice, these people should now be driven to support action against child poverty for economic reasons.

For full prosperity for a company or country can only be delivered – and Britain properly equipped for the future – if we get the best out of all people – developing the full potential of all our young people, and that cannot happen without continuous and accessible equality of opportunity. And this means that we must break down all the old barriers that in Britain hold people back and deny opportunity. Too often in the old Britain – the old Britain characterised by the old-school tie and the old-boy network – what counted was the privilege you were born to when what should have counted was the potential you were born with. What mattered too often was where you came from when what should have mattered was what you aspired to. What was valued was often the connections you had when what should have been valued was the contribution you might make. What was re-warded in the old Britain was too often background, class, inheri-tance, when it should have been merit, effort and contribution to the community.

So in the interests of opportunities for all our children and the health of our economy, I want Britain to move from the closed society it has been to the open society it can become; from élitism in education to excellence that is accessible to all; from enterprise too often confined to a closed circle of that élite to enterprise opened up to all; from entrenched privileges for the few that disadvantaged the many to opportunity for all that benefits the whole country. And once we take this view that what matters on both ethical and economic grounds is genuinely equal opportunities to realise po-tential, we are challenged not only to remove barriers of class, race, sex and other discrimination, but to positively shape and implement policies that will equalise opportunities for all. And in each case there must be a permanent duty on government not only to actively seek this objective, but to set out our national economic goals, as we have done, to achieve this.

Let us recall that in 1942 – fifty-eight years ago – Sir William Beveridge identified five evils – ignorance, squalor, want, idleness and disease – which a new Welfare State had to confront. He wrote about 'an attack upon five giant evils – upon the physical want with which it is directly concerned, upon disease which often causes that want, and brings other troubles in its train, upon ignorance which no democracy can afford among its citizens, upon squalor . . . Upon idleness which destroys wealth and corrupts men'.

Our goal today must be even more ambitious than the one Beveridge set us when he attacked these five giant evils. In each of the areas he defined we must move forward from the Beveridge policies for subsistence and minimum standards to modern policies for maximum opportunity and fulfilment. Instead of just securing freedom from want – sufficiency and minimum standards – our goal is prosperity for all, that by 2010 by committing ourselves to achieve a faster rise in productivity than our competitors and thus a faster rise in living standards, we can spread the benefits of prosperity to everyone. In this way economic stability and growth can be the foundation for social justice.

Second, instead of simply attacking unemployment, the goal of full and fulfilling employment; that by 2010 by opening employment opportunity to all, with a permanent duty on government to pursue this objective, we can have more in work than ever before.

Instead of simply attacking ignorance, the goal of lifelong education for all; that by 2010 by expanding educational opportunity we achieve permanent, recurrent or lifelong education – for any course, any study, any age – and fully extend educational opportunity to all so that no one is written off.

Instead of simply tackling disease, not just an NHS there when you need it but health and social policies that can prevent as well as cure disease and promote good health.

And – what I want to concentrate on today – the fifth goal: policies that will ensure the best possible start in life for every child.

But with this commitment to new opportunities and new rights come also new obligations and new responsibilities upon all of us. And I believe that as advocates for this coming decade of economic and social renewal we should reclaim not only the value of fairness, as we root out economic and social injustice, but we should affirm the value of personal responsibility.

In the past we correctly accused the right of concentrating exclusively on individual responsibility and refusing to recognise social injustice – a neat device that allowed them to blame the victim, and abandon the poor. But in the past as the left correctly called for social justice, we were accused of understimating the importance of personal responsibility. Indeed it was because we were caricatured as advocating rights without responsibilities that we were vulnerable to the attack of the right and their revolt against collective action, to the right's dogma that individuals – even children – should be left to their destiny, that the state should stand aside if not wither away and that there was no such thing as society.

Now, with our understanding that individual responsibility matters within a responsible society, the argument of the right has fallen. And the way is open for that responsible society to draw support from the public as we tackle the structural injustices that exist. So just as our commitment to responsibility means that governments should not seek to substitute for, but instead should support, stable intact families, so too our commitment to social justice means that communities and governments must play their part in strengthening the capacity of parents to raise children, helping people struggling to balance work and families and tackling child poverty.

And to tackle child poverty we will first provide increased financial support for families. Second, we will offer new help for parents in a national childcare strategy. Third, we will invest more in education and strengthen our schools. Fourth, in areas of need, we will expand Sure Start help – and help for children of all ages most at risk – by investing more in education, health and services to tackle the causes of poverty and we will do so by encouraging local action. Fifth, starting with our new children's fund, a new alliance for children bringing together national and local government and voluntary and community groups.

. . .

On 8 July 2004 the Chancellor gave the Joseph Rowntree Centenary Lecture, entitled 'Our Children Are Our Future'. This is a *tour de force* piece and no apology is given for including it, albeit it repeats some earlier material. It covers the background and the philosophy underpinning all aspects of the action being taken by the government on child poverty. It is also a powerful argument for doing more to create equality of opportunity and equity of outcome for this crucial sector. And it is also a recognition that action at this level needs a new compact between the state and those who benefit from the measures. In the speech the Chancellor clearly endorses the radicalism of the approach being taken in Sure Start under which services for the under-fives not only involve voluntary and charitable action at a local level – even more so than there has been in the past – but also the running of these local groups is being passed to community control, with hugely impressive benefits which the Chancellor clearly recognises.

The speech is also noteworthy for its appraisal of what more needs to be done in this area. The Chancellor explains that (even) after seven years of government he is not less idealistic but more idealistic about what can be achieved. He wants Sure Start to be rolled out to all parts of the country, and building on this, perhaps even to tackle an even greater challenge – the poverty of aspiration amongst children and young people and their parents.

It is a privilege to be here today to deliver the Joseph Rowntree Foundation Centenary Lecture and let me begin by paying tribute to one hundred years of service to our community by the Rowntree Foundation: born out of Joseph Rowntree's concern and Christian outrage about poverty and deprivation; built by the dedicated commitment of people who had a vision of the world not as it was but as it could be; and today widely acknowledged to be at the heart of what I can call the nationwide crusade for justice for the poor, with not just an established and well-deserved reputation for authoritative research that consistently shines a spotlight on the needs of our country's families but a path-breaking role in finding practical solutions – that started with pioneering developments in housing and community regeneration and now extends into not just housing and community regeneration but innovative forms of care for the young, the elderly and the disabled.

So in a century of service, the Rowntree Foundation, always rooted in values of public service, always driven forward by ideas and often painstaking research, always a tangible national expression of compassion in action – taking its rightful place as one of the great British national institutions. So I want today at the outset to congratulate all of you – board, staff, supporters, campaigners – on your years of progress and achievement. And I hope you can be proud that your concern – poverty; your mission – to shock the nation into action against poverty; and your driving ambition – the eradication of poverty – for far too many years a call for justice unheard in a political wilderness, is the ambition now not just of your organisation but the ambition of this country's government. And let me also say today that I am humbled not just to deliver this lecture to this Foundation but to address a gathering of so many people who have served our communities and country with such distinction, men and women here today in this audience so distinguished in their own spheres of service – charity workers, social workers, community activists, academics, researchers, NGO leaders. You have not only worked year after year to tackle social evils but have worked tirelessly in some of the most difficult circumstances, keeping the flame of compassion alive often in some of the least propitious times and in some of the darkest and most challenging corners of our community. So especially for those who have toiled at the front line – often with few resources and little support – let me place on record my appreciation of the service so many of you give – of the work you do, the contribution you make, the dedication you show and the real difference you make.

Let us think back to the conditions Joseph Rowntree surveyed one hundred years ago: the first building blocks of the modern Welfare State yet to be established, the Lloyd George People's Budget still a few years away, but Victorian and Edwardian society starting to discover the full scale of poverty in their midst; and Winston Churchill – who went on to introduce the first minimum wage – appalled by the huge gap between what he called the excesses of accumulated privilege and the gaping sorrows of the left-out millions. And about Joseph Rowntree we could have no doubt: an idealist not a dreamer; an enthusiastic reformer not a reluctant donor; and in his lifetime and through the Foundation he created we can genuinely say that he led the way in four areas vital to the development of our social services and the fabric of our community life.

First, his plea – and I quote – that we 'search out the underlying causes of weakness or evil in the community rather than remedying their more superficial manifestations'. You might call it tough love: his rightful insistence that we tackle the sources of poverty and not just their consequences; that we should focus on the eradication of the evil of social injustice and not just compensate people for its existence.

Second, Rowntree's insistence on an evidence-based approach. Indeed his Foundation is a monument to one man's conviction that the lives of countless fellow citizens can be improved by the intelligent application of knowledge and then policy to one of the greatest social evils and one of the greatest moral challenges of the day.

And that led, thirdly, to an understanding of the multiple causes of poverty, and the multidimensional nature of poverty. And although there have been many changes in the last one hundred years – for when he began there was no sickness benefit, no state pensions, no unemployment benefit and no National Health Service – I am struck by the fact that the multiple challenges that Rowntree identified in his 'Founder's Memorandum' still remain relevant today – the challenge of poverty itself, of bad housing, poor education, neighbourhood renewal. And you could say that he understood what was meant by multiple deprivation long before the term was even invented. And finally it led him – and the Foundation – to pioneer an understanding of the life cycle of poverty. In 1904, Rowntree described that tragic life cycle – of poverty during childhood, poverty for parents when they had children and poverty during old age: a life cycle of poverty broken only by the short periods when you were an adult before your children were born or an adult whose children had grown up and left home.

And the striking truth about what we found in 1997 was how firmly and how widely this 'life cycle of poverty' had returned. And I believe that Rowntree would agree that addressing the multiple causes of poverty and the life cycle of poverty in our times, demands we be far bolder than the philanthropists of 1904. Let us recall that in 1942 – nearly forty years after the Rowntree Foundation was set up and in response to some of its pioneering work – Sir William Beveridge identified five evils – want, idleness, ignorance, squalor and disease – which a new Welfare State had to confront. But because we are interested in the potential of every person, our goal today – inspired by Rowntree – must be even more ambitious than the one Beveridge set us in 1942 when he listed his five evils:

- instead of simply attacking idleness and unemployment, our goal is the genuinely challenging goal of full and fulfilling employment;
- instead of simply attacking ignorance, our goal is the more ambitious goal of lifelong education for all;
- instead of simply attacking squalor, our goal is high-quality affordable housing for all and not just houses but strong and sustainable communities;
- instead of simply tackling disease, our goal is not just an NHS there when you need it but health and social policies that can prevent as well as cure disease and promote good health; and
- instead of just securing freedom from want – which meant sufficiency and minimum standards – our goal is the development of the potential of all to secure prosperity for all.

And in addressing these great challenges, our objective must be to ensure not only dignity for the elderly in retirement and the chance for all adults to realise their potential but that every child has the best possible start in life. And it is on the needs of children and the challenges ahead that I want to concentrate my remarks on policy today.

. . .

The return in the last three decades of the life cycle of poverty – indeed the great and unacceptable concentration of poverty amongst households with young children – is the greatest indictment of our country in this generation and the greatest challenge of all. The facts are that in the two decades before 1997 the number of children growing up in workless households – households where no one had a job – rose to almost 20 per cent. One in every five children did not have a parent earning any income from work. The numbers of children in low-income households more than doubled to over 4 million. And you must never forget that the UK – one of the richest countries of the industrial world – suffered worse levels of child poverty than nearly all other industrialised nations. Indeed, anyone reading reports on the condition of Britain will be shocked by one straightforward but disgraceful fact. When we came into government one in every three babies born in Britain were being born into low-income households; born not into opportunity but into poverty.

This is the 'condition of Britain' question we had to confront one hundred years after the Joseph Rowntree Foundation was set up. And it is the 'condition of Britain' question still with us fifty years after Beveridge and the creation of the Welfare State. Not only was child poverty endemic by 1997 but social mobility had slowed – in some respects, gone into reverse. And while more room existed at the top, a child from the lowest social class was a quarter as likely to make it to that place at the top as the child from the highest social class. But during these years when child poverty grew, so too did our understanding of all that we had to do to tackle child poverty – and in particular just how crucial the first months and certainly the first years of a child's life are in determining life chances. Indeed recent research suggests that much of children's future prospects can be predicted within twenty-four months of them being born. Leon Feinstein has shown how psychological and behavioural differences varying strongly by social class can be seen in children as young as twenty-two months and continue to have a systematic – and increasingly significant – effect on employment and earnings patterns right through to later life. Research undertaken in the US shows that pre-school experiences in language and literacy are strong predictors of later development in language and literacy. And the Effective Provision of Pre-School Education project in the UK found that children who participated in some sort of early learning made significantly more progress than those who didn't. Abigail McKnight concludes that individuals who experience childhood poverty tend to suffer a penalty in labour-market earnings in adult life, and that the size of this penalty has grown over time. For we now also know from your research that an infant who then grows up in a poor family is less likely to stay on at school, or even attend school regularly, less likely to get qualifications and go to college, more likely to be trapped in the worst job or no job at all, more likely to be trapped in a cycle of deprivation that is lifelong . . . less likely to reach his or her full potential: a young child's chances crippled even before their life's journey has barely begun.

I believe that action to eradicate child poverty is the obligation this generation owes to the next. Children may not have votes – or the loudest voices . . . or at least their voices are not often heard in our politics – but our obligation is, if anything, greater because of this.
. . .

So in 1999, determined to ensure that each child has the chance to realise his or her potential, the government set an ambitious long-term goal to halve child poverty by 2010 and eradicate it by 2020. Tackling child poverty is, for us, the critical first step in ensuring that each child has the chance to develop their potential to the full. And as a first step, we have sought to reduce the number of children in low-income households by April 2005 at least a quarter. So far, measured by absolute low income, 2 million children have been lifted out of poverty; so far too, measured by relative low income, half a million children have been lifted out. And I think there is general agreement that having allocated resources to raise our Child Tax Credits for the poorest families, we are on track to meet our target of reducing child poverty by a quarter by April next year. But we are not complacent in any way nor will we relax our efforts or allow them to be stalled. The next step – our goal of, by 2010, reducing child poverty by half – is even more challenging and how we reach this goal is the subject of the remaining observations I want to share with you.

I can tell you today that in the Spending Review next week we will set out the detail of the target for 2010 – to halve the number of children in households in relative low income compared to 1998. As many of you have proposed to us, next Monday we will also set out an additional target to halve the numbers of children suffering from material deprivation – children lacking basic necessities the rest of us take for granted. And because we know from your research that the quality of housing is critical in tackling poverty, we will – as part of this new material-deprivation measure – be monitoring the quality of a child's housing conditions. Acting, I believe, in the spirit of Rowntree.

And so let me point you to the policy changes that I believe are now necessary if we are to meet this anti-poverty target, the means by which we seek to develop the potential of millions of British children.

. . .

While universal Child Benefit is the foundation, it is the introduction of the Child Tax Credit – now benefiting 6 million families and 10 million children – that allows us, while giving more to every child, to give most to those who need it most, and is thus the front line of our attack on child poverty. So with the addition of the Child Tax Credit the nine out of ten families who would in 1997 have received just £11 in Child Benefits now receive more than twice as much – £27 a week. For the poorest families tax credits go even further: with one child under eleven, financial support which was £28 in 1997 is now £58.22 – a near doubling in real terms. And a family with two children under eleven can now receive in children's benefits over £100 a week.

Indeed, progress is being made to meeting our child-poverty target because the poorest 20 per cent of families have received not 20 per cent of all additional money but over 40 per cent. And, as a result, while all families with children are on average £1,350 a year better off now than they were in 1997, the poorest 20 per cent of families are £3,000 a year better off. For the rest of this parliament we will continue to uprate the child element of the Child Tax Credit in line with earnings – and I can tell you today that in future Pre-Budget Reports and Budgets we will assess progress towards our 2010 goal. As a government we have also come to realise that if we are to meet our child-poverty goals and ensure that there is equality in opportunity but also fairness in outcome, assets matter as well as income. So to each child born after September 2002 an initial contribution to their own individual Child Trust Fund of £250, with twice as much – £500 – for the poorest third of children; and then again a contribution at seven and then perhaps at later ages to enable all young people to have more of the choices that were once available only to some. With the new Child Trust Fund worth twice as much for the poorest child; with the Child Tax Credit worth four times as much for the poorest child; and with five times as much for the poorest infant – our anti-poverty commitment is based on a progressive principle which I believe that all decent-minded people can and should support: more for every child, even more help for those who need it most and at the time they need it most, equality of opportunity and fairness of outcome applied in new times and with tax credits the principal new means.

And as we develop our policies on financial support over the coming years, I recognise from your research and policy proposals that we have not done enough in a number of important ways and that there are major issues which now need to be addressed including:

- first, the costs faced by larger families and the consequences for benefits and tax credits; and
- second, the housing costs faced by the low-paid, and this requires us also to evaluate the way housing benefit interacts with the tax and benefit system and the impact of the pilots for paying flat-rate housing benefit.

So looking ahead we will continue to address the issue of children's benefits but we have also always been clear about the importance of the contribution of family employment to meeting our child-poverty targets. And of course we must get the balance right between supporting mothers to stay at home, particularly in the early years, and creating opportunities for employment. Again it is because of tax credits – which create a new tax system whose rates start at 40 per cent at the top but go to as low as minus 200 per cent for the lowest-income earners – that a lone parent with one child working thirty-five hours at the minimum wage is now £73 a week better off in work than on benefit. And a couple with one child and one parent working thirty-five hours at the minimum wage is now around £38 a week better off in work than on benefit. Because the starting wage for the unemployed man or woman returning to work is typically only two-thirds of the average hourly rate, the Child and Working Tax Credits have been designed not just to help people into work but to help people in work move up the jobs ladder and into higher incomes. Under the old system of family credit, 740,000 households faced marginal tax and benefit withdrawal rates of over 70 per cent; now the new credits have cut this figure by nearly two-thirds, helping people keep more of every extra pound they earn.

In total, 1.8 million more people are in jobs now than in 1997, with unemployment reduced to its lowest level in thirty years. But if we are to meet our child-poverty targets we must advance further and faster to full employment in every community and we must make it a priority to reach the still-large number of households with children where no adult works. And of crucial importance in meeting our child-poverty target for 2010 will be employment opportunity for lone parents. It is a striking fact that lone-parent households contain a quarter of all children but account for nearly half of those in poverty. As a result one and a half million of the country's poorest children are today living on benefit in lone-parent families where no one has a job. Since 1997 250,000 more lone parents have gone into work. Because of the New Deal, the minimum wage, the Working Tax Credit and other initiatives, the lone-parent rate of employment in the UK has increased to 53 per cent. But in the US lone-parent employment is more than 60 per cent, in Sweden above 70 per cent and in France in excess of 80 per cent. Our target is 70 per cent lone-parent employment by 2010. And let me explain the significance of this ambition. If we meet our target to raise lone-parent employment, this one success alone could reduce the number of British children living in poverty by around 300,000. And if we went even further to French levels we could reduce the number of children in poverty by a total of approaching half a million.

Now research shows most lone parents would like to combine paid work with the vital job of being a parent. But they face real barriers to doing so. And those who work with lone parents – and lone parents themselves – have rightly called on us to do more to help them get the skills they need for work and to ease the transition between income support and paid work. So while all lone parents are now invited in for work-focused interviews, we are also piloting new lone-parent 'work discovery weeks' – run by employers in London, Glasgow, Liverpool, Manchester, Leeds and Birmingham – that are providing introductory and preparatory courses for work in some of our best-known retail stores, hotels and companies – and are backed up by help with child care. Where local employers identify a demand for skills lone parents in these six cities also have access to free NVQ Level 3 training – and funds to buy work clothes or equipment. And because we recognise that the time of transition from benefits to employment can be difficult, from October lone parents will benefit from a new job grant of £250 when they move into work and they will enjoy a four-week extension of Housing Benefit.

So what does the success of our recent measures mean in practice for tackling child poverty? It means that with the new help with Housing Benefit, lone parents on a typical rent of £50 a week and working part time will receive at least £217 a week for around sixteen hours' work a week. The effective hourly rate is not the minimum wage of £4.50 but £13.50 an hour – making them far better off working part-time than not working at all. And so we have come to recognise that central to tackling child poverty – as well as to the importance of helping families balance work and family life – is the provision of adequate child care. And while we have since 1997 created over a million more childcare places, the greatest help for low-income families has been the third element of tax credits that we have introduced – the tax credit for covering the costs of child care – up to £95 each week for families with one child in qualifying child care and up to £140 for those with two or more children. When we started in 1997 it was claimed by just 47,000 families; it is now benefiting 320,000, with maximum help given to lone parents. And while we ensure that by 2008 nearly 2.5 million children a year will have access to good-quality child care, again for poor families the next stage in the extension of the childcare tax credit is of greatest importance – from April 2005 extended to a wider range of eligible child care including, in some cases, at home. And the tax credit will be supported by a new incentive for employers – to give their employees up to £50 a week, free of income tax and National Insurance, to help with childcare costs.

So tax credits have been and will continue to be the key to tackling child poverty. But as a government we also have a duty and role to play in encouraging the development of the potential of Britain's children through the provision of high-quality public services – and Bruce Katz has this morning shown why one of our priorities must be to drive up the performance of public services in our most deprived neighbourhoods and thus break long-established cycles of deprivation. And I do not underestimate the critical role that new investment in housing can play. Of all the services that contribute to the development of potential, a good education – the subject of the government's five-year plan today – is clearly the most fundamental. So as I announced in the Budget, we are investing over three years an additional £8.5 billion in education; raising average spending per pupil from the £2,500 a year we inherited to £5,500 by 2008 – and, as a sign of our commitment to tackling disadvantage – by even more in the 1,400 schools that benefit from our extra support for leadership and excellence to combat deprivation.

We have, indeed, a long way to go in ensuring for today's poor children a decent start in life but it is important to record that the greatest improvement so far in reading, writing and maths has been in the primary schools of the poorest areas. And I can tell you that the next stage is to help at an early stage the very pupils most in danger of falling behind – and with extra money for their books, and their classrooms, equipment and staffing drive up their literacy and numeracy. I can also inform you that secondary schools with more than 35 per cent of their fourteen-year-olds eligible for free meals are now making the biggest gains in maths and science results at Key Stage 3. Indeed the number of secondary schools with less than 25 per cent of their pupils achieving five or more good GCSEs has fallen from over 600 in 1997 to 224. And today's five-year plan sets out our next steps – with the very pupils most in need offered more personalised learning, including new vocational options, and greater access to them.

I can tell you also that in the Spending Review there will be new, more challenging floor targets for the poorest areas. And as part of the review of the local formulae used to distribute schools funding – due to take place later this year – I would like to identify even more effective ways to target resources at tackling deprivation: measures to help children in the bottom-income quintile catch up, particularly in primary school, and measures to enable schools to meet the higher costs of educating children from poorer backgrounds who may have lower levels of early educational attainment and who may have far less parental support.

Tragically Britain has, for decades, had one of the poorest staying-on rates of the industrialised world. In Britain more young people leave school early, more leave without qualifications and more never reappear in the world of education. So again to tackle both poverty and lack of opportunity – and to seek to tackle perhaps an even greater challenge, the poverty of aspiration amongst children and young people and their parents – we have reformed the careers service, introduced summer schools, encouraged better links between schools and universities and colleges. And we have piloted an Education Maintenance Allowance: up to £1,500 a year on top of Child Benefit and the Child Tax Credit for those young people who need financial help to stay on in education and get the qualifications they need. And so successful has the allowance been in raising staying-on rates that from September this year it will be available nationwide; and as it goes nationwide be made available not just for school and further-education courses but for training too – once again helping all young people, but doing more for those who need help most so that no child is left behind.

I said at the outset that while we are committed to social security from the cradle to the grave, too many children have already lost out within months of being born – condemned to poverty because not enough has been done to help them from the cradle to the nursery school. Indeed for fifty years while there was undoubtedly much innovation in the voluntary and charitable sector, Welfare State support for the country's youngest children consisted of maternity services, vaccinations and a requirement to appear at school at age five. Yet while the provision remained inadequate the evidence grew that the first four years of a child's life are critical to their personal development; that children who went to nursery or other early education before they attended school were likely to have significantly improved social, emotional and cognitive development; that the longer children attend pre-school – and the higher the quality of the service – the greater the positive influence; and that such intervention was particularly beneficial for the poorest children. And so it is clear that a strategy of counteracting disadvantage must begin right from the start of a child's life and that the earliest years – once the lowest priority – are now rightly becoming among the highest priority: not just the biggest gap in provision and next frontier for us to cross, but one of the single most important investments the Welfare State can make.

The Sure Start Maternity Grant – once just £100 – has been raised to £500, a five-fold rise in five years. Reversing a long-standing policy that more Child Benefits went to older rather than younger children, we doubled the Child Tax Credit for the first year of a child's life. To help parents stay at home with their children, maternity leave and pay has been substantially extended and paternity pay now exists for the first time. And earlier than planned, nursery education is now available for all three-year-olds as well as all four-year-olds.

Now, in the past to identify a problem – the need to expand provision for infants from birth to three – would probably have led simply to the creation of a new state service. But I believe that what today is happening in the area of under-five provision shows how what we do – in the spirit of Rowntree – is based upon evidence; how the best approach is multi-dimensional – across the services – and the range of provision mixed; and how, instead of a narrow focus on what central government can do, voluntary and community organisations, and parents, and government – local and national – through not just one service but a range of services – child-health services, social services, and early learning – are now all part of the solution.

I often say that Sure Start is today one of the best-kept secrets of government, but it is also one of the unsung successes of the voluntary and community sector. And there are now over 500 Sure Start or children's centres providing services for 400,000 children across the country, including a third of all children under four living in poverty. And you have only to visit local Sure Start projects – as I did in Bristol a few weeks ago and then in Birmingham last week – to capture a very real sense of the difference they are making: and already evidence from individual projects in some of Britain's most deprived areas shows that Sure Start is having a notable effect on children's language development and social skills, and on the interaction of parents and their children.

What is then exciting about Sure Start and the approach it represents? I believe that what is exciting is what Rowntree himself would have approved of – and what Rowntree Foundation research has pointed towards: first, a coordinated approach to services for families with young children, tackling the multi-dimensional causes of poverty – physical, intellectual, emotional and social – by adopting an integrated approach with child care, early education and play, health services and family support at the core of Sure Start. It reflects a growing recognition that housing, health, transport, social services, youth and many other services are vital in tackling child poverty and developing young people's potential. And the new Public Service Agreements we will be publishing alongside our commitment to new investment for these services will reflect this.

Second, the emphasis within this approach on health and inequality highlighted by today's report of the Health Care Commission. And later this year there will be a new public-health White Paper – refocusing our attention on preventive health – which will emphasise once more the importance of tackling the unacceptable health inequalities – including infant life chances – which distort our country.

Third, Sure Start is emphasising the central role of parents in tackling child poverty – and that is why parents are enlisted in the very running of the Sure Start projects. We must never forget that it is parents who bring children up, not governments, and our emphasis is on the opportunities now available to parents and the responsibilities they must discharge. So we are not only increasing the financial support available to parents – and exploring options for future further increases in maternity and paternity pay – but making available wider support for parents, including expanding parenting classes and providing access to practical parenting advice in a wider range of locations.

Fourth, the central role of voluntary community and charitable organisations from mothers-and-toddlers' groups to the playgroup and childcare movement to a vast and impressive range of specialist organisations throughout our country. It is a humble recognition of the limits of government – that child poverty cannot be removed by the action of government alone but by government, working with parents, voluntary, charitable and community organisations – and a celebration of the vital role of the voluntary and community sector in every city and town of our country. And let us not forget that alongside traditional voluntary organisations – like the churches and uniformed organisations for young people – that have been declining in numbers, there has been a mushrooming of young mothers' groups, playgroups, and groups and clubs associated with children locally and nationally. And let us be clear about the radicalism of our approach. For Sure Start also enacts an important new principle into action – that services for the under-fives not only involve voluntary and charitable action at a local level – even more so than we have done in the past – but either in partnership or in sole control, the very running of these local groups can be and is being passed to community control. And it is a recognition that we must all accept our responsibilities as parents, neighbours, citizens and community leaders, in the battle against child poverty.

And of course there is a fifth innovation: the far greater emphasis on early learning – so early that it can start with the local school contacting the mother not in the months before the child's fifth birthday but just a few weeks after the child is born – backed up by innovations like Bookstart offering children the books they might not otherwise have, to start in their first months to learn to read.

And we can see now how, combined with the improved income support for the under-fives that I have described, the additional cash resources for early learning and the support for the specialist groups – many represented here – that deal with disability, special needs and other challenges, a new more comprehensive approach not just to tackling child poverty but to developing the potential of every child is taking shape. And as we approach the Spending Review next week and advance to the Pre-Budget Report, I can tell you that what I have described this morning can only be the start of what we have yet to do. Building on Sure Start, the next stage is to fund the creation of new Children's Centres across the country – again providing a combination of good-quality child care, early-years education, family support and health services. By 2006, 650,000 children will be covered by Sure Start or Children's Centres. And there will be new funding – despite our other representations – to ensure 1,700 Children's Centres by 2008 – one in each of the 20 per cent most deprived wards in England, as we advance towards our goal of a Children's Centre for every community.

But Sure Start – and related services – point the way for a new agenda for services for young children: greater encouragement for local initiatives and community action in the war against child poverty; offering government money to back non-government initiatives to tackle disadvantage; partnership with both the biggest voluntary and community organisations and the smallest; the emphasis on prevention, not simply coping with failure; greater parental involvement in the running of services. And anyone who like me has attended a Sure Start conference – and seen the dynamism, energy and determination of parents, volunteers and carers in action – can begin to understand the transformative power that organisations from the playgroup movement to the childcare campaigns can have. And I look forward to the 'little platoons' in our communities becoming veritable armies demanding we do more.

So new finance, like tax credits; new initiatives, like the New Deal for lone parents; new dimensions, like support for child care; new services, like Sure Start; new approaches, whole services managed by the voluntary sector; new directions, engaging parents in the running of programmes. All weapons in the war against child poverty, all evidence that parents, voluntary organisations and government can, acting together, make a real difference. All evidence also that, informed by knowledge, working with the best of caring organisations, public action can transform young lives. Go to a Sure Start programme, as I did a few days ago – and see the bright new investments that are starting to change the face of some of the most deprived areas of our country. Listen to a mother, once feeling trapped in her home, telling you how Sure Start has introduced her to other mothers with similar stories to tell. Hear the views of children of lone parents – telling of their pride that their mother now has a job. And hear the responses of parents on the Child and Working Tax Credits – describing how what they can spend on their children has been raised by £50 a week.

And so I tell you: after seven years of government I am not less idealistic but more idealistic about what we can achieve working together. Because we now have evidence of what can be done by Sure Start in some areas of the country, we want to apply the lessons to all parts of the country. And because we have evidence of the good that is done for some children, then we want to extend these opportunities to all children. And what started, for us, seven years ago as an article of faith about what might be achieved is now a conviction based on clear evidence about what can and must be done. Because what has been done shows us what more can be done, because the evidence of small successes shows what even larger successes are possible, it must make us more even more ambitious to do more. So my experience of government has not diminished my desire to tackle child poverty but made me more determined to do more. For what has happened so far does not begin to speak to the limits of our aspirations for developing the potential of Britain's children, but challenges us to learn from the changes now being made and strive in future years to do even more. So on Monday I will be able to announce the next stage in our policies for tackling child poverty and for helping the development of the potential of every child – and I believe as a country we are ready to do more to tackle old injustices, meet new needs and solve new challenges.

But what we can achieve depends upon the growth of a nationwide sentiment of opinion – indeed, a shared and concerted demand across communities, across social classes, across parties, across all decent-minded people – that the eradication of child poverty is a cause that demands the priority, the resources, and the national attention it deserves. It is not usual for governments to welcome the growth of pressure groups that will lobby, demonstrate, embarrass, expose and then push them to action. But I welcome the New Alliance for Children – the broad coalition of community organisations, the voluntary and charitable sector determined to push further to end child poverty. For the emerging evidence – and the growth in a nationwide public opinion – emboldens me to believe it can indeed be this generation of campaigners, charity workers, child carers, Sure Start organisers, working together, that will right the social wrongs that impelled Joseph Rowntree to action and ensure every child has a fair start in life.

So let us continue to follow the lead given by the pioneers who brought the Rowntree Foundation into being. And inspired by a generation of reformers like Rowntree who had a vision; driven forward – as the Rowntree Foundation has always been – by the evidence of what is happening around us; never losing sight of the vision that inspired a whole generation; our eyes fixed firmly on the goal that if every child has the best start in life, we can build a better Britain.

7

MODERN PUBLIC SERVICES

'When I was a boy,' Gordon said, 'my father told me story after story about the fear which illness brought to families as they faced up to the crippling costs of seeking treatment for loved ones.' Clearly, removal of that fear was a wonderful release and had a huge impact on people's lives. And a big impact on Gordon, as it had on me. As he spoke, I could hear my own parents telling me similar stories about their own experiences in their early years in the North East of England.

His pride shone through that his party had changed Britain so substantially, with such benefit for so many, after 1948. So did his passionate belief that our National Health Service played a crucial role in defining 'Britishness'. The NHS was, as described in the Bevan Lecture, a clear, enduring and practical expression of those shared values which shape our country. Equally clear was his determination that he and his colleagues in government, the 'successors of Bevan' who were likely to be in power for a good few years, should reform health services to ensure successful delivery for decades to come, meeting the challenges of changing demographics and new treatments.

Would I, he asked, be prepared to review the resources needed, long term, for UK health services to continue to provide comprehensive, high-quality services? For the first but not the last time, I encountered a steely stare as I suggested that these terms of reference would have to change. 'Continue to provide comprehensive, high-quality services', I said, seemed to make too many assumptions about the adequacy of the quality being delivered in 2000. Surely he wanted to aim much higher? A warm smile returned. He did indeed have concerns about the service being delivered; he had a vision of a much better service and it was that which he wished to play his part in creating: innovative, using new technologies well and playing an important role in developing a healthy and skilled UK population.

When, a year later, I presented the findings to him, his view was clear that the prudence of his early years as Chancellor had, indeed, been for a purpose.

This was no mere slogan but an important part of his strategy falling into place. But what the findings showed was that some other countries had combined equality of access with better delivery. The defining difference of 1948 had been lost. And, by 2006, it is a measure of his own success that the Conservative Party has apparently accepted all he said. No longer can he claim that a free NHS at the point of need is the central dividing line between the political parties. The debate, and no doubt Gordon Brown's speeches, will move on to the issue of how to achieve successful implementation and reform. Have the processes and the measurement systems delivered? Has his trust in colleagues to produce results borne sufficient fruit? That is where the eventual judgement will be made.

Sir Derek Wanless

As a medical practitioner and heart specialist, I spent almost the entire first half of my professional career focused on learning, practising and developing my specific branch of medicine. I was soon to realise that achieving the potential and morals of medicine both now and in the future depends critically on having the appropriate system of health-care delivery and investing heavily in research. Having had first-hand experience with different systems around the world and working for a long time (more than forty years) for the NHS left me with no doubt about the unique nature and superiority of the NHS, both as a concept and in practical terms.

The speeches of the Chancellor, Gordon Brown, published in this book indicate clearly his commitment, coupled with deep understanding of the NHS as a whole, and the practicalities involved, including investing in basic science and applied research. Having listened to Gordon on more than one occasion, I am convinced that upholding the principles of the NHS and planning for the future is one of his main overall targets. As he repeatedly affirms, the NHS says a lot about the morals and aspirations of people of this country and is a unique model for the rest of the world and therefore must be preserved and developed in spite of the continuous changes and challenges.

Sir Magdi Yacoub, FRS

A recurring theme in the speeches of the Chancellor has been the question of the role to be played by the state in the provision of public services. However, as the Chancellor explains in the speeches collected in this chapter, this issue is also a debate about what kind of country we are, because it is a debate not just about the right choice of health-care system, or the technicalities of how best to finance public services, but about the national values the people of Britain hold to be important. And in the Aneurin Bevan Memorial Lecture the Chancellor argues that social policy has always to be rooted in the shared experience of the nation. Asserting that Bevan's philosophy was not abstract or theoretical, the Chancellor argues that Bevan's social-inclusion policies started from what he saw around him in Welsh communities, and were based on real needs found in the real lives of the real people he grew up with and worked with in South Wales. Taking off from this interesting analysis, the Chancellor argues that we need to find specific policy solutions to unique British problems which are rooted in people's experiences and histories. People from Bevan's community believed that the injustices they suffered should not just not happen to them, they should not happen to anyone. They had a vision, and in this powerful speech the Chancellor argues that this might translate, for our time, into five social-justice objectives, to be met by modern public services; a commitment to full employment; the collective provision of the best modern public services; an end to child and pensioner poverty; to ensure the best educational opportunity including higher education for the majority of young people; and to forge a new global deal for the developing world.

The following speech was given by the Chancellor on 20 March 2002 to the Social Market Foundation. Entitled 'Economic Stability and Strong Public Services', it uses health care as an example of a service which should not be left solely to market pressures. The Chancellor said at the time of the first review of the NHS (carried out for the Treasury by Sir Derek Wanless) that 'for me the NHS is a clear, enduring and practical expression of our shared values as a country – that all our citizens should have decent health care and that an NHS with quality service for all, based on need irrespective of income, should represent the realisation of this ideal'. His conclusion is that the NHS is a unique British institution that has marked Britain out in the world. This speech is a powerful exposition of why the NHS is still a good choice for Britain, fifty years after its establishment, despite huge changes in technology, public expectations and demography. He also reviews the possible funding systems

against considerations of efficiency, equity and choice. He concludes that
user-charging, social insurance and private insurance systems all fail these
tests, and unlike the NHS, fail to help those with the greatest needs, as
well as being likely to fail to deliver for those on higher incomes.

The challenge of next month's Budget is not just to build a stronger
more enterprising economy but to put the National Health Service
on a solid foundation for the long term. Our five Budgets since 1997
have pursued a consistent course: to entrench economic stability and
fiscal discipline; to cut unemployment and debt, releasing new
resources to invest in the NHS and vital public services; and, by
insisting strings are attached that match new resources to better
results, to set a proper framework for better public services.

The Secretary of State for Health has already shown – and will
continue to show in the coming months – how, to put patients first,
there will be new national standards and improved accountability,
devolution to front-line services and greater choice and flexibility. My
role as Chancellor is to ensure not just that our public services are
properly funded, but that funds are raised in a fair and efficient way
which ensures value for money. We have not come this far to put our
hard-won economic stability and fiscal discipline at risk and – with
low inflation and low unemployment again today – we will not
compromise on our economic stability. The something-for-nothing
days are over in our public services and there can be no blank
cheques.

Our ambition for the Budget and Spending Review is to put the
NHS on a sound long-term financial footing; and this must be based
on tough choices between and within departments, matching resources with reform. In the coming Budget and Spending Round,
before committing the Treasury to additional expenditure, we will
need to know of Health and all departments whether extra spending
is a priority, whether there is a clear strategy of reform to deliver value
for money, and the track record of increased resources leading to
improved results.

Today – in the run-up to the Budget and Spending Review – I want
to advance the debate on how we finance health care. It is a debate
crucial to the wider debate on the future shape of our public services.
Indeed it is a debate about what kind of country we are, because it is a

debate not just about the technicalities of finance but about the national values we – the people of Britain – hold to be important. It was because of our concern about the demographic, technological and other pressures on health-care services in Britain that in 2000 the Treasury announced a major review on long-term health-finance needs and appointed Mr Derek Wanless to conduct it.

Having received his interim report at the time of the Pre-Budget Report, the government urged that a national debate should take place. In the same way there was a national consensus after 1948 on the funding of the NHS, a new national consensus should be sought for the future funding of health care, one that matches greater reform and modernisation of the NHS with greater resources. I said at the time of the Wanless Review that for me the NHS is a clear, enduring and practical expression of our shared values as a country – that all our citizens should have decent health care and that an NHS with quality service for all, based on need irrespective of income, should represent the realisation of this ideal. Indeed I was brought up to believe that the NHS reflected what Professor Richard Titmuss called the 'gift relationship', giving practical effect to people's altruistic as well as self-interested impulses – a unique British institution that has marked Britain out in the world.

My own experiences have confirmed that instinct and that belief: that the uniqueness, indeed the greatness, of the NHS as a British institution is that – with its dedicated and expert staff – it is designed to be there when you need it, open to all, no matter what your circumstances. And there is evidence that this view of the NHS is shared by the majority of British people too. But at a time when its values, its affordability and even its right to existence are being questioned, it is proper – indeed essential – for us to examine all our assumptions about the future of health care and its funding here in Britain. At the time of the Pre-Budget Report, I asked those who advocate a different way to pay for health care in Britain to come forward with their specific proposals.

Today, having examined the main alternatives – user charges, private insurance and social insurance – I want to set out the government's own analysis. And I want to set out our views not just by reference to the past and the present. For what we need is not just a funding system able to meet the health-care needs of today but one that meets the challenges of the long-term future – particularly the increasing cost of technology, demographic change and rising expectations.

There was an assumption after 1948 that, once health care was free at the point of delivery, demand would fall as the backlog was cleared. But for a whole range of reasons, that did not happen. In 1948 the NHS offered 400,000 operations in NHS hospitals and 1 million outpatients were seen. Today there are 6.5 million operations each year, with over 40 million outpatient appointments. The first reason for this is the growth in availability of new treatments and drugs as a result of technological advance. It has been suggested that this huge expansion in technology and in its costs calls into question the entire nature of the health service. Over the last half-century technology has opened up vast new areas of diagnosis and treatment. We know more, we can do more, so we can deal with many more illnesses and save many more lives. And as a result of the progress of the last fifty years, many illnesses and injuries that were not then survivable can now be treated with confidence and a new certainty of success.

So the medical miracles of a generation ago are commonplace occurrences today. And of course the rate of accumulation of new knowledge – and new abilities to intervene – continues to increase. We are in the midst of a pharmaceutical and biomedical revolution with – looking to the future – new techniques from genetics to stem-cell therapy and new drugs to prevent, alleviate or cure conditions like Alzheimer's and HIV/AIDS.

But costs are increasing too. For while a maturing technology often brings rising cost effectiveness, each emerging technology that is proved effective brings new demands for its use. Many new technologies, like minimally invasive surgical procedures, are cheaper than the old technologies which they replaced – largely because they are less traumatic and hospital stay has fallen accordingly – but their convenience has substantially increased referral and uptake, leading to greater costs too.

And as drug efficacy and acceptability improves, more patients will be treated over the longer term to prevent harm and disease: for example, with statins to lower cholesterol – where the numbers using them are expected to rise dramatically from 1 million to over 6 million by 2010 – or anti-hypertensives to reduce the likelihood of strokes. Overall, the average annual increase in the cost of medicines, dressings and appliances dispensed in the community rose by nearly

10 per cent per year during the 1990s. Some drugs – such as those used to treat metabolic disorders – can now cost up to £8,000 per prescription. We should never lose sight of the overwhelming trend: the good – even great – news that many more lives can be saved, many more diseases cured, many more serious and complex injuries survived.

But what challenges us is that the same new treatments, surgical procedures and curative and preventive drugs carry costs from which – in other countries – individuals and families are not protected: costs that can overwhelm family budgets, bringing poverty and bankruptcy simply from paying for health care. After more than fifty years of the NHS, it is easy for us in Britain to forget that for an individual or a family unprotected by a system such as ours the cost of catastrophic illness or an acute condition can be – and often is – literally catastrophic. And many would suggest that the last thing people who have the anxiety and fear of being sick need is the added anxiety and fear of whether they can pay for treatment.

The second challenge to health-care systems is changing demography, and with long-term care increasingly an issue of concern there is a case for looking at health and social services together. The British population is not only larger than in 1948, rising from 50 million to nearly 60 million, but older. And these trends are set to continue. The population is forecast to grow by one-fifteenth to 64 million over the next twenty years with the number of the people over sixty-five increasing by nearly a third over the same period to 12.5 million. We know that, because much of ill health is age-related, health-care costs rise with age and that the average annual cost to the NHS of a person aged over 85 is approximately six times the cost for those aged between 16 and 44. But because such systematic evidence as is available suggests that, as life expectancy rises, people will be less severely ill for longer at the end of their lives, Derek Wanless suggested in his interim report that, overall, demographic pressures will only add around 1 per cent a year to Britain's total health-care bill.

The third challenge is the increase in expectations about standards of care in hospitals and health care generally – and an increasing demand for patient choice. We know of health gaps between Britain and our main European comparators in life expectancy, infant mortality, premature mortality and survival rates from cancer and heart disease. And recent surveys show what we all know: that as well as safe, high-quality treatments, taxpayers rightly expect improvements in the quality of service the NHS offers. They want improved use of new technology, shorter waiting times, more time with their GP, a more joined-up service, and better accommodation and facilities. In fact, to move towards meeting these needs, one-third of beds in new hospitals will be in single rooms. All this reflects the fact that people want greater choice with services designed around their individual needs – the end of a 'one size fits all' approach.

Changing technology, demography and expectations provide the context within which we are considering the twenty-year funding needs of the health service. It is within this context that I want to test each possible system of health-care funding – user-charging, private insurance and social insurance – on their capacity not just to meet today's needs but future needs. And I will suggest that those who use rising expectations and new demographic and technological demands to make the case for user charges or private insurance are conveniently misusing new challenges to pursue ancient prejudices. Of course, most countries rely on a mix of different funding streams for health care but most are based predominately on one financing system. And I will examine in detail the case of those who contend that a different system would be better for Britain. There are those who argue that the NHS, while valid for the more basic needs of the 1940s, is out of date for the more sophisticated needs of today. But I will argue that the future impact of new technology makes the case for a revenue-funded National Health Service even more valid today than it was in 1948.

The first alternative to examine is user-charging – requiring patients to pay directly for all or part of the cost of a particular treatment or service. In Britain we already have user charges for dentistry and prescriptions but in other countries this phenomenon is much more extensive. At the heart of the theoretical case for widespread charging in health is the assumption that health care is a commodity to be purchased like any other – individuals paying the full price for what they consume, each household freely choosing their pattern of consumption, with the supply of health care permanently and rapidly adjusting to the pattern of preferences: a pure free-market position.

But many influences impact upon demand in health care in a way that is different from an ordinary market. Health consumption is, of course, unpredictable and can never be planned by the consumer in the way that – for example – weekly food consumption can. It does not reflect free choice in the way that consumer demand does for other commodities: we demand health care not principally because we want it but because we need it. And, unlike a conventional market, the consumer will normally have less information and less expert knowledge to seek out the best product at the lowest price than in an ordinary buyer-and-seller's arrangement. Patients are not doctors and they generally have less knowledge than in other markets to make informed judgements about what care they need, where to obtain that care, or easily compare the price and quality of the services on offer. At the most extreme, there could be an added danger where the professional whose expertise the patient relies on for medical judgement also has the power to set the price of their service.

Moreover, there is clearly a public-interest question that means health care cannot be treated like a normal market. 'Tackling contagious diseases cannot be left to the ordinary operation of supply and demand,' Aneurin Bevan said in 1948, 'the maintenance of public health requires a collective commitment.' And whether it is in preventing contagious diseases and other risks to public health or, more generally, in advancing the economic benefits of a healthy workforce, governments have an interest in ensuring that individuals receive treatment which may have a small personal benefit but a large social gain.

There is strong evidence that not only would charges discourage people from using preventive care – and divert demand to other areas of the health system where charges aren't levied – but that they would discourage some people, particularly the least well-off and the elderly, from seeking treatment altogether. According to a recent survey in New Zealand – where there is a system of charges for GP visits – 20 per cent of respondents said they had a medical problem but did not visit a doctor due to cost, compared to 3 per cent in the UK. Fourteen per cent didn't get a test, treatment or follow-up care due to cost, compared to 2 per cent in the UK. About 80 per cent of patients in France – where GPs charge around £20 per visit and hospitals £6.50 a day – take out supplementary insurance to pay for the charges. Until 2000, the other 20 per cent who couldn't afford private insurance were left to pay the charges themselves and one in four people surveyed said that they were put off seeking care for financial reasons. In response to this inequity, the French government now provides free supplementary insurance for those on low incomes.

If people are discouraged from seeing the doctor, they may simply end up back in the system at a later time with more severe health problems that require more intensive and costly treatments – a result which is potentially more painful for the individual and less cost-effective for national health care. So exemptions would have to be introduced to ensure those with a clinical need are not discouraged or prevented from receiving treatment. But these exemptions would inevitably make a charging system even more complicated and less efficient, with higher administration and collection costs. In New Zealand hospital charges were introduced but eventually dropped because the large number of exemptions and high administration costs meant that the scheme raised less than 0.5 per cent of total health-service costs in extra revenue.

In his interim report, Derek Wanless concluded that there could be cases where the use of charges did not result in such significant equity or efficiency problems but did give greater choice. He suggested that this might be the case with charges for non-clinical services, such as access to computer facilities or digital TV in hospital rooms. But we in Britain reject user charges for GP and hospital care because of the effects they would have on the poorest and most vulnerable in our society. Put starkly, user charges would mean the sick pay for being sick. So making health care reliant on charges is not a road we will take.

The fact is that none of us know when we will be in a position to need health care. We don't know in advance what all our health-care needs will be, or when we are going to be sick. It is to deal with precisely these risks that individuals, families and entire societies seek to insure themselves against the eventuality of being ill. And why most systems of financing health care – either public or private – are based primarily around the insurance principle. The essential idea of insurance is always the same – the pooling of risks – but the reach of the insurance and the method of finance determine whether health care is treated as a commodity or as a right. Before discussing public insurance models, I want to examine the advantages and disadvantages of the second funding system – private insurance.

To move to a British health-care system reliant on private insurance would mark a dramatic shift for our country. Like most of Europe, Britain has never had a strong tradition of private insurance in health. Even today only 3 per cent of adults buy their own insurance and with company schemes only 11 per cent have it. And the advisability of making such a change would have to be tested against considerations of equity – the large number of citizens who, in other countries, cannot afford such schemes – and efficiency, including the higher administrative costs of private schemes. As with charges, the paradox of health-care systems based on private insurance is that the people who need health care the most are the least likely to be able to afford it. We know that the poorer and older someone is, the more likely they are to fall ill. And in the United States – as with private insurance more generally – the less healthy pay the highest insurance premiums, with premium costs climbing sharply with age. According to the American Consumers' Union, the sickest 10 per cent of the American population spends six to seven times what the average person does on health care.

As a result, over 26 per cent of families in the US report that they have foregone necessary medical treatment over the last year because of prohibitive medical costs, and about 250,000 people each year give up insurance for cost reasons. In total, 18 per cent of adults of working age and 12 per cent of children do not have any insurance in the US – over 40 million people in all. Eighty per cent of these are in working families, many of them in small businesses or self-employed. The elderly and very poor are covered through public insurance schemes – Medicare and Medicaid.

So adopting private insurance as the UK health-care system would clearly fail to help those with the greatest needs, but paradoxically it is also likely to fail to deliver for those on higher incomes. Even comfortably-off families in the United States can be faced with huge additional bills because insurance packages tend to exclude high-cost chronic care altogether and have co-payments of 20 per cent or more. Someone with a private insurance policy covering 80 per cent of charges can face additional costs of nearly $2,000 for hospitalisation for childbirth and up to $5,000 for a heart-bypass operation. In Germany, where people on higher incomes have a choice between the public insurance offered by sickness funds and private insurance, two-thirds choose the public option because it is considered to be cheaper and less risky.

No private scheme covers every treatment an individual might need for life at a price they could afford. Private insurance policies currently on offer in the UK usually exclude primary care and emergency care – which currently accounts for over 90 per cent of patient contact – including GP visits, outpatient drugs and dressings, and hospitalisation for childbirth, as well as treatment for HIV/AIDS or other pre-existing or chronic conditions. Indeed the UK website for Medibroker states: 'In general, private medical-insurance plans do not cover chronic or critical illness which cannot be cured. For example, multiple sclerosis, asthma or diabetes.'

Rising knowledge of genetics also seems likely to further exacerbate the problems already present in private insurance systems. People with a predisposition for a particular disease will be open to discrimination and may face excessive premiums, reductions in coverage or find it impossible to obtain private insurance altogether. In fact, advances in genetics make the case for the widest possible pooling of risk. The more accurately you can predict risks the greater the case for risk-pooling.

But does private insurance meet the test of efficiency? Because of poor cost control, fragmentation of service and high management and administration costs, private insurance systems in other countries are consistently more expensive for both consumers and taxpayers than publicly funded health systems. In the United States, the cost of private insurance premiums is high and rising. In April 2001, it was estimated that annual premiums for employer-sponsored plans were over $2,500 for single coverage and over $7,000 for family coverage, with employees paying between 50 and 70 per cent of these costs. During 2001, premiums rose in price by 11 per cent, compared with general inflation of only 3 per cent and are forecast to rise by a further 13 per cent in 2002. Administrative costs in the US are twice as high as in Canada – a system based predominately on general taxation – largely due to the cost of insurance companies selling and handling policies, processing claims and pre-approving procedures, in some cases overruling doctors and denying needed care.

Of course there are models of best practice in the private sector from which we can learn – such as Kaiser Permenante in California. But the evidence suggests that Kaiser offers a better service not because it is funded through private insurance but because of its innovative use of resources including IT, the wider range of treatment offered in primary-care settings and the coordination of health and social care. These are lessons which can be applied in the public as well as the private sector.

And simply moving towards a private insurance system is not guaranteed to reduce the amount of money spent by the state on publicly funded health care. Despite a large private insurance sector, the public-sector cost of health care in the US is still significant. Medicare and Medicaid cost $400 billion a year and, with tax relief for private insurance, US public expenditure on health is $500 billion a year, about 7 per cent of national income. The irony is that the United States spends nearly as high a share of national income covering some of the health needs of some of its people as the United Kingdom spends on covering all the health-care needs of all its people. At the end of the day, 90 per cent of private insurance policies in the United States are taken out by employers for their employees – costing employers nearly $100 billion a year. And there is evidence that workers themselves are reluctant to change jobs for fear of losing cover. This leads to a less flexible and less mobile workforce, with subsequent knock-ons to the economy as a whole. In different US surveys at least 10 per cent and up to 30 per cent reported that they or a family member remained in a job at some time because they did not want to lose health-insurance coverage.

So private insurance fails the equity test. It does not pass the efficiency test. What of choice? Although the United States probably has the most market-driven system of health care – which in theory should give consumers greater choice – in practice the position is less clear cut. To ensure that the cost to the employer is minimised, many companies enrol their employees in health-maintenance organisations, or managed care plans. These narrow the choices patients have about the doctors and hospitals at which they can be treated. So far from the issue being – as some imply – the statist NHS denying choice versus the pro-choice private systems, the private insurance systems are essentially managed systems which restrict consumer choice.

Currently, private insurance does play a part in providing some supplementary cover for a small minority in Britain so even if there is not a case for a wholesale shift to compulsory private insurance, is there a case for extending tax relief for those who wish to take up private insurance – either generally or for elective surgery – on a voluntary basis? A study was conducted by the Treasury and the first and significant cost is a deadweight cost – at least £500 million – of providing tax relief for those who would take out private insurance policies anyway. Even when tax relief was available in the UK during the early 1990s it wasn't particularly successful in encouraging people to subscribe to voluntary health insurance. It cost £1 billion in subsidies but the number of people with private insurance rose by only 50,000 in seven years – an increase of 1.6 per cent. As the then Chancellor Nigel Lawson said at the time the tax relief was introduced,

> if we simply boost demand . . . by tax concessions to the private sector without improving supply, the result would not be so much a growth in private health care but higher prices . . . increasing demand in the private sector pushes up prices and therefore pay. That would inevitably spread across all staff costs in the NHS and we would end up getting less value for money.

The third alternative funding system is social insurance – the model in France, Germany and the Netherlands. There, health care is predominately financed by compulsory contributions from employers and employees, calculated as a proportion of earned income, paid into and managed by independent, not-for-profit, sickness funds. Fifty years ago, Bevan rejected a system funded in this way. He said that a contributory system would have denied some a full range of benefits; endless anomalies, he said, resulted; and such restrictions or exclusions were out of place for a national scheme. He said it would create a two-tier NHS.

Some countries still have a two-tier social insurance system which restricts equity of access. In Belgium, 88 per cent of people are included in a scheme which provides comprehensive benefits and 12 per cent in the alternative scheme for the self-employed where the benefits package covers major risks only. And in France reforms were introduced in 2000 as a response to fears that the previous structure was harming access to care amongst low-income groups. The Universal Health Coverage Act entitles everyone legally resident in France to public health insurance, regardless of their contribution status. The Act also provides free supplementary insurance for those on low incomes. So even insurance-based systems, which nominally link benefits to contributions, have had to find ways – financed through general taxation – of tackling the two-tier system and including the uninsured.

Those in favour of social insurance argue that it encourages people to pay more for their health care because the sickness funds are independent from government, giving a greater sense of ownership and therefore greater support for the system as a whole. But in fact, it is often employers who end up footing much of the bill. In France employers contribute 12.8 per cent of their earnings – on average, around £60 per week per employee. And in Germany, they contribute around 7 per cent, with average weekly payments per employee of around £30. Of course, it is right for employers to contribute on the grounds that ill health could have significant effects on the productivity of their business. But it should be noted that one advantage of the National Health Service is that employers are not expected to pay all or most of their own employees' health-care costs.

Furthermore, introducing local insurance funds could not easily be done in the UK, where our national service represents a very different tradition of health care from Germany, the Netherlands and France, whose insurance has been regionally and locally based. It was to move from a patchwork of local provision that in 1948 a unified national service was created. Indeed while some theorists argue that Britain should move from a tax-funded system towards social insurance, in practice countries such as France are moving from social insurance towards greater use of general taxation, in part because of concerns about people being excluded but also to widen the revenue base of the funds. In these circumstances, it would be perverse to go through the administrative upheaval of totally reorganising along Continental social insurance lines. As the French funding system moves towards Britain, it would seem strange for the British funding system to move towards the French.

Finally, some argue that social insurance systems give people greater choice – first, because they can choose between social insurance or opt out, and second, because they can choose between funds within the social insurance system. In fact, apart from in Germany, very few people have the choice of opting out of the state system – and in some cases, such as the Netherlands, higher-income groups are simply compulsorily excluded. And the choice provided between different funds within the social insurance system can, in practice, be constrained. In Germany, for example, there are over 400 different insurance funds but what they cover is strictly defined in law, leaving little room for choice.

In addition to our findings on social insurance, we have so far found that charging fails both the equity and efficiency tests. And we have discovered that because of the exemptions, restrictions and its partial coverage, private insurance fails the equity test without being either more administratively efficient or, in practice, as conducive as might appear in principle to choice.

So let me now turn to the NHS, the National Health Service. The question is whether in a reformed NHS the system of NHS funding is, in principle, sound for today's and tomorrow's world. In the original document sent to every citizen in 1948 the promise was unequivocal: the new health service will 'provide you with all medical and nursing care', it said. 'Everyone – rich or poor, man, woman or child – can use it or any part of it. There are no charges, except for a few special items. There are no insurance qualifications. But it is not a "charity". You are all paying for it, mainly as taxpayers, and it will relieve your money worries in time of illness.' There could be no clearer statement of the principle of equity: the NHS was built around the cornerstone of universal access to health services, regardless of ability to pay. And at its core is the recognition of health care as a fundamental human right, not a consumer commodity.

But in the intervening years between 1948 and now Britain did not invest as other countries invested in health care. Indeed, Derek Wanless pointed out in his interim report that between 1972 and 1998 a cumulative £220 billion less was invested in UK health care compared to the European Union average. But while the idea has been underfunded, is the NHS idea of funding universal access and universal provision itself still valid? Do we still support a health service free at the point of use, available to all, not just out of sentiment but as the rational choice for Britain's future?

While other models of insurance involve different levels of coverage for different individuals, the unique value of the NHS idea is that, no matter your circumstances or needs, risks are universally pooled and everyone is included. There is no doubt that the NHS is a good deal over the life cycle. Health-care costs are most expensive in the last years of an individual's life – at precisely the time when people generally have less money than during their working lives. Unlike private insurance, where premiums rise with age, the way the NHS is financed means that elderly people actually contribute significantly less for health care than those of working age.

While private insurance – as we have seen – involves exclusions, access and provision by the NHS is designed to be more comprehensive than any other, covering GP visits, GP house calls, nurses, health visitors, the whole primary-care team, elective surgery, accident-and-emergency cover and the medical costs of catastrophic illness. While private insurance covers some of the people some of the time, the evidence is that what people want is a health-care system that covers all of the people all of the time.

So people want the NHS at its best to combine the universality of access with universality of provision – and thus offer the best insurance policy in the world, without the ifs and buts and small print of private insurance policies but with, as far as possible, everything and everyone covered. And just as the principles of access to the NHS are fair and equitable, so is the system of funding it. Eighty per cent of the NHS is funded from general taxation, which means the charge for the NHS is broadly based, not falling on one particular group. Unlike systems of charging, it does not charge people for the misfortune of being sick. Unlike systems of private insurance, the NHS does not impose higher costs on those who are predisposed to illness, or who fall sick. And unlike social insurance systems, while the NHS does rightly ask employers to make an additional contribution in recognition of the benefit they receive from a healthy workforce, it does not demand that employers bear the majority burden of health costs.

In France, the amount contributed by employers to health care is around £60 a week for an employee on average earnings; in Germany it is around £30 a week. The amount contributed by UK employers to health care through national insurance is around £5 a week for an employee on average earnings. Even taking into account the contribution made by employers through general taxation, this would be no more than £10 a week per employee.

So the NHS scores well on equity; what of efficiency? Some people say that the cost of equity is inefficiency, indeed abuse. Because, for example, GP visits are free of charge, the system is abused. Even with a free GP system, the number of GP visits per person tends to be lower in the UK than in America, France or Germany. With the GP system an essential gatekeeper for access to the rest of the NHS – doing so by coordinating a wide provision of primary care with its hospital-based services – the NHS avoids much of the inefficiency of systems based much more on open access to hospital-specialty care. Moreover, while those who advocate charging argue that they would make financing health care more efficient because they would encourage the more responsible use of resources, the truth is that most of the costs of health care are initiated by the doctor, not the patient. As we have also seen, the fragmented nature of other systems of funding, particularly private insurance, is a source of additional administrative costs.

Of course, the NHS can be more efficient and productive. As Derek Wanless has already pointed out in his interim report, NHS productivity could be far higher than it is; for example, with the right investment in it and the reforms the Health Secretary is making, including improved triage schemes, better use of nurses and booked admissions, designed to make greater efficiency and productivity possible. But the key point is that there is no reason to think that the funding system for the NHS itself makes for a less efficient service.

Finally, choice. As we have seen, all systems in fact restrict choice – even private insurance systems. I would argue that greater choice will increasingly become possible in the NHS as we improve its capacity, and that is what the current reforms are designed to achieve. That is why we are committed to increasing not just the number of GPs but improving their premises and facilities as well. Patients will not simply be empowered with greater information, but also be given more choice than in the past. As we made clear in our election manifesto, by the end of 2005, every hospital appointment will be booked for the convenience of the patient, making it easier for patients and their GP to choose the hospital and consultant that best suits their needs. And finally, there is already some degree of choice about non-clinical services – people can pay for a single room for maternity services, for example. So I believe the evidence suggests that the NHS can accommodate greater choice and expectations in the future.

But some say that the NHS will be overwhelmed in the future, in particular by the costs of new, high-tech treatments. However, I believe that these rising costs actually make the NHS system of funding more valid today than at its creation. In 1948 the argument for common funding and pooled risk centred on the unpredictability of health needs and the expense of health care. At that time, much of what could be offered was a standard and, in practice, rather modest service. At that time, the scientific and technological limitations of medicine were such that really high-cost interventions were rare or very rare. There was no chemotherapy for cancer. Cardiac surgery was in its infancy, intensive care barely existed. Hip and knee replacement was almost unknown. A whole range of diagnostic and treatment techniques that today we take for granted were simply not available. Now – because the more effective treatments that can be offered today are far more expensive and because, of course, we still do not know when we or members of our family will need health care – the argument for common funding and pooled risk is in my view stronger than ever. And immeasurably stronger than it was in 1948.

Look at what is possible medically – and what, in the absence of the NHS, would too often be impossible financially for almost every family. Treatments ranging from serious heart abnormalities in a new-born baby to the cost of care for longer-term problems, such as behavioural disorders, diabetes and HIV/AIDS. Many of these illnesses and injuries come unexpectedly. No one budgets for them, and very few could. The standard of technology and treatment is now such that, unlike 1948, some illnesses or injuries could cost £20,000, £50,000 or even £100,000 to cure. Because the costs of treatment and drugs are higher than ever, the risks to family finances are greater than ever, and therefore the need for comprehensive insurance cover of health-care needs stronger than ever. Because none of us ever know in advance whether it is you or your family that will need that expensive care – for acute or chronic illness – the most comprehensive insurance cover is the best policy to cope with unpredictability. Insurance policies that, by definition, rely for their viability on ifs, buts and small print can cover only some of the people some of the time.

In a world of expensive treatments and even more expensive drugs, charging is simply making the sick pay more for being sick. So more than ever families need a system of funding that insures everyone as comprehensively as possible against the risks of huge medical bills. And this is true for the most comfortably-off members of our society as it is for the poorest. Why? Because charges for any one of these treatments could impoverish individuals, households, and families far up the income scale, it is now not just in the interests of a lower-income family but those on middle or higher incomes to be insured in the NHS's comprehensive way.

Some present the current NHS system of funding as an ideological hand-me-down from the immediate post-war era, to be supported only out of sentiment rather than hard-headed calculation. Others dismiss the NHS funding system as an impossible dream – 'fine in principle, a failed experiment in practice'. But far from being a hangover from a distant age or an unrealisable vision, the NHS system of funding is demonstrably the modern rational choice. Not just for poor or low-income families in Britain, but for the vast majority of families in Britain. Not just for today but for tomorrow too. And far from it being valid for the needs of the 1940s but not for now, a tax-funded system is Britain's better way forward for coping with the three challenges facing health care: the rising costs of new technology, the increase of 3 million by 2020 in the elderly population, and the ever rising expectations for higher standards of personal care.

If we can match reform and results to resources, our Budget and Spending Round offer a historic opportunity to put NHS funding on a sustainable footing – not just for a year or two but for the long-term; upholding and improving the NHS not just because it is an institution that is part of our history and our shared values but because, reformed and renewed, it can be the most efficient and equitable guarantee of health care for millions, provide the better choices and service they need and become, for the British people, the best insurance policy in the world: the best for each of us and the best for all of us.

This is the time for people to join the debate. I believe that, following this debate, we can build a national consensus around making the NHS the best insurance policy in the world.

In the Aneurin Bevan Memorial Lecture given on 23 May 2003 the Chancellor argues that social policy has always to be rooted in the shared experience of the nation. Asserting that Bevan's philosophy was not abstract or theoretical, the Chancellor argues that Bevan's social-inclusion policies started from what he saw around him in Welsh communities, and were based on real needs found in the real lives of the real people he grew up with and worked with in South Wales. Taking off from this, the Chancellor argues that we need to find specific policy solutions to unique British problems which are rooted in people's experiences and histories. People from Bevan's community believed that the injustices they suffered should not just not happen to them, they should not happen to anyone. They had a vision, and in this powerful speech the Chancellor argues that this might translate, for our time, into five social-justice objectives, to be met by modern public services: a commitment to full employment; the collective provision of the best modern public services; an end to child and pensioner poverty; to ensure the best educational opportunity including higher education for the majority of young people; and to forge a new global deal for the developing world.

. . .

2002, now, is the right time to honour the memory of Aneurin Bevan. Because the NHS, which he created just fifty years ago, which has endured for fifty years, is this year being renewed, I hope, for the next fifty years under the same principles he set out with the same objective he set out: free to all at the point of need, irrespective of wealth. And it is appropriate we are meeting here today because Bevan's great book *In Place of Fear* – which showed the insights and inspiration which led him to create the NHS – was published exactly fifty years ago this year.

In place of fear there should, he said, be security and, in his words, serenity. Bevan's philosophy was not abstract or just theoretical, but started from what he saw around him here in Welsh communities; was founded on unshakeable beliefs; was driven forward by a clear mission for change; and was built on a passion for justice. That he started not from textbooks or abstracts, but from real needs found in the real lives of the real people he grew up with and worked with here in South Wales, can be seen from the inspiration he received from the Tredegar Medical Society – the contributions of miners and steelworkers who employed their doctors and nurses and whose collective endeavour, each contributing to the health of all, became the inspiration for the National Health Service we enjoy today.

And from his starting point of where people found themselves – as he said 'a free people will always refuse to put up with preventable poverty' – Bevan built his philosophy not – as the Conservatives accused him – around violating rights but around righting wrongs: a demand for a correction of a generation of injustices: 'the sense of injustice' that, as he said, 'does not derive solely from the existence of inequality. It arises from the belief that the inequality is capricious, unsanctioned by usage and, most important of all, senseless.' And what he called his philosophy's driving force was utterly positive and life-enhancing: the promotion and liberation of the potential of all – as he said in a memorable phrase, the conviction that 'free men can use free institutions to solve social and economic problems of the day, if they are given a chance to do so'. And his objective – as he said, quoting his favourite philosopher José Enrique Rodó: 'not to reduce all to the lowest common level but to raise all towards the highest levels'. His aim: not to level people down, but to enable people to lift themselves up.

High ideals about the extraordinary potential of ordinary people: enduring values to be reapplied by each generation – indeed, as he said, 'modernised' because 'policies are often blunted in use' and may have to be renovated or even discarded in each era to meet the needs of the times. And in our time I believe it means five social-justice objectives:

- first, a commitment to full employment;
- second, to renew the collective provision of not just basic but the best modern public services;
- third, to secure for the first time an end to child and pensioner poverty;
- fourth, to ensure the best educational opportunity including higher education for young people – not just for the privileged but, for the first time, for the majority;
- and fifth, to forge a wholly new global deal for the developing world – for few would deny that we have in our hands the power, never given to any other generation at any other time in human history – and thus the obligation – to banish ignorance and poverty from the earth.

So I believe that for Labour this is not a time to slow down or pause or to be complacent. For as long as there is poverty, unemployment and deprivation; as long as prosperity bypasses a single family or community; as long as there is opportunity denied in education; as long as there is injustice not just in Britain but round the world; our work has only just begun.

I believe that the experience here in South Wales that shaped Bevan's beliefs and his political programme made Bevan's starting point the goal of full employment. As Michael Foot has put it in his magnificent biography of Bevan, 'unemployment was the great issue on which all else hinged'. For Bevan, the mass unemployment of the 1930s was 'the biggest human problem parliament has ever had to handle'. Bevan came from a Wales which, both by inclination and by necessity, depended upon strong communities. Communities which had together endured war, depression, and would live through war again. Communities which together had suffered closure, unemployment, poverty and deprivation but, despite all that, communities that remained resilient and strong. Communities from which thousands had been forced to emigrate and travel tens of thousands of miles – but still, from whatever extremity of the world they found themselves in, they saw their village or valley as home. For our parents and grandparents, community was never artificial, never an afterthought, never an unreal or false togetherness for the sake of appearances. In a mining area where, not least when a mine's safety was an issue, the lives of each depended upon the support of all. Community – or what we sometimes call solidarity – was of the essence. We owe obligations to neighbours, even strangers, because they are part of what we are.

As here, so in Scotland and in the industrial communities, hard times – the harsh and bitter experience of industrialisation – taught the parents of the men and women I grew up with not just solidarity in preference to individualism but also compassion in preference to selfishness. Out of a sense of community – and a respect each for the other – came a hatred of injustice and a demand for social justice.

As William McIlvanney – a great Scottish writer – says, our ancestors were not fools. They knew how much easier it was to be a Conservative than a socialist; easier to conserve than to change; easier to succumb to vested interests than to take them on; easier to take your own share than fight for everyone to have a fair share; easier to see progress as moving up on your own than ensuring everyone moves up together. But Bevan's generation – as McIlvanney says – sensed their lives were part of a worthwhile struggle, believed that the injustice they suffered should not just not happen to them, it should not happen to anyone. And they rose above the bleakness of their daily struggle and blessed it by transforming their hardships into a vision: a society where there is not indifference but care; not cruelty but kindness; not endless competition but regular cooperation; not selfishness but sharing; not the pursuit of élitism but of excellence; not class but classlessness. And it was this that gave purpose to their lives. For them, as he says, democratic socialism was an honest attempt to fulfil what is best in human nature: people choosing quite deliberately to develop the best aspects of their nature and to keep in check the worst.

They were not, in the main, Marxists. For them, McIlvanney concludes, Marxism was a demand to be something you are not, which our individual natures could not honestly answer. Instead democratic socialists say you must be the most you can be while allowing others to be the most that they can be – an attempt to share as justly as we can with each other the terms of human existence. But this did not mean that for Bevan social justice was an abstraction. Social justice was houses free of damp, teachers in our classrooms, nurses in our hospitals . . . and, as a precondition, work for people. For unemployment he saw as not only immoral but an economic waste, hence the demand not that each be left isolated and stranded to fend for himself but that we organise a society where there is work for all – full employment.

So in Bevan's generation, so in ours. Since the time I went to school and grew up beside a mining community – and for a whole genera- tion – our political life has been dominated by unemployment – long- term unemployment, youth unemployment, the fear of unemploy- ment, the poverty and insecurity caused by unemployment. Unem- ployment is an impassable barrier to people realising their potential and an implacable source of poverty. An unemployment, as Bevan said, that 'eats like acid into the homes of the poor'. Bevan's dream was to rebuild the towns and villages around him so that – in the words of an American – young children could again get up in the morning and look out of their windows to see whole communities going to work.

If the 1920s and 1930s of Bevan's time are remembered for adults standing around street corners, the 1980s will be remembered for young people sleeping rough in cardboard cities, young people without jobs, prospects or hope. It has not only been our party's dream for a century that full employment should be a central goal but that the driving force of any successful economic policy should be a commitment to full employment not just for a year or two but on a sustainable basis. For years in opposition we could do nothing about it. All we could do was protest. We marched for jobs, we rallied for the right to work, we petitioned for full employment. But out of government we could not deliver jobs.

After I became Shadow Chancellor in 1992 Labour set out proposals for taxing the excess profits of the privatised utilities to pay for jobs for the unemployed. If only one person had benefited from the New Deal that would have made it worth while. But in total 660,000 young people, two-thirds of a million of our fellow citizens, nearly 50,000 in Wales, have benefited. And when I tell you that, under Tony Blair, one and a half million men and women denied jobs under the Tories are now in jobs under Labour, I do not say this in a spirit of congratulation, but in a spirit of resolve. In the mid-1980s, 350,000 young people had been out of work for more than a year. Today it is 5,000. Youth unemployment is down two-thirds; long-term unemployment by three-quarters, now the lowest since the 1970s. For the first time in years, the majority of lone parents are now able to work. Twenty-six thousand more people are in work in Wales today than in 1997.

But this is only a start. For one in six working-age households still has someone who is not working and our goal is full employment for our generation: employment opportunity for all. So we are:

- entrenching monetary and fiscal stability and discipline to help create jobs;
- pushing forward with a challenging economic reform agenda not just for stability but for productivity in Britain and Europe;
- investing in skills to improve employability;
- extending the New Deal, its opportunities and its responsibilities, to all the remaining 95,000 long-term unemployed, with – in twenty of the highest-unemployment communities of Britain – in return for the responsibility to accept the offer, guaranteed jobs with proper wages;
- and to help more long-term unemployed people in Wales into jobs, we have set up two employment zones, including the Head

of the Valley's employment zone, to help tackle the problems in the areas where long-term unemployment has remained consistently high.

Because women have suffered most from injustice in employment opportunities, we are pushing forward with a new programme of 'choices' for lone parents – to push up employment rates from just over 45 per cent when we came to power to 70 per cent, underpinned by a national childcare strategy – extending, for the first time ever, the right of childcare to all those who need it. And we are seeking to make a reality of the right to work for disabled men and women when they wish to work: disabled people cruelly denied their chances under the Tories, now under Labour given the right to develop their talents and fulfil their potential. And recognising that, in high-unemployment communities which prosperity has for too long passed by, we need more economic activity and enterprise, we will be working with the Welsh Assembly and Scottish Parliament to regenerate run-down high streets and industrial sites, cut the cost of investing in small businesses and in entrepreneurship, deliver special help for growing enterprises and provide funds for training and education in the new skills we need.

And we are not just determined to create jobs but, in a world of fast-moving change where people will tend to move between jobs and have to acquire during their working life new skills for jobs, we will make sure there are continuous and recurring opportunities for work, and will make work pay: next year building on the minimum wage, a new Working Tax Credit to tackle poverty in work. For the first time from next April a Minimum Income for all those in work over twenty-five, creating a tax system where the rates range from 40 per cent at the top to minus 200 per cent as we create fairness and justice in the workplace.

But the new Britain worthy of Bevan's vision will be built not only around a goal of full employment but around the goal of world-class public services. Just as it is only because people have forgotten the unemployed standing on street corners in the thirties that they undervalue the deliverance from evil that came with full employment and the Welfare State, so too it is only because some people have forgotten the chaos and patchwork of voluntary, charitable and municipal health care that Aneurin Bevan swept away – and the unmitigated good that comes from a National Health Service – that anyone can contemplate its withering away. Yet many of you will look back, like me, and recall that so many of the opportunities we have had – the best schooling, the best of health care when ill, for many of us the best chances at university – so many of the opportunities we have enjoyed – owe their origin to the decisions of the 1945 Labour government to create a Welfare State that takes the shame out of need, to fund a National Health Service free to all, to build decent public services worthy of a civilised society – in health, transport, education and the important fight against crime – public services that are an expression of something more than the material – of an ethic of service that reflects our obligation each to the other in society.

A National Health Service, Bevan said in a famous speech introducing the National Health Service Bill in 1946, would

> lift the shadow from millions of homes. It will keep very many people alive who might otherwise be dead. It will relieve suffering. It will be a great contribution towards the well-being of the common people of Britain. No society can legitimately call itself civilised if a sick person is denied medical aid because of lack of means. The essence of a satisfactory health service is that rich and poor are treated alike, that poverty is not a disability, that wealth is not an advantage.

For me the National Health Service is a clear, enduring and practical expression of these shared values which shape our country: the NHS built upon the conviction that the health of each of us depended upon a contribution by all of us. And let me say that I believe that the case for the NHS system of funding and thus a renewed and reformed NHS is not weaker but stronger now than even it was in Bevan's day. In 1948 when the NHS was founded, the scientific and technological limitations of medicine were such that high-cost interventions were rare or very rare. There was no chemotherapy for cancer, cardiac surgery was in its infancy, intensive care barely existed, hip and knee replacement was almost unknown. Now, the standard of technology and treatment is such that unlike in 1948 some illnesses or injuries could cost £20,000, £50,000 or even £100,000 to treat and cure. Because the costs of treatment and of drugs are higher than ever, the risks to family finances under a paying system are greater than ever not just for poorer families but for comfortably-off families up the income scale and therefore the need for comprehensive insurance cover of health care stronger than ever. Private insurance policies that, by definition, rely for their viability on ifs, buts and small print can cover only some of the people some of the time. Because none of us ever knows in advance whether it is you or your family that will need that expensive care – for acute or chronic illness – the best policy to cope with unpredictability is clearly an insurance policy that offers cover to all of the people whatever their income for all illnesses and diseases without the ifs, buts and small print of other policies.

So while some present the current NHS system of funding as an ideological hand-me-down from Bevan's days as Health Minister, to be supported only out of sentiment rather than hard-headed calculation; and while others dismiss the NHS funding system as an impossible dream – 'fine in principle, a failed experiment in practice', the NHS system of funding – comprehensive and inclusive insurance with treatment free at the point of need – is demonstrably the modern rational choice: the best insurance policy in the world not just for poor or low-income families in Britain, but for the vast majority of families in Britain. Not just for today but for tomorrow too, and more so than in 1948.

So we believe in a reformed and renewed NHS free at the point of need where, as we see in Wales, there is local devolution and then greater local choice; local accountability and improved service; a health service that has to be reformed and renewed to meet the three great challenges facing health care: the rising costs of new technology, the increase of 3 million by 2020 in the elderly population, and the ever rising expectations for higher standards of personal care. I believe, just as it was in 1948 when Bevan had to wage war against the Conservatives, a free NHS free at the point of need is now the central dividing line between the political parties in British politics and will be a central theme in Welsh and Scottish elections next year.

The Conservatives – in fact, their Shadow Chancellor Michael Howard, that well-known Welshman – now tell us that the NHS was a Stalinist creation, in other words that it was wrong in principle from the very start, and that when he said under the Thatcher government the NHS was safe in their hands he never really meant it. He and his party now explicitly refuse to commit themselves to an NHS free to all at the point of need. Their hatred of the NHS is such that they would prefer a private sector performing inefficiently to a public service delivering well.

I believe we should now expose the costs and inequity of private insurance under which typical family premiums cost £100 a week, are rising by 13 per cent a year and leave 40 million Americans uninsured; and the costs and inequity of charging for clinical services – £8,000 for a hip replacement, £40,000 for a heart transplant, £10 for a visit to a GP or to stay in hospital for a day – the unfairness of the sick paying for being sick. And I want to ask you today to help us ensure that, just as in Bevan's generation private health was decisively rejected in favour of the NHS system of funding, so too in our generation we reject a system under which poverty would bar the entrance to the best hospitals; where the only health care you could be sure of is the health care you were able to pay for; where, for today's Tories, one person on BUPA matters more to them than 50 million people covered by the NHS.

Let us affirm that it was Aneurin Bevan who helped us escape from a world where nurses had to leave the beds of their patients to run charity flag days to pay for their hospital buildings and their doctors' salaries. And we are not returning to that. And so let us affirm that it is because we recognise the unpredictability of health needs, the rising costs of health technology, and the equity and efficiency of the NHS tax-funded system that, for us, the renewed NHS – with the largest sustained increased investment in any decade of its fifty-year-long history – will remain a National Health Service: a public service free at the point of use with decisions on care always made by doctors and nurses on the basis of clinical need – the best insurance policy in the world.

But, for Bevan, democratic socialism was not just about work, however important, and the provision of public services, however critical. Democratic socialism was – yes – about teachers in classrooms, roofs above people's heads, doctors and nurses when needed, money in people's pockets. But power, wealth and opportunity in the hands of the many not the few meant something more. It was also about the liberation of human potential. Bevan's starting point was a fundamental belief in the equal worth of every human being. As he said in *In Place of Fear*: 'it is commonly said that we are all born unequal, but surely that is the wrong way of expressing it. It would be

more correct to say that we are born with different potential aptitudes than that we are born unequal.' And as his favoured philosopher Rodó said, 'our duty is to help each and every one develop their
potential to the full – in other words, to bridge the gap between what
we are and what we have it in ourselves to become.'

Bevan believed that nobody's potential should be written off at
birth, seven, eleven or sixteen. As Bevan said in *In Place of Fear*,
'whether the special aptitudes, qualities or temperament we are born
with turn out to be of later advantage, will turn upon whether they
are sufficiently cultivated'. It was simply a denial of any belief in
equality of opportunity and a waste of human potential if we were to
assume that there is one type of intelligence, one means of assessing
it, only one time when it should be assessed and just one chance of
succeeding. We have to act on the consequence of recognising these
facts about human worth: that people have a richness and diversity of
potential, that their talents take many forms – not just analytical
intelligence but skills in communication, language, and working with
other people – and that these talents can develop and flourish over a
lifetime. And should all be valued.

In the central scene in Trevor Griffiths' play *Food for Ravens*,
commissioned to mark the fiftieth anniversary of the NHS and
the centenary of Bevan's birth, the old dying Bevan talks to the
young enquiring Bevan: it is a moment, as Hywel Francis has
recorded in a recent speech, 'of magic, pathos and controlled anger':

> Schooling for our people [said the old Bevan] has always been
> constructed misery, from which a true education has been
> deliberately excluded – obedience and cringing servility in;
> imagination and mental daring out. That's always been our
> sort of schooling, a human dog-training.
>
> Once I asked a simple question, 'What do we put in place of
> fear?' If we let ourselves believe that reading and writing and
> painting and song and play and pleasure in the imagining, good
> food, good wine, good clothes and good health are the toff's
> turf, boy, haven't we lost the battle already? They're ours, our
> human right, all right?

There it is: the driving force in Bevan's philosophy – tackling what
was called the 'poverty of aspiration' and challenging people every-

where to accept the equal right, what he called the human right, of the poorest citizen to develop their potential to the full. Not – as he says – the old one-off opportunity of schooling up till age sixteen: a single chance to get your foot on a narrow ladder – one opportunity at school till sixteen, a chance if missed that was gone for ever – followed by an opportunity for just 10, 20 or 30 per cent to go into higher education. But instead recurrent, permanent, lifelong opportunities at any time, education at any age at any place, and not just education but the liberation of potential with new opportunities in employment, the economy and across our society and culture.

While mining communities like yours and mine have always understood the importance of education as a means of financial and personal liberation, for too long since 1945 the Welfare State tried to compensate people for their poverty instead of ensuring the opportunities were delivered to tackle the causes of poverty, and providing routes out of poverty to the liberation of potential. So while we reject equality of outcome because it is statist, centralising, against human nature, and – as I said earlier – demands we be something we are not, an equality of outcome that would level down, we support an equality of opportunity that lifts people up and helps answer Bevan's worries about the poverty of aspiration. It is an equality which demands not just that individuals enabled by opportunity also accept responsibility to make the most of their talents for their community – rights and responsibilities the modern expression of community, of solidarity – but that we have a duty to remove all the old barriers – whether it be lack of nursery schools, under-investment in schools, old-fashioned élitism in our higher-education system or failure to take adult education seriously. The challenge, because we waste too much of the talent of Britain: to open up opportunities for education to an extent never before seen in this country so that every child will have the best possible chance in life. And because today the most important resource of a country is not its raw materials but the talents of its people – now the essential means of production – and because economies that work only for the few and do not bring out the best in all their people will ossify and be left behind – the equality of opportunity that we have always argued for as an ethical imperative is today also an economic necessity.

The old walls of privilege for some must be replaced with new paths of opportunity for all. We said in our manifesto that we would put schools and hospitals first. This summer, in the Spending Review, we will honour our commitments not just to health but to education – which will receive the priority it requires to deliver further substantial improvements in standards in our schools, colleges and universities. Having raised the share of education in our national income during the last parliament, we are pledged to increase significantly the share of national income devoted to education over the course of this parliament – not just because education is crucial for social justice but because it is key to improving the productivity of the British economy. We must promote opportunity not just for some of the people some of the time but opportunity for all of the people all of the time.

And one focus in our Spending Review will be not just on resources but on reforms to break down the educational barriers that, at whatever point in the life cycle, deny opportunity and hold people back. Because for Britain to be the best society it can we must tackle the challenge of low aspirations – by reminding young people of the new opportunities to go as far as their talents will allow them, to make the most of themselves, and to be all that they can be, to fulfil the potential they have, just as we remind them of their responsibilities – the modern expression of community and solidarity – to others to use their talents well.

The first barrier is poverty – for child poverty is a scar on the soul of Britain. So Labour's goal is to halve child poverty in ten years on the road to abolishing child poverty in our generation. Our approach is universal and progressive – it starts with Child Benefit for every family, but is designed to help families most when they need help most and when their children are youngest. So payments for the first child, which in 1997 started at £11 and rose to £28, now start at £15.75, for 5 million families are nearly £26, and for the poorest families are £48.25 a week – a near doubling of cash support since 1997.

And as the next step in meeting our poverty targets, we are bringing together all these related payments for children in a new Child Tax Credit, paid through the tax system, introduced next April – a new seamless system of support, built on universal Child Benefit, with one single payment – improving work incentives and ensuring for the first time that all child payments are paid to the main carer.

And it is exactly the same progressive universalist principles that we are applying to pensions with our £1.5 billion rise in pensions next year: the universal state pension rising each year, pensioners with modest occupational pensions and savings gaining up to an extra £14 a week from the pension credit rising each year faster than earnings, with a Minimum Income Guarantee rising in line with earnings that takes thousands of pensioners out of poverty – our aim that in our generation we abolish pensioner poverty and ensure every pensioner has dignity and security in retirement.

So from removing the barrier of poverty, the second barrier to remove is that too many children go to school not ready to learn. By 2004, Sure Start will be helping 400,000 children, ensuring they are given the opportunity to flourish and are ready to learn when they get to school. I want Sure Start in the UK to be as central to defining Britain as a country of opportunity as Head Start in the USA. And with nursery places already increasing by over 200,000 since 1997, by 2004 all three- and four-year-olds will have access to nursery schools – the early learning that was once the privilege of a minority now under Labour becoming available for all.

Third, the task is now to achieve for secondary schools what we are achieving for primary schools – setting higher standards, and demanding results in return for the new resources. If we can reach out to the fifth of children denied opportunity before they leave school, we will all gain; fail and we all fail. But even then we have more to do. Today in Britain most of the children of rich families go to university but most of the children of poor families do not. In fact, 76 per cent of children of the wealthiest fifth of our families go into higher education, while only 14 per cent of the children of the poorest fifth do. And our aim is not to reduce the numbers from rich families but to increase the number from poor families. This is not only right and fair; it is essential to our economy – with higher productivity and higher-paid jobs increasingly dependent on higher levels of education. For too long too many in this country have believed college and university are not for them, a sad reflection of a poverty of aspiration. That day must end. The Secretary for Education is right to examine measures that will help broaden intake so we will help more pupils stay on at school after sixteen and get the necessary qualifications for university or college:

- extending the successful experiment of providing targeted financial grants via Educational Maintenance Allowances, which has raised school staying-on significantly to cover more sixteen-, seventeen- and eighteen-year-olds – and in Wales the assembly is introducing a similar scheme; and
- in doing so ensuring that all young people have access to the advice and support they need to make the most of college and university opportunities.

And we in the UK administration are looking at the success of the Welsh Assembly's student-grant scheme as it develops

We want to give new support for the colleges supporting 4 million students now in further education. And to back up 'Learndirect' to improve workplace adult skills we will, in a new pilot experiment, ask employers, in return for our financial support for paid leave, to offer their employees time off to obtain the qualifications they need, and we will continue to back TV learning. And we will encourage a programme of open access in which teams go regularly to all schools to explain both the opportunities and importance of university to young people early on in their secondary education.

For as we tackle the inadequacy of provision and the poverty of aspiration it is time to leave behind for ever what Aneurin Bevan would have called the old Britain of the old-boy networks where too often the privilege you were born to mattered more than the potential you were born with. It is time to leave behind the old Britain where too often the school your parents went to counted more than the skills you were prepared to acquire. And it is time to leave behind the old Britain which too often valued the connections you had when what matters is the contribution you can make.

But a tribute to Aneurin Bevan would be incomplete, especially in front of Michael Foot, and wholly inadequate, if we did not understand that the challenges we have to address for Britain – poverty, inequality, access to education and health, the challenges of economic and social development – we have to address for the world. As Bevan said so eloquently in *In Place of Fear*, 'if it is by now irrefutable that most, if not all, the peoples of the world are linked together in an endless variety of reciprocal activities, then the condition of each of us becomes the concern of all of us.'

Martin Luther King put it this way: 'we are each strands in an inescapable network of mutuality, together woven into a single garment of destiny', not here as self-interested individuals sufficient unto ourselves, with no obligations to each other, but all part of a community bound together as citizens with shared needs, mutual responsibilities and linked destinies – not only across our nation but also across our world, our fates and interests bound together. Bevan's vision was not national, it was international: not just international but cosmopolitan – his belief not just that an injury to one is an injury to all but that an injustice anywhere is a threat to justice everywhere. A minister in the post-1945 government and then Foreign Affairs Spokesman for Labour in the fifties, he was one of a generation of leaders who had known both the greatest of depressions and the greatest of wars and who had resolved that the failed policies of *laissez-faire* which resulted in vast inequities and recurring depression from the 1870s to the 1930s and had contributed to war and conflict should not be repeated. Untrammelled, unregulated market forces had brought great instability and even greater injustice. In the post-war era governments had to work collectively if they were to achieve both stability and justice. For Bevan's generation knew that just as peace could not be preserved in isolation, prosperity could not be maximised in isolation, that prosperity like peace is indivisible. And that prosperity, to be sustained, had to be shared. Bevan said in *In Place of Fear*: 'either poverty will use democracy to win the struggle against property, or property, in fear of poverty, will destroy democracy'. Or as John F. Kennedy put it, if a free society cannot help the many who are poor, it cannot save the few who are rich.

And having built in Bevan's time for the post-war world of distinct national economies new international institutions and a commitment to growth and prosperity for all, now we must do it for the post-national global economy – where economically no nation is an island; and where the new frontier is that there is no frontier. And the way forward for tackling poverty and injustice in the new global economy is not to retreat from globalisation – to a 1930s-style *laissez-faire* or to protectionism or old national controls but to ensure by cooperation and modernising our international institutions that it is possible to envisage a world free of hunger, poverty and deprivation and meet development goals:

- that by 2015 we halve poverty;
- end avoidable child mortality, cutting it by two-thirds; and
- achieve universal education, giving every girl and every boy in every part of the world the right to schooling.

Look at the challenge: the 113 million children – two-thirds of them girls – who are not going to school today because they have no schools to go to; the 200 million young people working as child labourers; the 150 million children who are malnourished, living on the knife's edge of bare existence; and the 30,000 children facing death each day from diseases we could prevent. In total 600 million children in developing countries living in the most disfiguring, grinding poverty imaginable – condemned to failure even before their life's journey has begun.

The global campaign for debt relief in which many of you through churches, NGOs and local organisations have been engaged is now lifting the burden of unpayable debt from twenty-six of the most highly indebted countries, cancelling $62 billion in debt. And as we have seen with Uganda, pupil–teacher ratios as a result of debt relief will fall from 100:1 to 50:1 and every child at school will have a roof above their head.

But what drives us forward are not the achievements we can point to – important as they are – but the gains still to be made. And I want to propose what is a new deal for the global economy, that is also a new deal for the world's poor, that ensures no country genuinely committed to good governance, poverty reduction and economic development is denied the chance to cut infant mortality and poverty and achieve schooling for every one of its children. The new deal is that in return for developing countries pursuing corruption-free policies for stability and for creating a favourable environment for investment, developed countries should agree to increase vitally needed funds to achieve the agreed Millennium Development Goals. Let me briefly mention the four areas in which progress is urgent.

First, hunger is a fact of life for too many children. And in some countries – and not just Malawi – it is tragically getting worse not better. Even when there is adequate food available, poverty often prevents poor people from feeding their children. And as Tony Blair's African partnership recognises, Africa is getting poorer. So the

British government proposes today to take not only short-term immediate action – as our International Development Secretary is doing – to help those countries currently affected by food shortages, including Malawi, Zimbabwe and Zambia, but that we finally recognise the importance of the trade round for long-term food security – opening up agriculture in all our countries to fair competition, opening up trade in everything but arms.

Second, because we have been far too slow in advancing our education goals – because as things stand eighty-eight countries will not achieve primary education for all by 2015 and indeed because instead of raising educational aid as a share of national income the world has been, disgracefully, cutting it – our government's proposal today is that the richest countries back the new World Bank initiative with the funds it now needs to fast-track our commitment to meeting the goal of primary education for all by 2015 and to ensuring that in all countries education is not subject to fees but free for everyone.

Third, half child deaths are from four avoidable diseases – acute respiratory-tract infection, diarrhoea, malaria and measles – a loss of millions of children's lives unnecessarily each year. So building on this year's new global health fund for drugs and treatments in HIV/AIDS, malaria and TB, I propose that just as we fast-track investments in education for countries who have a plan, so too for health we should fast-track support for helping to build health-care systems.

Fourth, because too often the world has set goals like the Millennium Development Goals and failed to meet them; because, too often, we have set targets, reset them, and recalibrated them again; because too often our ambitions, in the end, only measure our lack of achievement, this time, it can be – and must be – different.

So to build a virtuous circle of debt relief, poverty reduction and sustainable development for the long term, I propose we step up our commitment to making debt relief a success, by driving forward with HIPC implementation and pledging to ensure its full financing – something that will need a further $1-billion contribution from the richest countries. And I propose we do far more than that. That we accept that the cost of meeting the Millennium Development Goals is $50 billion a year more; and that to achieve this we ask Europe and

America to maximise their development spending by examining as a matter of urgency the means by which the currently planned $12-billion-a-year boost to aid can be made to go much further and its benefits maximised.

Every time we lift one child above the squalor of the slums . . . every time we rescue one teenage soldier pressed into combat or one young girl pushed into prostitution or forced labour . . . every time we cure one mother afflicted by disease, and give her and her children a chance in life . . . we are making a difference. But if we can lift not just one child, but millions of children, and then all children, out of poverty and hopelessness, we will have achieved a momentous victory for the cause of social justice on a global scale and the values that shape our common humanity.

Every child the best possible chance, every young person the prospect of education, every adult the reality of a job, every pensioner dignity in retirement, every citizen the best public services, every country playing its part in a just and inclusive world. Not just some but everyone – whatever their birth, background or race – has the chance to achieve their potential. Five national and international goals which show the sheer scale of our ambitions for Britain – goals that for economic as well as equity reasons we cannot postpone or defer, goals that taken together can advance a new progressive consensus for Britain that no opponent could ever erode; goals for our country worth fighting for, goals that show there is purpose in politics, inspired by the same principles that shaped the creation of our labour movement a century ago.

Here tonight in South Wales I ask you to look back on not just the life of Aneurin Bevan but on the lives of our pioneers: men and women in communities like this who one hundred years ago got together in small groups, initially against the odds, to form the labour movement we know today. And their sacrifices, their struggles, their hard-won gains, their great achievements – full employment, an NHS, a Welfare State, a belief in equality and justice – and their conviction that power need not be won at the expense of principle but could not be won without unity and solidarity, must inspire us, here from Wales this evening, to rededicate our efforts to achieve in our time the realisation of their dream:

- a society based on need rather than greed;
- a society where individuals stand free of paternalism and privilege;
- a society where each person has the chance to realise their potential to the full;
- not just here in Britain but in our world.

There are good causes worth fighting for – the same yesterday, today and tomorrow. There is a purpose in politics. We can build a Britain worthy of our pioneers; we can build a Britain worthy of our ideals.

8

BRITISHNESS

Twenty-first century Britain faces momentous change of a scale probably not encountered since the start of the nineteenth century. Then, the combination of the Industrial Revolution and the establishment of Britain as an unrivalled imperial power unleashed economic, social and cultural transformation. Today, the ocean of change created by three forces – globalisation, demography and technology – threatens to overwhelm us. But just as in the nineteenth century, it is the task of politics to offer a coherent account of these world-shaking movements; and to propose routes by which democratic societies can negotiate their own transformation, rather than being drowned by seemingly irresistible natural forces.

The response of many on the unrejuvenated left, shared by many on the far right, is what you might call the 'Canute' strategy: to stand on the shore of this sea of change and to try to command the waves to retreat. In this context that would mean attempts by governments to restrict flows of capital; efforts to throw up barriers to migration; and a retreat to narrow, nationalistic cultural norms. But as King Canute demonstrated, all that such a posture is likely to deliver is a severe soaking or worse. A second approach, favoured by the centre right, is simply to surrender to the ocean, to provide minimal protection against the storms and to wish everyone good luck. The strongest may survive, but I do not believe that even they can be sure of survival without a basic solidarity coming into play at the moments of greatest stress.

That is why Gordon Brown's appeal to the British people to think hard about the values that sustain our commitment to the common good is much more than an invitation to cheery flag-waving. It is why his speeches on Britishness should not be trivialised by cynics as just another canny Caledonian ploy. Nor should his exploration of national identity be seen as just a knee-jerk response to alarming outbreaks of interethnic conflict across Europe, or to the gathering strength of extremism in our own country.

The questions that Brown asks do encompass all of these events, but they are larger and more profound. And so is his answer. At the heart of his approach lies a simple but powerful proposition, stated in his Spectator Lecture: 'The British way is not to fear change but to embrace it.' The important point about this statement is that it isn't just politician's optimism. It tells, first, that this is one politician who has grasped Bill Clinton's dictum that 'Globalisation isn't a policy; it's a fact. What matters is what we do about it.' And, second, that his response to the challenge, though it draws on universal values, is rooted in the traditions of these islands.

In these speeches, we see the emergence of a coherent left response to the challenge of identity politics. It may be that it is Brown's very Scottishness that has opened his mind to the value of an overarching national identity in cementing social solidarity. The Commission for Racial Equality's recent research on British identity showed that ethnic minority Britons find it easier to identify as Scots or Welsh than they do as English. That suggests that these are inclusive civic identities which do not pose ethnic hurdles for the Scottish Asians, or the black Welsh; it allows them to be just as Scottish and as Welsh as their white neighbours – and just as committed to the success of their nations. In the same way, it may be that a vital aspect of our response to the challenge of globalisation is a progressive assertion of British identity.

Finally, however, it is vital to distinguish that inclusive assertion of identity from the ethnically based exclusiveness put forward by the right. And here again, Brown offers a persuasive alternative; put simply, 'British is as British does.' In essence we define Britishness by our values, by our behaviour towards each other and by the nature of the institutions which define our community. No matter where you came from – or when – you too can be truly British. The route to the creation of an inclusive national identity could become, along with our language, our most valuable export in years to come. British experience and insight will be vital in a world desperately in need of the map across a sea of change.

Trevor Phillips

This chapter contains a selection of the Chancellor's speeches on a topic that he has spoken about and returned to on a number of occasions since 1997. There is no doubt that the Chancellor has developed a distinctive and well-regarded analysis of Britishness. Three of the many speeches which deal with this topic are included here, and the intention is to show how the thinking develops from initial considerations of the values and institutions which constitute what might be called a British consciousness; through historical reflections on how an absence of an agreed view of Britishness has caused problems (for both political parties) in relation to both domestic policy and the UK's relations with Europe and the wider world; to a position arrived at through analysis of the writings of many thinkers across the political spectrum, which might be described as a programme, responding to the views of the progressive consensus, for a future manifesto. In proposing this far-reaching programme, the Chancellor argues that the British way is to embrace, not fear, reform, and that the challenge of the twenty-first century is not just to express our Britishness in the evolutionary reform of individual institutions but to work towards a constitutional settlement that recognises both our rights and aspirations as individuals and our needs and shared values as a community.

In the first speech, the Spectator Lecture, given in November 1997, the Chancellor takes three themes as he approaches the question of what Britishness means to new Labour: the first starts from a phrase adapted from George Orwell about the 'British genius', which he argues is 'not just inventive and creative, adaptable and hard-working, with a strong sense of fair play and public service; but is also outward-looking, tolerant and internationalist'. He goes on to argue that if the government wants to respond to the hopes of the British people and to help realise their aspirations, it needs to develop modern institutions, decentralise power, and establish a new settlement between the individual, the community and the state. The second theme is that people's sense of 'Britishness' is not to be found in the use of that word, particularly when it is opposed to terms such as 'Scottish' or 'Welsh', but rather through understanding the shared values and shared pride in British institutions like the NHS. We need a stronger and more secure sense of ourselves if we are to achieve a modern society and constitution, and build a role in the world. The third theme makes the point that in the new global economy, where raw material, capital and inventions can be bought from anywhere at any time, the unique resources of a nation lie in the potential skills and talents of its people. Because we are a creative, inventive, adaptable people – steeped in the ethic of hard work, self-improvement through education, and fair play – we are well placed to take advantage of a revolutionary shift in the patterns of the world economy.

The second speech was to a Smith Institute special conference on Britishness held in April 1999, and here the Chancellor focused particularly on the nations of the UK, and their contribution to Britain in the forthcoming century. Recalling the enduring British values of creative enterprise and hard work, of outward-looking tolerance and fairness, he used new research to argue that the British people believe that we are stronger as one Britain together, weaker apart; that this belief in Britain is rooted not so much in old institutions as in enduring values; and that the reason that in the eighties and early nineties the divisive forces of separatism grew – and uncertainty about Britain developed – was not because different values were driving the peoples of our country apart but because our unreformed institutions had ceased to reflect our shared values. This leads the Chancellor to suggest that it is time to modernise our constitution; to renew the settlement between individual, community and state because power has become over-centralised and must be redistributed. And it also leads him to argue that communities and the government should do more to empower those who have been denied the opportunity of participating in modern Britain, whether this is by geography, race, disability, ethnicity or gender. As he says:

> The British way is to break up centralised institutions that are too remote and insensitive and so devolve power . . . to restore and enhance local initiative and mutual responsibility in civic affairs and thus to strengthen local institutions . . . to encourage and enhance the status of voluntary and community organisations in the service of their neighbourhoods . . . to develop a strong cohesive society in which in return for responsibility there is opportunity for all . . . to examine how best in this generation we advance individual potential through a supportive community . . . to encourage the creative talents of all and in the interests of fair play to offer the unemployed new opportunities . . . to adapt the Welfare State to new needs around the work ethic: modernising Britain's institutions and society to meet new challenges in line with the British qualities we have always demonstrated in our past.

The third speech is the 70th British Council Anniversary Lecture, given on 7 July 2004. In this impressive speech the Chancellor points out that on some of the bigger issues of our time, such as Europe, or the reform of the second chamber, or devolution, or asylum and immigration, there is still no consensus about what we should stand for as a country, or even how the British national interest is defined. Early on in the speech, the

Chancellor analyses the contributions of many writers, journalists and politicians who have written and spoken about Britishness over the years. He is hard on Thatcherism, and its stress on individualism over corporatism, arguing that it left unresolved all the big questions about Britain's future, including devolution, our constitution, and our relationship with Europe and the rest of the world. He quotes the views of many contemporary commentators, including Andrew Marr, Neil Ascherson, Tom Nairn, Norman Davies, Roger Scruton, Simon Heffer, Ferdinand Mount and Melanie Phillips and others representing all parts of mainstream opinion, but concludes that beyond certain individual issues, some common ground does exist: it is 'the recognition of the importance of and the need to celebrate and entrench a Britishness defined by shared values strong enough to overcome discordant claims of separatism and disintegration'.

In this speech, the Chancellor takes the Britishness arguments further than he has done before, not least in addressing the question of how Britain should relate to Europe and the rest of the world. He concludes that, for all the changes wrought by globalisation, national identity is still a vital force; and that only by understanding our Britishness, and the very things that bind our country together, will we be able to meet the challenges of the future. He argues that while the nation state must continue to represent our national interest, it is through a close constructive relationship with our European partners that Britain will not only enjoy greater prosperity but continue to have influence and continue to make a positive contribution on the world stage. As he says: 'The more influence we have in Paris and Berlin, the more influence we have in Washington. Equally, the less influence we have in the European capitals the less influence we have around the world.'

And his analysis of Britishness also leads the Chancellor to conclude that British values have much to offer Europe as it develops. Being in and leading in Europe means we can contribute British ideas to the development of the European Union. Our British qualities that will help Europe are openness to trade and our outward-looking and internationalist instincts and connections which stretch across the world; our creativity as a nation and our adaptability; our insistence on the importance of public service and openness in the running of institutions; and other values we share which stress the importance of hard work, self-improvement through education, fair play, and opportunity for all.

In the Spectator Lecture given on 4 November 1997, the Chancellor

takes three themes as he approaches what Britishness means to new
Labour: the first starts from a phrase adapted from George Orwell about
the 'British genius' which he argues is 'not just inventive and creative,
adaptable and hard-working, with a strong sense of fair play and public
service; but is also outward-looking, tolerant and internationalist'. The
second theme is that people's sense of 'Britishness' is not to be found in
the use of that word, particularly when it is opposed to terms such as
'Scottish' or 'Welsh', but rather through understanding the shared values
and shared pride in British institutions like the NHS. The third theme
makes the point that in the new global economy, where raw material,
capital and inventions can be bought from anywhere at any time, the
unique resources of a nation lie in the potential skills and talents of its
people. Because we are a creative, inventive, adaptable people – steeped
in the ethic of hard work, self-improvement through education, and fair
play – we are well placed to take advantage of a revolutionary shift in the
patterns of the world economy.

I want to argue this evening that the qualities of Britishness – being
creative, adaptable and outward-looking, believing in liberty, duty
and fair play – that taken together amount to a British genius, can
help us to tackle the biggest challenges we face and place modern
Britain at the forefront of a new era. I will argue, in particular, that
the British way is not to retreat into a narrow insularity and defensive
isolationism, but to be confidently outward-looking and to lead by
example. The British way is not to fear change but to embrace it,
confident in the knowledge that the British people, more than any
other, have the practical creativity and innate adaptability to master
change and turn it to our advantage. The British way is not to exalt
self-interested individualism but, throughout the centuries, has been
to foster a uniquely rich and continuously evolving relationship
between individual, community and state. At its best it creates a
vibrant civil society, one that is enterprising, cohesive and strong. My
conclusion will be that to lead as a country, and to achieve a modern
society and constitution and build a role in the world, we need a
stronger and more secure sense of ourselves.

The post-war period in Britain can be seen, in retrospect, as a
period of soul-searching and – from the independence of India in
1947, to the Hong Kong handover half a century later – a fifty-year

quest to define a new identity for ourselves in the world in the face of profound changes around and affecting us. Of course, all European nations had to embark on similar journeys after the apocalypse of the Second World War. But with a larger empire to steer towards independence, and a past of historic power and greatness, it has, for Britain, been a more protracted and troubled journey.

In the 1950s, Harold Macmillan tried to give us a role as civilised Athens to the thrusting Rome of the United States. In the 1960s, Harold Wilson tried to persuade us that we could transcend history as the white heat of the technological revolution would create a new modern Britain out of the ashes of the past. By the 1970s, it was clear that neither approach had succeeded in forging a new modern identity for Britain. And Margaret Thatcher arrived with the promise that she – and only she – could make us great again by stripping away the post-war accretions of corporatism to reveal the true Britain beneath. To her great credit she recognised the need for Britain to reinvent itself and rediscover a new and vital self-confidence; and understood that we could gain strength from the glories of our past which could point the way to a glorious future. In reaction to the failures of the post-war corporatist state, she argued for a full-blooded individualism as the British way, indeed that all that was needed was a rediscovery of 'Victorian values', which she construed as a minimal state (no such thing as society) and a culture of self-help. These things, she argued, had once made us great and would make us great once more.

But while the Thatcherites exalted individualism over collectivism, a moment's consideration tells us that even Victorian society was grounded in a more complex interplay between the claims of self-interest, duty and fairness. In counterpoising self-interest to collectivism without considering the importance British people attached to fair play and to belonging to a society, the Thatcherites mistook historical circumstances – the retreat from old-style collectivism – for eternal truths. And, in response to the Cold War, and in her attempt to rebuild Britain's post-imperial position, Margaret Thatcher believed our post-war status could be resurrected by being a junior partner, albeit one which, in her view, supplied ideological backbone, to the United States in a Cold War crusade. Britain, it was argued, could afford to ignore Europe. For a time it seemed to many of her supporters that she had succeeded in reinventing Britain in this way. But once the Communist threat evaporated, there was little left to validate our international position. And the attempts to replace the old threat from Moscow with a new kind of threat from Bonn found no long-term resonance. While the Thatcherites were left telling us Britain did best when it stood alone, a little considera- tion of our history would find we have been – historically – outward- looking, internationalist and European.

So advances, achievements and important changes to Britain under the Thatcher government there were. But now in 1997, it is clear that its ideology left all the great questions about Britain's future unresolved: the relationship between the nations of the United Kingdom, the future of our constitution, our cohesiveness as a community, and our relationship with Europe and the rest of the world. The Thatcherites understood that Britain had to change. They knew that the answer lay in a modern idea of Britishness – under- standing our roots and strengths as a nation. But in rebuilding the concept of Britishness from individual self-interest and mistrust of foreigners, a very narrow base indeed, they misunderstood what sort of nation Britain is and the source of our greatest strengths. In other words they learnt wrong lessons from our past. They did not, in my view, appreciate that our most glorious achievements flowed from a Britishness that is far more complex and sophisticated than the one Mrs Thatcher and her supporters mythologised.

So what does being British mean to me? First, we should be clear that our sense of being British matters as much as ever. Of course cultural and economic globalisation has had a profound effect on our sense of ourselves. When capital crosses national frontiers at the push of a key, air travel has made the outside world personally familiar to millions, television has brought it into the homes of millions more and suprana- tional organisations like the European Union and the World Trade Organisation play an increasingly important role in the world, it is natural to look again at what it means to be British. For some global challenges the nation state may be too small, hence the fashionable but in my view erroneous view that the concept of national identity has declining relevance. For some local challenges it may be too big, hence the interest in and support for devolution and, in particular, a Scottish Parliament and the Welsh Assembly.

But the Scottish people, for the most part, have no difficulty in being Scottish and British. Indeed the lesson of devolution is that it is because national identity resides essentially in people, that reform of institutions can take place without diminishing British national identity. So what is the essence of Britishness for me? I believe that when we talk about the character of a country, we are not talking about some mystery of the blood or a pattern on a flag just as we are not talking only about its traditional institutions. We are talking about the qualities of a people, of the collective experience they have shared over time, qualities that are rooted in their geography and their history. Britain's island position has, for some, been an excuse for insularity of mind, but it is precisely because we are a group of small islands, bounded by the sea, that we have always looked beyond our own horizons. As much as one quarter of our GDP arises from imports and exports – 25 per cent against America's 10 per cent. The open seas have always been for Britons more of a highway to the wider world than a moat cutting us off from it.

Our history is not, as John Major once famously – and erroneously – said, one of 1,000 years of union between our peoples but – and this is the real historical point – one of 2,000 years of successive waves of invasion, immigration, assimilation and trading partnerships that have created a uniquely rich and diverse culture. Through these 2,000 years – out of these tidal flows of history – certain forces emerge again and again which make up a characteristically British set of qualities – qualities which, taken together, George Orwell once described as the British genius. Because these islands have always been remarkably outward-looking and open, this country has fostered a vigorously adaptable society and has given rise to a culture both creative and inventive. But an open and adapting society also needs to be rooted and Britain's roots are on the most solid foundation of all – a passion for liberty anchored in a sense of duty and an intrinsic commitment to fair play. Taken together these qualities – being creative, adaptable and outward-looking, our believing in liberty, duty and fair play – add up to the British genius, a genius that has been manifest throughout our history.

First, a creativity and inventiveness: from the first agricultural revolution to the pioneering work of Babbage and Turing that made possible the computer and information revolution; in science, discoveries from Newton to DNA and cloning; in engineering from the steam engine to the TV; and, in medicine, from penicillin to interferon. An inventiveness that has ranged right across medicine and science to the arts and music. And now today British dynamism is leading the world in some of the most modern and creative industries – communications, fashion, film, popular music and art, architecture, and many areas of science and the environmental technologies. Second, a willingness and ability to adapt that enabled Britain to embrace the opportunities of the Industrial Revolution with unprecedented vigour and success, and to mobilise from peace to war to survive and triumph in two world conflicts. Thirdly, an outward-looking internationalism that made us not just the workshop of the world but the greatest trading nation the world has ever seen. Fourth, a passion for liberty matched by a strong sense of duty; a belief that rights and responsibilities go together; which made Britain lead the way in democratic reforms to restrict arbitrary power from 1689 and for 300 years. Finally, a belief in fair play, a tolerance that has enabled us to welcome successive waves of immigrants – from Saxons and Normans to Huguenots and Jews and Asians and Afro-Caribbeans – into what today is a thriving, multicultural nation. And a belief in treating people fairly: rewarding hard work, encouraging self-improvement through education, for nearly half a century reflected in a cross-party consensus in favour of equality of opportunity, all of this captured in George Orwell's word 'decency'.

Now, in highlighting an alternative view of British history, one which places intrinsically British qualities at its centre, I do not want to claim moral superiority for Britain or romanticise the past. Of course lots of abuses existed. Lots of men and even more women remained unfree and poor. No one should gloss over the dark sides of our past or its inequities. We have had our failures. All nations have. But I believe these qualities, which together have been responsible for the best of our past and thus provide a unique insight into our history, must inform and guide any debate of the central questions for our future. Creative by being adaptable and outward-looking – with a strong sense of what is fair, grounded in liberty and duty. These are the qualities of an old country with the strength to continuously renew itself. It is our understanding of them that guide the modernisations now being undertaken by new Labour.

That is why, for example, our Budget sent the first important signals that we want to encourage creative talents in Britain and to do so by extending opportunities to develop them. The British way is not to neglect them in the interests of some crude free-market dogma but to encourage and support them. Indeed in a world where capital raw materials can be bought from anywhere, the one indigenous national resource that remains – the creative talent of British people, from our scientists to our musicians – holds the key to future economic success. Future Budgets will continue to encourage creative talent.

And in tackling the two biggest political challenges we face as a country – the settlement between individual, community and state within Britain and the relationship between Britain and the rest of the world – I believe we must now draw strength from our British qualities.

The British way: the individual and the community: not individualism. There is a golden thread which runs through British history of the individual standing firm against tyranny and the arbitrary use of power. It runs from that long-ago day in Runnymede to the Bill of Rights in 1689 to not just one but four great Reform Acts within less than a hundred years. The great tradition of British liberty has, first and foremost, been rooted in the protection of the individual against the arbitrary power of the state. But it is a golden thread which has also twined through it a story of common endeavour in villages, towns and cities, men and women with shared needs and common purposes, united by a strong sense of duty and often an even stronger sense of fair play. And their efforts together produced uniquely British settlements that, from generation to generation, have balanced the rights and responsibilities of individuals, communities and state.

The two ideologies that have dominated the histories of other countries have never taken root here. On the one hand an ideology of state power, which choked individual freedom, making the individual slave to some arbitrarily defined collective interest, has found little or no favour in Britain. On the other hand an ideology of crude individualism – which leaves the individual isolated, stranded, on their own, detached from society around them – has no resonance for a Britain which has a rich tradition of voluntary organisations, local democracy and civic life. So whenever rulers have tried to impose state control or a crude ideology of individualism, they have never for long enjoyed the support of the British people. Instead, because of our sense of social obligation and fair play the British people never, for long, lost sight of a middle way: the good that can be done when the individual is empowered by the community around him or her, whether it be public health, welfare or education.

So the British way has always been more than self-interested individualism as, even in the heyday of free-market philosophy, writers like Adam Smith and Samuel Smiles recognised. Victorian prosperity and improvement were founded on something more and something greater than harsh organised selfishness. Entrepreneurial vigour – the very creativity that I have singled out – went hand in hand with a spirit of responsibility and mutuality. Victorian Britain was successful when that creativity and economic drive which went with it were combined with the sense of social obligation – often infused with religious values – and a broad moral commitment to civic improvement. If we want an emblem of real Victorian values, we only have to think of the Great Exhibition at Crystal Palace in 1851, the very first world trade fair. It was funded largely by private enterprise, yes, but it was also driven and supervised by government. It celebrated our creativity in British industry and innovation, yes, but it was in no way insular: it also welcomed exhibits and competitors from the rest of the world. Employers nationwide paid for their workers to travel to London to see what they had achieved. It trumpeted the achievements of British industry, yes, but contemporaries also called it a temple of labour. Self-help was not so much a belief in an ethic of self-interest which might benefit only a few but a commitment to an ethic of hard work and self-improvement that could unite all.

And in this way Britain benefited not just from pioneering inventors, entrepreneurs and financiers, but from a pioneering commitment to education, and to municipal provision of public amenities from libraries to parks and the basic infrastructure of our towns and cities. Long before the idea of national insurance was taken up by the state, individuals and communities were showing the way. Miners were forming self-insurance unions, docking part of their pay in order to provide some kind of security for each other in sickness, injury and death. From craft unions and credit unions, through collective contributions to hospitals and schools, right through to the great and unique achievement of a National Health Service and our Welfare State, our society has evolved through this realisation that we can act more effectively in concert than we can ever do alone.

But it is not just the British commitment to liberty and mutual responsibility that have informed our political settlements. It is also our adaptability. For me, the remarkable lesson of British history is our bold and often fearless and imaginative ability to adapt to change. To have managed change for 300 years without violent revolution is unique. I find it extraordinary that some appear to believe that it is somehow British to defend the idea of a constitution that never changes: it is precisely our ability to change our constitution that characterises the British way. Stability in our society does not come from rigidity: it comes from the ability to accommodate (and master) change – as earlier Conservatives recognised. As Benjamin Disraeli said in 1867, 'change is inevitable in a progressive society. Change is constant.' In the past this nation led the world in responding to political and economic change. And even Conservatives celebrated that. 'A state without the means of change', Edmund Burke famously declared, 'is without the means of its conservation.'

So the British way is to embrace, not fear, constitutional reform. That is why the new Labour government believes that our plans to modernise our constitution build upon our inheritance rather than threaten it. The British way is to recognise when we need to renew the settlement between individual, community and state and act upon that recognition. Today, we recognise that power has become overcentralised and must be redistributed. And today also, we recognise that too many have been denied opportunity, and communities and government can do more to empower them. The British way is thus to break up centralised institutions that are too remote and insensitive and so devolve power. The British way is to restore and enhance local initiative and mutual responsibility in civic affairs and thus to strengthen local institutions. The British way is to encourage and enhance the status of voluntary and community organisations – Burke's 'little platoons' – in the service of their neighbourhoods. The British way is to develop a strong cohesive society in which in return for responsibility there is opportunity for all. The British way is to examine how best in this generation we advance individual potential through a supportive community. This is what lies behind our programme for educational and employment opportunity and 'welfare to work'. This is one example of new ways and different methods in keeping with British traditions – our programme for modernising the Welfare State, taking unemployed men and women from welfare to work. The British way is to encourage the creative talents of all and in the interests of fair play to offer the unemployed new opportunities as we are doing. It is to offer these rights in return for the duty to take up the rights as we are doing. It is to move from centrally imposed schemes and construct a programme based on local initiative with community and voluntary organisations and private companies at its forefront as we are doing. And it is to adapt the Welfare State to new needs around the work ethic it is reinventing the idea of welfare for the modern age as we are doing. This in my view is the British way: modernising Britain's institutions and society to meet new challenges in line with the British qualities we have always demonstrated in our past.

I turn to the second central issue facing our country: relations between Great Britain and the wider world. The end of the Cold War inevitably intensified the uncertainty about our role in the world. Up till 1989 we had seen ourselves as partners with the US fighting the Cold War – an assessment that postponed any real creation of a post-imperial role. The end of the Cold War has sparked off calls to reassess our whole relationship with Europe as part of a wider rethinking of our role in the world. The questioning of our role in Europe did not therefore start with Maastricht. It started with the end of Empire and intensified with the end of the Cold War. In other words, the starting point is not Europe but our view of ourselves in the world. The European question can only be answered properly after we have addressed the British question.

As I said earlier, one view of Britishness starts from the proposition that Britain does best when we stand alone, free of long-term continental attachments. Indeed, recently there has been a wholesale rewriting of history to suggest that joining Europe was one of many wrong turnings in our twentieth-century history, that Britain's traditional way of life and sovereignty are in danger of being submerged, and that Britain's future lies outside Europe. Of course, Britain's relationship with Europe has neither been exclusive nor constant. Any study of the history of Britain in Europe shows we have always taken a pragmatic rather than dogmatic view of the best relationship with Europe. Indeed we have always been European; from waves of settlers who came to these islands from Europe – whether Celts, Romans, Anglo-Saxons, Vikings or Normans – to our central role in the dynastic struggles where we sought a stable balance of power in Europe to counteract any one nation's ascendancy. When a new world role came in the seventeenth and eighteenth centuries as maritime power became imperial power, this did not replace our

European role, but was added to it. In the mid-nineteenth century Palmerston was preoccupied not with India but with Europe. In the nineteenth century this pragmatism became formalised as the balance-of-power thesis. Hence Palmerston said we had no eternal allies, no perpetual enemies. Our aim was always to moderate extremes in the interests of stability. In British foreign policy no less than in our domestic settlements British qualities of openness and adaptability have held sway. Our history shows not just that we have always been a European power but that Britain has been European for good pragmatic reasons. So we should dismiss the notion that our history suggests being British is synonymous with being anti-European.

As the experience of the first half of this century showed – in two world wars – Britain did not and would not relinquish our role in Europe or abdicate responsibility for the progress of the Continent. Europe, by virtue of history as well as geography, is where we are. And our approach must be guided by, as always, a common-sense engagement in pursuit of our national interest. Rigid and inflexible ideology has never been the British way and under this government will never be. The idea that we could withdraw from Europe or be outside Europe's mainstream and instead become a Hong Kong of Europe – a low-wage competitor with the Far East – or a tax haven servicing major trading blocs – the idea of a Greater Guernsey – only needs a minute's consideration to be rejected. Britain, which has been a European first-rank power for several centuries, often holding the balance of power within Europe, would become a spectator in Europe's future development. That, in my view, is not the British way.

Of course, the nation state is and will remain the focus of our British identity and our loyalty. It is entirely right that the test of whether we want to be part of any future European venture is whether it is good for Britain's national interest. The nation state will and must continue to represent our national interest. That is why we reject federalism. But I believe that it is through a close constructive relationship with our European partners that Britain will not only enjoy greater prosperity but continue to have influence and continue to make a positive contribution on the world stage. The more influence we have in Paris and Bonn, the more influence we have in Washington. Equally the less influence we have in the European capitals the less influence we have around the world. Our Atlantic alliance is not in contradiction with our European commitments. British interests are best served by being strong in Europe.

And those who say there is a constitutional objection to a single currency have failed to take on board that where a pooling of political and economic sovereignty has been in the British interest – as in NATO and indeed in the existing single market of the European Union – we have been willing and sufficiently adaptable to embrace it in the British interest. Just as before, the test of the single currency will be pragmatic; clear and unambiguous economic benefits in the national interest.

Of course Europe needs to modernise as Britain is modernising. We want Europe to be more open, more competitive, more flexible, to set its sights as we have done on higher growth and employment, moving beyond the sterile debate between regulation and deregulation with a new emphasis on skills, productivity and employment opportunity. Europe needs structural economic reforms alongside its enlargement. But I believe that British values have much to offer Europe as it develops. Being in and leading in Europe means we contribute British ideas to the development of the European Union. Our British qualities that will help Europe are openness to trade and our outward-looking and internationalist instincts and connections which stretch across the world; our creativity as a nation and our adaptability; our insistence on the importance of public service and openness in the running of institutions; and other values we share with others which stress the importance of hard work, self-improvement through education and fair play and opportunity for all.

These are all British qualities – qualities many of which we share with other countries, qualities that I want to bring to British engagement in Europe. These are the very qualities that can help the nations of Europe go forward together into a more prosperous twenty-first century. So to those who say that the future means Britain submerged in Europe, I say the opposite: with an emphasis on these qualities Europe can learn from Britain, just as we in Britain can learn from the rest of Europe. It is strange therefore that the Conservative Party, which has normally taken a pragmatic view of British national interest, should now tell us that even if the economic arguments for joining a single currency were compelling they would not necessarily support it; and that the national economic interests may now come second to their ideological objections. If they believe a single currency wrong in principle why do they not oppose it for one hundred years? If they believe the test is whether it is good for the economy why do they rule it out, without any economic rationale, for ten years?

Previous Conservative governments have sensibly supported the pooling of sovereignty not just in NATO but in the single market, where it is in the British interest to do so. My conclusion is that anti-Europeanism in the Conservative Party rather than concern for the constitution is now precluding a more sensible position. Dogma is triumphing over the national interest. History suggests to me – and I have explained this evening why it does so – that there are no grounds for believing that to be pro-British it is necessary to be anti-European. Indeed, history suggests that, far from being isolationist, Britain has always thrived when it is outward-looking and internationalist. So I believe the right-wing view – that to be pro-British you have to be anti-European – is not only wrong but increasingly irrelevant to the debate about how best we pursue Britain's economic interest. And it is increasingly out of touch with the pro-European mainstream national consensus about the single currency that we are now building.

This is where the debate must lie. For years now the right have claimed they are the only patriotic party, the British party, and in every election I have fought they have scorned the left and patriotic people on the left, who are proud of their Britishness, for being anti-British. Today, as I suggest, this old and bogus dividing line in British politics has been swept aside. The old caricature – patriotic right versus disloyal left – is exposed as hollow, a card that can never be played again. Our patriotism – outward-looking and internationalist – reflects British traditions and British qualities. Just as this has been the traditional British way it is the modern British way. Indeed it is only if, as a country, we retreat into our shell – into a narrow-minded isolationism – that people will conclude that Britain has had its day. And it is because I believe that isolationism will never, for long, be anything other than a marginal influence in British politics that I consider that a new consensus that is outward-looking and internationalist and European is not only the British way forward but can and will be built in this country: a national consensus that can stretch across the country, and throughout business and industry.

So from our past we find our future, the key to the modernisation of Britain's institutions and our role in the world. And starting from what

I have called the British genius – to be creative by being outward-looking and adaptable, with a strong sense of fair play founded on liberty and duty – we find the way to the new Britain. Our history teaches us the British way is not to fear change but to embrace and master it. The British way is not a self-interested individualism but to build a strong cohesive society where there is opportunity for all. The British way is not to retreat into a narrow insularity and defensive isolationism, but to be open, confidently outward-looking and to lead by example. The British way, the way forward, the way ahead to a modern Britain in which we all can have pride.

At a Smith Institute Conference on Britishness held in April 1999, the Chancellor focused particularly on the nations of the UK, and their contribution to Britain in the forthcoming century. Recalling the enduring British values of creative enterprise and hard work, of outward-looking tolerance and fairness, he used new research to argue that the British people believe that we are stronger as one Britain together, weaker apart; that this belief in Britain is rooted not so much in old institutions as in enduring values; and that the reason that in the eighties and early nineties the divisive forces of separatism grew – and uncertainty about Britain developed – was not because different values were driving the peoples of our country apart but because our unreformed institutions had ceased to reflect our shared values.

This leads the Chancellor to suggest that it is time to modernise our constitution; to renew the settlement between individual, community and state because power has become over-centralised and must be redistributed. And it also leads him to argue that communities and the government should do more to empower those who have been denied the opportunity of participating in modern Britain, whether this is by geography, race, disability, ethnicity or gender. As he says:

'The British way is to break up centralised institutions that are too remote and insensitive and so devolve power . . . to restore and enhance local initiative and mutual responsibility in civic affairs and thus to strengthen local institutions . . . to encourage and enhance the status of voluntary and community organisations in the service of their neighbourhoods . . . to develop a strong cohesive society in which in return for responsibility there is opportunity for all . . . to examine how best in this generation we advance individual potential through a supportive community . . . to encourage the creative talents of all and in the interests of fair play to offer the unemployed new opportunities . . . to adapt the Welfare State to new needs around the work ethic: modernising Britain's institutions and society to meet new challenges in line with the British qualities we have always demonstrated in our past.

. . .

I will show how a Britain, previously held back by what has often been a disabling nostalgia for a story-book uniformity, for things that are lost and things that never were, can and must yield to a Britain increasingly strengthened, not divided, by the reality of our diversity and by the shared values that flow from the rich interaction of our traditions, experiences and peoples. I will suggest that the whole of Britain will benefit from the birth of new centres of power and initiative throughout our country and that we can be proud of a Britain which becomes the first successful multicultural, multi-ethnic and multi-national country in the world. Indeed, when diversity becomes a source of strength and when British values are given new expression in modern British institutions, Britain will not only become a more culturally confident, and socially cohesive country, but a more economically successful one too.

Two years ago when I gave the Spectator Lecture on 'the British genius' I argued that Britain is best defined not by ancient institutions but by living values that British people shared. I suggested that the old order of unreformed institutions that was once 'the ground of Britain's being' was passing into history. And I said that by rediscovering great British qualities – being creative, adaptable and outward-looking, believing in liberty, duty and fair play – what I called, in Orwell's words, the British genius – Britain will be best placed to tackle the great challenges of a global economy.

Professor Linda Colley argues that Great Britain was an eighteenth-century construct. It was crafted in response to perceived external threats – religious and military – and then subsequently reinforced in the expansion and defence of the British Empire and the perceived benefits it brought. For two centuries Britishness was most commonly expressed in this imperial role and in deference to the institutions which embodied empire, from the monarchy down-wards. This traditional view of Britishness – bound up with imperial ambitions and responsibilities – could not indefinitely survive the end of empire.

Linda Colley has written:

> The factors that provided for the forging of the British nation in the past have largely ceased to operate . . . different kinds of Britons no longer feel the same compulsion to remain united in the face of the enemy from without . . . and crucially both commercial supremacy and imperial hegemony have gone . . . and no more can Britons reassure themselves of their distinct and privileged identity by contrasting themselves with impover-ished Europeans or by exercising authority over manifestly alien peoples.

Indeed the post-war period in Britain can be seen, in retrospect, as a time of soul-searching. Of course, all European nations had to embark on similar introspections amid the ruins left by the Second World War. But for us the task seemed to be longer, harder and more complex. From the independence of India in 1947 to the Hong Kong handover half a century later as it shed the old Empire, Britain has been engaged in a protracted and agonising quest to define a new identity, a new sense of ourselves and a new purpose.

. . .

When Margaret Thatcher came to power, she strove to resurrect our pre-war status by creating a Britain defined by what she saw as a return to nineteenth-century individualism, an unchanging constitu-tion and mistrust of foreigners. Mrs Thatcher certainly understood the need for change. She recognised the importance of an appeal to enduring British values. Sadly her view of Britishness was far too narrow, and she learnt the wrong lessons from the past. In defining Britishness in terms of individual self-interest, an unchanging con-stitution and distrust of foreigners, she ignored our greatest strengths – the great British qualities of tolerance, fair play, public service and a practical outward-looking internationalism. And instead of respond-ing to the need to modernise our institutions around our values, she mistook an unwritten constitution for an unchanging constitution and became the apostle of constitutional rigidity. We should not forget that by the time she left office the great questions about our future – questions about our future relationship with Europe and the world, the future relationship between the nations of the United Kingdom, the future of our constitution, and indeed questions about the very cohesion of our society – were all unresolved. So, in the end, Mrs Thatcher's project foundered on too narrow a concept of Britishness, and on her stubborn faith in unreformed institutions that increasingly failed to reflect British values or respond to the demands of a new era.

By 1997, when new Labour came to power, Britain's traditional institutions were no longer able to command the loyalty they once did – to function as a sufficiently powerful cohesive force binding Britain together. Indeed unreformed institutions – based on an antiquated and indeed deferential view of British society – could not and cannot meet the challenges and pressures of our day. It is this old unreformed Britain that evoked the new nationalism, a nationalism an unreformed Britain found it difficult to contain. It is in these circumstances that we have embarked on a programme of constitutional economic and social reform. We recognise that our unity as a country cannot be based merely on memory or geography. Indeed, anyone trying to build the Britain of the twenty-first century solely on institutional change will fail unless that change is rooted in deep-seated and long-held beliefs of the British people. We must not forget that what went wrong for Britain is not that different communities in our country rejected values we had shared in common but that our institutions have ceased to reflect these values. And we must not forget either that these shared values come not from the imposition of a narrow uniformity of values or in institutions but from the interaction and cross-fertilisation of all the peoples, experiences and nations of our islands. The old Empire of interests must now be succeeded by the new Britain of shared values. And British institutions must be reformed and re-founded explicitly on British values.

What are these? Not least because of our geography – our island status – and our history I believe that the peoples of our islands have always been remarkably outward-looking and open. I believe that this country has, at its best, fostered a vigorously adaptable society that has given rise to a culture both creative and inventive. And I believe also that our open and adapting society is rooted in a passion for liberty anchored in a sense of duty and an intrinsic commitment to fairness. Taken together these qualities which add up to the British genius – being creative, adaptable and outward-looking, our belief in liberty, duty and fair play – are not only important in understanding our past but give us new direction for the future – new social and economic purpose. So in my view the British way is not to fear change but to embrace it, confident in the knowledge that British people have the practical creativity and innate adaptability to master change and turn it to our advantage. The British way is not to exalt a self-interested individualism but throughout the centuries to foster a uniquely rich and continuously evolving relationship between individual, community and state, a strong vibrant civil society where there is opportunity for all. The British way is not to retreat into a narrow insularity and defensive isolationism but to be open and tolerant, confidently outward-looking and to lead by example.

This notion of Britishness is more important than ever in the new context of globalisation. Forty of the top one hundred economies are now companies not countries. The lightning speed of technological transformation – while bringing us closer together in many ways – is also challenging our sense of ourselves and putting national identity to the test. Changes in the global economy are creating a world-wide culture – global communications and travel, global brand names, global music, films and entertainments and global media outlets. But many people also seek refuge from these homogenising forces in a reassertion of their own distinctiveness.

Arthur Schlesinger writes:

> The more people feel themselves adrift in a vast impersonal, anonymous sea, the more desperately they swim towards any familiar, intelligible protective life raft; the more they crave the politics of identity. Unless a common purpose binds nations together, tribal antagonisms will drive them apart. In the century ahead civilization faces a critical question – what is it that holds a nation together?

Today Britain has been under greater pressure because the new forces are beating against unreformed structures. One response to global changes – what Anthony Giddens calls in his current Reith Lectures 'our runaway world' – is to let Britain break apart: for those who are separatists the answer is not a better Britain but a shattered

Britain. Just as in the nineteenth century the response to industrialisation and uneven development was political nationalism, so too in
the late twentieth century, one response to globalisation is to retreat
into political nationalism. So the separatists call forth a different
future for our islands – divided into separate national states and
taught that their separateness is what matters most.

Yet the progressive response to global change is not to look
inwards, to cut ourselves off, to erect new barriers or in the face
of profound change to retreat to forms of factionalism. What Mario
Cuomo has written of America is true of Britain today: 'Most can
understand both the need to recognise and encourage an enriched
diversity as well as the need to ensure that such a broadened multi-
cultural perspective leads to unity. And not a destructive factionalism
that would tear us apart.'

And the unity we are talking about is not one forced upon all of us
by the imposition of a narrow and crude uniformity of values or
institutions. It is instead one that knows diversity can give us strength,
a multi-national Britain in which we are enriched and strengthened
by our different contributions and cultures. The loss of any of them
would diminish all of us.

So let us examine the values and then the common endeavours
that bind us together and what they mean for us in this new world. All
countries share values in common, values that are not necessarily
unique to them but which in combination can give rise to a special
and unifying identity. I have said that the reality is not simply that we
share a common island, a common language and a common history
but a broad range of defining values – a commitment to openness
and internationalism, to public service and fair play, to creativity and
inventiveness, to democracy and tolerance.

Not only does our survey evidence suggest that most people see
British identity as important to them – that being British matters –
and that they can happily accommodate being Scottish and British,
Welsh and British, English and British, or Cornish, English, and
British, but that their attachment to Britain is more than sentimental.
Interestingly what defines Britain for people is not so much past
glories or even ancient institutions as shared values, and the modern
institutions that reflect them. I note that in the survey carried out for
this conference 75 per cent agree 'the people of Britain derive
positive benefits from living and working together'. And this is as

true in Scotland where 73 per cent agree, and in Wales where 76 per cent do. Indeed 84 per cent agree that it is important for England, Scotland and Wales to work together to be a strong force in the new global economy (including 81 per cent in Scotland and 89 per cent in Wales). So people not only think we are better united, worse off divided, but also believe that the set of common values and concerns shared by England, Scotland and Wales is a good argument for the Union. Eighty-five per cent describe these values of tolerance and fairness as important, including 88 per cent in Scotland and 82 per cent in Wales.

And, interestingly, the important institutions most favoured for creating a distinctive identity for Britain were not those which would have resonated a century ago. We might expect the House of Commons to be chosen as very important by only 33 per cent. The BBC is indeed chosen as very important in defining Britain by more – 36 per cent. The army is chosen by 51 per cent. And of all British institutions the NHS was chosen most often as representative of Britain – chosen by 71 per cent. And if we look at these three British institutions – institutions promoting social provision, defence and culture – and the values that underpin them, we discover a great deal of what Britain means to people.

The National Health Service was, of course, not a specifically English or Scottish creation. If anything it was created by a Welshman, and it grew out of the demands from mining and industrial communities in all parts of Britain, that we should never again return to the indignities of the thirties where nurses had to leave the beds of their patients to run charity flag days. Today when people talk of the National Health Service, whether in Scotland, Wales or England, people think of the British National Health Service: here national is unquestionably 'British'. And its most powerful driving idea is that every citizen of Britain has an equal right to treatment regardless of wealth, position or race, and, indeed, can secure treatment in any part of Britain.

And at the heart of the National Health Service is a concept defined by Richard Titmuss when he wrote about blood donorship in Britain as the 'gift relationship'. Blood freely given by a citizen in any part of Britain is available to any British citizen in every part of Britain. This is a simple life-sustaining proof of a central truth: when we pool and share our resources and when the stronger help the weak it makes us all stronger. I believe that the ideal of common bonds and mutual interests linking our destinies together is as real for other public services: the ideal that every child in Britain should have equal opportunity in education. And the equally strong belief, widely felt throughout the country, that everyone in Britain who can work has both the right and responsibility to do so. When Scots, English or Welsh talk of the right to work, they do not normally distinguish between the rights of the Scottish, Welsh or English miner, computer technician, nurse or teacher.

People also believe that we are stronger in securing and defending our islands when we do so together. So it is not surprising that in our survey 83 per cent agree that it is important for the nations of Scotland, England and Wales to work together to guarantee peace and security (83 per cent in Scotland and 93 per cent in Wales). The British islands have for centuries formed a single natural strategic unit. It is only common sense ratified by centuries of experience and supported by all the polling evidence that Scotland, Wales and England benefit from the economies of scale inherent in a common approach to defence. Our people know that separate defences would cost more and be less effective and that a separate English, Welsh and Scottish foreign policy would leave each and all of us more vulnerable. This idea that we are stronger together, that no citizen of Britain should be a foreigner in Britain, no neighbour a stranger in Britain is quite distinct from the nationalist position as is of course the view of a common culture, our view that the culture of the whole of Britain should be equally accessible to the whole of Britain, and that no barriers, geographical, social, or cultural should stand in the way of opportunity for every citizen of Britain.

If we take but one example, the BBC: it was created by a Scot, but healthy devolution should not obscure the fact that it is a service that operates for the whole of Britain, is paid for by a sharing of costs by all the people of Britain, and is seen as a defining feature of Britain. Scotland or Wales could not, of course, afford the same service on today's licence fee. But the real question is how would Scotland or any other part of the United Kingdom benefit by excluding itself from the gains that come from being part of a broader mix of cultures. Most people believe that we gain from access to a common culture and the diversity of our distinctive contributions to it.

Indeed the survey evidence shows that people see that Britain is more than the sum of its parts and that there are direct and palpable gains from sharing. Of course the British idea of national insurance has changed over time. But no one can deny that the sharing of risks among 58 million citizens is a more durable and resilient support for the poor and thus for social justice than the sharing of risks among 5 million. And this is as true of the economy generally, where barriers should be coming down instead of going up.

Many of the consequences of Scottish or Welsh divorce from the rest of the United Kingdom can already be identified: higher taxes, lost jobs, businesses driven away and a huge fiscal deficit. In face of mounting evidence of the costs of separation the Welsh and Scottish Nationalists appear to be at odds. The Scottish and Welsh Nationalists appear to be separating from each other. The Scottish Nationalists insist on independence but have failed to publish their promised analysis of the fiscal position of a separate Scotland. I challenge the SNP to end the dishonesty of their campaign and to come clean with the people of Scotland about the costs of divorce – the black hole in their plans. It is time they published their long-promised, never-delivered independence manifesto. It is the missing manifesto of the current elections.

But the Welsh Nationalists are also trying to avoid the questions about the costs of separation; having, for years, put up posters arguing for independence, they are now trying to deny they support independence and have even removed from this year's party-membership card its previous commitment to self-government and separate representation at the United Nations.

Neither Scottish nor Welsh Nationalists can reconcile themselves to the realities of the new Britain the new government is forging – its inclusiveness, its commitment to participatory democracy, and its recognition that all citizens have a contribution to make. Every day the credibility gap grows between the essentially nineteenth-century nationalist view of isolated nation states divided against each other – and the twenty-first-century reality of interdependent economies and societies working together. I believe that the answer to nationalism, the case for Britain is, in the end, quite straightforward and even more compelling in the age of the global economy where barriers are coming down than in the age of Empire – that we gain from common services and are diminished without them; that we achieve more working together than working apart; that unity, out of diversity, gives us strength; that solidarity, the shared endeavour of working and cooperating together, not separation, is the idea of the future, and an idealism worth celebrating. And the sum is greater than its parts. Because Britain gains greater strength from the rich interaction of cultures and experiences, and thus from its pluralism, and because underpinning our institutions are shared values which have wide support.

We are, of course, talking not just about what Britain has been but what Britain can become. Not the old unionism, a legacy of empire, with its monolithic view of the state, an old order which, in its present form, cannot meet the challenge of separatism. We must build a constitution which reflects British values – and that requires a new and resilient relationship among individuals, communities and state – individuals as full citizens, pluralistic cultures as contributing communities, and the state as a guarantor of freedoms, empowering rather than dominating.

. . .

Much remains to be done but the establishment of Scottish, Welsh and Northern Irish democratic parliaments and assemblies represents a radical devolution of power from the centre. This creates, for the first time in hundreds of years, a new plurality of law-making institutions. So devolution does not create new identities: it gives existing identities an institutional form, whether it be Scotland, Wales or Northern Ireland. This is made explicit in the Good Friday Agreement, which for example states 'the birthright of all the peoples of Northern Ireland to identify themselves and be accepted as Irish or British or both'. What Deborah Mattison's survey evidence shows is that people in mainland Britain are comfortable with the idea of being Scottish or Welsh or English and also British at the same time. So the essence – the idea of union – remains and is indeed strengthened – that we are Scottish and British, Welsh and British, and English and British.

Within England, Regional Development Agencies and regional chambers arise from similar sentiments – that we are, for example, Cornish, English and British, from Yorkshire, England and Britain, loyalties that are not in conflict with each other but reinforce and enrich each other. None of these complex realities about regional and national – and, potentially, even European identities – are remotely reflected by the old constitutional arrangements – an old centralised state that was long portrayed but can no longer be defended as the eternal expression of Britishness. And we should not forget that the party that in 1997 supported an unchanging constitution lost all its parliamentary seats in Scotland and Wales.

The new plurality of institutions is not a redistribution of power in favour of one nationality and against another but the constitutional expression of a Britain which recognises diversity can be a source of strength and ensures that at each and every level people can participate and are now not subjects but citizens. The Britain of citizens will gain even more vitality in the Bill of Rights, which for the first time in Britain's history enshrines in law the basic principles of civil rights; in the Freedom of Information Act, which makes the state accountable for information held about its citizens; in the reform of local government, which gives substance to a very British idea, that decisions should be made by the people at the level closest to the people; and in the reform of the House of Lords, where heredity is no longer permitted to command voting power. These reforms are not simply protections for the individual against an overbearing state. These measures embody a new relationship between individual citizens, self-governing communities and enabling state in which the individual is enhanced by membership of their different communities and the state empowers rather than controls or directs. And with constitutional reform Britain now possesses not just a past to be proud of but a relevance for our future rooted in where people are from, in what they have long believed and what they feel themselves to be.

So when people say we have embarked on constitutional innovation without thinking, under pressure from this interest group or that, or that we have no coherent overall plan of reform, the challenge is easily answered. Those critics fail to understand that the modernisation of British institutions is rooted in our pride in Britain – applying enduring British values to a new era – and rejecting the constitutional rigidity that would leave us defending as eternal expressions of Britishness ancient institutions like the House of Lords that had long ceased to reflect British values. Our entire constitutional programme is designed to ensure modern British institutions that reflect enduring British values.

Can a Britain of citizens make the next leap forward in our history and become the first successful multi-cultural, multi-ethnic, multi-national country? For this we need not just tolerance but a new set of constitutional arrangements and a unifying and inclusive idea of citizenship – the challenge being to acknowledge and celebrate diversity in a way that strengthens our shared values and common institutions. America is, at its best, a strong multi-cultural, multi-ethnic country. As Trevor Philips has written: 'Americans have had to construct an idea of their nation from huge groups of people who had barely heard of each other before landing on American soil. By contrast, Britain has a thousand or more years of nation-building behind it, and historically speaking, we have had ripples, rather than waves, of immigration; change has been incremental.'

While America has absorbed and transcended the diverse ethnicities that came to its shores, America – unlike Britain – has never really been a multi-national state, with large contiguous areas of distinct national history and heritage. For Britain to succeed as multi-cultural, multi-ethnic and multi-national we must not only tolerate our differences. We must welcome them in a Britain of diversity where our shared life is enriched and reshaped by the very act of citizens, communities and nations freely and actively participating in it. In this way Britain is welcoming not only to the old nationalities which make up British citizenship but to the new nationalities which do so as well. To realise ourselves as a multi-cultural, multi-ethnic and multi-national country, colour must never be a badge of citizenship, an invitation to second-class treatment, or an excuse for discrimination. The Stephen Lawrence case illustrated the risks to all of us of institutionalised racism – and the public response to it demonstrated the prize for all of us if everyone, no matter their colour or race, is treated equally. Britain has the chance to escape the long night of racism that has blotted other democracies. And to do so the new Britain must not only demonstrate its values of tolerance to old and new nationalities and its determination to root out all discriminatory practices, but also show that out of the interaction of races as well as cultures we become a richer, stronger society.

Britain must also move – as it now is – from the Britain of old-fashioned economic and social policies which stifled creativity, work, and fairness to modern policies which make our economy stronger and liberate the potential of our people. Every economic and social reform we are making is creating a new Britain where from the foundation of these enduring values we harness modern technology for the benefit of all. The British belief in the virtues of hard work and self-improvement is sustained and extended in the new 'welfare to work' programme, our expansion in educational opportunity and investment, our programme for lifelong learning and our programme of making work pay. The British values of creativity and enterprise – the Britain of Newton, Watt, Fleming and Turing – is given new expression in innovative twenty-first-century industries, from fashion design, music and communications to British breakthroughs in medicine, biotechnology, information technology and modern manufacturing itself.

And Britain's history as outward-looking, open and tolerant is reaffirmed in our European and international policy. So after fifty years of soul-searching I believe that Britain is ready to be ambitious again and reach for big things; in Tony Blair's words, a beacon to the rest of the world. In 200 days we celebrate the year 2000. What matters is not that we cross the divide into a new century but what we decide to do with the next decade and next century. And I see a Britain where new centres of powers in Edinburgh, Cardiff and Belfast become vibrant forces pioneering change. And with Regional Development Agencies and chambers, centres in the north, north west, midlands and south too. London too will have its own authority. In the new multi-national Britain, Wales, Scotland and Northern Ireland and London are of course leading Britain in the fact and manner of devolution. But Regional Development Agencies and regional chambers are strengthening cities from Manchester and Liverpool to Newcastle and Bristol as centres of power and initiative too.

This is not just about institutions. It is about changing people's lives. Let me give one example – in the scale of educational opportunity, as devolution manifestos make clear, Scotland and Wales have ambitions to lead Britain. For Scotland and Wales the dream of educational opportunity for all – the democratic intellect – has been as important for our journeys as peoples, as the American dream has been for the American people. Now they must reflect that in the era of lifelong education. Scotland will have not just Britain's but Europe's first drugs enforcement agency. Northern local authorities have pioneered in new services from child care to crime prevention, and we are now seeing their innovations followed throughout Britain not least in our national childcare strategy and our policies for policing. The midlands have been leading Britain in linking universities and colleges and industry to develop modern manufacturing strength. Wales is pioneering a new bilingualism. And in culture, for example, British popular music has been successively reinvigorated from different centres of energy – from Bristol to Manchester, Liverpool to London.

So Britain is becoming a country where we can talk of Scotland leading Britain, Wales leading Britain, the north leading Britain – not only London leading Britain: new centres of leadership, new and vibrant forces for creative change. So while the old Britain is going, enduring British values are creating the new Britain – British people reaffirming our values, reshaping our institutions to express them, and making our country more confident in our culture, more cohesive in our society, and more successful in our economy. Britain – its citizens, its communities, its institutions – instead of growing apart – are ready once again to grow together.

In the 70th British Council Anniversary Lecture, given on 7 July 2004, the Chancellor's analysis of Britishness has developed. He points out that on some of the bigger issues of our time, such as Europe, or the reform of the second chamber, or devolution, or asylum and immigration, there is still no consensus about what we should stand for as a country, or even how the British national interest is defined.

In an important passage early on in the speech, the Chancellor analyses the contributions of many writers, journalists and politicians who have written and spoken about Britishness over the years. He is hard on Thatcherism, and its stress on individualism over corporatism, arguing that it left unresolved all the big questions about Britain's future, including devolution, our constitution, and our relationship with Europe and the rest of the world. He quotes the views of many contemporary commentators, including Andrew Marr, Neil Ascherson, Tom Nairn, Norman Davies, Roger Scruton, Simon Heffer, Ferdinand Mount and Melanie Phillips and others representing all parts of mainstream opinion, but concludes that beyond certain individual issues – some common ground does exist: it is the recognition of the importance of and the need to celebrate and entrench a Britishness defined by shared values strong enough to overcome discordant claims of separatism and disintegration.

In this important speech, the Chancellor takes the Britishness arguments further than he has done before, not least in addressing the question of how Britain should relate to Europe and the rest of the world.

He concludes that, for all the changes wrought by globalisation, national identity is still a vital force; and that only by understanding our British-ness, and the very things that bind our country together, will we be able to meet the challenges of the future. He argues that while the nation state must continue to represent our national interest, it is through a close constructive relationship with our European partners that Britain will not only enjoy greater prosperity but continue to have influence and con-tinue to make a positive contribution on the world stage. As he says: 'The more influence we have in Paris and Berlin, the more influence we have in Washington. Equally, the less influence we have in the European capitals the less influence we have around the world.'

And his analysis of Britishness also leads the Chancellor to conclude that British values have much to offer Europe as it develops. Being in and leading in Europe means we can contribute British ideas to the devel-opment of the European Union. Our British qualities that will help Europe are openness to trade and our outward-looking and internation-alist instincts and connections which stretch across the world; our creativity as a nation and our adaptability; our insistence on the im-portance of public service and openness in the running of institutions; and other values we share which stress the importance of hard work, self-improvement through education, fair play, and opportunity for all.

. . .

In the last half of the last century, post-imperial Britain came to be defined to the world by perceptions of national economic decline. In the first years of this new century we can begin to identify how:

- a once stop–go British economy is now stable;
- a once corporatist British business and industrial culture is seen now as more enterprising and more flexible;
- a country once characterised by high unemployment now enjoys record employment;
- a country on a rising tide of confidence can now aspire to become one of the great success stories of the new global economy.

But if we are to fully realise the economic potential of Britain my view is that we need something more. For the twelve years I have been

Shadow Chancellor or Chancellor, I have felt that our country would be better able to meet and master the challenges of ever more intense global competition if we could build a shared sense of national economic purpose. Indeed, over half a century, Britain has been damaged by the absence of agreement on economic purpose or direction: lurching for narrow political reasons from one short-term economic panacea to another, often public sector fighting private, management versus worker, state versus market in a sterile battle for territory, that deprived British businesses and British workforces of confidence about the long term and held our country back.

So when in 1997 I made the Bank of England independent my aim was to build a consensus across all sections of society about the priority we all attached to economic stability. A shared purpose not just across macro-economic policy but across the whole range of economic questions is, I believe, even more essential now not just to face up to global competition from Asia as well as Europe and America but if we are to have the strength as a country to make the hard choices on priorities that will determine our success. Creating a shared national purpose also reflects a deeper need: to rediscover a clear and confident sense of who we are as a country. I believe that just about every central question about our national future – from the constitution to our role in Europe, from citizenship to the challenges of multi-culturalism – even the question of how and why we deliver public services in the manner we do – can only be fully answered if we are clear about what we value about being British and what gives us purpose and direction as a country.

Take the vexed question of Europe. I believe it has been a lack of confidence about what Britain stands for that has made it difficult for us to feel confident about our relationship with, and our potential role in, Europe. And as a result led many to believe – wrongly – that the only choice for Britain is between splendid isolation and total absorption. As with the debate over all international questions, the debate over Europe is, at root, about how the British national interest is defined and what we should stand for as a country.

Take our constitution and all the great and continuing debates about the nature of the second chamber, the relationship of the legislative to the executive, the future of local and central government. Our approach to resolving each of these questions is governed by what sort of country we think we are and what sort of country we think we should become.

Take devolution and nationalism. While the United Kingdom has always been a country of different nations and thus of plural identities – a Welshman can be Welsh and British just as a Cornishman or -woman is Cornish, English and British – and may be Muslim, Pakistani or Afro-Caribbean, Cornish, English and British – the issue is whether we retreat into more exclusive identities rooted in nineteenth-century conceptions of blood, race and territory, or whether we are still able to celebrate a British identity which is bigger than the sum of its parts and a union that is strong because of the values we share and because of the way these values are expressed through our history and our institutions.

And take the most recent illustration of what challenges us to be more explicit about these issues: the debate about asylum and immigration – and the debate about multi-culturalism. Here the question is essentially whether our national identity is defined by race and ethnicity – a definition that would leave our country at risk of relapsing into making a misleading 'cricket test' or, worse, colour the determination of what it is to be British. Or whether there are values which shape our national identity and which all citizens can share – thus separating citizenship from race – and which can find explicit expression so that they become a unifying and strengthening force.

And this is important not just for tackling these questions – central as they are – but for an even larger reason. In a growingly more insecure world people feel a need to be rooted and they draw strength from shared purpose. Indeed if people are to cope successfully with often bewildering change then a sense of belonging is vital. And that, in turn, depends on a clear shared vision of national identity. And I want to suggest that our success as Great Britain – our ability to meet and master not just the challenges of a global marketplace but also the international, demographic, constitutional and social challenges ahead – and even the security challenges facing a terrorist threat that has never been more challenging and demands upon those charged with our security never greater – depends upon us rediscovering from our history the shared values that bind us together, and on us becoming more explicit about what we stand for as a nation.

But if these issues around national identity are so important, my starting question must be: why over decades have we as a country singularly failed to address them and yet we see – as Jonathan Freedland has so eloquently described – other countries, principally America, successfully defining themselves by values that their citizens share in common? The real answer, I believe, lies in our post-war history – in a loss of self-confidence and direction, even a resignation to national decline, a loss of self-confidence that is itself now becoming part of our history.

I was born in mid-century in what you might now call middle Scotland – in 1951. And while much was changing around us, Britain was still a country of fixed certainties that – echoing Orwell's *The Lion and the Unicorn* – were well understood, virtually unquestioned and barely stated. The early 1950s was the world of Sir Winston Churchill, a coronation that was reported with almost religious enthusiasm, an unquestionably United Kingdom, and around us symbols of an imperial Britain. I grew up in the fifties and sixties on maps of the world with a quarter of it pink and on British books and comics and then films which glorified the Blitz, the Spitfires, Sir Douglas Bader and endless reruns of *The Guns of Navarone*. This was, of course, a Britain whose confidence was built – unlike the USA – not on aspirations about the future but on real achievements of the past:

- the Britain that could legitimately make claim to be the first country in the world to reject the arbitrary rule of monarchy;
- the Britain that was first to make a virtue of tolerance and liberty;
- the Britain that was first in the Industrial Revolution;
- the Britain that was centre to the world's largest empire – the global economy of its day;
- the Britain that unlike continental Europe was never subject to revolution;
- the Britain that had the imperial mission which made us a world power and then a 'defence of the west' mission which appeared to justify a continuing sense of ourselves as a world power;
- the Britain that – unlike America, which as a country of immigrants had to define itself by its belief in liberty and opportunity for all – did not feel its exceptionalism called for any mission statement, or defining goals, or explicit national ethos. Indeed we made a virtue of understatement or no statement at all.

This is a long way from the image of Britain of recent decades – what now goes for 'post-war Britain' – that long half century of uncertainty: the Britain of managed decline – at home and abroad; of failing corporatism; of sterile self-defeating struggles between public and private sectors, management and unions, state and market (in the fifties it was said we had managed decline, in the sixties mismanaged decline, and in the seventies we declined to manage); the Britain of doubts and hesitations about Europe; of the growth of secessionist movements in Scotland and Wales; of, as immigration rose, a retreat by some into defining Britishness through race and ethnicity, what was called the 'cricket test'; and then, as the sun set on the Empire, the failed attempts to root our post-1945 identity simply in the longevity of our institutions alone – indeed in the idea of unchanging institutions.

It was almost as if we looked backward with nostalgia because we could not look forward with hope. And so as the gap between imperial myth and reality grew, so too the view grew that Britain was not, in fact, underpinned by any strong sense of Britishness at all. And it led to a questioning of the very existence of Britain, right across mainstream opinion. Indeed Andrew Marr, now the political editor of the BBC, chose to entitle his 'state of the nation' book *The Day Britain Died*, writing: 'I have a profound belief in the likelihood of a British union dissolving within a decade.' For Neil Ascherson, from the liberal left, all that remains of Britishness is 'a state, a flag and armed forces recruited from every part . . . just institutions . . . not social reality'. And with a similar eloquence his fellow Scottish writer Tom Nairn has argued that because there was little that is British left to underpin Britain, what he called 'the break-up of Britain' was inevitable.

Professor Linda Colley, whose ground-breaking historical research had demonstrated that the 'United Kingdom' was founded on great but ultimately transient historical forces – the strength of anti-French feeling, the bonds of empire and Protestantism – concludes:

> The factors that provided for the forging of the British nation in the past have largely ceased to operate. Protestantism, that once vital cement, has now a limited influence on British culture, as indeed has Christianity itself. Recurrent wars with the states of continental Europe have in all likelihood come to an end, so

different kinds of Briton no longer feel the same compulsion to remain united in the face of the enemy from without. And crucially both commercial supremacy and imperial hegemony have gone. And no more can Britons reassure themselves of their distinct and privileged identity by contrasting themselves with the impoverished Europeans or by exercising authority over manifestly alien peoples. God has ceased to be British and providence no longer smiles.

And the historian Norman Davies even lists eighteen British institutions which according to him have defined Britishness and which he now suggests have lost their authority, putting the existence of Britain in doubt. And this view of decline and decay – and then a profound sense we have lost our way as a country – is, if anything, held more forcibly today by writers and thinkers from the right – Roger Scruton (whose highly challenging study of Englishness is entitled 'an elegy'), Simon Heffer and Ferdinand Mount. For them the final nails in the coffin of Great Britain are not just devolution but Britain succumbing to multi-culturalism and to Europe. For Mount, quoting Orwell that 'England is perhaps the only great country whose intellectuals are ashamed of their own nationality', our nation could become 'one giant cultural mall in which we would all wander, free to choose from a variety of equally valuable lifestyles, to take back and exchange purchases when not given satisfaction or simply to window-shop'. And Melanie Phillips concludes 'the big political divide in the country is now clear . . . it is over nothing less than the protection of liberal democracy and the defence of the nation itself'.

Yet as I read these writers and thinkers I detect that beyond the battleground on individual issues – our relationship with Europe, devolution and the constitution, asylum and immigration – some common ground does exist: it is the recognition of the importance of and the need to celebrate and entrench a Britishness defined by shared values strong enough to overcome discordant claims of separatism and disintegration. Take David Goodhart's recent contribution to the multi-culturalism debate. In questioning whether there is an inherent conflict between the need for social cohesion and diversity he argues that he wanted to emphasise that what we need is 'a core set of social norms . . . who are we does matter'. And while Melanie Phillips argues that a culture war is raging she has a remedy rooted in shared values of Britishness. There is hope, she says, because 'if citizenship is to mean anything at all, ministers must sign up to an overarching set of British values'. Interestingly, while Sir Herman Ousley, former chairman of the Commission for Racial Equality, directly assails her views and indeed those of David Goodhart, he too returns to that same starting point – that there are British values all can share. Echoing Orwell's *England, My England*', his biographer Sir Bernard Crick argues that British 'people should have a sense of allegiance, loyalty, law and order, and political tolerance'. Even Tom Nairn writes of Britishness that 'there is a residual and yet still quite comfortable non-smallness about the term'.

But when we ask what are the core values of Britishness, can we find in them a muscularity and robustness that neither dilutes Britishness and British values to the point they become amorphous nor leaves them so narrowly focused that many patriotic British men and women will feel excluded? Of course, a strong sense of national identity derives from the particular, the special things we cherish. But I think we would all agree that we do not love our country simply because we occupy a plot of land or hold a UK passport but also because that place is home and because that represents values and qualities – and bonds of sentiment and familiarity – we hold dear. And it is my belief that out of tidal flows of British history – 2,000 years of successive waves of invasion, immigration, assimilation and trading partnerships that have created a uniquely rich and diverse culture – certain forces emerge again and again which make up a characteristically British set of values and qualities which, taken together, mean that there is indeed a strong and vibrant Britishness that underpins Britain. I believe that because these islands – and our maritime and trading traditions – have made us remarkably outward-looking and open, this country has fostered a vigorously adaptable society and has given rise to a culture both creative and inventive. But an open and adapting society also needs to be rooted and Britain's roots are on the most solid foundation of all, a passion for liberty anchored in a sense of duty and an intrinsic commitment to tolerance and fair play. The values and qualities I describe are of course to be found in many other cultures and countries. But when taken together, and as they shape the institutions of our country, these values and qualities – being creative, adaptable and outward-looking, our belief in liberty, duty and fair play – add up to a distinctive Britishness that has been manifest throughout our history, and shaped it. 'When people discard, ignore or mock the ideals which formed our national character, then they no longer exist as a people but only as a crowd,' writes Roger Scruton. And I agree with him.

For there is indeed a golden thread which runs through British history, of the individual standing firm for freedom and liberty against tyranny and the arbitrary use of power. It runs from that long-ago day in Runnymede in 1215 to the Bill of Rights in 1689 to not just one but four great Reform Acts within less than a hundred years. And the great tradition of British liberty has, first and foremost, been rooted in the protection of the individual against the arbitrary power of first the monarch and then the state. But it is a golden thread which has also twined through it a story of common endeavour in villages, towns and cities – men and women with shared needs and common purposes, united as neighbours and citizens by a strong sense of duty and of fair play. And their efforts – and that sense of duty and fair play – together produced uniquely British settlements that, from generation to generation, have balanced the rights and responsibilities of individuals, communities and state and led to a deeply engrained British tradition of public service.

First, liberty: it was Montesquieu who wrote in the eighteenth century that ours was 'the freest country in the world'. I would suggest that it is because different ethnic groups came to live together in one small island that we first made a virtue of tolerance, welcoming and including successive waves of settlers – from Saxons and Normans to Huguenots and Jews and Asians and Afro-Caribbeans, and recognising plural identities. Today 85 per cent believe a strong sense of tolerance is important to our country's success. And I would suggest that out of that toleration came a belief in religious and political freedom – illustrated best by Adam Nicolson's story of the creation of the King James Bible: different denominations coming together in committee to create what was called 'irenicon', which means a symbol of unity for the whole nation.

Liberty meant not just tolerance for minorities but a deeply rooted belief – illustrated early in our history by trial by jury – in the freedom of the individual under the law and in the liberty of the common people rooted in constantly evolving English common law. When Henry Grattan – the eighteenth-century Irish politician – attempted to sum up our unique characteristics, he said that you can get a parliament from anywhere but you can only get liberty from England. Indeed so powerful were the ideas contained in the 1689 Bill of Rights which led to liberty associations all over Britain that both sides in the American War of Independence fought 'in the name of British liberty' and before America took the word to be its own, liberty was, in fact, identified with Britain.

Of course liberty is, in Matthew Arnold's words, 'a very good horse to ride, but to ride somewhere'. And history is strewn with examples of how we failed to live up to our ideals. But the idea of liberty did mean, in practice, that for half a century it was Britain that led the worldwide anti-slavery movement with engraved on the badge of the Anti-Slavery Society a figure of a black man and the quote, 'Am I Not a Man and a Brother'. Indeed at home no slave was ever permitted and abroad the Royal Navy searched the world to eradicate slavery.

And this view of liberty not only produced the Bill of Rights and the anti-slavery movement but caused Britain to lead the way in restricting the arbitrary power of monarchs and then onward to the far-reaching democratic reforms of the nineteenth and twentieth centuries. And at every point this British belief in liberty has been matched by a British idea of duty as the virtue that reinforces neighbourliness and enshrines the idea of a public realm and public service. A belief in the duty of one to another is an essential element of nationhood in every country but whether it arose from religious belief, from *noblesse oblige*, or from a sense of solidarity, duty in Britain – for most of the time an unwritten code of behaviour rather than a set of legal requirements – has been, to most people, the foundation of rights rather than their consequence.

And the call to civic duty and to public service – often impelled by religious convictions – led to the mushrooming of local and national endeavour, of associations and clubs, a rich tradition of voluntary organisations, local democracy and civic life. From the guilds, the charities, the clubs and associations – which bred amongst other things the City of London's unique structure – and from the churches, to the municipal provision of public amenities like libraries and parks and then to the mutual insurance societies, trades unions and non-governmental organisations, the British way is to recognise and enhance local initiative and mutual responsibility in civil affairs and to encourage and enhance the status of voluntary and community organisations – Burke's 'little platoons' – in the service of their neighbourhoods.

Alongside that passionate commitment to duty, Britishness has also meant a tradition of fair play. We may think today of British fair play as something applied on the sports field, but in fact most of the time it has been a very widely accepted foundation of social order: treating people fairly, rewarding hard work, encouraging self-improvement through education and being inclusive. In his last speech to parliament in March 1955 – the speech that urged the British people to 'never flinch, never weary, never despair' – Churchill described the essential qualities of the British people and at the forefront was fair play. For other nations, he said, 'The day may dawn when fair play, love for one's fellow men, respect for justice and freedom, will enable tormented generations to march forth triumphant from the hideous epoch in which we have to dwell.'

And this commitment to fair play – captured in Orwell's word 'decency' – has animated British political thought on both left and right over the centuries, right through to the passion for social improvement of the Victorian middle classes and the Christian socialists and trade unions who struggled for a new welfare settlement in the twentieth century. It was a settlement – making opportunity available to all, supporting the most vulnerable in society, inclusive, and ensuring what we would today call social justice – which over nearly half a century brought forth agreement across party and across social classes. So the British way has always been more than self-interested individualism. Even in the heyday of free-market philosophy society was always thought to rest on something greater than harsh organised selfishness. In his *Theory of Moral Sentiments* Adam Smith described the 'helping hand' that matched the 'invisible hand' of his *Wealth of Nations.* And he believed that the drive for economic success should be combined with traditions of social obligation, public service and a broad moral commitment to civic improvement. And this has brought forth tens of thousands of local neighbourhood civic associations, unions, charities, voluntary organisations – the space between state and markets in a Britain that has always rejected absolutism and crude selfish individualism – that together embody that very British idea – civic society – that was discovered in Britain long before 'social capital' ever entered our dictionary. And it is an idea that Chief Rabbi Jonathan Sacks captures eloquently for our times when he talks of British society and citizenship not in terms of a contract between people that, in legalistic ways, defines our rights narrowly on the basis of self-interest; but a British 'covenant' of rights and responsibilities born out of shared values which can inspire us to neighbourliness and service to others.

So while we talk in economics of the Anglo-Saxon model – the pursuit of economic individualism through free markets – Britishness has always been more than just the 'freedom from' restraint but also stands for civic duty and fairness and these two qualities of British life – the notion of civic duty binding people to one another and the sense of fair play which underpins the idea of a proper social order – come together in the ethic of public service. And this gave rise to great British public institutions admired throughout the world – from the National Health Service and our army, navy and air forces to our universities, including the Open University, and the expression of civic purpose and social inclusion in culture and arts – our great national and municipal art galleries, museums and the BBC – not least the BBC World Service and the British Council.

Alongside these values have been found what I regard as essentially British qualities: an ability to adapt, and an openness to new ideas and new influences which have made us, as a country, both creative and internationalist in our outlook. To have managed change for 300 years without violent revolution is unique. I find it extraordinary that some appear to believe that it is somehow British to defend the idea of a constitution that never changes. It is precisely our ability to evolve our constitution that characterises the British way. So stability in our society does not come from rigidity: it comes from the ability to accommodate and master change: 'a state without the means of some change', Edmund Burke famously declared, 'is without the means of its conservation'. 'Change is inevitable', Benjamin Disraeli said in 1867: 'in a progressive society change is constant'. And a willingness and ability to adapt enabled Britain to embrace the opportunities of the Industrial Revolution with unprecedented vigour and success and, more than a century later, to mobilise from peace to war to survive and triumph in two world conflicts. And our very openness to new ideas and influences also means that at the heart of British qualities are a creativity and inventiveness – from the first agricultural revolution to the pioneering work of Babbage and Turing that made possible the computer and information revolution; in science, discoveries from DNA to cloning; in engineering, the work of Brunel and the inventions from the steam engine to the TV; and in medicine, from penicillin to interferon – an inventiveness that has ranged right across medicine and science to the arts and music. And so it is not surprising that as we rediscover these qualities, British dynamism is leading the world in some of the most modern and creative industries – communications, fashion, film, popular music, art, architecture, and many areas of science and the environmental technologies.

And out of that same openness to new ideas and influences, an outward-looking internationalism that made us not just the workshop of the world but as a country of merchant adventurers, explorers and missionaries the greatest trading nation the world has ever seen. Many people have made much of the fact that Britain was a set of islands. But unlike some other island nations Britain's history has never been marked by insularity. We are an island that has always looked outwards, been engaged in worldwide trade and been open to new influences – our British qualities that made us see, in David Cannadine's words, the Channel not as a moat but as a highway. An island position that has made us internationalist and outward-looking and not – as other islands have become – isolationist and inward-looking.

Of course all nations lay claim to uniqueness and exceptionalism and many would choose or emphasise the qualities of the British people in a different way from me. And in highlighting this view of British history – one which places what I regard as intrinsically British values and qualities at its centre – I do not want to claim moral superiority for Britain nor romanticise the past. And I do not gloss over abuses which also characterised our past. Nor do I claim the values and qualities I have described are not to be found in other nations. But I believe that they have shaped our institutions and together they have been responsible for the best of our past – creating a distinctive British identity that should make us proud of, and not reticent or apologetic about, our history. But most of all these values and qualities should inform any discussion of the central questions affecting our future. In fact the two ideologies that have characterised the histories of other countries have never taken root here. On the one hand an ideology of state power – which choked individual freedom, making the individual slave to some arbitrarily defined collective interest – has found little or no favour in Britain. On the other hand an ideology of crude individualism – which leaves the individual isolated, stranded, on their own, detached from society

around them – has no resonance for a Britain which has a strong
sense of fair play and an even stronger sense of duty and a rich
tradition of voluntary organisations, local democracy and civic life.

And this is my idea of Britain today. Not the individual on his or
her own living in isolation 'sufficient unto himself' but a Britain of
creativity and enterprise which is also a Britain of civic duty and
public service. And in this vision of society there is a sense of
belonging that expands outwards as we grow from family to friends
and neighbourhood; a sense of belonging that then ripples outwards
again from work, school, church and community and eventually
outwards to far beyond our home town and region to define our
nation and country as a society. And we should not only be explicit
about our British values but express them fully in the way we organise
our institutions. Let me suggest the agenda that flows from this.

First, start with Burke's 'little platoons', which reflect both a British
desire for liberty and a strong sense of civic duty and fair play. If the
British way is to encourage and enhance the status of voluntary and
community organisations in the service of their neighbourhoods
then we should recognise that aspects of post-war centralisation fell
short of our vision of empowered individuals and vibrant communities. The man in Whitehall never knew best; the woman in the
WRVS and local community service usually knew much more. And so
the question is how, from the foundation of British values, we
refashion the settlement between individual, community and government. Today in Britain, there are more than 160,000 registered
charities, more than 200,000 non-charitable voluntary and community organisations, around 400,000 in total, one for every hundred of
the adult population – defining Britain as such a thing as society: an
estimated 16 million people who do some kind of voluntary work –
and nearly two adults in every five who give of their time to help
others at least once in the year – and we best reflect our British
traditions of civic duty and public service by strengthening our
community organisations and making them more relevant to the
challenges of today. Take community service by young people. If
America has its Peace Corps and now its Americorps, South Africa its
national youth service, France its 'Unis-cité', the Netherlands its
'Groundbreakers Initiative', Canada its Katimavik programme,
should not Britain – with far greater and deeper traditions of
voluntary and community service – be building on those traditions

to engage a new generation of young people in service to their communities? And should we not be doing far more to provide nationally and locally the means by which young people find it easy to participate?

I am sure that, following the Russell Commission on young people, we will wish to consider establishing a National Youth Community Service; to ensure that poverty should not be a barrier to a gap-year option for a young person; to promote a range of opportunities nationally and internationally that back up the marvellous work already done by volunteering organisations; and to secure a business engagement in this that can translate the widespread social concern that exists among employers and employees alike into effective action for the common good. And I am sure we will also want to do more to translate community values into meeting new needs through new means like the internet and community television and so carry on the British tradition of voluntary service into the next generation. Take mentoring – underdeveloped in Britain – where I can envisage a new initiative for the future of Britain where through the internet, TV, local organisations and personal contact, we could establish a new network of mentors to befriend, advise, support and link those who need help and advice to those who can help. And because sporting activity is so important to defining our country's view of itself I believe we should also look in detail at the proposal to revive and expand participant sports in our country for a new National Sports Foundation.

It follows secondly that if the British way is to restore and enhance local initiative and mutual responsibility in civic affairs we should be doing far more to strengthen not just voluntary organisations but local institutions of government. Rather than asking people to look upwards to Whitehall to solve all their problems, the British way is surely to encourage more and more people, from their own localities, to take more charge of the decisions that affect their lives. Today, with devolution, elected mayors and new local energy and enthusiasm, many cities in England, Scotland, Wales and Northern Ireland are undergoing a renaissance and, as they become centres of initiative influencing our whole country, the whole of Britain can learn and draw from the energy of each of its parts. And a reinvigorated local democracy can, I believe, emerge to empower people in their own neighbourhoods to deal with the challenges they face:

- anti-social behaviour, where the engagement of the whole community is paramount;
- schooling, where the participation of parents and the local community is vital;
- the health service, where the direct involvement of patients and prospective patients matters.

Third, a Britishness that thrives on a strong sense of duty and fair play and a commitment to public service means taking citizenship seriously. And like the Home Secretary, who will also focus on these issues in a speech today, I would welcome a national debate on what the responsibilities and rights of British citizenship mean in practice in the modern world. I believe strongly in the case for citizenship lessons in our schools but, for citizenship to matter more, these changes to the curriculum must be part of a far more extensive debate – a debate that, like the wide-ranging debate we see in America about what it is to be an American and what America stands for, includes our culture and history as well as our constitution and laws. And I believe we would be stronger as a country if there was, through new literature, new institutes, new seminars, new cross-party debate about our Britishness and what it means.

And what of the institutions and symbols that best reflect citizenship and thus give importance to national identity? These must be symbols that speak to all our citizens so I believe that we should respond to the undermining of an inclusive citizenship by the British National Party by not only fighting their racism but by asserting at every opportunity that the union flag does not belong to a vicious minority, but is a flag for all Britain – symbolising inclusion, tolerance and unity; and that England, Scotland and Wales – whose celebration of national identity is to be welcomed and encouraged – should also honour not just their own flags but the union flag for the shared values it symbolises. There is also a more substantive issue about the importance of integration set against respect for diversity. Of course we live in a multi-ethnic as well as multinational state but because a multi-ethnic Britain should never ever have justified a crude multiculturalism where all values became relative, surely the common values that we all share should be reflected in practical measures such as those the Home Secretary is outlining today to avoid religious hatred and to encourage – and in some cases require – the use of the

English language. Take an economic example. Because many cannot find work because of language difficulties, it is surely right to pilot mandatory language training for those jobseekers whose language needs are preventing them from getting jobs. Upholding British values summons us to do far more to tackle discrimination and promote inclusion. And I believe that there should now be greater focus on driving up the educational attainment of pupils from ethnic minorities and a more comprehensive New Deal effort to tackle unacceptably high unemployment in areas of high ethnic minority populations.

If I am right, the British way is to develop a strong cohesive society in which in return for responsibility there is opportunity for all. And our British belief in fairness and our commitment to public service makes the NHS, founded on health care based on need not ability to pay, one of the greatest British institutions – an NHS that both reflects the values of the British people and is being modernised for our times in accordance with these very values. And we should never lose sight of the importance of the NHS not just to our view of Britishness but to the world's view of Britain. If, in the twenty-first century, we cannot make the NHS work in Britain we must ask what hope there is for millions in developing countries struggling with ill health and disease who cannot afford private health care. But if we can show that the NHS, health care based on need not ability to pay, is indeed the best insurance policy in the world then we give to the developing countries a model of modern health care – and hope.

Rediscovering the roots of our identity in our shared beliefs also allows us to address complex questions about our relationship with the rest of the world. This is not a subject for today – not least because it will be discussed endlessly for many months to come – but a far more detailed speech. But two observations follow from my remarks today. The first is that globalisation is fundamentally changing the nature of Europe. In the past, European integration was built on the idea of a European trade bloc dominated by European flows of capital, European-wide companies and European brands. Today we are in a completely different world of global movements of capital, global companies and global brands. As a result, the old integra-tionist project – the single market and single currency followed by tax harmonisation, federal fiscal policies and a quasi-federal state – the vision of a trade-bloc Europe – is fatally undermined. For to succeed economically Europe must move from the old model – the trade-bloc or fortress Europe – to a new globally oriented Europe that champions economic liberalisation, a reformed social dimension and a more open rather than protectionist approach to trade with the rest of the world.

The second observation is that while we must continue to learn from successes in other European countries, British values and qualities – particularly our outward-looking internationalism that led us to pioneer free trade – have a great deal to offer in building the Europe of this new global era. Indeed British qualities and values can play a leading part in shaping a Europe that must reform, be flexible, be competitive, be outward-looking and build better trading and commercial relationships with the USA. So being fully engaged in Europe need not threaten Britain with subjugation inside an inward-looking trade bloc but can mean Britain and British values playing a full part in leading a global Europe. A Britain that thinks globally not only builds from our traditions of openness and outward-looking internationalism but builds upon huge British assets and strengths – the British Council itself, the BBC, the BBC World Service, our universities and our long-felt sense of obligation to the world's poor. And in addition to our well-known proposals for international development – including debt relief and the International Finance Facility for development – that represent a new deal between the richest and the poorest countries, I believe with you that we should build on the great success of the British Council internationally and do more to put one of our greatest assets – the English language, now the language of the internet and business – at the service of the world. One and a half billion people now speak English. Our aim should be that that no one in any continent is prevented by poverty, exclusion or educational disadvantage from learning the English language.

Thinking globally in an insecure world – and, more importantly, in the world since September 11th – requires us of course to take necessary steps to discharge a British government's first duty – the defence of its citizens, the people of Britain. And as we look forward to next week's Spending Review, I will make available the resources needed to strengthen security at home and take action to counter the terrorist threat at home and abroad. Those who wish to cut in real terms the Budget even for security will need to answer to the British people. We will spend what it takes on security to safeguard the British people.

I started this lecture by asserting that the British way is to embrace, not fear, reform and the challenge of the twenty-first century is not just to express our Britishness in the evolutionary reform of individual institutions but to continue to evolve towards a constitutional settlement that recognises both our rights and aspirations as individuals and our needs and shared values as a community. But as we discuss how our evolving British constitution can best reflect our British values, what is very clear to me is that even if a significant section of the Conservative Party has ceased to see itself as the Conservative and Unionist Party, our Labour Party must stand resolute as the party of the union. And indeed all decent-minded people should, I believe, stand for and champion a union that embodies the very values I have been discussing: a union that, because it reflects shared values, has achieved – and will in future achieve – far more by us working together than we could ever achieve separate and split apart.

So, in conclusion, there are good economic reasons for a new and rising confidence about the future of Britain. There are social and cultural reasons too for a new British optimism, a rising British confidence. We should think of Britain as a Britain discovering anew that its identity was never rooted just in imperial success or simply the authority of its institutions, nor in race or ethnicity. We should think of a Britain rediscovering the shared values that bind us together. Indeed the ties that today bind us are the same values and qualities that are at the core of our history . . . the values that should shape our institutions as they adapt, change and modernise to meet and master future challenges. So standing up for Britain means speaking up for British values and qualities that can inspire, strengthen and unify our country. And we can stop thinking about a post-war Britain of decline – the Britain that was – and start thinking about the Britain that we can become: Britain, a great place to grow up in; a Britain believing in itself; a new era of British self-confidence; not just a Britain that is a beacon for economic progress but a Britain proud that because of its values and qualities, progress and justice can advance together, to the benefit of all.

9

LIBERTY, RESPONSIBILITY
AND FAIRNESS

For someone who is a historian and an academic to comment on speeches by a major politician may seem strange. Politicians have to work with the present; historians' chosen territory is the past. Politicians deal in power; academics generally possess none. Yet, as these two speeches demonstrate, a keen interest in academic history writings is one of Gordon Brown's characteristic strengths. History is rarely a wholly reliable guide to the future, but an instinctive sense and informed understanding of the past can help politicians (and everyone else) to place contemporary challenges and debates in a much broader context, and to move beyond obscurantist myths, glib slogans and easy generalisations. As Brown recognises, for instance, while its scale and many of the forms it takes today are entirely new, globalisation itself is not, and neither is Britain's exposure to it. Great Britain is a small island, but since the seventeenth century, and for good as well as ill, its inhabitants have had more to do with other continents than most other peoples. Extreme openness to an interconnected world, to its risks and to its opportunities, is part of our present, but it is nothing new.

But what is most striking about these two speeches is their resurrection of and insistence upon liberty in the British political tradition. Most seventeenth-, eighteenth- and nineteenth-century commentators took this for granted. They believed that this polity possessed an 'Ancient Constitution', which was not contained in a single document but did manifest itself in significant statements of individual and legal rights, as well as in institutions. In historical fact, of course, Brown's 'golden thread' of British liberties has sometimes unravelled, and was often tied in the past so as to exclude the majority: those who were female, or poor, or non-white, or not Protestant. None the less, bringing words like 'liberty' and 'rights' firmly back into British political vocabulary, and thinking in terms of new documents that will embody both them and civic responsibilities, is very important. One of the things that strikes me as a Briton living abroad is the contrast between the admittedly uneven, but none the less conspicuous, prosperity of Britain, and the cynicism, frequent lack of self-confidence, and – occasionally – even outbursts of self-hatred that often characterise its media. A sense of emptiness and frustration often comes over. I am not so naïve as to believe that a new cult of liberty and new constitutional initiatives can be the whole solution. But people need political ideals in order to flourish as well as better incomes, and now that Britain has emerged from its post-imperial blues and its post-war economic malaise, paying attention to the former is overdue.

Countries in drift and in stress – and given the state of the world at present that is all of them – easily succumb to over-authoritarian leaders or to slick, media-friendly figures who seem to offer reassurance and quick fixes. By contrast, Gordon Brown deals in and is not afraid of ideas and debate. He urges us to think constructively about this country, by taking the trouble to think hard and creatively himself.

Linda Colley

In two important speeches delivered at the end of 2005 and at the beginning of 2006 the Chancellor has been developing some of the themes which occur in his speeches on Britishness, set out in Chapter 8. In these, he introduces a wide-ranging discussion of the way the British people have engaged over time with the principle of liberty, and how, in contrast with other countries, liberty has been linked to responsibility and fairness. His case is that it is only in Britain that the links between these three principles (liberty for all, responsibility by all and fairness to all) find wide applicability and acceptance amongst citizens. He argues that a progressive politician who can develop polices which derive from the interaction of these principles can set a new agenda for a modern view of Britishness, and that will lead to a new range of policy initiatives aimed at addressing the major challenges facing our country – our relationships with Europe, America and the rest of the world; how we equip ourselves for globalisation; the future direction of constitutional change; a modern view of citizenship; the future of local government, ideas of localism; our community relations and the balance between diversity and integration; and the shape of our public services.

Starting with the writings of Scottish Enlightenment thinkers, and drawing from a wide range of political philosophical texts, Gordon Brown asks questions about our nation's relationship to liberty: why is it that our passion for liberty did not lead, at least for most of our history, to a cult of self-interested individualism or to a British libertarianism? What prevented the triumph of the idea of the 'isolated individual free from ties or allegiances'? What kept alive the idea of the importance not just of family but also of community? His conclusion is that at the centre of our British heritage, the idea of liberty has always been linked to the equally powerful ideas of responsibility and fairness. People are not just 'individual islands entire of themselves', but citizens where identity, loyalty and a moral sense determine the sense of responsibility and fairness we all feel to each other.

The Chancellor's thesis is that Britain is defined not by race nor ethnicity; not by our ancient institutions; not by the various national traits for which we are famous across the world; but by our shared values – formed and expressed in the best of our history. He feels that a distinctively British set of ideas about ourselves and our role in the world has emerged from the long tidal flows of our national experience – the 2,000 years of successive waves of invasion, immigration, assimilation and trading partnerships that have both created a uniquely rich and diverse culture and made us stable, outward-looking and open.

In the first Hugo Young Memorial Lecture, given to an invited audience in Chatham House on 13 December 2005, Gordon Brown used the opportunity to reflect on the life and writings of the distinguished *Guardian* journalist to discuss liberty, responsibility and fairness in the context of internationalism. In particular he argues that at different points in our history, in peace and war, in ascendancy and adversity, we have always emphasised the importance of liberty, responsibility and fairness. But he extends the argument, making the point that, to an extent that has not been fully appreciated, each depends upon the other and all of them are necessary to our nation's future. He suggests that Britain has a choice as we prepare and equip ourselves to address the opportunities and the insecurities of globalisation:

> Britain can either retreat into the old narrow view of liberty as a form of libertarianism, responsibility as little more than paternalism, fairness as just formal rights before the law – leaving people and communities not only ill-equipped for challenges ahead, but with too little liberty, too little responsibility, and too little fairness. Or by meaning what we say about building a Britain of liberty for all, responsibility by all, and

fairness to all, we can actively work for a new constitutional settlement, a strong vibrant civic society, and a reformed and renewed public realm delivering security and opportunity for all.

. . .

Today in tribute to the man who got nearer to the truth than any commentator of his time, I want to talk about the ideas I judge mattered deeply to Hugo Young, and the ideas I judge matter to our future: liberty; responsibility; fairness; and of course internationalism: ideas that are absolutely central to the view of the world in which I too was brought up; ideas that have become central to my view of our country and its future in global society; ideas that I want to discuss not as abstract political theory – and far less as an exercise in hindsight and historical revisionism – but as ideas that should in my view be the foundation for a new agenda of political, economic, social and constitutional reform, a new settlement that will enable us to face up to the scale and size of the global challenges; ideas that are not unique to the British culture – indeed all cultures value liberty, responsibility and fairness – but when taken together, charted through our history, are at the heart of a modern Britishness, central elements of a modern and profoundly practical patriotism: the surest way in which our nation can succeed economically and socially in the twenty-first century will be by building a society in which there is liberty for all, responsibility by all and fairness to all.

Our values do not, of course, float freely without roots; they are rooted in the best of our history. And because they can inspire us we can unite around them: they give us shared purpose. Liberty, responsibility and fairness have each a resonance that echoes from our nation's past. At different points in our history, in peace and war, in ascendancy and adversity, we have emphasised the importance of liberty, responsibility and fairness. But today I want to argue that, to an extent that has not been fully appreciated, each depends upon the other and all of them are necessary to our nation's future. My argument is that it is only by understanding the critical place of liberty, responsibility and fairness together that Britain can meet and master the changing tides of the future. The society which will not only prosper but flourish in these islands in the twenty-first century will be one which draws strength from these values side by side: liberty for all, responsibility by all, fairness to all.

I want to show how a long-term reform agenda for the renewal of our country – the reform and modernisation of institutions and policies – flows from these tested and enduring values. What is my central thesis? It is the view that Britain is defined not by race nor ethnicity – as those who would impose a cricket test would have us do – nor by our ancient institutions, nor just the various national traits for which we are famous across the world, but by our shared values formed and expressed in the best of our history. It is the view that a distinctively British set of ideas about ourselves and our role in the world has emerged from the long tidal flows of our national experience – the 2,000 years of successive waves of invasion, immigration, assimilation and trading partnerships that have both created a uniquely rich and diverse culture and made us an island – stable, outward-looking and open – for whom the Channel was – in David Cannadine's words – 'never a moat but a highway' for commerce and ideas.

The first value I want to highlight is liberty, one I emphasised in a British Council lecture I gave on Britishness last summer – liberty as both the rights of the individual protected against an arbitrary state and, more recently, as empowerment. Ask British people what they think important about our country – and one quality they highlight is our tolerance – ask about a characteristic that makes them ashamed and it is intolerance. Although it took until 1829 for Catholic emancipation, even later for rights for the Jewish community, women and ethnic minorities, John Locke led the way when he said beliefs cannot be compelled and the government existed for the advance-ment of civil interests. Out of the practice of toleration came the pursuit of liberty. And it was the battle for freedom from the old, from ancient hierarchical obligations – from the arbitrary rule of kings, from the overbearing power of bishops, from a wasteful mercantilism – that inspired seventeenth-, eighteenth- and nine-teenth-century philosophers from Locke to Adam Smith and then to John Stuart Mill.

'The civil wars of Rome ended in slavery and those of the English in liberty,' Voltaire wrote. 'The English are the only people upon earth who have been able to prescribe limits to the power of kings by resisting them.' And he added, 'The English are jealous not only of their own liberty but even of that of other nations.'

So powerful did the British idea of liberty become that – perhaps ironically – the American War of Independence was fought by both sides 'in the name of British liberty'. Wordsworth wrote of 'the flood of British freedom'. Hazlitt thought an Englishman 'has and can have no privilege or advantage over other nations but liberty'.

I stress how contemporaries here and elsewhere thought of our country as the home of liberty, because I believe that the idea of Britain defined as the home of liberty had as much power at that time as, in our time, the idea of America as land of liberty has for the USA. It was indeed Macaulay's whole theme that under what he called 'the new settlement', 'the authority of law and the security of property were found to be compatible with a liberty of discussion and of individual action never before known'.

There is, of course, the danger of seeing past villains as heroes and I do not wish to do so; for we should not forget the abuses, the discrimination, the injustices done; and it would be wrong to glorify or distort the past, particularly to uphold a particular view of the present. But in British debate after debate, in resolving controversy after controversy, contemporaries appealed to the British idea of liberty as their judge and jury. In 2007 we will celebrate the two-hundredth anniversary of Britain leading the world in the abolition of the slave trade. When Charles Darwin challenged Britain on slavery, it was precisely because slavery was an affront to national values which championed liberty. 'He trembled to think that we Englishmen and our American descendants with their boastful cry of liberty have been and are so guilty.' Or as the Scots author of the verses 'Rule Britannia' put it, 'Britons never, never, never shall be slaves.' And nearer our own times, George Orwell summed up the idea of liberty when he wrote that 'The totalitarian idea that there is no such thing as law – there is only power – has never taken root [here]. In England such concepts as justice, liberty and objective truth are still believed in.'

Some, however, would define British liberty as no more than constraining executive power, and – as some on the right argue – that because all the individual craves is to be left alone, the best government is no government. But I believe that across the centuries Britain evolved a far more generous, expansive view of liberty which, even if the concept of citizen did not, in theory, replace that of subject, focused not just on the abuse of power but on the empowerment of the individual – first only men of property and then all the people. While French politics focused on curbing the power of the monarch but not that of the state, the British idea was that rulers should yield power so that parliament and the people could wield it, shaping the decisions that affected their lives.

And British liberty came to mean liberty for all: a democratic view of liberty. So in this century a consensus has evolved that liberty is not just passive, about restricting someone else's powers, but active, people empowered to participate. And I believe that when in our generation Robert F. Kennedy argued for citizen participation and community self-government, and gave us a modern idea of the empowered citizen, he echoed a strong British tradition of civic engagement I would like to recapture.

But ever more so in this century, a consensus is also emerging that our liberties, equal and compatible with the liberties of all, should be tested against the extent to which they enable each individual not just to have protection against arbitrary power or the right to political participation, but to realise their potential. In Britain, this idea of liberty as empowerment is not a new idea. J.A. Hobson asked, 'Is a man free who has not equal opportunity with his fellows of such access to all material and moral means of personal development and work as shall contribute to his own welfare and that of his society?'; and before him T.H. Green stated, 'When we speak of freedom as something to be so highly prized, we mean a positive power or capacity of doing or enjoying something worth doing or enjoying, and that, too, something that we do or enjoy in common with others.'

I have previously talked about our history as both the triumph of the human spirit and yet the story also of the tragic waste of human potential. I was remembering, from a classroom long ago, Gray's 'Elegy Written in a Country Churchyard', and that lying there was – as he put it – some 'mute inglorious Milton': our history the story not just of great creative genius in action, but of men and women of talent or even genius who might have been so much more – poets, philosophers, scientists, doctors, inventors – but were forever denied the freedom to develop their potential.

Perhaps in a pre-industrial or an industrial society we could afford to disregard that loss; but in a post-industrial society where what gives you competitive advantage and wealth is your creative ability, prosperity will depend upon our ability, through investment in education, to tap the potential and bring out the best not just in the few but the many.

In each generation we have found it necessary to renew the settlement between individual, community and state and I cannot see how the long-term credibility of our institutions or our policies can be secured unless our constitutional, social and economic reforms are explicitly founded on these British ideas of liberty. Our long-held commitment to liberty must of course be the starting point for any future discussion of the British constitution and for a new settlement. Because a central feature of our tradition and the protection of our liberties within it is the limits we place on executive power. I am pleased that on my first day in office I took on that challenge, giving up government power over the Bank of England. I made the same point during the general-election campaign when I suggested there was a case for a detailed consideration of the role of parliament in the declarations of peace and war. I would apply this same approach to constitutional questions such as the issue of House of Lords reform, left unfinished by the 1911 Act, which – in the words of its own preamble – was only a temporary step.

Our long-held commitment to liberty demands also that we break up any centralised institutions that are too remote and insensitive, devolving and decentralising power, encouraging structures and initiatives so that the power so devolved brings real self-government to communities. My own view is that new politics cannot be a reality unless we make local accountability work by reinvigorating the democratically elected mechanisms of local areas – local government. And I believe it is in the same spirit that we explore a new pluralism in our politics, searching for not just consensus but for a shared sense of national purpose, seeking new ways of involving people in shaping the decisions that affect them – from citizens' juries to local citizen forums – where the evidence is that participation does not just enthuse those directly involved, but makes the public generally feel more engaged.

But as Hugo was first to acknowledge, our passion for liberty which runs through and defines much of recent British history did not lead, at least for most of our history, to a cult of self-interested individualism or to a British libertarianism. And why not? What prevented the triumph of the idea of the isolated or self-interested individual free from ties or allegiances and made us instead praise Edmund Burke for his love of the 'little platoon'? What kept alive the idea of the importance not just of family but also of community even when Hume, separating 'is' from 'ought', appeared to devalue the very idea of duty? When the thrust of eighteenth-century Enlightenment philosophy was its 'relentless focus on the unique and the individual' – appearing to deny the importance of belonging, what kept not just the family but neighbourhood, community and local associations and loyalties right at the forefront of our view of Britishness, and made most of us reject both Mill's extreme view of liberty and, more recently, a crude libertarianism which demanded freedom irrespective of our responsibilities to others? What made us think, in the words of Roosevelt, that 'the man who seeks freedom from responsibility in the name of individual liberty is either fooling himself or trying to cheat his fellow man'.

When we think about it the answer becomes clear. It is because at the heart of our British heritage, alongside the idea of liberty are the equally powerful ideas of responsibility and duty. So that people are not just individual islands entire of themselves, but citizens in whom identity, loyalty and indeed a moral sense determine the sense of responsibility we all feel to each other. 'Liberty means responsibility, that is why most men dread it,' Bernard Shaw wrote. In her recent book *The Roads to Modernity* the historian Gertrude Himmelfarb compares and contrasts the contribution France, America and Britain made to the modern world. She finds that while France and America both had revolutions in the name of freedom, it is Britain and British ideas that led the way into the modern world by focusing on benevolence, improvement, the civic society and the moral sense as necessary for social progress.

And because this comes alive not only in families, but through voluntary associations, churches and faith groups and then on into public service, we, the British people, have consistently regarded a strong civic society as fundamental to our sense of ourselves – that moral space, a public realm in which duty constrains the pursuit of self-interest. As John Stuart Mill had to concede, 'there are many positive acts to the benefit of others which anyone may rightfully be obliged to perform.' 'All for ourselves and nothing for other people' is 'a vile maxim', wrote Adam Smith. Coming from Kirkcaldy as Adam Smith did, I have come to understand that his *Wealth of Nations* was underpinned by his *Theory of Moral Sentiments*, his invisible hand dependent upon the existence of a helping hand. Of course Smith wanted people freed from the shackles of obedience to kings and vested interests, hence the 'wealth of nations'; but while he wanted people freed from the old constraints he certainly did not envisage people free of civic bonds and civic duties, hence his theory of moral sentiments. 'Whenever we feel the fate of others is our personal responsibility we are less likely to stand idly by,' he wrote. For Smith the moral system encompassed the economic system, generating the responsible virtues of industry, honesty and reliability – and the stable associations in which we accept our responsibilities each to one another, habits of cooperation and trust, the moral sense upon which the market depended. So he always believed that the centre of a town is far more than a marketplace. And it is true to say that, even when Enlightenment philosophers – like Smith – stood under the banner of freedom, they did not argue that their view of freedom gave men immunity from their responsibilities to serve their society: the British way always more than self-interested individualism, at the core of British history the very ideas of 'active citizen', 'good neighbour', civic pride and the public realm.

So there is indeed a golden thread which runs through British history, of the individual standing firm against tyranny and then of the individual participating in their society. It is a thread that runs from that long-ago day in Runnymede in 1215 and on to the Bill of Rights in 1689 to not just one but four great Reform Acts within less than a hundred years. And the tensile strength of that golden thread comes from countless strands of common continuing endeavour in our villages, towns and cities, the efforts and achievements of ordinary men and women, united by a strong sense of responsibility, who, long before de Tocqueville found civic associations to be at the heart of America, defined Britain by its proliferation of local clubs, associations, societies and endeavours – a Britain where liberty did not descend into licence and where freedom was exercised with responsibility.

So the two ideologies that have dominated the histories of other countries have never taken root here – neither state power, which chokes individual liberty; nor crude individualism, which has no resonance for the Britain of thousands of voluntary associations, the Britain of mutual societies, craft unions, insurance and friendly societies and cooperatives, the Britain of churches and faith groups, the Britain of municipal provision from libraries to parks and the Britain of public service – mutuality, cooperation, civic associations and social responsibility.

Of course, as Jonathan Sacks explains so eloquently, this popular idea of responsibility and civic engagement was, more often than not, taught in narratives, less the subject of philosophical texts but celebrated in poetry and song, enacted in rituals, embodied in traditions, passed on in families. And we can track the change from a Britain proud of pioneering citizen responsibility through jury service to a Britain today where responsibility by all means: corporate social responsibility expected of business, the obligations accepted by the unemployed to seek work, the challenge to residents in poor neighbourhoods to break from a dependency culture, and local initiative and mutual responsibility coming alive in new areas of community life from child care, to drug rehabilitation, to the greatness of our hospices.

So one of the great challenges ahead is the encouragement and renewal for the coming generation of that rich British tradition of voluntary organisations, local democracy and civic life. And it is to make this ideal of responsibility real for a new generation that I announced last week private and public funding for the first British National Youth Community Service that will provide part-time and full-time community service at home and abroad, including the offer of gap years to those who could not otherwise afford them. Just as from America in the 1960s came the Peace Corps which, like the British VSO before it, caught the imagination and harnessed the idealism of that generation, so now from Britain in the first decade of a new century, National Youth Community Service can engage and inspire the coming generation of young people. Our voluntary organisations should neither be captured by the state nor used as a cut-price alternative to necessary public provision – and so we should reject any old left idea of the state assuming the responsibilities of civic society – and reject any new right view of the voluntary sector as a weapon in the battle against any role for government – a view that takes us backwards into an old world of paternalism.

In advance of our Spending Review, I want to energise a new debate on the vital future role of the voluntary, charitable and community sector in our country and how we can do more to encourage the giving of both time and money and to make the necessary decisions to support both. I want this generation to recognise their unique and often irreplaceable qualities – the skill at one-to-one contact, the knowledge of what's happening on the ground, the pioneering of new ways, the encouragement of citizenship. And I believe that any new constitutional settlement should recognise the importance we attach to both their independence and their role as innovators in meeting new needs in new areas, in bringing to life in our times the idea of responsibility by all.

Let us recap: in an old world of hierarchy, in feudal and later periods, responsibility was defined narrowly as no more than *noblesse oblige*; in a world of deference in the pre-industrial age, responsibility was little more than a form of paternalism. But we can see the evolution of the idea of responsibility through the great social movements of the last 200 years to today, when it is defined primarily through the concept of fairness. The great Britain we all need cannot be wholly cohesive or successful if built around liberty alone or responsibility alone or even liberty and responsibility together, important as these values are. A modern successful Britain must be built around liberty, responsibility and fairness.

In the 1950s in his last speech to parliament, Churchill spoke of a Britain defined by its sense of fair play. In the 1940s Orwell talked of a Britain known to the world for its 'decency'. A YouGov survey in July 2005 showed that as many as 90 per cent of British people thought that fairness and fair play were very important or fairly important in defining Britishness. Britishness today, as Michael Ignatieff concluded, is parliamentary democracy, rule of law, fairness and decency. Of course the appeal to fairness runs through British history. The call, of course, of the oppressed, the disadvantaged and the left-out, with Raineborough asserting in the 1647 Putney Debates that 'the poorest he that is in England hath a life to live as the greatest he'; but the call throughout the generations of all decent-minded people demanding wrongs be righted in the interests of justice.

The twentieth-century innovation has been to give new expression to fairness as the pursuit of equality of opportunity for all, unfair privileges for no one. And in this century there is an even richer vision of equality of opportunity challenging people to make the most of their potential through education, employment and in our economy, society and culture. Charities can and do achieve great transformative changes, but no matter how benevolent, they cannot, ultimately, guarantee fairness to all. Markets can and do generate great wealth, but no matter how dynamic, they cannot guarantee fairness to all. Individuals can be and are very generous but by its nature personal giving is sporadic and often conditional.

So fairness can be advanced by but cannot, in the end, be guaranteed by charities, however benevolent; by markets, however dynamic; or by individuals, however well meaning, but guaranteed only by enabling government. Take a movement all of us have seen grow from thousands to millions and all of us admire greatly. The organisers of Live Aid 2005 / Live 8 concluded that, however worthy, right and timely Live Aid 1985 was, even these immense efforts were not wholly sufficient. They concluded that while Live Aid 1985 could offer charity through individual donations it needed action by governments to guarantee justice, hence their theme 'From Charity to Justice'. As Bob Geldof said, Live Aid 2005 / Live 8 is not about charity, nor protest, but about making things happen, persuading governments to act. So just as good government is not inimical to civic society, so civic society is not inimical to good government, but complementary to it. For the good society to flourish to the benefit of all, private endeavour must be matched by public endeavour. And while changing needs often require government to withdraw from areas where it should not be – as in the management of interest rates – they can also mean government, aware that as a nation we need to be equipped for a global future, discharging fresh responsibilities too.

Let us recall that in the fifty years after 1945, just about the only services most under-fives and their parents received were basic maternity provision, vaccination and a letter asking you to turn up at school at five. Now we know that the first forty-eight months of a child's life are probably more important than later years to that young child's educational and social development. We also know just how unfair it was that nursery education was restricted to just the few who could pay for it. Because of that – and because of the changing needs of parents to balance work and family life – a whole new frontier of the Welfare State, a revolution in services, is being opened up with government able to guarantee what no other organisation could ever guarantee – maternity and paternity rights, and Sure Start services for children before three and the right to free nursery education from the age of three.

I am both impressed and excited by the vast range and mixed economy of Sure Start, voluntary, charitable and private-sector providers, and the high level of innovation in this new sector; and we need to do more to encourage new providers. But it is because my underlying philosophy is that every child is special, every child precious and therefore that no child should be left behind – in other words to ensure we empower every child and not just some with opportunity – that we need to recognise the enabling role of government. Parents who want to do best by their children want both the flowering of local initiative in Sure Start, civic society at its best, and the helping hand of public purpose: from the local nursery school, the local Sure Start centre, whoever runs it, to the Child Tax Credit and maternity leave, supportive local and national services that empower from a government on people's side. That a strong civic society needs a good enabling government on people's side to deliver fairness – and that to enlarge the civic space you do not need to eliminate the rest of the public realm – is a lesson we must learn and relearn in every generation.

Take the New Deal for jobs and skills, the modern expression of a big idea, society accepting its responsibility for the goal of full employment and of individuals empowered and equipped to realise their potential, a positive view of liberty for all, the freedom to work. But the modern British way is of responsibility by all: of new opportunities matched by the obligation of the unemployed to work or to learn new skills. In the coming decades – as technological change forces people to make, on average, seven big job changes across their working lives – a New Deal that equips people with the new skills they will need will become more, not less, essential. Of course there are issues of cost and how private, voluntary and community organisations can help deliver the New Deal. But to oppose the principle of the New Deal is for society to walk away – leaving people on their own, helpless, facing change and insecurity, condemning us to a Britain of liberty for some but not all, responsibility demanded of some but not all, fairness to some but not all.

The same is true of the environment, where private, voluntary and charitable endeavour should not exclude government's responsibilities in this area but complement them. So whether it be enduring responsibilities for full employment, or new frontiers balancing work and family life, or caring for our environment or, more generally, addressing poverty and investing in schools, hospitals, science and infrastructure to equip our country for all the global challenges ahead – if you will the ends, fairness to all, you must be prepared to will the means – enabling, empowering government to make fairness possible.

At the outset I cited Gray's 'Elegy Written in a Country Church-yard', and talked of liberty as empowerment. And does this not come alive today in the idea of individuals challenged to make the most of their potential – challenged to bridge the gap between what they are and what they have it in themselves to become? Let us recall Gray musing in the year 1750 about a 'mute inglorious Milton', a guiltless Cromwell, a village Hampden. Recalling the tragic waste throughout our history of the might-have-been: the great music never composed; the great art never realised; the books never written; the science that never saw past the edge of known truth; the medical breakthrough that never was to save a life; the contributions never made; the potential never realised.

Yet today with China and India turning out 4 million graduates a year and in a race with us not to the bottom but to the top, a small country like ours cannot afford to neglect the potential of any or write off the talents of any young person and if we do so will be left behind by globalisation. So instead of, as in the past, developing only some of the potential of some of the people, our mission for liberty for all and fairness to all summons us to develop all of the potential of all the people. And instead of condoning what Aneurin Bevan called 'a poverty of aspiration' that restricts success to the few, our view of responsibility by all should mean we challenge all young people to make the most of themselves. And we should champion the idea of Britain as a country not diminished by 'a poverty of aspiration' but energised by a wealth of ambition in all areas of our country. That is why education – public investment in it and continuing reform of it – and an assault on the denial of potential, and the abolition of the culture that tolerates a poverty of aspiration, must and will remain at the heart of our mission.

So tonight I have set out an idea of a Britain far better equipped for the global challenge because its future is built upon the most solid foundation of all – enduring values we can readily rediscover and embrace – a passion for liberty for all, anchored in an ethic of responsibility by all, which comes alive for our generation in a commitment to fairness for all. And I have argued that by applying these values of liberty, responsibility and fairness to the modernisation and renewal of British institutions and policies we will best meet the global challenges ahead. Britain does indeed have a choice of two roads as we prepare and equip ourselves to address the opportunities and the insecurities of globalisation. Britain can retreat into the old narrow view of liberty as a form of libertarianism, responsibility as little more than paternalism, fairness as just formal rights before the law – leaving people and communities not only ill-equipped for challenges ahead, but with too little liberty, too little responsibility, and too little fairness. Or by meaning what we say about building a Britain of liberty for all, responsibility by all, and fairness to all, we can actively work for a new constitutional settlement, a strong vibrant civic society, and a reformed and renewed public realm delivering security and opportunity for all.

In January 2006, Gordon Brown delivered the keynote speech to the Fabian Society annual conference. In this remarkable speech, much of the subsequent press comment focused on the rather narrow question of whether Britain should do more to celebrate Britishness, perhaps through greater use of flags, public holidays and the like. But in fact this speech, properly read as an extension of the Hugo Young Memorial Speech given a month earlier, sets out some interesting ideas for the future, and perhaps more than a hint of what might be in the manifesto for a fourth-term Labour government.

In this speech the Chancellor argues that our success as a nation, our ability to meet and master not just the challenges of a global economy but also the international, demographic, constitutional, social, and security challenges ahead, requires us to rediscover and build from our history and apply in our time the shared values that bind us together and give us common purpose. He develops the argument that there is a fundamental relationship that links liberty, responsibility and fairness to a modern definition of patriotism, and to Britishness. And taking off from that, the Chancellor sets out a range of policy initiatives aimed at addressing the major challenges facing our country – our relationships with Europe, America and the rest of the world; how we equip ourselves for globalisation; the future direction of constitutional change; a modern view of citizenship; the future of local government, ideas of localism; our community relations and the balance between diversity and integration; and the shape of our public services.

Being clear what Britishness means in a post-imperial world is essential if we are to forge the best relationships with the developing world and in particular with Africa. But take Europe also: there is no doubt that in the years after 1945, faced with relative economic decline as well as the end of empire, Britain lost confidence in itself and its role in the world and became so unsure about what a confident post-imperial Britain could be that too many people defined the choice in Europe as either total absorption or splendid isolation; and forgot that just as you could stand for Britain while being part of NATO, you can stand for Britain and advance British national interests as part of the European Union.

Let me also suggest that it is because that loss of confidence led too many to retreat into the idea of a Britain that was little more than institutions that never changed – so for decades, for fear of losing our British identity, Britain did not face up to some of the great constitutional questions, whether it be the second chamber, the relationship of the legislative to the executive or the future of local government. Take also the unity of the United Kingdom and its component parts. While we have always been a country of different nations and thus of plural identities – a Welshman can be Welsh and British, just as a Cornishman or -woman is Cornish, English and British – and may be Muslim, Pakistani or Afro-Caribbean, Cornish, English and British – there is always a risk that, when people are insecure, they retreat into more exclusive identities rooted in nineteenth-century conceptions of blood, race and territory – when instead we, the British people, should be able to gain great strength from celebrating a British identity which is bigger than the sum of its parts and a union that is strong because of the values we share and because of the way these values are expressed through our history and our institutions.

And take the most recent illustration of what challenges us to be more explicit about Britishness: the debate about asylum and immigration and about multiculturalism and inclusion, issues that are particularly potent because in a fast-changing world people who are insecure need to be rooted. Here the question is essentially whether our national identity is defined by values we share in common or just by race and ethnicity – a definition that would leave our country at risk of relapsing into a wrongheaded 'cricket test' of loyalty.

Equally, while the British response to the events of July 7th was magnificent, we have to face the uncomfortable fact that there were British citizens, British born, apparently integrated into our communities, who were prepared to maim and kill fellow British citizens, irrespective of their religion – and this must lead us to ask how successful we have been in balancing the need for diversity with the obvious requirements of integration in our society. But I would argue that if we are clear about what underlies our Britishness and if we are clear that shared values – not colour, nor unchanging and unchangeable institutions – define what it means to be British in the modern world, we can be far more ambitious in defining for our time the responsibilities of citizenship; far more ambitious in forging a new and contemporary settlement of the relationship between state, community and individual; and it is also easier too to address difficult issues that sometimes come under the heading 'multiculturalism' – essentially how diverse cultures, which inevitably contain differences, can find the essential common purpose without which no society can flourish.

So Britishness is not just an academic debate – something just for the historians, just for the commentators, just for the so-called chattering classes. Indeed in a recent poll, as many as half of British people said they were worried that if we do not promote Britishness we run a real risk of having a divided society. And if we look to the future I want to argue that our success as Great Britain, our ability to meet and master not just the challenges of a global economy but also the international, demographic, constitutional and social challenges ahead, and even the security challenges, requires us to rediscover and build from our history and apply in our time the shared values that bind us together and give us common purpose.

I believe most strongly that globalisation is made for a Britain that is stable, outward-looking, committed to scientific progress and the value of education. And that by taking the right long-term decisions Britain can stand alongside China, India and America as one of the great success stories of the next global era. But it is also obvious to me that the nations that will meet and master global change best are not just those whose governments make the right long-term decisions on stability, science, trade and education, but whose people come together and, sharing a common view of the challenges and what needs to be done, forge a unified and shared sense of purpose about the long-term sacrifices they are prepared to make and the priorities they think important for national success. And just as in wartime a sense of common patriotic purpose inspired people to do what is necessary, so in peacetime a strong modern sense of patriotism and patriotic purpose which binds people together can motivate and inspire. And this British patriotism is, in my view, founded not on ethnicity nor race, not just on institutions we share and respect, but on enduring ideals which shape our view of ourselves and our communities – values which in turn influence the way our institutions evolve.

Yet as Jonathan Freedland has written in his *Bring Home the Revolution*, Britain is almost unique in that, unlike America and many other countries, we have no constitutional statement or declaration enshrining our objectives as a country; no mission statement defining purpose; and no explicitly stated vision of our future. So I will suggest to you today that it is to our benefit to be more explicit about what we stand for and what are our objectives, and that we will meet and master all challenges best by finding shared purpose as a country in our enduring British ideals that I would summarise as – in addition to our qualities of creativity, inventiveness, enterprise and our inter-nationalism, our central beliefs are a commitment to – liberty for all, responsibility by all and fairness to all. And I believe that out of a debate, hopefully leading to a broad consensus about what British-ness means, flows a rich agenda for change: a new constitutional settlement, an explicit definition of citizenship, a renewal of civic society, a rebuilding of our local government and a better balance between diversity and integration. And around national symbols that also unite the whole country, an inclusive Britishness where, as a result of our commitment to liberty for all, responsibility by all and fairness to all, we make it possible for not just some but all people to realise their potential to the full.

So what do we mean when we talk about Britishness? Remember when we were young, we wrote out our addresses: our town, our county, our country, our continent, the world; like James Joyce jokingly at the start of *Portrait of the Artist as a Young Man*: Stephen Dedalus, Class of Elements, Clongowes Wood College, Sallins,

County Kildare, Ireland, Europe, The World, The Universe. I will say something more about the importance to identity of neighbour-hoods, towns, villages and communities and about our global re-sponsibilities. But, while a few years ago only less than half – 46 per cent – identified closely with being British, today national identity has become far more important: it is not 46 per cent but 65 per cent – two-thirds – who now identify Britishness as important. And recent surveys show that British people feel more patriotic about their country than almost any other European country.

So what is it to be British? What has emerged from the long tidal flows of British history – from the 2,000 years of successive waves of invasion, immigration, assimilation and trading partnerships; from the uniquely rich, open and outward-looking culture – is a distinctive set of values which influence British institutions. Even before Amer-ica made it its own I think Britain can lay claim to the idea of liberty. Out of the necessity of finding a way to live together in a multi-national state came the practice of toleration and then the pursuit of liberty. Voltaire said that Britain gave to the world the idea of liberty. In the seventeenth century, Milton in *Paradise Lost* put it as 'if not equal all, yet all equally free'. Think of Wordsworth's poetry about the 'flood of British freedom'; then Hazlitt's belief that we have and can have 'no privilege or advantage over other nations but liberty'; right through to Orwell's focus on justice, liberty and decency defining Britain. 'We can get a parliament from anywhere,' said Lord Grattan, 'we can only get liberty from England.'

So there is, as I have argued, a golden thread which runs through British history – that runs from that long-ago day in Runnymede in 1215; on to the Bill of Rights in 1689 when Britain became the first country to successfully assert the power of parliament over the king; to not just one but four great Reform Acts in less than a hundred years – of the individual standing firm against tyranny and then – an even more generous, expansive view of liberty – the idea of govern-ment accountable to the people, evolving into the exciting idea of empowering citizens to control their own lives.

Just as it was in the name of liberty that in the 1800s Britain led the world in abolishing the slave trade – something we celebrate in 2007 – so too in the 1940s in the name of liberty Britain stood firm against Fascism, which is why I would oppose those who say we should do less to teach that period of our history in our schools. But woven also into that golden thread of liberty are countless strands of common, continuing endeavour in our villages, towns and cities – the efforts and popular achievements of ordinary men and women, with one sentiment in common – a strong sense of duty and responsibility: men and women who did not allow liberty to descend into a selfish individualism or into a crude libertarianism; men and women who, as is the essence of the labour movement, chose solidarity in preference to selfishness; thus creating out of the idea of duty and responsibility the Britain of civic responsibility, civic society and the public realm.

And so the Britain we admire of thousands of voluntary associations; the Britain of mutual societies, craft unions, insurance and friendly societies and cooperatives; the Britain of churches and faith groups; the Britain of municipal provision from libraries to parks; and the Britain of public service. Mutuality, cooperation, civic associations and social responsibility and a strong civic society – all concepts that after a moment's thought we see clearly have always owed most to progressive opinion in British life and thought. The British way always – as Jonathan Sacks has suggested – more than self-interested individualism – at the core of British history, the very ideas of 'active citizenship', 'good neighbour', civic pride and the public realm. Which is why two-thirds of people are adamant that being British carries with it responsibilities for them as citizens as well as rights.

But the twentieth century has given special place also to the idea that in a democracy where people have both political, social and economic rights and responsibilities, liberty and responsibility can only fully come alive if there is a Britain not just of liberty for all, and responsibility from all, but fairness to all. Of course the appeal to fairness runs through British history, from early opposition to the first Poll Tax in 1381 to the second; fairness the theme from the Civil War debates – where Raineborough asserted that 'the poorest he that is in England hath a life to live as the greatest he'; to the 1940s when Orwell talked of a Britain known to the world for its 'decency'. Indeed a 2005 YouGov survey showed that as many as 90 per cent of British people thought that fairness and fair play were very important or fairly important in defining Britishness. And of course this was the whole battle of twentieth-century politics – whether fairness would be formal equality before the law or something much more, a richer equality of opportunity. You only need look at the slogan which dominated Live Aid 2005 to see how, even in the years from 1985 to 2005, fairness had moved to become the central idea – the slogan in 2005 was 'From Charity to Justice': not just donations for handouts, but, by making things happen, forcing governments to deliver fairness.

Take the NHS, one of the great British institutions – what 90 per cent of British people think portrays a positive symbol of the real Britain – founded on the core value of fairness that all should have access to health care founded on need not ability to pay. A moment's consideration of the importance of the NHS would tell us that you don't need to counterpose civic society to government and assume that one can only flourish at the expense of the other or vice versa. Britain does best when we have both a strong civic society and a government committed to empowering people, acting on the principle of fairness. And according to one survey, more than 70 per cent of British people pride ourselves in all three qualities – our tolerance, responsibility and fairness together. So in a modern progressive view of Britishness, as I set out in a speech a few weeks ago, liberty does not retreat into self-interested individualism, but leads to ideas of empowerment; responsibility does not retreat into a form of paternalism, but is indeed a commitment to the strongest-possible civic society; and fairness is not simply a formal equality before the law, but is in fact a modern belief in an empowering equality of opportunity for all.

So in my view the surest foundation upon which we can advance economically, socially and culturally in this century will be to apply to the challenges that we face, the values of liberty, responsibility and fairness – shared civic values which are not only the ties that bind us, but also give us patriotic purpose as a nation and a sense of direction and destiny. And so in this vision of a Britain of liberty for all, responsibility from all and fairness to all we move a long way from the old left's embarrassed avoidance of an explicit patriotism. Orwell correctly ridiculed the old left view for thinking that patriotism could be defined only from the right: as reactionary; patriotism as a defence of unchanging institutions that would never modernise; patriotism as a defence of deference and hierarchy; and patriotism as, in reality, the dislike of foreigners and self-interested individualism. We now see that when the old left recoiled from patriotism they failed to understand that the values on which Britishness is based – liberty to all, responsibility by all, fairness for all – owe more to progressive ideas than to right-wing ones. But more than that, these core values of what it is to be British are the key to the next stage of our progress as a people: values that are capable of uniting us and inspiring us as we meet and master the challenges of the future. So we in our party should feel pride in a British patriotism and patriotic purpose founded on liberty for all, responsibility by all, and fairness to all. And, as we address global challenges, the modern application of these great enduring ideas that British people hold dear offers us a rich agenda for change, reform and modernisation true to these values.

First, start with the constitution and test the current condition of Britain against our principles of liberty for all, responsibility by all and fairness to all. And just as each generation needs to renew the settlement between individual, community and state, so too we should recognise that we do not today meet our ideal of liberty for all if we are to allow power to become over-centralised; we do not achieve responsibility by all if we do not encourage and build a strong civic society; and we do not achieve fairness to all if too many people feel excluded from the decision-making process.

So the British way forward must be to break up, in the name of liberty, centralised institutions that are too remote and insensitive, and so devolve power; to encourage, in the name of responsibility, the creation of strong local institutions; and, in new ways in the name of liberty, responsibility and fairness, to seek to engage the British people in decisions that affect their lives. So I believe it is imperative that we reinvigorate the constitutional reform agenda we began in 1997. And I cannot see how the long-term success, legitimacy and credibility of our institutions or our policies can be secured unless our constitutional, social and economic reforms are explicitly founded on these ideas. Just as on the first day I was Chancellor I limited the power of the executive by giving up government power over interest rates to the Bank of England, I suggested during the general election there was a case for a further restriction of executive power and a detailed consideration of the role of parliament in the declarations of peace and war. And, of course, founding our constitution on liberty within the law means restricting patronage, for example, in matters such as ecclesiastical and other appointments so that we prevent any allegation of arbitrary use of power. I would apply this same approach to constitutional questions such as the issue of House of Lords reform, where, in my view, the two principles that should guide our approach are the primacy of the House of Commons and the need for the accountability of the second chamber. At the same time the next stage of our discussions of human rights should, as people such as Francesca Klug have argued, also take more fully into account the very British idea that individual rights are rooted in ideas of responsibility and community.

We must apply also our principles of liberty for all, responsibility by all and fairness to all to the future of our civic society and the responsibilities of citizenship, and we will therefore want to do more to encourage and enhance voluntary initiative, mutual responsibility and local community action. For two centuries Britain was defined to the world by its proliferation of local clubs, associations, societies and endeavours – from churches and trades unions to municipal initiatives and friendly societies. And I believe that we should, for this and the coming generation, do more to encourage and empower new British organisations that speak for these British values. A modern expression of Britishness and our commitment to the future is the creation of the British National Youth Community Service: engaging and rewarding a new generation of young people from all backgrounds to serve their communities; demonstrating our practical commitment to a cohesive and strong society. So just as from America the Peace Corps – and before it, in Britain, British Voluntary Service Overseas – harnessed for the 1960s and beyond a new spirit of idealism and common purpose, in 2006 a new British National Youth Community Service can galvanise and challenge the energies and enthusiasm of a fresh generation of teenagers and young people. For example, gap years should not be available just for those who can afford to pay, but to young people who cannot afford to pay themselves but want to make the effort to serve their communities at home and abroad. And we should think of gap months, gap weeks as well as gap years. Time to serve the community, not just for people going on to higher education but for people whatever their skills.

And we should consider how we can link up with Asia, Africa and America and I will meet the airlines to ask what more they can do to help sponsor this idea. In return for service for their country in the USA in the 1940s the GI Bill helped thousands through college and university and we should consider and debate another idea: helping those who undertake community service with the costs of education, including help with Education Maintenance Allowance and tuition fees for those undertaking community work. The Russell Commission has recommended a prominent role for British business in this new community endeavour. I am meeting all faith groups to discuss community service. And shortly I will meet business organisations. And I thank businesses who have already signed up as pioneer sponsors for this idea and today I invite and urge businesses to match-fund £100 million – £50 million each from government and business – for long-term funding for this new idea. Britain can lead the world with a modern national community service.

Responsibility by all in Britain today means also corporate social responsibility – business engagement in voluntary activity, translating the widespread social concern that exists among employers and employees alike into effective action for the common good. And with corporate social responsibility not as an add-on but at the core of a company's work, Britain can lead the way in a modern approach to corporate responsibility. We set up Futurebuilders to help existing charities adapt to the modern world. I believe we need to examine how we might do more to encourage new charities and social enterprises, locally and nationally, to start up, develop and flourish, perhaps with a fund for seed-corn finance. Take mentoring, which is about befriending people, especially, in a more isolated society, the most vulnerable. While underdeveloped in Britain in contrast to other countries, mentoring is a modern expression of civic society at work. And we should explore innovative ways – through the internet, TV, local organisations and personal contact – of recruiting and training mentors and linking those who need help and advice to those who can help and advise.

Next, test our principles of liberty, responsibility and fairness and apply them to how we think about local government. And if, as I argue, the British way is to restore and enhance local initiative and mutual responsibility in civic affairs, we should be doing more to strengthen local institutions. While all governments have proved to be cautious in devolving power, I hope we can say that – as the Scottish Parliament, Welsh Assembly and mayor in London bear witness – this government has done more to devolve power than any other. But we must now look to further devolution of power away from Westminster, particularly to a reinvigoration of local government and to schools, hospitals and the self-management of local services, the emphasis on empowerment, communities and individuals realising their promise and potential by taking more control over their lives. And in doing so we must recognise that people's local sense of belonging is now focused on the immediate neighbourhood. So I welcome the debate on what some call 'double devolution' – on how we reinvigorate democracy at the most local of levels. For example, neighbourhood councils could help harness that sense of belonging and involve people directly in decisions about the services that they use every day. Just as neighbourhood policing – being pioneered here in London as well as elsewhere – is showing, greater local engagement and improved public services can go hand in hand: the police able to respond more quickly to local concerns and local people taking greater responsibility for working with the police to tackle these concerns.

And I believe a genuinely British approach to representative and participatory democracy should explore new ways of involving people in decisions. In various places in Britain and around the world local, regional and even national governments have been experimenting with new ways of involving the public in decision-making – not the usual suspects, the vested interest – but groups of citizens who come together, sometimes in small groups such as citizens' juries, sometimes in large deliberative exercises, to examine important issues of public policy. And I look forward to the considerations of the Power Commission.

A commitment to the British values of liberty, responsibility and fairness also means taking citizenship seriously. From the quality of citizenship lessons in our schools; to building on the introduction of citizenship ceremonies; to defining not just the rights of citizenship, but the responsibilities too; to finding the best ways of reconciling the rights to liberty for every individual with the needs for security for all; and, of course, an issue we will discuss in detail today – getting the balance right between diversity and integration. July 7th has rightly led to calls for all of us, including moderates in the Islamic community, to stand up to extremism. At one level, when suicide bombers have connections with other countries and can, in theory, use the internet or be instructed through mobile phones, we know that defeating violent extremists will not be achieved through action in one country alone or one continent, but only globally, through all means: military and security means but also debate, discussion and dialogue in newspapers, journals, culture, the arts and literature. And not just through governments but through foundations, trusts, civil society and civic culture, as globally we seek to distance extremists from moderates. But, at another level, terrorism in our midst means that debates, which sometimes may be seen as dry, about Britishness and our model of integration clearly now have a new urgency.

I believe in your discussions today you will conclude that it does entail giving more emphasis to the common glue – a Britishness which welcomes differences but which is not so loose, so nebulous, that it is simply defined as the toleration of difference and leaves a hole where national identity should be. Instead I have no doubt that a modern commitment to liberty, responsibility and fairness will lead us to measures that bring all parts of the community together to share a common purpose and linked destinies. Clearly we will have both to tackle prejudice, bigotry and the incitement to hatred and to do far more to tackle discrimination and promote inclusion. I believe we must address issues about the incitement to hatred just as I believe that there should now be greater focus on tackling inequalities in job and educational opportunities, driving up the educational attainment of pupils from ethnic minorities and a more comprehensive New Deal effort to tackle unacceptably high unemployment in areas of high ethnic minority populations. Indeed, we should do more to help integration. Take the example of those who cannot find work because of language difficulties. Here we should look at expanding mandatory English training. And for those who are trapped in a narrow range of jobs where their lack of fluency in English makes it hard for them to make progress in their careers, we should examine the case for further support. And to back up this effort there should be a national effort for volunteers as well as professionals to mentor new entrants. And we should also think of what more we can do to develop the ties that bind us more closely together.

The Olympics is but one example of a national project which is uniting the country. But think for a moment: what is the British equivalent of the US Fourth of July, or even the French Fourteenth of July for that matter? What I mean is: what is our equivalent for a national celebration of who we are and what we stand for? And what is our equivalent of the national symbolism of a flag in every garden?

In recent years we have had magnificent celebrations of VE Day, the Jubilee and, last year, Trafalgar Day. Perhaps Armistice Day and Remembrance Sunday are the nearest we have come to a British day that is – in every corner of our country – commemorative, unifying, and an expression of British ideas of standing firm in the world in the name of liberty, responsibility and fairness?

And let us remember that when people on the centre left recoiled from national symbols, the BNP tried to steal the Union Jack. Instead of the BNP using it as a symbol of racial division, the flag should be a symbol of unity, part of a modern expression of patriotism. So we should respond to the BNP by saying the union flag is a flag for Britain, not for the BNP; all the United Kingdom should honour it, not ignore it; we should assert that the union flag is, by definition, a flag for tolerance and inclusion.

And we should not recoil from our national history – rather we should make it more central to our education. I propose that British history should be given much more prominence in the curriculum – not just dates, places and names, nor just a set of unconnected facts, but a narrative that encompasses our history. And because citizenship is still taught too much in isolation I suggest in the current review of the curriculum that we look at how we root the teaching of citizenship more closely in history. And we should encourage volunteers to be more involved; to help schools bring alive the idea of citizenship with real engagement in the community. Rediscovering the roots of our identity in our shared beliefs also gives us more confidence in facing difficult questions about our relationship with the rest of the world. And – instead of a Britain still characterised by doubts about our role in the world, and in particular, grappling uncertainly with issues of integration in a European trade bloc; instead of a Britain seeing the battle as Britain versus Europe, not Britain part of Europe; instead of thinking the European choice is between non-engagement and total absorption; a Britain failing to see we can lead the next stage of Europe's development – I believe that, more sure of our values, we can become a Britain that is an increasingly successful leader of the global economy; a global Britain for whom membership of Europe is central; and then go on to help a reformed, more flexible, more outward-looking Europe play a bigger part in global society, not least improving the relationships between Europe and the USA.

And, of course, true to our ideals of liberty, responsibility and fairness, Britain leading the way in new measures to make the world safer, more secure and fairer – not just debt relief, the doubling of aid and, reflecting our openness as a nation, by securing a world deal on trade. But, from that foundation, proposing, true to our internationalism, a new way forward: a global new deal – universal free schooling for every child, universal free health care for every family – where the richest countries finally meet our commitments to the poorest of the world.

So a modern view of Britishness founded on responsibility, liberty and fairness requires us to:

- demand a new constitutional settlement;
- take citizenship seriously;
- rebuild civic society;
- renew local government;
- work for integration of minorities into a modern Britain; and
- be internationalist at all times.

10

PROTECTING AND IMPROVING
THE ENVIRONMENT

I want to say before I begin my substantive comments that it is a deep honour for me to be introduced by Gordon Brown. I am an unabashed and enthusiastic admirer of Gordon, and have been for a long time. I know personally it's possible to be responsible for a great many good things and then see others take virtually all the applause . . .

Gordon and I share a Calvinist heritage and a Scottish gene pool, though my forebears were not Presbyterian. He is a global leader and I say in all sincerity that his vision and scope and breadth, as well as depth, of thought is truly extraordinary and unique . . . You know, when the Labour Party tackled the difficult social issues of old-age pensions, health care for working families and so many other policies now taken for granted that were difficult at the time, it was because the Labour Party saw the need for social justice in a larger context, and dealing with social justice one year at a time, one Budget at a time, is insufficient if you really want to reach the goal. They thought freshly and now we are in a new era when we have to think freshly about the relationship between the global environment and social justice.

Al Gore
John Smith Memorial Lecture, London
November 2005

When I received the Nobel Peace Prize in December 2004, I called on industry and global institutions to appreciate the value of economic justice, equity and ecological integrity. I also urged them to recognise that extreme global inequities and prevailing consumption patterns at the expense of the environment and peaceful coexistence cannot be sustained for long.

Gordon Brown is one who understands these linkages. As his speeches on the environment, development and security show, he is one of the few world leaders who understand that environmental concerns cannot be placed in a category separate from the economy and from economic policy. Through this understanding, he is saying that a threatened environment threatens future economic activity and growth. Soil erosion, the depletion of marine stocks, water scarcity, air pollution – all these problems endanger all of us.

As the Green Belt Movement has been arguing, he goes further and acknowledges that the poorest members of the community – those most dependent on the natural world for their survival, and those with the fewest resources to buy their way out of unhealthy environments – suffer the most. And he knows that such suffering can lead to further suffering – to violence and war. As do I, Gordon Brown believes that we can overcome the many kinds of injustice. And, as so many others and I do, he has the courage to hope.

Like the Green Belt Movement, Gordon Brown, through his words and actions, is planting seeds for peace. I hope that you will read his words and honour his actions.

Wangaari Maathai

In March 2005, the Treasury made protecting and improving the environment an explicit part of its objectives and performance targets. Objective 8 now reads: 'to protect and improve the environment by using instruments that will deliver efficient and sustainable outcomes through evidence-based policies'. Since the implications of this decision are substantial, and accounted for major initiatives in the 2006 Budget, a speech the Chancellor gave on 15 March 2005 is included here. It was given to an Energy and Environment Ministerial Roundtable, rather than to a public gathering: had it been public it surely would have got more coverage than it did, particularly for the way it links the environmental and economic cases for government intervention; and because it recognises the impact of these initiatives on developing countries, particularly in Africa. As the Chancellor argues:

climate change is an issue of justice as much as of economic development. It is a problem caused by the industrialised countries, whose effects will disproportionately fall on developing countries . . . We must help the poorest countries adapt to those effects of climate change which are already occurring and which cannot be avoided to ensure that all the Millennium Development Goals are met – not at the cost of economic growth but to achieve it. And we must offer assistance where it is wanted to emerging economies whose emissions are rising, to help them provide energy for development and for poverty reduction – not at the cost of economic growth but to achieve it in ways which contribute to tackling, rather than exacerbating, the problem of climate change.

In a sense the key message here is that environmental issues can no longer be separated from the economy and economic issues. Whether it is soil erosion or the depletion of marine stocks, water scarcity or air pollution – not only is previous economic activity their cause, but these problems significantly threaten future economic activity and growth. As far as climate change is concerned the Chancellor is convinced by the evidence, and he accepts that as economic instability increases risk and undermines investment, so climate change will come to threaten our economic development and growth. And on energy, he believes that the task facing the world is to ensure that the energy investment decisions we make now contribute to addressing the need to reduce carbon usage. These policy objectives will have a major impact on all economies, but as the Chancellor concludes – we have no choice in the matter. In future, we have to build our economies on a platform of economic growth, full employment *and* environmental care. We have to make climate stability, energy investment and energy security central to economic policy.

. . .

More than sixty years ago, in 1944, the great British economist John Maynard Keynes laid down what he believed were the foundations of economic policy – that it was for government to ensure the twin objectives of high and stable levels of growth and employment.

Today we know that there is a third objective on which our economies must be built – and that is environmental care. If our economies are to flourish, if global poverty is to be banished, and if the well-being of the world's people is to be enhanced – not just in this generation but in succeeding generations – we must make sure we take care of the natural environment and resources on which our economic activity depends. And we now have sufficient evidence that human-made climate change is the most far-reaching – and almost certainly the most threatening – of all the environmental challenges facing us. As you know, the UK government – led by Prime Minister Tony Blair and by Margaret Beckett and Patricia Hewitt – has made climate change one of the two central priorities – along with global poverty – of our 2005 G8 Presidency. And I want to explain today why I believe that climate change is an issue for finance and economic ministries as much as for energy and environmental ones – and why all these parts of individual national governments – and indeed all governments internationally – must work together to tackle it.

Environmental issues – including climate change – have traditionally been placed in a category separate from the economy and from economic policy. But this is no longer tenable. Across a range of environmental issues – from soil erosion to the depletion of marine stocks, from water scarcity to air pollution – it is clear now not just that economic activity is their cause, but that these problems in themselves threaten future economic activity and growth. And it is the poorest members of the community – those most dependent on the natural world for their survival, and those with the fewest resources to buy their way out of unhealthy environments – that suffer the most. Indeed, it is in the issue of climate change that we can see this interaction of economic development, environmental degradation and social inequity most clearly. As you know, the impact of climate change will depend on how far and how fast temperatures rise, and on the nature of accompanying changes to rainfall, sea levels and extreme weather events. But even at global mean temperatures of 1 degree centigrade above pre-industrial levels – 0.2 degrees warmer than now – the evidence now shows that economic impacts are likely to be significant. And at a global average of 2 degrees or more the consequences – for agricultural productivity, water stress, ecosystems and human health – become potentially devastating. The Intergovernmental Panel on Climate Change suggest that the global economic costs associated with an increase in average global temperature of 2.5 degrees could add up to between 1.5 and 2 per cent of global GDP a year. As these costs unfold, an unstable climate could lead to instability in some societies and economies. And as economic instability increases risk and under-mines investment, so climate change will come to threaten our economic development and growth.

But climate change is an issue of justice as much as of economic development. It is a problem caused by the industrialised countries, whose effects will disproportionately fall on developing countries. Climate change is a consequence of the build-up of greenhouse gases over the past 200 years in the atmosphere, and virtually all these emissions came from the rich countries. Indeed, we became rich through those emissions, although of course we did not know this then. But at the same time it is now clear that the largest impacts of climate change will occur in the great land masses of Africa, Asia and Latin America. Indeed many are already occurring, from reduced rainfall in the Sahel to floods in Bangladesh. So as the Commission for Africa concluded in its report published last week, economic development in the poorest countries is going to take place in the context of a changing climate, and development strategies are going to have to adapt to meet this new challenge. This is not a question of making climate change a priority over poverty reduction – that would be absurd as well as immoral. It is precisely economic development and growth which will provide the resources and technological advance to enable economies to adapt to and mitigate climate change. The task is to ensure that poverty-reduction strategies and our quest to meet the 2015 Millennium Development Goals are not overwhelmed and reversed by the impact of climate change.

At the same time we must acknowledge where the responsibility lies for tackling climate change. This was set out in the 1992 United Nations Framework Convention on Climate Change, agreed by over 180 countries. The convention clearly sets out the principle of 'common but differentiated responsibilities' – that the industrialised countries must take responsibility first in reducing their emissions of greenhouse gases. For the UK's part, we are aiming to meet not only our Kyoto target of reducing greenhouse gas emissions by 12.5 per cent by 2012. We have also set ourselves a stretching national target of moving towards a reduction in carbon-dioxide emissions of 20 per cent over 1990 levels by 2010, and a longer-term goal to put ourselves on a path to cut the UK's carbon-dioxide emissions by 60 per cent by 2050. And we are making progress. But at the same time we have to acknowledge that no country can solve this problem on its own. The UK is responsible for only 2 per cent of global emissions of greenhouse gases, so our actions will have little impact on climate change unless they are part of a concerted international effort.

That is why the UK supports the Kyoto Protocol which came into force last month. And why we are working with other countries to establish both a consensus around the need for change and firm commitments to take action to reduce carbon emissions world-wide. The European Union accounts for about 15 per cent of carbon emissions; the G8 as a whole, about half. So the action of the richest countries can make a huge difference on their own. However, in due course, as the UN Convention recognises, we will need a comprehensive global response. We will need the cooperation of all countries with significant energy needs and emission levels if – for the benefit of all of us – we are going to tackle this global challenge comprehensively and cost-effectively. In a globally competitive economy a multilateral approach is the only way forward.

Now, controlling greenhouse gases requires policy action in a number of areas but for the remainder of my remarks today I want to focus on energy policy. I believe that economic-policy makers now need to pay much greater attention to this – not just because the pace of global economic growth is demanding investment in energy supply and distribution on an unprecedented scale, but because new challenges have emerged in energy policy in the last few years:

- every nation today is concerned about energy security;
- higher energy prices are requiring industry and commerce to examine the costs and efficiency of energy use;
- the growing evidence of climate change is forcing attention on carbon emissions and their reduction.

And in terms of policy these challenges all point now in the same direction: towards a reduction in the carbon intensity of energy production and greater efficiency in its use. Over the next twenty-five years, the International Energy Agency estimates that global economic growth and development will require investment in the world's energy infrastructure of some $16 trillion. Around 1,500 large generating plants will be built, most using fossil fuels, over a third of them in China alone. And, with the lifespan of a power station itself at up to forty or fifty years, the decisions we make now, and over the next two decades, will affect our energy options – and the climate change impacts these will have – for at least the next half a century. So the task facing the world is to ensure that the energy investment decisions we make now contribute to addressing these challenges, and do not exacerbate them. Over the last few years the United Kingdom government has set our energy policy on such a path. In particular, we have used a variety of market-based policies designed to stimulate energy efficiency and to encourage the development of low-cost renewable sources of energy supply:

- the Climate Change Levy and associated Climate Change Agreements which – as new research we are publishing tomorrow confirms – have been more successful in saving energy than we anticipated on introduction;
- the renewables obligation, which has led to a significant increase in renewable-energy generation;
- the UK Emissions Trading Scheme – the world's first economy-wide greenhouse-gases trading scheme – which is achieving emission reductions well above expectations;
- enhanced capital allowances to encourage take-up of innovative energy-efficient technologies;
- incentives for cleaner cars; and
- support for research and development in sustainable energy – now rising to over £100 million a year.

Through these and other measures we have sought to reduce carbon emissions in the most cost-effective way, stimulating technological innovation, and harnessing entrepreneurialism. And, overall, the UK government is on course not just to achieve but to go beyond its Kyoto target. But in fact the greenhouse-gas emission numbers do not tell the whole story. Since 1997 the British economy has enjoyed high growth, averaging growth of 2.8 per cent a year, or 17 per cent in total. In the same period carbon-dioxide emissions have remained about the same. So the carbon intensity of the British economy – carbon emissions per unit of GDP – has fallen by nearly 15 per cent. This is not to be complacent. We know that we have much further to go. But it is to point to one of the crucial lessons of the UK's and other countries' experience over the last eight years – that climate-change policy *is* compatible with strong economic performance. For well-designed policies can actually stimulate innovation and improve productivity, particularly in the field of energy efficiency. The evidence shows that in the UK most businesses and public-sector organisations could easily achieve up to 20 per cent reductions in their energy bills in short payback periods, often without any capital investment at all – which in turn would have a positive effect on profitability and competitiveness.

So the first task of climate change policy is to release these productive benefits. Many companies have already taken action in response to the policies that we have put in place to encourage more efficient use of energy. But others have not. In the global economy, as pressure on global resources and prices increase, I believe that no business can now ignore this challenge. For the UK my ambition is that British businesses should become world class in their energy-efficiency performance, in the same way that they must become world class in their performance in productivity, skills, and research and development. And yet, as our energy-efficiency innovation review has found, there is a clear market failure in energy efficiency in this country. There are profitable, cost-saving measures which can be taken in the management of energy which are currently going to waste. In most of our economy and in most of our public sector we continue to buy and sell energy rather than energy services – the heat, light and power which are the real outputs. So I can announce today that the Treasury will host a summit in the coming year to explore how government and business can remove barriers to the development of energy-services markets in the UK.

And in making climate change a key priority of the UK's Presidency of the EU in the second half of this year, I want the energy efficiency and productivity of the European economy to be a principal focus. Today the Treasury is publishing a paper showing that, to succeed in the global economy, Europe needs to be more flexible, more adaptable and more enterprising. Facing the expansion of global competition and the explosive nature of technological change, and with developing countries on course to produce half the world's manufacturing exports, no country or continent can take its future prosperity for granted. Countries and continents will rise and fall depending upon their ability to adapt to change. The advanced industrial countries have important choices to make.

And as our Budget study published today on the restructuring of the global economy makes clear, their future cannot be founded upon low skill levels and low technology. All need to invest in science infrastructure and human capital. So to meet the challenge of the global economy Britain and Europe must remove unnecessary barriers to enterprise and make the necessary public investments in education and infrastructure. And one area where Britain and Europe excel is in environmentally friendly technologies.

It is now clear that – as well as renewable sources of energy – cleaner fossil-fuel technologies, including the capture of carbon dioxide and its long-term storage underground, are likely to become crucial elements of carbon-reduction strategies over the next few decades, particularly for emerging economies. These technologies have the potential to provide a step change in reducing emissions. I can therefore announce today that as part of the UK government's continuing support for research and development in this field we will now examine the potential of economic incentives to encourage carbon capture and storage. And in tomorrow's Budget I will also set out proposals for a new high-level energy-research platform which will bring together public and private funders of energy research to enhance opportunities for collaboration and to set shared priorities for research. I believe that in both energy efficiency and the development of low-carbon energy sources there are major economic opportunities for business. But climate-change policy must also take into account its impact on business competitiveness. This must therefore be carefully monitored and managed. I know that, for business investment, certainty in the long-term policy framework is very important. I am therefore issuing a challenge today to the business community, in the UK and beyond: to join us in putting in place a long-term framework to meet our climate-change goals in the most cost-effective way and with the lowest impact on competitiveness.

It is clear that a key requirement of this will be to work internationally. And that it is why the Kyoto Treaty and the EU Emissions Trading Scheme are so important. They make the economic opportunities of a climate-friendly energy policy real and tangible. Carbon now has a price. Carbon-saving is now a way of making money. And as the EU trading scheme sets Europe on course to meet its Kyoto targets, businesses across the continent have an unprecedented opportunity to benefit from carbon reduction – and through the Kyoto Treaty mechanisms this is as true for countries in the trading of carbon credits as it is for firms. The UK is a strong advocate of carbon-trading and of the economic opportunities it brings. I am delighted that the City of London has become a centre of carbon-trading activity. And having seen the interest in cap and trade schemes in the north-eastern states of the US and in California, and elsewhere, I hope that in due course that we can extend the hand of trading from Europe to other parts of the world.

And while we take these measures in the UK and in Europe, I also believe we must support emerging economies and developing countries in their efforts. As the Commission for Africa demanded, we must help the poorest countries adapt to those effects of climate change which are already occurring and which cannot be avoided to ensure that all the Millennium Development Goals are met – not at the cost of economic growth but to achieve it. And we must offer assistance where it is wanted to emerging economies whose emissions are rising, such as those represented at this conference today, to help them provide energy for development and for poverty reduction – not at the cost of economic growth but to achieve it in ways which contribute to tackling, rather than exacerbating, the problem of climate change. And so I am delighted that Chinese Minister Liu is here to speak following me on this subject. It is clear that both technical assistance and financing will be part of this: and there are barriers to both that must be overcome. We want to develop, through the G8 process, a package of practical measures, focused on accelerating technological development, to cut emissions. And we must look at what more support the international financial institutions, including European institutions like the European Investment Bank, can provide to promote greater investment in climate-friendly energy production and energy efficiency.

So, in conclusion, I believe we must build our economies on a platform of economic growth, full employment *and* environmental care. We must make climate stability, energy investment and energy security central to economic policy. I believe this is within our power, if we have the will. But it will require us to act together and I hope that this conference can be the start of a process to bring together, not just energy and environment ministries from our countries, but finance and economic ministries too, to explore how we can together address these issues. In the mid-twentieth century, John Maynard Keynes played a key role in shaping the new international institutions – the United Nations, the IMF, the World Bank – believing that international cooperation was the only way to solve the economic challenges of the post-war world. I believe that today – at the start of the twenty-first century – international cooperation is again the only way forward. Here, as elsewhere, we must live up to the ideal of an international community acting for the public good – for the present generation, and for generations to come.

On 20 April 2006, the Chancellor addressed the United Nations Ambassadors in New York. He opened the speech by suggesting that how we protect our environment, secure our planet and safeguard our future for our generation and for generations to come is one of the greatest international challenges of our time.

This speech, like the earlier one above, stresses the need for environmental priorities – including climate change – to be considered in future alongside economic priorities. The Chancellor argues that they are not mutually exclusive: we simply cannot have a situation in the future where economic growth is prioritised at the expense of the environment, or environmental care at the expense of growth and prosperity. But in this speech he takes his arguments about the interrelation of economic objectives and our environmental objectives a step further, arguing not only that jobs, economic growth and prosperity now increasingly reinforce each other, but that this is the way to develop social justice as well.

He also argues that since climate change is a global problem, it requires a global solution, and he suggests that it will be necessary to build a global consensus for tackling environmental change. Appropriately enough, given the location of the speech and the audience, he concludes by suggesting that just as the post-1945 international institutions were founded for the world problems of that generation and their times, we need to find ways for our global institutions – primarily the UN and the World Bank – to meet and master the challenges of our generation and our times.

The Chancellor uses his substantial experience of successful policy-making within the UK to set out in this speech some concrete steps which can be taken at country and at global level to make an impact on climate change. As he says, 'I know from experience of the long but ultimately successful journey to debt relief for the poorest countries that to build a consensus for environmental action founded on detailed practical policies for change will take time but is an essential element for success.' Building on his experience as one of the longest-serving and most experienced finance ministers in the world, his chairmanship of key World Bank committees, and his membership of the UN Review Committee, the Chancellor is in an extremely powerful position to make progress on what he calls 'a new framework for environmental progress at a global level'. As he concludes, great challenges require great acts of statesmanship. We are indeed lucky to have him in the right place at the right time to move us all from words to a commitment to deliver practical policies that can unite world opinion in a new and broad-based consensus that could bring about change: 'so that we can make the world anew'.

. . .

Environmental sustainability is not an option – it is a necessity. For economies to flourish, for global poverty to be banished, for the well-being of the world's people to be enhanced – not just in this generation but in succeeding generations – we have a compelling and ever more urgent duty of stewardship to take care of the natural environment and resources on which our economic activity and social fabric depends.

So the new synthesis we need is that economic growth, social justice and environmental care advance best when they all advance together. This imperative applies most strongly of all to the greatest of the environmental challenges we face, that of climate change.

It is now clear that, if current trends are left unchecked, the economic costs of climate change will be far greater than previously thought. And yet at the same time it is becoming evident that the means of tackling it are increasingly available and the costs could become affordable – and that tackling it offers real economic benefits and opportunities to developed and developing countries alike. So I want to argue today that it is through the new economics of climate change that a new global consensus for tackling environmental change can be built. Whether we agree with *Time* magazine, which observed last week that 'the serious debate has quietly ended' or not, the real question now is not whether climate change is happening or indeed what are its causes: the question is how fast it is happening and how we address these causes.

Since the start of the Industrial Revolution global greenhouse gases have risen by 30 per cent. In the last century alone, global temperatures have risen by almost one degree Celsius – probably the fastest rate of increase for a thousand years. And the rate of change has been speeding up. The ten hottest years since records began over 150 years ago have all occurred in the past twelve.

The consequences of this warming are now evident right across the world. In the past century, almost all the major ice caps have started melting – adding 20 billion tonnes of water each year to the oceans. Since 1900, global sea levels have risen by 10–20 centimetres. And the Intergovernmental Panel on Climate Change suggests that, by the end of this century, sea levels could rise by up to a further 90 centimetres and temperatures could rise by a further five to six degrees. And with rising sea levels and temperatures on this scale, we must assess the consequences for agricultural productivity, for water stress, for ecosystems, for flood defences and for human health. Studies for the UK Environment Department suggest that by 2050 African cereal production could fall by 10–30 per cent, up to 3 billion people could live in areas of increased water stress and millions could be at increased risk of malaria and dengue fever. Already we are seeing changing rainfall patterns and increased weather extremes. And the Intergovernmental Panel estimates that the global economic costs of a temperature rise of just 2.5 degrees could be up to 2.5 per cent of global GDP.

So climate change is not just an environmental issue, but most definitely an economic issue. And the time lags between greenhouse-gas emissions and climatic impacts mean that, to affect climate in twenty years' time, we have to act now. This is why, last year, I asked Sir Nicholas Stern – former Chief Economist at the World Bank and Head of the British Government Economic Service – to report on the economics of climate change. And what his initial findings suggest is that the risks of climate change will not be evenly spread, but will hit poorest countries most. This makes the issue of climate change one of justice as much as of economic development: a problem whose causes are led by industrialised countries but whose effects will disproportionately fall on developing countries – most recently drought in the Sahel and the Horn of Africa. And because we are now spending $6 billion in aid simply to respond to this humanitarian crisis, resources are being diverted to tackle the short-term consequences of environmental change and away from dealing with the causes of underdevelopment and environmental neglect. So it is right that anti-poverty campaigners have taken up the environmental as well as the poverty challenge. Round the world, as they know, it is the poorest – those who depend most upon the natural world for their survival, and those with the fewest resources to buy their way out of unhealthy environments – that suffer the most.

'Today, we understand that respect for the environment,' Kofi Annan rightly said, 'is one of the main pillars of our fight against poverty,' and thus essential for achieving the Millennium Development Goals. Indeed an unstable climate can lead to economic instability, thus threatening investment and economic development and growth.

So we must start from the profound truths: that economic development in poor countries is going to take place in the context of a changing climate, that underdevelopment and environmental neglect go hand in hand, that future development strategies are going to have to adapt to meet this new twin challenge. This is not a question of making climate change a priority over poverty reduction, it is ensuring that policies for growth offer the technological advance and necessary resources to overcome both poverty and underdevelopment and environmental degradation.

Climate change is therefore a global problem. And it requires a global solution. This is not to say that countries do not individually have a responsibility to act. We do. And we will. But it is to acknowledge the reality that no country can solve this problem on its own. Britain produces only 2 per cent of the world's greenhouse gases; even America – the single largest source – produces less than one quarter. The message that global problems require global solutions underpinned the United Nations Framework Convention on Climate Change agreed at the Earth Summit in Rio nearly fifteen years ago. And, whatever its shortcomings, this also underpins the Kyoto Protocol – now ratified by over 160 countries, representing over 60 per cent of the world's emissions. And now I believe it is not just more urgent than ever before but also more possible than before to build a global consensus for tackling environmental change.

Such a consensus is not easy. It must be founded first on a shared understanding of the challenge ahead. But under Tony Blair's chairmanship, the G8 began a process of dialogue with other major energy-consuming nations on climate change and clean energy. Agreement at the UN Convention in Montreal shows that the will is potentially there. And I believe that this global consensus, which over recent years has often seemed impossible, is now within our grasp – because the policies we need to meet economic and environmental needs are now converging.

First, as Kofi Annan said last month: 'Today's high oil prices make the economic and environmental arguments even more mutually supportive.' And with the trebling of oil prices over three years, the demand for a supply of energy that is secure, stable and sustainable is more broadly based than ever. Indeed, a more sustainable and efficient use of energy resources was the focus of discussions among both consuming and producing nations' discussions at the opening of the new headquarters of the International Energy Forum in Saudi Arabia which I attended last November. President Bush's State of the Union Address in January highlights both America's dependence on oil and the need for change. But the concern goes far beyond America. Previous shocks have been triggered by supply shortages. And indeed today's high prices can be attributed in part to uncertainty of supply from political instability in major producers to the impact of hurricanes. But few doubt that the underlying issue is one of demand – with a rising Asia now consuming one-third of the world's oil. Higher prices are now requiring countries and businesses to examine their energy costs, in particular greater efficiency of use and diversification of supply.

Of course major advances in the efficiency of the use of oil have been made since the last oil-price spike in the 1970s. New technology has made drilling more successful and increased the yield from fields. In addition to this continued advance, new finds in oil and gas will almost certainly give us greater supply than previously documented. But even with this progress, we cannot escape the conclusion that more environmentally sensitive uses of energy must become an essential element of delivering future economic growth rather than being seen as at odds with it. And in Washington tomorrow – with global oil prices now again above $70 a barrel – based on the plan Britain set out last year, I will ask the G7 to discuss not only how we ensure greater security of energy supply but support alternative sources of energy and greater efficiency of energy use. So, reducing carbon emissions is an energy, and thus an economic, imperative as much as it is an environmental imperative.

But, second, the economic agenda and the environmental agenda are not only now converging: the one now reinforces the other more than ever before. So while, of course, there will be costs to reducing greenhouse-gas emissions, preventing climate change can contribute to the next stage of economic growth. It is a lesson we are learning from Britain's recent experience. We are on course not just to achieve but to go beyond – indeed nearly double – our Kyoto target for greenhouse-gas emissions. But these numbers do not tell the whole story. For in the last decade our economy has grown much faster than in previous decades and faster than the rest of Europe. Yet in Britain in this period of high growth, greenhouse-gas emissions have not risen. So without being complacent about what more we have to do, which we are not, it is correct that the carbon intensity of the British economy – carbon emissions per unit of GDP – has fallen by a third.

If in the future all countries are to both change and grow, we must set the common framework that allows this to happen:

- by acting multilaterally, we can ensure in the new global economy that there is no race to the bottom in business competitiveness;
- by developing long-term incentives, we provide the certainty that business requires to invest; and
- by working with the grain of the market, we free innovation, flexibility and entrepreneurship that promotes growth rather than holding it back.

This is why we strongly support the innovation of carbon-trading. It offers us a way to reinforce economic and environmental objectives. It gives carbon an international price. It means carbon-saving can be a way of making money and increasing returns on investment. And it makes the economic opportunities of a climate-friendly energy policy real and tangible.

We first saw the potential of trading in America with sulphur and nitrous-oxide trading in the 1990s – reducing acid-rain emissions by one million tonnes. In Britain, our voluntary carbon scheme, with more than thirty companies, helped reduce carbon emissions by more than 1.6 million tonnes. And the City of London is now a global centre for carbon-trading. And now in Europe, we have adopted a scheme that will cut emissions across all twenty-five Member States. And Britain is now proposing to extend and strengthen the European scheme beyond 2012. By matching it with an extension of the Clean Development Mechanism beyond 2012 – our aim is for it to support investment not just in Europe, but in developing countries. So we will examine how we can guarantee a continued market for carbon credits up to and beyond 2012. And by linking it with other initiatives now being developed across the world from states in America and Australia to countries such as Canada and South Korea, our aim is for it to become the driver for a deep, liquid and long-term global carbon-trading system. Our ultimate goal must be a global carbon market.

And with a global framework in the making, the environment can itself become a driver of future economic growth. Economic competitiveness can actually increase by improving environmental efficiency as we secure more wealth from less energy and fewer resources. Increasing labour productivity has always been a core goal of all successful businesses. Now, as energy costs rise and materials become more scarce, we need to pay the same attention to resource productivity.

Perhaps the most promising development is that new jobs, new industries and new exports come from rising investment in new, low-carbon technologies. In Britain alone, the environment market has increased from £16 billion, 170,000 jobs and 7,000 companies in 2001; to £25 billion, 400,000 jobs and 17,000 companies in 2004. Over the next ten years it is estimated that a further 130,000 jobs could be created. In Europe, the environment sector already accounts for 1.3 per cent of employment – 2 million jobs. And in 2010 the global environmental market – clean energy, waste and water – could be worth almost $700 billion – a sector as big as the successful aerospace or pharmaceuticals sectors.

In this field the role of governments – in partnership with business and science – is to harness market power and dynamism by stimulating the discovery and development of these technologies. Because while the technologies that will set us on the path to the low-carbon economy of the next twenty years exist now, those of the following twenty do not. America is the world's largest investor in environmental R&D. And is now joining in a new Asia-Pacific technology initiative with Australia, India, Japan, China and South Korea. Europe's environmental research funding is the basis for a new partnership with China on a virtually zero emissions coal power plant. For our own part, Britain already spends over £800 million a year on environmental research, backed up with tax breaks and capital allowances to encourage innovation. And Britain is jointly working with Norway on developing the potential of carbon capture and storage in the North Sea.

In my Budget last month, I announced proposals for a new National Institute of Energy Technologies, a public–private partnership – with the aim of raising finance of £1 billion – to create a new facility at the cutting edge of research and innovation. Its mission is to bring together the best engineers, scientists and companies from around the world – our investment in science and technology going hand in hand with the new market incentives.

And thus with a developing global environment market, the new global consensus I believe to be possible grows into more than a shared understanding of a shared problem, and becomes a set of shared solutions in the shared interest of us all. And it is this that underpins the next driver for consensus: all of us – countries, consumers and companies – are increasingly realising our responsibilities for environmental care. So just as a growing sense of personal and social responsibility which is more than just enlightened self-interest paved the way in the past to socially responsible growth, so today in the twenty-first century such personal and social responsibility can be the basis for mutually beneficial environmental and economic progress.

With the scientific evidence now clear, we are as individuals increasingly aware of what we can do. Encouraged by market solutions, companies are also increasingly aware of their corporate responsibilities. And with internal carbon markets, commitments to become carbon neutral, and energy efficiency initiatives, the world's leading firms are already showing that the flexible will invariably defeat the inflexible. And with many new and smaller far-sighted firms emerging into these markets the companies that look like leading tomorrow are those that are already investing in a low-carbon economy today. And as the market increasingly pioneers answers to climate change – governments also need to act with imagination and initiative, recognising our responsibilities – by putting in place the right long-term policy framework with clear, credible and forward-looking signals.

Of course even within a multilateral framework, no two countries will have the same policies for their own specific needs. But the principles are common: ranging from the most basic – that consumers have the information they need to make informed choices about their environmental impact; to introducing fiscal and other incentives for environmentally friendly behaviour; and then to setting, where it is right to do so, standards for environmental protection, including our proposed annual carbon report. In this way not just the Department of Environment but every department of government from transport to foreign affairs, from education to overseas development, becomes a department of the environment.

In Britain our new Climate Change Programme, published last month, sets out the details of our approach. And our Energy Review, concluding this summer, is examining our future energy options – including renewables and nuclear – and will set our future strategy.

Central to our approach has been our willingness to take the difficult decision to introduce a Climate Change Levy. By incentivising better energy use, the levy has increased the energy efficiency of British business by over 2 per cent each year. Alongside the levy there are now 5,000 Climate Change Agreements to increase business energy efficiency, and we have created the Carbon Trust, which has already provided advice and support to over 3,000 businesses. At the same time we have recycled the revenues from the levy into reductions in businesses' National Insurance contributions. So by targeting the marginal use of energy, the Climate Change Levy has provided real market incentives to energy efficiency, while showing how by taxing 'bads' (emissions) we can reduce taxes on 'goods' (jobs). Together, in each of the next five years, these climate change measures will cut emissions by more than 6 million tonnes, accounting by 2010 for a third of our total carbon reductions.

Nearly a quarter of carbon emissions come from vehicles. So we are incentivising fuel-efficient cars with measures that range from variable rates of vehicle duty (starting with no duty at all for the cleanest cars) to support for bio-fuels. Our new obligation in electricity supply

– now underpinned by new support for micro-generation technologies – is increasing the share of renewables to 10 per cent.

The energy used by buildings and the products in them account
for half of our emissions. So far bolder new regulations introduced
this month will make new buildings 40 per cent more energy efficient
than they were just ten years ago – showing that, alongside exhortation, information and incentives, targeted standards can make a
difference, in the same way that new regulations for fridges cut CFCs
and ozone damage twenty years ago; and the Clean Air Acts did away
with London's infamous smog fifty years ago.

But our new approach also offers a way out of the trap that so often
governments round the world have fallen into: we are pioneering
risk-based regulation which means increasingly that only on the basis
of risk will we demand information, form-filling and inspection. We
are recognising too that even the most basic addition of information
can play a powerful role in making self-driven change happen:
providing people with their right to information can play a powerful
role in making self-driven change happen. In Britain, for example,
we are now piloting better labelling on electronic goods and smart
meters in homes. But here too with a global goods market – with
more products than ever made in one country but bought in another
– we also need global action. Today consumer goods left on standby
world-wide are responsible for 1 per cent of global emissions. So
Britain will propose that the EU and the International Energy Agency
bring together leading manufacturers and countries to speed up the
international implementation of the one-Watt standard for energy
efficiency.

Finally, I believe that a global consensus for action on climate
change is possible because we can see how all countries can share in
the benefits from it. For this to happen, developed countries must be
prepared to support, with public investment, through grants or loans,
the efforts of developing countries. And we have a special responsibility to help the poorest countries both to adapt to climate change
and to invest in climate-friendly energy production and energy
efficiency. Only in this way can we ensure that all the Millennium
Development Goals are met – not at the cost of economic growth, but
to achieve it. Indeed new alternative-energy technologies offer not
only the possibility of meeting Africa's growing needs, but also the
potential of new exports to the rest of the world. And when I was in

Africa last week, Britain began discussions with Mozambique and South Africa on a new partnership with Brazil – today the world's largest producer of renewable bio-fuels – on how southern Africa could become a leader in bio-fuels production as well.

Yet globally there is an estimated $60 billion annual shortfall in energy investment in developing countries. So at the G8 meeting in Gleneagles in Scotland last year, Britain proposed a new global energy investment framework. The aim of the framework is to remove the barriers that prevent investment, by developing new financing mechanisms which leverage private and public finance from both within and outside developing countries. And in Washington tomorrow, I will propose a new public–private partnership, a World Bank-led facility, a $20 billion fund for developing economies to invest in alternative sources of energy and greater energy efficiency. I believe it is by providing in these ways for a flow of public and private investment funds for developing countries that we will be able to bring these countries into the global consensus on climate change that I am calling for today.

But globally we can do more. For just as the post-1945 international institutions were founded for new world problems of their time, we need to find ways for our institutions to meet and master the challenges of our generation. Our international institutions are essential to global action on the environment because, as I have said, the impact is global and felt disproportionately by the poor and there can be no development without environmental care. In the review Kofi Annan has constituted, chaired by three prime ministers – of Mozambique, Norway and Pakistan – and of which I am privileged to be a member, the United Nations is testing its global remit against the challenges ahead and it is clear that if we were starting afresh, environmental stewardship would play a more dominant and central part. The UN Environment Programme based in Nairobi plays a key global role in setting global standards and ensuring that the environment is properly integrated into the UN's development and humanitarian work. And next month the Commission for Sustainable Development will launch its next two-year energy strategy. Increasingly, as a sister international organisation, the World Bank has become the key financier of environmental standards and programmes in the developing world.

If we are to encourage lower-carbon energy supply, energy efficiency and adaptation to climate change, we must do more at a global level. Take one example – while we are in the process of forming national institutes for environment and energy, research into the environment remains underdeveloped in contrast to medical and IT research work and we lack a global network. The UN's uniqueness lies in its representativeness, and thus accountability and legitimacy. The World Bank has financial power and experience of long-term project investment to make the right connections between tackling environmental neglect and addressing poverty and underdevelopment. Both can be both voices for the poor and vehicles for action against poverty. So I believe that to meet and master the scale of the challenges ahead together the UN and the World Bank must work to create a global environmental presence that exhorts, incentivises, researches and monitors change and most of all is in a position – alongside the private sector – to invest in change. So I hope that the UN review, which will report later this year, will make concrete recommendations on this new framework for environmental progress at a global level.

Great challenges require great acts of statesmanship. And this is the right time to move from words to a commitment to deliver practical policies that can unite world opinion in a new and broad-based consensus that could bring about change. In facing up to the challenges of their times, the world leaders of sixty years ago created new international institutions – the United Nations, the IMF, the World Bank – and demonstrated by their actions that international cooperation was the best way to solve the economic challenges of the post-war world. But such path-breaking statesmanship and leadership also brought the Marshall Plan of the 1940s. Starting from Communist threats in Greece, Turkey and the Balkans, the statesmen of the day quickly realised that there was an even bigger challenge: the political, economic and social reconstruction of Europe. For four years America contributed 1 per cent of its GDP to the rebuilding of Europe. But the greatest contribution was in the transatlantic trade and commerce and flows of people and ideas between both continents. I believe that today – in the first decade of a new century – international cooperation built on bold innovative statesmanship is again the best way forward. And by our actions we could in reality realise the ideal of an international community acting for the public good – for the present generation, and for generations to come.

But this is an endeavour that, because it has not yet been met, challenges us to reach out in dialogue and debate. The visionaries of the 1940s understood also that the global challenges they faced required them not just to have the right policies but that they should seek to build a consensus for stability and change across the world. And I know from experience of the long but ultimately successful journey to debt relief for the poorest countries that to build a consensus for environmental action founded on detailed practical policies for change will take time but is an essential element for success. I have suggested today how a progressive consensus can be built for sustainable, stable and equitable growth for both developed and developing countries: how a new paradigm that sees economic growth, social justice and environmental care advancing together can become the common sense of our age. The scale of environmental challenge we now face brings home to us that working apart we will fail but working together we can make progress. And by acting boldly together, it is in our power to achieve for our times what the post-1945 pioneers achieved for theirs. In our generation we can indeed make the world anew.

FURTHER READING

Annan, Kofi, *We the Peoples: The Role of the United Nations in the 21st Century*, United Nations Millennium Report, 2000

Arnold, Matthew, *Poems*, 1853; *Poems*, 2nd Series, 1855; *Merope*, 1858; *New Poems*, 1867; *On Translating Homer*, 1861 and 1862; *On the Study of Celtic Literature*, 1867; *Essays in Celtic Literature*, 1868, 2nd Series, 1888; *Culture and Anarchy*, 1869; *St Paul and Protestantism*, 1870; *Friendship's Garland*, 1871; *Literature and Dogma*, 1873; *God and the Bible*, 1875; *Last Essays on Church and Religion*, 1877; *Mixed Essays*, 1879; *Irish Essays*, 1882; *Discourses in America*, 1885; *Essays in Criticism*, 1865 and 1888; *Culture and Anarchy*, 1888

Balls, Ed, Foreword to *New Localism: Refashioning the Centre-Local Relationship*, by Dan Corry and Gerry Stoker, New Local Government Network, 2002

Bellah, Robert, *Habits of the Heart*, 1985; *The Good Society*, 1992

Berlin, Isaiah, 'Two Concepts of Liberty', Inaugural Lecture, Oxford, 1958

Bevan, Aneurin, *In Place of Fear: A Free Health Service*, 1952

Beveridge, William, *Unemployment*, 1909; *Social Insurance and Allied Services*, 1942

Blendon, Robert J., Cathy Schoen, Catherine M. Desroches, Robin Osborn, Kimberly L. Scoles and Kinga Zapert, *Inequities In Health Care: A Five-Country Survey*, Health Affairs 21, 2002

Bono, speech to Labour Party Conference, Brighton, September 2004

Boswell, James, *Life of Samuel Johnson*, 1791

Burke, Edmund, *Philosophical Inquiry into the Origin of Our Ideas of the Sublime and Beautiful*, 1756; *Reflections on the Revolution In France*, 1790

Bush, George W., 'Remarks by the President on Global Development', The White House, 14 March 2002

Butler, R.A., *The Art of the Possible*, 1971

Campbell, Joseph, with Bill Moyers, *The Power of Myth*, 1988

Carlisle, Thomas, *An Occasional discourse on the Negro Question*, 1849

Churchill, Winston, House of Commons speech, 1 March 1955

Coalition Government Report, *Full Employment*, 1944

Colley, Linda, *In Defiance of Oligarchy: The Tory Party 1714–1760*, 1982; *Britons: Forging The Nation, 1707–1837*, 1992

Crosland, Anthony, *The Future of Socialism*, 1956; *The Conservative Enemy: A Programme of Radical Reform for the 1960s*, 1962; *Socialism Now and Other Essays*, edited by Dick Leonard, 1974

Dahrendorf, Ralf, *Class and Class Conflict in Industrial Society*, 1959

Darwin, Charles, *Voyage of the Beagle*, 1839; *On the Origins of Species by Means of Natural Selection*, 1859; *The Descent of Man*, 1871

Davies, Norman, *Europe: A History*, 1996; *The Isles: A History*, 1999

Eskimo poem of Netsilik origin called 'Magic Words', as recorded in Jerome Rothenberg's *Shaking the Pumpkin* and in Robert Bly's *News of the Universe*

Feinstein, Leon, 'The Relative Economic Importance of Academic, Psychological and Behavioural Attributes Developed in Childhood', in *What Do We Know about Brain Development and Childhood Interventions?*, Centre For Economic Performance, London School of Economics, July 2000

Ferguson, Adam, *Essay on the History of Civil Society*, 1767; *Principles of Moral and Political Science*, 1792

Foot, Michael, *Aneurin Bevan: A Biography*, 1973

Freedland, Jonathan, *Bring Home the Revolution*, 1999

Gaitskell, Hugh, 'Public Ownership and Equality', in *Socialist Commentary*, 1955

Giddens, Anthony, BBC Reith Lectures, 1999

Goodhart, David, 'Too Diverse/Discomfort of Strangers', *Prospect*, February 2004

Gore, Al, *Earth in the Balance: Forging a New Common Purpose*, 2000; *An Inconvenient Truth*, 2006

Gray, Thomas, *Pindaric Odes*, 1757; 'Elegy Written in a Country Churchyard', in Arthur Quiller-Couch (ed.), *The Oxford Book Of English Verse: 1250–1900*

Green, T.H., *Lectures on Liberal Legislation and Freedom of Contract*, 1881

Griffiths, Trevor, *Food for Ravens*, television film for BBC Wales, 1997

Gutmann, Amy, *Democracy and Disagreement*, 1998

Hammarskjold, Dag, *Markings*, translated by Sjoberg & Auden, 1964

Hazlitt, William, *Principles of Human Action*, 1805; *Political Essays*, 1819; *Table Talk*, 1821; *The Spirit of the Age*, 1825

Heffer, Simon, *Nor Shall My Sword: The Reinvention of England*, 1999

Himmelfarb, Gertrude, *The Roads to Modernity*, 2004

Hobhouse, L.T., *Liberalism*, 1911; *Labour Movement*, 1893; *Theory of Knowledge*, 1896; *Morals in Evolution*, 1906; *Development and Purpose*, 1913; *The Elements of Social Justice*, 1922

Hobson, J.A., *Problems of Poverty*, 1891; *Problem of the Unemployed*, 1896; *Evolution of Modern Capitalism*, 1894; *John Ruskin: Social Reformer*, 1898; *The Industrial System*, 1909; *Towards International Government*, 1914

Hume, David, *Treatise of Human Nature*, 1739; *Essays Moral and Political*, 1741; *Political Discourses*, 1752; *History of England*, 1754–62

Hutcheson, Francis, *A System of Moral Philosophy*, 1755

Ignatieff, Michael, 'Identity Parades', *Prospect*, April 1988

Jenkins, Roy, *Churchill: A Biography*, 2001

Joyce, James, *A Portrait of the Artist as a Young Man*, 1916; *Ulysses*, 1922

Kant, Immanuel, *An Answer to the Question: 'What is Enlightenment?'*, 1784

Kinnock, Neil, *The Future of Socialism*, Fabian Pamphlet no. 509, 1986

Kennedy, President John F., statement upon signing order establishing the Peace Corps (Executive Order 10924), 1 March 1961; Inaugural Address, 20 January 1961

Kennedy, Robert, Day of Affirmation Address, University of Cape Town, 6 June 1966

Keynes, John Maynard, *The General Theory of Employment, Interest and Money*, 1936; *Economic Consequences of the Peace*, 1919; *Treatise on Probability*, 1921; *Tract on Monetary Reform*, 1923; *Treatise on Money*, 1930; *Essays in Persuasion*, 1931

King Jr, Martin Luther, 'I Have a Dream' speech, Washington DC, 28 August 1963; 'Letter from a Birmingham Jail', 16 April 1963; sermon delivered at Ebenezer Baptist Church, Atlanta, Georgia, February 1968; 'The Drum Major Instinct' sermon, Ebenezer Baptist Church, 4 February 1968

Lawson, Nigel, *The View From No.11: Memoirs of a Tory Radical*, 1992; Mais Lecture, 1984

Lincoln, Abraham, First Inaugural Address, 4 March 1861

Macaulay, Thomas Babington, *History of England, from the Accession of James II*, 1852

Maathai, Wangaari, *The Canopy of Hope: My Life Campaigning for Africa, Women, and the Environment*, 2002; *The Green Belt Movement – Sharing the Approach and the Experience*, 2004

Mandela, Nelson, *Nelson Mandela Speaks: Forging a Democratic, Non-racial South Africa*, 1993; *Long Walk to Freedom: The Autobiography of Nelson Mandela*, 1994

Marr, Andrew, *The Day Britain Died*, 2000; *My Trade: A Short History of British Journalism*, 2004

Marshall, George, Harvard speech, 5 June 1947

Marshall, T.H., *Citizenship and Social Class*, 1992

McNair, John, *James Maxton: Beloved Rebel*, 1955

McIlvanney, William, *Docherty*, 1975

McKnight, Abigail, *Trends in Earnings Inequality and Earnings Mobility, 1977–1997: The Impact of Mobility on Long-Term Inequality*, DTI Employment Relations Research Series, No. 8, February 2000

Mill, John Stuart, *A System of Logic*, 1843; *On Liberty*, 1859; *Utilitarianism*, 1863; *Three Essays on Religion*, 1874

Milton, John, *Paradise Lost*, 1667; *Paradise Regained*, 1671; *Samson Agonistes*, 1671

Montesquieu, Charles de Secondat, baron de, *The Spirit of the Laws*, 1748

More, Sir Thomas, *Utopia*, 1895

Morris, William, *Letters on Socialism*, 1888

Morrison, Toni, *James Baldwin: His Voice Remembered*; 'Life in His Language' featured in the *New York Times*, 20 December 1987

Mount, Ferdinand, *Property and Poverty: An Agenda for the Mid-80s*, 1984; *The Recovery of the Constitution: The Second Sovereignty Lecture*, 1992; *The British Constitution Now: Recovery or Decline?*, 1992; *Mind the Gap: Class in Britain Now*, 2004

Nairn, Tom, *The Break-up of Britain: Crisis and Neo-Nationalism*, 1977

Okun, Arthur, *Equality and Efficiency: The Big Tradeoff*, 1975

O'Neil, Onora, 'A Question of Trust', BBC Reith Lectures, 2002

Opinion Leader Research, published in *New Britain*, a Smith Institute pamphlet, 1999

Orwell, George, *The Lion and the Unicorn: Socialism and the English Genius*, 1941; *The English People*, 1947

Osborne and Gaebler, *Reinventing Government*, 1982

Owen Robert, *A New View of Society*, 1814

Paine, Thomas, Common Sense, 1776; *The Rights of Man*, 1792; *Age of Reason*, 1795

Pope John Paul II, '*Pacem In Terris:* A Permanent Commitment', Message of His Holiness for the Celebration of the World Day of Peace, 1 January 2003

Pope Paul VI, *Encyclical Populorum Progressio* (On the Development of Peoples), 1967

Phillips, Anne, *Which Equalities Matter?*, 1999; *The Politics of Presence: Political Representation of Gender Race and Ethnicity*, 1998

Phillips, A.W., 'The Relation between Unemployment and the Rate of Change of Money Wage Rates in the United Kingdom, 1861–1957', *Economica*, 1958

Phillips, Melanie, 'The need to defend the nation', column in the *Daily Mail*, 5 April 2004

Powell, Colin, remarks at the Development, Democracy and Security Conference, Washington DC, 30 September 2004

Priestley, J.B., *English Journey*, 1934

Raineborough, Thomas, speech in *The Army Debates About Democracy*, 1647

Rawls, John, *Theory of Justice*, 1971; *Political Liberalism*, 1993

Riddell, N., *Labour in Crisis: The Second Labour Government, 1929–31*, 1999

Rodo, José Enrique, *Ariel*, 1900

Roosevelt, Franklin D., Annual Message to Congress, 3 January 1938

Rousseau, Jean Jacques, *The Social Contract*, 1762; *Confessions*, 1782

Rowntree, Joseph, Founders Memorandum, 1904

Sacks, Rabbi Sir Jonathan, *The Politics of Hope*, 1997; *The Dignity of Difference*, 2002; *To Heal a Fractured World: The Ethics of Responsibility*, 2005

Sandel, Michael, *Liberalism and the Limits of Justice*, 1982; 'The Moral Limits of the Market', in the Tanner Lectures on Human Values, delivered at Brasenose College, Oxford, 11 and 12 May 1998

Schlesinger, Arthur, *The Disuniting Of America*, 1998

Schumpeter, Joseph A., *Capitalism, Socialism and Democracy*, 1943

Scruton, Roger, *England: An Elegy*, 2001

Sen, Amartya, *Development as Freedom*, 2000; *The Argumentative Indian:*

   Writings on Indian History, Culture and Identity, 2005; *Rationality and Freedom*, 2004

Shaw, George Bernard, *Man and Superman*, 1903; *Major Barbara*, 1905

Shenefield, John H., and Irwin M. Stelzer, *The Antitrust Laws, A Primer*, American Enterprise Institute, 2001

Skidelsky, Robert, *John Maynard Keynes*, 2001

Smiles, Samuel, *Self-Help*, 1859

Smith, Adam, *The Theory of Moral Sentiments*, 1759; *An Inquiry into the Nature and Causes of the Wealth of Nations*, 1776

Smith, John, Labour Party Conference speech, 1992

Social Justice Report, *Strategies for National Renewal, the Report of the Commission on Social Justice*, 1994

Stelzer, Irwin (ed.), *The Neocon Reader*, 2005

Tawney, R.H., *Equality*, 1931

Thomson, James, *The Seasons*, 1730; 'Rule Britannia', put to music by Thomas Augustine Arne, circa 1740; *The Castle of Indolence*, 1748

Titmuss, Richard, *The Gift Relationship: From Human Blood to Social Policy*, 1970

Tocqueville, Alexis de, *Democracy in America*, 1835/1840

Voltaire, François-Marie Arouet, *Letters on the English*, 1778

Walzer, Michael, *Spheres of Justice*, 1984

Webb, Sidney and Beatrice, *The History of Trade Unionism*, 1894; *Industrial Democracy*, 1897

White, E.B., on the death of John F. Kennedy, *The New Yorker*, 30 November 1963

Williams, Raymond, *Culture and Society, 1780–1850*, 1958

Williams, Rowan, Archbishop of Canterbury, Richard Dimbleby Lecture, 19 December 2002

Wilson, James Q., *The Moral Sense*, 1993

Winstanley, Gerard, *The Law of Freedom in a Platform*, 1652

Wolfensohn, Jim, speaking at Woodrow Wilson International Centre for Scholars, Washington DC, 6 March 2002

Wollstonecraft, Mary, *A Vindication of the Rights of Women*, 1792

Wordsworth, William, *England* ('It is not to be thought of . . .'), 1802

Young, Hugo, *But, Chancellor: Inquiry into the Treasury* 1984; *One of Us: Life of Margaret Thatcher*, 1989; 'Thatcherism: did society survive?', the Maisie Ward Sheed Memorial Lecture, 1992; *This Blessed Plot: Britain and Europe from Churchill to Blair*, 1998; *Political Lives*, 2001; *Supping with the Devils*, 2004

APPENDIX

Dates and occasions of the speeches reproduced in this book

BIOGRAPHICAL NOTES ON THE CONTRIBUTORS

Kofi Annan is the seventh Secretary-General of the United Nations, and the first black African to hold the position. Mr Annan's priorities as Secretary-General have been to revitalise the United Nations through a comprehensive programme of reform; to strengthen the organisation's traditional work in the areas of development and the maintenance of international peace and security; to encourage and advocate human rights, the rule of law and the universal values of equality, tolerance and human dignity found in the United Nations Charter; and to restore public confidence in the organisation by reaching out to new partners and, in his words, by 'bringing the United Nations closer to the people'.

Helen Clark MP is Prime Minister of New Zealand. She joined the NZ Labour Party in 1971, has been an MP since 1975 and in the cabinet since 1987. She was elected Leader of the Labour Party in December 1993 and served as Leader of the Opposition until the general election in November 1999, when Labour was elected to government, and she has led her party to two further election victories since then.

Linda Colley is a British historian, widely known for her 1992 study *Britons: Forging the Nation, 1707–1837*, which explored the development of a British national identity following the 1707 Acts of Union. She was a Fellow of Christ's College, University of Cambridge, before taking a position at Yale University in 1982, and later being Richard M. Colgate Professor of History there. From 1998 she held the Senior Leverhulme Research Professorship in History at the London School of Economics, moving to become Professor of History at Princeton University in 2003.

Lord Ralf Dahrendorf is a German-British sociologist, philosopher, political scientist and politician. From 1969 to 1970 he was a member of the German parliament for the Freie Demokratische Partei, and a Parliamentary Secretary of State in the Ministry of Foreign Affairs. In 1970 he became a Commissioner in the European Commission in Brussels. From 1974 to 1984 he was Director of the London School of Economics. He returned to Germany to become Professor of Social Science at Konstanz University (1984–86). He became Warden of St Anthony's College at Oxford University in 1986. He sits in the House of Lords as a crossbencher.

Al Gore is an American politician, businessman and author, who served as the 45th Vice President of the United States from 1993 to 2001. He ran for President in 2000 following Bill Clinton's two four-year terms, and was defeated in the Electoral College vote, while winning the popular vote. He currently serves as President of the American television channel Current and as Chairman of Generation Investment Management, sits on the board of directors of Apple Computer, and serves as an unofficial advisor to Google's senior management.

Alan Greenspan is an American economist and former Chairman of the Board of Governors of the Federal Reserve of the United States. First appointed chairman in 1987, he was reappointed at successive four-year intervals until retiring in 2006, and is considered by many to be the leading authority on American domestic economic and monetary policy. Following his retirement as Fed chairman, he accepted an honorary position at the UK Treasury.

Wangaari Maathai founded the Green Belt movement in Kenya in 1977, which has planted more than 10 million trees to prevent soil erosion and provide firewood for cooking fires. The programme has been carried out primarily by women in the villages of Kenya, who through protecting their environment and paid employment for planting the trees are better able to care for their children and their children's future. In December 2002 Wangaari Maathai was elected to Parliament, and became Deputy Minister in the Ministry of Environment, Natural Resources and Wildlife in January 2003.

Nelson Mandela, in his own words, personifies struggle. He is still leading the fight against apartheid with extraordinary vigour and resilience after spending nearly three decades of his life behind bars. He has sacrificed his private life and his youth for his people, and remains South Africa's best-known and loved hero. He was inaugurated as the first democratically elected State President of South Africa on 10 May 1994, retiring from public life in June 1999.

Trevor Phillips was appointed Chair of the Commission for Racial Equality in March 2003. A former president of the National Union of Students, he has been a broadcaster, a member of the Greater London Authority, and is the author of many newspaper articles and comment pieces as well as co-writer of *Windrush: The Irresistible Rise of Multiracial Britain*, and *Britain's Slave Trade*.

J.K. Rowling is the author of the Harry Potter books. After she graduated from Exeter University, she found work as a secretary, and later spent time teaching English in Portugal before moving to Edinburgh, Scotland, with her daughter. She currently resides in Scotland with her husband and three children. She is active and passionate in her support of single-parent families.

Sir Jonathan Sacks is the Chief Rabbi of the United Hebrew Congregations of the Commonwealth and is widely recognised as one of the world's leading contemporary exponents of Judaism. A gifted communicator, the Chief Rabbi is a frequent contributor to radio, television and the national press. He is the author of a number of books, and a frequent contributor to the national press and also to 'Thought for the Day' on BBC Radio 4's *Today Programme.*

Sir Derek Wanless was Group Chief Executive of NatWest from 1992 until 1999. In April 2002 he produced the report *Securing Our Future Health: Taking a Long-Term View* for the Chancellor of the Exchequer. He undertook further work on this topic for the UK government in April 2003, and has recently completed a study *Securing Care for Older People* for the King's Fund. He is currently a director of Northern Rock plc and Business in the Community, a Commissioner at the Statistics Commission and a Trustee of the National Endowment for Science, Technology and the Arts.

Sir Magdi Yacoub is an eminent heart surgeon, who was consultant cardiothoracic surgeon at Harefield Hospital (1969–2001), Director of medical research and education (from 1992), and was involved in the development of the techniques of heart and heart–lung transplantation. In 2002 he was selected to spearhead a government recruitment drive for overseas doctors. Although retired, he continues to act as a high-profile consultant and ambassador for the benefits of transplant surgery.

INDEX

A NOTE ON THE EDITOR

Wilf Stevenson, a former Director of the BFI, is the Director of the Smith Institute, an independent think tank set up to undertake research and education in issues that flow from the changing relationship between social values and economic imperatives.

A NOTE ON THE TYPE

The text of this book is set in New Baskerville, which is based on
the original Baskerville font designed by John Baskerville
of Birmingham (1706–1775). The original punches he cut for
Baskerville still exist. His widow sold them to Beaumarchais,
from where they passed through several French foundries
to Deberney & Peignot in Paris, before finding their
way to Cambridge University Press.

Baskerville was the first of the 'transitional romans' between
the softer and rounder calligraphic Old Face and the 'Modern'
sharp-tooled Bodoni. It does not look very different to the
Old Faces, but there's a crisper differentiation between
thick and thin strokes, and the serifs on lower-case letters
are closer to the horizontal with the stress nearer the
vertical. The R in some sizes has the eighteenth-century
curled tail, the lower-case w has no middle serif, and
the lower-case g has an open tail and a curled ear.